Empirical Research on the German Capital Market

Contributions to Management Science

Harald Dyckhoff/Ute Finke
Cutting and Packing in Production and Distribution
1992. ISBN 3-7908-0630-7

Richard Flavell (Ed.)
Modelling Reality and Personal Modelling
1993. ISBN 3-7908-0682-X

Michael Hofmann/Monika List (Eds.)
Psychoanalysis and Management
1994. ISBN 3-7908-0795-8

Rita L. D'Ecclesia/Stavros A. Zenios (Eds.)
Operations Research Models in Quantitative Finance
1994. ISBN 3-7908-0803-2

Mario S. Catalani/Giuseppe F. Clerico
Decision Making Structures
1996. ISBN 3-7908-0895-4

M. Bertocchi/E. Cavalli/S. Komlósi (Eds.)
Modelling Techniques for Financial Markets and Bank Management
1996. ISBN 3-7908-0928-4

Holger Herbst
Business Rule-Oriented Conceptual Modeling
1997. ISBN 3-7908-1004-5

Constantin Zopounidis
New Operational Approaches for Financial Modelling
1997. ISBN 3-7908-1043-6

Klaus Zwerina
Discrete Choice Experiments in Marketing
1997. ISBN 3-7908-1045-2

Giovanni Marseguerra
Corporate Financial Decisions and Market Value
1998. ISBN 3-7908-1047-9

WHU Koblenz – Otto Beisheim Graduate School of Management (Ed.)
Structure and Dynamics of the German Mittelstand
1999. ISBN 3-7908-1165-3

Armin Scholl
Balancing and Sequencing of Assembly Lines
2nd rev. ed. 1999. ISBN 3-7908-1180-7

Wolfgang Bühler · Herbert Hax
Reinhart Schmidt (Eds.)

Empirical Research on the German Capital Market

With 38 Figures
and 60 Tables

Physica-Verlag
A Springer-Verlag Company

Series Editors
Werner A. Müller
Martina Bihn

Editors
Prof. Dr. Wolfgang Bühler
Universität Mannheim
Fakultät für Betriebswirtschaftslehre
Lehrstuhl für Finanzierung
Schloß
D-68131 Mannheim, Germany

Prof. Dr. Dr. h.c. Herbert Hax
Universität zu Köln
Wirtschafts- und Sozialwissenschaftliche Fakultät
Albertus-Magnus-Platz
D-50923 Köln, Germany

Prof. Dr. Reinhart Schmidt
Universität Halle-Wittenberg
Wirtschaftswissenschaftliche Fakultät
Lehrstuhl für Finanzwirtschaft und Bankbetriebslehre
Reichardtstr. 11
D-06099 Halle, Germany

ISBN 3-7908-1193-9 Physica-Verlag Heidelberg New York

Cataloging-in-Publication Data applied for
Die Deutsche Bibliothek – CIP-Einheitsaufnahme
Empirical research on the German capital market: with 60 tables/Wolfgang Bühler; Herbert Hax; Reinhart Schmidt (ed.). – Heidelberg: Physica-Verl., 1999
(Contributions to management science)
ISBN 3-7908-1193-9

Printed in Germany

Cover design: Erich Kirchner, Heidelberg

SPIN 10712528 88/2202-5 4 3 2 1 0 – Printed on acid-free paper

Preface by the Editors

Resorting mainly to US data academic researchers in the USA have become world-wide leaders in capital market empiricism. It therefore seems necessary to investigate whether the results of this research are universally valid; or, whether other explanatory models are needed for capital markets elsewhere.

In the mid 'eighties' a group of German professors initiated an intensive program of empirical research on the German capital market. A nation-wide research program was established with generous financial support from the *Deutsche Forschungsgemeinschaft* (DFG). More than fifty researchers, including fifteen professors of finance, began a cooperative research program. The program objectives included the development of expertise in modern methods of empiricism in financial economics and the derivation of results that might be specific to the German capital market.

A crucial prerequisite for the implementation of the research program was the creation of reliable and adequate data bases. Unlike the American counterparts, the German researchers did not have efficient data bases at their disposal. Thus, as a necessary first step, the researchers had to establish data banks. Capital market researchers are now able to access three important data banks which, only as a basis for academic research, are option to academic researchers world-wide. Data banks of German stock and bond prices and listed company financial statements have been established by Hermann Göppl, University of Karlsruhe, Wolfgang Bühler, University of Mannheim, and Peter Möller, RWTH Aachen, respectively. As a result of these efforts, the conditions for empirical research in finance and accounting in Germany have been improved immeasurably.

This volume includes fifteen contributions which document the final part of research undertaken by those participating in the research program. The diverse nature of the issues reissued by these contributors is indicative of the broad spectrum of the German empiricists in the area of financial economics. The work in the earlier stages of the research initiative on the German capital market was published in *"Zeitschrift für betriebswirtschaftliche Forschung", Special Volume No. 31 (1993).* As the coordinators of the central research program we have partitioned the contributions in this volume into four sections.

The first part of the book is dedicated to problems of market structure and organization. New experimental approaches are reported including, in particular, those for investigating the specific attributes of different institutional designs under idealized *ceteris paribus* conditions. Additionally, the relationships between market structure and cost of immediacy are compared for floor trading and electronic trading system. A further study demonstrates that the creation of a new market segment may generate positive abnormal returns because of lower transactions costs.

The second part deals with information and capital market. A macroeconomic analysis shows that systematic relationships between interest rates are able to transmit central bank policy actions into the real sector of the economy. A microeconomic investigation into the effects of financial reporting suggests that German investors well understand German financial reporting whilst, compared with disclosure based on U.S.GAAP, traditional German financial reporting reveals both lesser amounts and alternative forms of information.

The third part is concerned with risk and return. Arbitrage pricing theory is investigated by reference to the German stock market as are, within a somewhat broader context, risk, return and liquidity. Additionally, beta estimates are derived with different estimation procedures using both market and accounting data. The results reveal a weak relationship between accounting numbers and systematic risk in the case of German stocks. An investigation into the performance of German mutual funds, using a variety of performance measures, reveals that no fund's performance is superior to that of a broadly based index.

The fourth and final part of this volume addresses problems concerning futures and options. The call policy of three German governmental institutions in respect of their bond market issues is analyzed with two different analytical models. The time-lags between price changes characterizing the relationships between stocks and stock options are also investigated. Apropos of the DAX futures market, research findings suggest that extraordinary arbitrage profits can be earned from a strategy which allows for the seasonally of dividend payments. Finally, results are presented on the impact of stock price jumps on option values for representative model parameters and the historical impact of jumps on option values.

We are grateful to Professor Gerald H. Lawson, formerly of the Manchester Business School, who proposed numerous linguistic and other changes to the original texts of the contributions to this volume which were written in English by their German authors. We are also indebted to Dr. Annemarie Sapusek and Doris Storch for their help in preparing the final version of the text.

The editors hope that this research gives a good insight into the special institutional and empirical realities of the German capital market and that the academic community will profit from the special approaches and extended methods that are reported here. The results should prove to the equally important to academic research and in the realm of investment banking.

Mannheim/Cologne/Halle

Wolfgang Bühler
Herbert Hax
Reinhart Schmidt

Table of Contents

A Market Structure and Organization

Market Design, Trading Behavior and Price Discovery - An Experimental Stock Market Model

Wolfgang Gerke and Horst Bienert
University of Erlangen-Nuremberg

1. Introduction

Empirical capital market research is not restricted to observing existing markets. It has long been acknowledged that experimental markets, purposefully created, controlled and observed in the laboratory, are a valuable complement to both empirical field research and theoretical models (Smith 1989, Hey 1991, Friedman/Sunder 1994, Davis/Holt 1991).

This article reports on several series of market experiments. These experiments were developed and conducted in the context of a 5-year-project with financial support from the Deutsche Forschungsgemeinschaft (DFG). They extend, and modify, the design of previous "asset market" experiments in order to capture some additional salient features of the microstructure of stock markets. These extensions include an indefinite time horizon and a somewhat more complex institutional market structure than in standard experimental double auction asset markets. We also discuss the derivation of the experimental design from a general model of stock markets and the validity of the experimental model.

In the second part of this paper we discuss the objectives and considerations that led to the development of our experimental stock market, and describe the resulting experimental procedure. The third part illustrates the use of this approach to investigate questions of trading behavior and market design. The first section presents evidence that the disposition effect, well established in individual decision-making, persists in an interactive market setting. Furthermore, we investigate its impact on market level variables. The second section compares markets with different degrees of order book transparency and traces differences in market performance to changes in individuals' decision situations. The final part contains a brief discussion of the results and of the potential validity of conclusions that can be drawn from experiments.

2. Designing a computerized experimental stock market

2.1 Basic design considerations

How does the organization of a stock market influence its performance? This general question characterizes the motivation for developing our experimental model of a stock market. Figure 1 indicates that there may be no simple answer to this question, but the simplified view of the complex interaction of market organization and market performance helps to identify potential approaches.

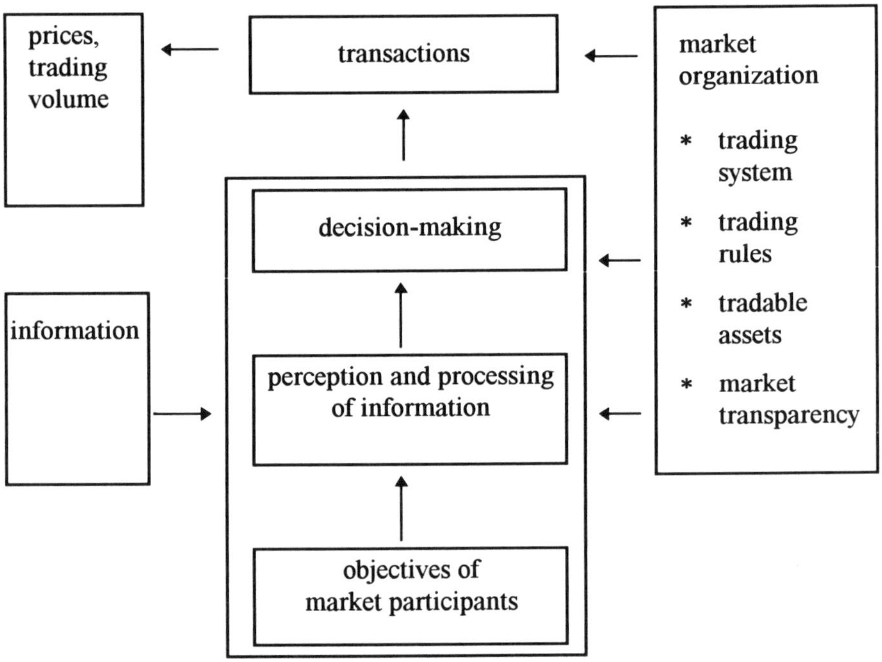

Figure 1: A general model of the market process

Figure 1 shows the general structure of the market process in financial markets. The market organization affects the decision situation of individual market participants, restricts their interaction and influences their use of outside information. Differences in market performance can only result from changes in this complex interaction between institution and behavior. Only a few steps in this process are observable for direct empirical studies. Most studies are restricted to some well-defined subset of the available information and market level outcome variables such as prices and trading volume. Inferences concerning the effects of different forms of market organization remain ambiguous because these effects are perturbed by other unobserved factors.

Experimental markets are intended to provide obervations on the interaction between an institution and human behavior in a controlled situation that is isolated from outside perturbations. In these experiments, efforts are made to control any variable that is not itself the object of investigation. Most asset market experiments have focussed on the information processing capability of markets with human traders and their cognitive limitations, and on the impact of different institutional variations on this capability. In repeated finite horizon market experiments with well-defined but uncertain liquidation values of the traded assets, market prices usually tend to reveal most of the available information after the first few repetitions. This result remains valid for different degrees of uncertainty and different distributions of information.[1]

In order to observe the aggregation of information with as little ambiguity as possible, these experiments employ a specific approach to the modelling of assets and markets. Usually, a single type of asset is traded for a short period of time. Before expiring worthlessly at the end of this period, the asset entitles its holder to receive payments. By giving participants well-specified uncertain information on these randomly determined payments, and by using real money, participants are confronted with the task of interpreting and inferring information on objectively defined "induced" values.[2]

In our experiments, we focus on a different dimension of many financial markets - and particularly of stock markets - that is not well captured by this experimental model of an asset market. What is so special about the stock market? The stock market contains a strong speculative element, i.e. individual valuations underlying today's bids, asks and prices are to a large extent determined by expectations of future prices, which in turn depend on expectations of other prices in the distant future. If the "value" of a stock is given by the present value of its future payoffs, investors' efforts to detect this value may not provide commensurate rewards. When individuals' time horizons are shorter than the lifetime of the asset, expected prices become more important than expected payoffs, and information on differences between value and price may be worthless.[3]

---

[1] A survey of asset market experiments is given by Sunder (1992)

[2] Smith (1972) explains the reasoning behind this so-called induced value theory.

[3] This aspect of the stock market is stressed by Keynes in his often-quoted "beauty contest" metaphor (Keynes 1936). An arbitrage-free deviation between price and value is also called a rational bubble (for rational bubbles with short horizon individuals see e.g. Tirole 1985). Arbitrage-resistant mispricing is also at the center of the so-called noise trader approach (Shleifer/Summers 1990).

The long lifetime of stocks, compared to individuals' time horizons, has a number of important implications. Prices become endogenous, i.e. exogenous determinants of value exert their influence on prices only through the decisions of present and future market participants. There is no predetermined point in time at which price and the fundamental value of a stock must converge, because nobody lives long enough to realize the fundamental value without reselling the stock. Furthermore, the fundamental value cannot even be detected, because the degree of uncertainty does not decrease over time. While the payment of dividends partially decreases the uncertainty of future payoffs before the dividend date, new uncertainty about other dividends still further in the future restores the uncertainty immediately thereafter.

This "revolving" uncertainty about the fundamental value of stocks and the speculative nature of decisions to buy, or to sell, may well play an important role not only in the behavior of participants in stock markets, but also in the way this behavior is influenced by the institution of a stock market. Hence, these factors may be critical when assessing the impact of institutional variations on the performance of a market.

An infinite time horizon cannot be implemented in a finite experiment. However, we try to approximate the essence of these stylized facts. In our experiments stocks pay risky dividends over an indefinite lifetime. By observing the demand for information, the orders placed together with the transactions and prices resulting from these orders under different market rules, we try to improve our understanding of the market process. Our objectives can be summarized in three questions:

- How do aggregate characteristics of the market process (prices and volumes) originate from the decision processes of market participants?
- What are the effects of changes in market organization, and how do these effects build up from individual decisions to the market level?
- Are there typical patterns in the behavior of market participants that could improve our understanding of real markets when replacing the standard assumption of fully rational behavior?

The design of the experiments is described in the next section. General features include an indefinite time horizon, revolving uncertainty about fundamental values, and fully endogenous price formation driven exclusively by the orders of the market participants. The trading system models institutional details of computerized stock markets quite realistically. In general, we employ a realistic framing of the experimental situation as a means of increasing the desired long term orientation and the motivation of subjects. However, within the structure determined by the underlying model of a stock market, priority is given to keeping things simple. The reduction of complexity remains the very nature of model-building and experiments, even if progress in understanding simple systems makes it both possible and sensible to proceed to more complex systems (Camerer 1992, p. 269, Hey 1991, pp. 208 and 226).

2.2 The trading system and experimental procedures

2.2.1 Basic design

In the experiment, a number of participants (usually 10) continuously face the decision to rebuild their portfolios. These portfolios consist of different stocks (usually 4), a fixed interest alternative and a cash balance. Stocks pay risky dividends over an indefinite lifetime and can be traded between subjects over a computerized trading system. The experiment runs for an indefinite number of consecutive 8-minute periods, and dividends influence the market value of stocks only through the prices of transactions between participants.

The following sections describe the characteristics of the assets, the rules of the trading system, the information available to the participants, and the instruction procedure used to prepare the subjects for their task.

2.2.2 Assets

At the start of the experiment, each participant is endowed with his share of the market portfolio, consisting of stocks of four fictitious firms, and a positive balance in currency units ("cash").

An increase in the total value of an individual portfolio can be attributed to dividends received, interest received on fixed-term deposits, or an increase in the market value of the shares held. Likewise, a decrease may result from transaction costs, interest paid on a negative cash balance ("overdraft"), dividends paid on short positions in stock, and a decrease in the market value of the shares in the portfolio.

No interest is paid on a positive cash balance. A negative cash balance is admissible up to a fixed proportion of total wealth, but the interest rate for this overdraft is higher than that received on fixed-term deposits.[4]

---

[4] In all experiments reported in this article, the interest rates were 10 percent per period on fixed term deposits and 14 percent per period on overdrafts.

The participants are free to invest any amount in fixed-term deposits at any time. The minimum duration of these non-tradable deposits is one period. The interest rate for deposits remains constant and publicly known throughout the experiment and is independent of the duration of the deposit. Interest and principal are paid together at the maturity of the contract. Maturity dates are always at the end of an 8-minute trading period.

Fixed-term deposits can be used as a safe investment alternative in assessing the value of the different shares traded in the market. These shares entitle their holders to receive dividends at the end of each period. The firms issuing these shares are not modelled in detail. They are wholly represented by a simple stochastic process that drives the behavior of earnings per share and dividends over time.

Dividends are derived from earnings. Earnings follow a random walk:

$$\text{earnings}_{t+1} = \text{earnings}_t + \text{innovation}_{t+1} \qquad (1)$$

Earnings innovations are drawn from a normal distribution with an expected value of zero. The standard deviation of the innovation variable is constant and publicly known for each firm. Earnings innovations are determined at the end of each period, and the resulting dividend is paid.

Equation 1 implies that the current level of earnings is also the expected amount of earnings for any future period. Earnings of each period are fully paid out as dividends, unless they are negative or needed to cover earlier losses. Negative earnings are cumulated and cause bankruptcy when a predetermined threshold is reached.[5]

For an investor, the dividend of the previous period is the best forecast of all future dividends. A risk neutral investor would compare the price of a stock with the amount needed for a fixed-term deposit yielding the same amount as the expected dividend.[6] Risk averse investors would require a risk-dependent discount on that price.

In the experiment, participants may buy, or sell short, up to 33 percent of the outstanding shares of any firm.[7] Short positions may be held for an indefinite time. They constitute an obligation to pay the dividends that are due for the shares sold short.

---

[5] Up to now, this bankruptcy has occurred only once in all our experiments.

[6] This applies if the probability of negative earnings is low (expected earnings are several standard deviations above zero) and if the expected change in stock prices is zero.

[7] This position limit is not frequently reached. Its purpose is to maintain a minimum degree of competition in each security and to prevent price manipulation.

The underlying "economic model" relies heavily on the basic ideas of capital market theory. The factors driving the dividend process are reduced to a multivariate normal distribution with known expected values, standard deviations and coefficients of correlation. This helps the participants with a background in capital market theory to understand the process easily.

2.2.3 Trading

All interaction within the market is transmitted and recorded by a computerized system. Figure 2 shows the trading screen of one participant.

A participant wishing to change the structure of his portfolio can take one of three actions. He can convert part of his cash holdings into a fixed-term deposit (F4) or submit an order to buy (F1) or to sell (F2) to the market.

The market is organized as a continuous double auction similar to stock exchanges, e.g. those in Paris or Toronto. Orders to buy, or to sell, must specify the type of stock, the number of shares and a price limit. They may be submitted as valid until cancelled, or as valid until the end of the current period. An incoming order is immediately matched with the opposite side of the order book. If price limits overlap, the new order is executed at the best price limits available in the order book. Any remaining part of the order that cannot be executed with the specified price limit enters the order book. When matching an incoming order, priority between orders from the book is determined first by price limit and then by waiting time. Any order in the book may be withdrawn at any time.

When two orders are matched, the resulting transaction is settled[8], and both parties are notified. The new market price is transmitted to all participants and displayed on their screens.[9] At the end of a period, interest and dividends are paid and received, and trading continues without a halt. After the end of the experiment, the final wealth of participants is calculated using the market values of their portfolios. The number of periods is not known in advance, but it is common knowledge that it is between 11 and 20. Whilst this indefinite time horizon does not fully implement the desired infinite time horizon, it nevertheless directs the participants' attention to an indefinite future.[10]

---

[8] This includes charging a transaction fee.

[9] When both orders are from the same participant, the transaction does not change the market price.

[10] For a similar approach, see Stanley (1994). An alternative approach to implementing an infinite horizon model in a finite experiment is used in Marimon/Sunder (1993).

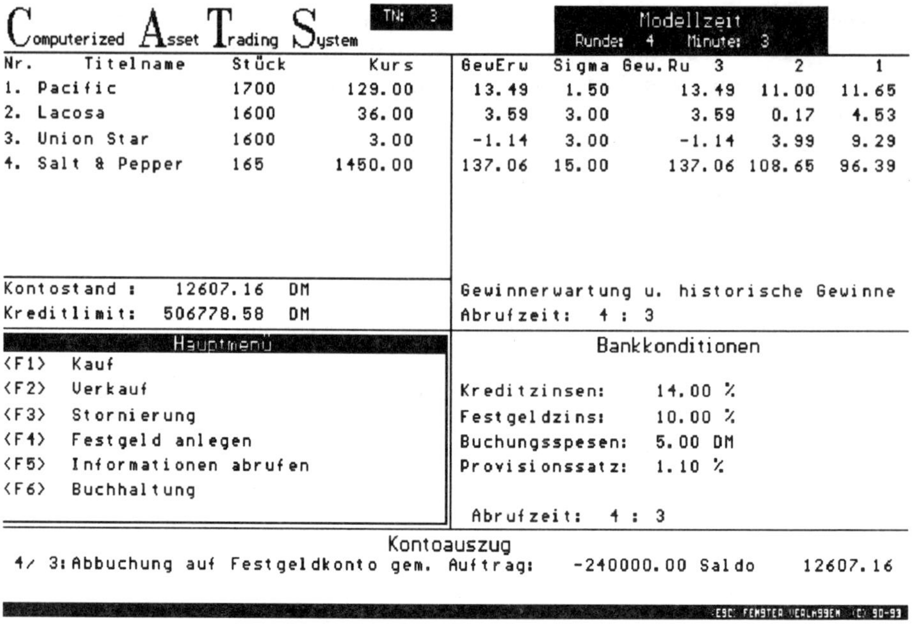

Figure 2: Trading screen

2.2.4 Information

The information available to market participants can vary between different experiments or between participants within an experiment. This section describes the standard version of a transparent market with homogeneous information supply.

The trader screen always shows the current time within the experiment, the individual stock portfolio, cash balance and the current market price of each stock. This information is updated by the system in real-time.

However, any other type of information is only displayed, or updated, on the trader's screen by special request on each occasion. Using these requests, the demand for different types of information can be analyzed in detail. The following types of information are offered:[11]

[11] In addition to those listed, there are information requests for individual data (account statements, outstanding orders, fixed-term deposits) and a summary of constant market parameters (interest rates, transaction costs).

- "Ticker": a table listing prices and size of the last three transactions for each stock.
- "Bid/ask-spread": a table listing the highest buy order limit and the lowest sell order limit currently in the order book for each stock.
- "Order book": a table listing the first five limit prices and corresponding volumes on both sides of the order book for one stock.
- "Earnings forecasts": a table listing expected earnings and the last three realized earnings for each stock. This table contains also the standard deviation of the earnings innovation for each stock. These standard deviations remain constant throughout the experiment.
- "Earnings correlation": this table lists the coefficients of correlation between the earnings innovation terms of different stocks. These coefficients remain constant throughout the experiment.

2.2.5 Instructions and framing

Subjects are prepared for participation in the experiments in three steps. If their recent educational background does not cover the basic concepts necessary to understand the experimental model, participants are given an intuitive summary of its important features.[12] The experiment is explained in a written detailed instruction. This instruction is also presented verbally, and questions may be asked. Answers are restricted to clarifications of the instructions. Every experiment is preceded by an introductory trading session of approximately 30 minutes to familiarize participants with the use of the computer system.

The instructions identify the experimental market as a model of a stock market and stock market jargon is used, e.g. "limit order", "order book", "portfolio", "fixed-term deposit" or "dividends". However, the abstract nature of the dividend process is common knowledge, and the "firms" have fantasy names that are unrelated to their characteristics or to the names of real firms.

To motivate our participants[13], we rely more on the intrinsic motivation created by the realistic framing of the experiment and their desire to do their best than on monetary rewards. The cash units used in the experiment are called "DM", but their value is restricted to the experiment. Contrary to most market experiments, laboratory money is not converted into real cash (or grades or any

---

[12] This summary covers the concepts of present value, normal distribution, standard deviation and the basic ideas of diversification and portfolio theory.

[13] Most of our participants are advanced students of business administration who participate in the experiments as part of an introductory course that covers basic aspects of the microstructure of stock markets and capital market theory.

other valuable outside good) at a predetermined fixed rate. However, participants have to pay a small amount at the beginning of the experiment. This sum is redistributed after the experiment in proportion to the individual's share of total market wealth.[14] Having observed a high level of visible dedication towards the objective of a "good performance", we believe that lack of motivation does not pose a problem.[15] The lack of monetary rewards may, however, distort the participants' attitudes towards risk, but there is no guarantee that moderate rewards prevent this distortion.[16] When trying to make general inferences from experimental results, the potential role of risk aversion must be considered with care.[17]

The instruction defines the objective of the participants as "a continuous and fast increase in wealth" using final wealth as the measure of success. The experiments that have been conducted hitherto seem to justify the conjecture that participants accept this objective as their own and try to identify profitable opportunities whilst attempting to avoid potential losses. Although we neither know nor induce the subjects' utility functions, we conclude that our markets are driven by individuals seeking profits in terms of laboratory wealth.

2.3 Applications and modifications

The system has been developed, tested and refined since 1990 with the support of the Deutsche Forschungsgemeinschaft (DFG). Including technical tests and exploratory pilot experiments, we have performed a total of 82 experiments using various constellations of parameters. The first series aimed at establishing a benchmark for subsequent variations and at investigating the stability and robustness of the observed market process.

---

[14] We view this procedure more as a symbolic illustration of individual success rather than a monetary incentive. With an initial deposit of 5 DM, most individual payoffs remain in the interval between 4 and 6 DM. Occasionally, extreme results are reached, such as 2 DM or 10 DM. The procedure is motivated by the hope that it provides some incremental motivation to perform well. A more detailed discussion of the incentive structure ist given by Gerke/Bienert (1994).

[15] This may cause severe problems in experiments where subjects are confronted with boring and repetitive tasks. In such cases, experiments without salient monetary rewards can yield invalid results. Such a case inspired the theory of induced value, see Smith 1972. On the other hand, many important results have been shown to obtain also in "hypothetical" situations (Tversky/Kahneman 1992, Jamal/Sunder 1991).

[16] The results in Kachelmeier/Shehata (1992) may be interpreted as indicating that small rewards induce a different inclination to risk compared with high rewards.

[17] There is no evidence that the low level of monetary rewards in our experiments causes a high proportion of risk-seeking behavior. Risk-seeking behavior should lead to extremely unbalanced portfolios, making the position limit in individual stocks a binding restriction in a high large of cases. This has not been observed.

So far, the experiments have been used to investigate a broad range of questions. These include differences between computerized trading and crowd trading in a similarly structured computer-assisted trading experiment (Gerke 1992), cultural differences between experimental subjects from different countries (Gerke/Schroeder-Wildberg 1993), learning from experience (Gerke 1994), the formation of bubbles (still in progress), and stock size effects (still in progress).

The remaining part of this article summarizes two investigations that illustrate two important perspectives on the experimental market process. The first focusses on patterns in the behavior of individual traders and how these affect the market as a whole. The second examines performance effects of institutional variations. Both approaches provide the foundation for ongoing research.

3. Some experimental results

3.1 Trading behavior: the disposition effect

3.1.1 Previous evidence and hypotheses

The "disposition to sell winners too early and ride losers too long" (Shefrin/Statman 1985) has become known as the "disposition effect". Such a disposition may be explained by an asymmetric valuation of gains and losses relative to a reference point. This asymmetric valuation is part of the prospect theory proposed by Kahneman/Tversky (1979). If the purchase price is assumed to be a natural reference point, the prospect of a reduction of a loss is valued more highly than the prospect of an increase in gains of the same size. This implies that - expectations assumed constant - people tend to sell stocks more readily after capital gains than at a loss.

Evidence of the disposition effect has been found in decision experiments where subjects buy and sell assets over a sequence of trading periods at exogenously given prices. Sales of assets are more likely to occur after capital gains than after losses (Weber/Camerer 1991, Schachter/Ouellette/Whittle/Gerin 1987). This induces a similar relation between price changes and sales of assets (Weber/Camerer 1991), because every price increase causes capital gains.

Both, the implied relation between capital gains and sales of stock (Shefrin/Statman 1985) and that between price changes and sales of stock are supported by empirical evidence. If data on price changes and trading volume are interpreted as evidence of the disposition effect (Ferris/Haugen/Makhija 1988, Lakonishok/Smidt 1986), this implies additional restrictions on the behavior of buyers:

If sellers are more willing to sell after price increases, this will only cause a higher trading volume if they find buyers for their sales. If buyers make their decisions independently of previous price changes, additional selling pressure will depress prices before causing a higher trading volume. The reluctance of sellers to sell at a loss will also exert a stabilizing influence on prices after they have fallen, preventing further decreases. Hence, under the assumption of independent buyer behavior, the disposition effect implies "sticky" prices that adjust reluctantly to new information.

The following section reports the main results of a series of experiments examining selling behavior and its interaction with the buying behavior of participants in experimental stock markets. We also use the observation of decisions to buy to distinguish between two possible explanations for asymmetric selling behavior.

3.1.2 Individual and market level results

The series comprises 16 experiments, conducted with advanced undergraduate students of the University of Mannheim.[18] The results were confirmed in 9 additional experiments with slightly different parameters and in 24 oral market experiments.[19]

In most experiments, there is a pronounced asymmetry between selling behavior in capital gain situations and in capital loss situations. Capital gains or losses of an individual are measured by comparing the current price with a volume-weighted moving average of his previous purchase prices in the same stock.[20] The number and volume of orders is adjusted for the relative frequency of capital gain or capital loss situations. In 14 out of 16 experiments, more sell orders come from participants in gain situations than from participants in loss

---

[18] These experiments employed the standard procedures described above, except that the detailed order book information was not available (only bid-ask information). However, in some experiments there were only 9 participants (5/16), 5 firms (11/16) or no short sales (4/16).

[19] Detailed results are reported in Gerke/Bienert (1993) and in Gerke/Bienert/Sun (1992). The 9 additional experiments did not offer automatic cancellation of orders at the end of a period.

[20] Hence, the individual analysis is restricted to previous buyers.

situations.[21] The same is true for the subset of "urgent" sell orders in 13 out of 16 experiments.[22] An "urgent" order is defined as an order that immediately triggers a transaction. Not surprisingly, there are also more sales in gain situations in 13 out of 16 experiments.[23] Thus, a disposition effect is found in aggregate selling behavior.

To investigate the selling behavior of individual participants, we calculate a coefficient that relates sales in gain situations to sales in loss situations for each participant:

$$\alpha = (S+ - S-) / (S+ + S-) \qquad (2)$$

S+ (S-) denotes the number of shares sold in gain (loss) situations, adjusted for the relative frequency of gain and loss situations for the respective individual. If decisions to sell were made independently of previous gains or losses, the expected value of the coefficient would be zero. Positive values indicate that the person's behavior is consistent with the disposition effect. Positive values are found in 81 out of 124 cases (65 %). Across all individuals, the mean value of α is 0.33.

How does this bias in individual selling behavior affect prices and trading volume of the market? Although the disposition effect is found at the individual level, it does not lead to systematic differences in trading volume between periods with price increases and periods with price decreases. One of the possible explanations for this puzzle is the close interrelation of selling pressure and price changes.[24] If capital gains have accumulated due to previous price increases, the sales triggered by these capital gains may stop, or even reverse, the increase in prices in the following period, creating high volume on a negative price change.

It is not possible to disentangle the influence of price changes on the order flow and the influence of the order flow on price changes. However, changes in the fundamental values of the stocks may be used as a proxy for "undisturbed" or ex ante expected price changes in a period. Deviations between changes in fundamental values and changes in prices would then be interpreted as indicating

[21] Across all experiments, the relation of orders to sell in gain situations to those in loss situations is 1.26.

[22] Here, the relation across all experiments is 1.57.

[23] The relative frequency of sales in gain situations is 1.63, when compared to loss situations.

[24] Alternative explanations can be constructed. For example, it may take more time than a period before capital gains increase the probability of a sale; or, the reduced selling volume from previous buyers may be offset by orders to sell (short) from other participants.

an asymmetric reaction of market participants towards anticipated price increases or decreases.

In the experiments, changes in fundamental values are equivalent to changes in earnings per share. We find weak evidence of a positive relation between the sign of the innovation in earnings and the trading volume in the subsequent period. This relation is positive in 11 out of the 16 experiments.[25]

While the number of sell orders does not differ much between periods with positive or negative earnings innovations, the number of buy orders differs considerably. In negative periods, orders to buy or to sell are equally likely, but the relation between buy and sell orders becomes 1.3 in positive periods. These results seem to reject the implications of a disposition effect, which ought to result in a reluctance to place sell orders when a decrease in prices is anticipated.

However, this reluctance to sell at falling prices shows up when the price limits of the orders are examined. Table 1 summarizes the average reaction of price limits to changes in earnings. While the relative price limits of buy orders - as a percent deviation from last period's price - are reduced by 1.18 percent for every percent of reduction in earnings, potential sellers react by increasing their price limits on average.

This striking reluctance to sell at falling prices creates a strong asymmetry in the reaction of prices to changes in earnings. A one percent increase in earnings results in an average price increase of 1.8 percent, whereas a one percent reduction of earnings is still accompanied by an average increase in prices of 0.48 percent.

Table 1: Price limits in periods with positive or negative changes in earnings

	Relative distance of price limits from last period's market price as a function of relative changes in earnings (elasticity coefficients)[26]	
Orders to ...	Positive (+ 1%)	Negative (- 1%)
... buy	+ 0.20	- 1.18
... sell	+ 2.89	+ 2.24

[25] According to the Mann-Whitney-U-test, the difference in trading volume between periods with earnings increases and periods with earnings reductions is significant at $\alpha = 0.05$.

[26] Denoting last period's market price P, the percentage change in earnings I, and the price limit L, the reaction coefficients in the table are computed as $((L - P) / P) / |I|$.

3.1.3 Discussion

Capital gains and losses for individuals seem to bias their subsequent decisions to sell stock in our experiments. However, this bias does not result in the positive relation between price changes and trading volume which is usually proposed as an empirical implication of the disposition effect.

Instead of an asymmetry in trading volume, we find a pronounced asymmetry in the reaction of prices to changes in fundamental variables. This asymmetry seems to result from a strong reluctance to sell at falling prices.

The results indicate that many participants may use the price of the previous period as their reference point rather than their own purchase price. If this is the case, the observed pattern supports the interpretation of the disposition effect as an asymmetric valuation as opposed to an irrational expectation of regaining earlier losses. Such expectations should influence the placement of orders to buy and to sell in the same way.

3.2 Market design: order book transparency in a continuous auction market

3.2.1 The role of order book transparency: theory and experimental design

Market transparency determines the information available for the strategic game played between market participants. The availability of information about the limit orders present on the market plays a key role in defining the decision situation of traders (Schwartz 1991, pp. 285-299, Harris 1990). At first sight, order book transparency seems to be a simple way of making a market more perfect by facilitating the public advertising of intentions to trade. But in an imperfect and speculative market, transparency may have some less obvious implications.

Traders can use their knowledge of other traders' orders to predict short term price movements. This prediction can be based either on the inference of underlying information that is revealed through the placement of an order or, more generally, on the mechanics of the market. Ceteris paribus, limit orders to buy work as barriers to price decreases, and sell orders tend to inhibit subsequent price increases.

Knowledge of the order book can be used to hide one's own information (Kyle 1985). Knowledge of other traders' intentions to trade is also valuable, if these intentions do not reveal any further information, because this knowledge can be used to attain a higher share of the potential gain from trade in an imperfect market.

Order book information does more than influence the reaction to the orders that are displayed. This reaction is also anticipated when orders are submitted thus creating a complex interaction between those creating the order book information by submitting orders and those observing the information. In general, participants can choose which of the two positions they take. This choice determines the abundance of limit orders and, hence, the liquidity of a market. The net effect of transparency on liquidity is not obvious, because it may be depend on different factors in a complex way.

First, a transparent order book does help to find the counterparty to an intended trade. An order signals an intention to trade, and the signal is observed by other traders. And a lack of limit orders becomes a visible opportunity to submit a new order with a restrictive price limit, offering immediacy at a price. The transparency of the order book fosters competition among potential providers of immediacy.

However, there are also factors reducing the attractiveness of submitting a limit order. An order may have an adverse effect on the order placement of other traders for two reasons. An order to buy may be perceived - rightly or not - as a signal of positive private information about the value of the stock. Furthermore, the order provides a fall-back option for traders who wish to sell and a protection against an immediate drop in prices for subsequent buyers at a marginally higher price. Hence, a buy order may create an incentive for others to submit bids just above its price limit and to increase the price limits of sell orders. More simply, a transparent order book reduces the necessity to submit limit orders, because it facilitates a "hit and run" strategy of waiting until an immediate trade becomes possible. With this strategy traders avoid the costs incurred by offering a "free trading option" to the market (Stoll 1992, p. 84).[27]

The relative weights of the two sides of the argument determine the net effect on traders' choices of order type and price limit and on market liquidity.

Two different trade-offs are involved in the decision to submit a limit order. Most models focus on informational aspects: traders try to avoid transactions

[27] An order to buy provides the market with a free put option at a strike price equal to the price limit of the order. The value of this option does not depend on the transparency of the order book (unless this influences the relative reaction time of market participants and thereby the maturity of the option).

with others who are better informed than themselves and seek to trade with those who have less precise information.[28] But there is also a bargaining trade-off which is independent of informational asymmetries: traders balance the anticipated terms of a possible trade against the danger of missing the trade altogether (Schwartz 1991). Both trade-offs may be influenced by a transparent order book. Hence, the net effect of order book transparency may depend on the relative weight that is attributed to issues of asymmetric information or bargaining.

Friedman (1991) reports on a series of short-term asset market experiments, that explore the impact of different degrees of market transparency, in continuous double auction markets in which there is an important degree of information diversity among traders. While order book transparency seems to increase the informational efficiency of these markets, the bid-ask spread becomes larger, indicating a reduction in liquidity (Friedman 1991).[29]

The fear of revealing valuable and clear-cut private information may be an important reason for not submitting competitive limit orders in these experiments. However, the implication of some piece of private information may be far from obvious, and differences in the valuation of information may make it difficult to infer private information from observed behavior. The following sections report on a series of experiments designed to observe the impact of different degrees of order book transparency when traders are homogeneously informed and trading is primarily driven by valuation rather than information.[30]

The experimental series comprises 20 experiments that differ only with respect to the availability of order book information (Gerke/Bienert/Schroeder-Wildberg 1995).[31] In 4 experiments with full order book information ("OB2"), both the summary information on bid-ask spreads and in-depth information on the order book of individual stocks were available as described in 2.2.4. In 10 experiments ("OB1"), the in-depth information was not available and traders were restricted to the bid-ask summary which offers only the market bid and ask for each stock without volume information. In 6 intransparent markets ("OB0") neither information was available. To learn about each other's inclination to trade, participants in these markets had to rely on information on past trades and on their own tentative orders.

---

[28] In most microstructure models (e.g. Glosten/Milgrom 1985), this is the problem of the market maker.

[29] In periodic call auctions, order book transparency seems to reduce both market depth and informational efficiency.

[30] This is in line with Smith (1991 p. 804): "I could give everyone in this room common, complete information, and yet each of you would face uncertainty concerning how others will behave, given this information."

[31] Parts of the results are summarized in Gerke/Garz/Schroeder-Wildberg (1994).

3.2.2 Transparency, order placement, liquidity, and pricing: results

The main results of the comparison between markets with different degrees of transparency refer to changes in order placement patterns, to subsequent changes in market liquidity and to the reaction of prices to fundamental information.

In OB1 and OB2 markets, participants can anticipate the position of their orders relative to the current market bid and ask. Therefore, they are less likely to enter orders with obviously low chances of execution than in OB0 markets. On the other hand, there will be some competition to hold the market bid or ask, and a "gravitational pull" (Cohen/Maier/Schwartz/Whitcomb 1981) towards accepting the market bid, or ask, rather than submitting a limit buy order just below the current ask, or a limit sell order just above the current bid.

Table 2 compares the average distance of newly entered price limits from the price at which an immediate transaction would be possible. A high distance reflects, either a large spread in the order book, or a cautious limit of the new order. In the second half of a trading period (minutes 5-8) there is more agreement on feasible transaction prices and trading becomes more urgent before the end of the period. Hence, the average distance decreases. On average, the price limit of a new sell order is 20.47 percent above the current market bid in the first 4 minutes of a trading period in OB0 markets, compared to only 7.21 percent in the second half of a trading period in OB1 markets.

Table 2: Average distance of newly entered price limits from the touch[32]

Average distance (percent)	OB0 (n=6)	OB1 (n=10)	OB2 (n=4)
Buy order			
Min. 1-4	15.57	9.06	10.64
Min. 5-8	12.36	7.88	9.43
Sell order			
Min. 1-4	20.47	9.31	9.53
Min. 5-8	12.03	7.21	7.89

[32] Average distance between the price limit of an order and the best available price limit on the opposite side of the order book. This measure is negative for orders with "overshooting" limit prices which lead to immediate transactions.

These figures illustrate both the convergence of price expectations during a trading period, which is delayed by a lack of transparency, and the competitive effect of the order book information.[33] In intransparent markets, transactions must be sought by placing tentative orders. These are often placed cautiously far off the touch and then improved step by step until a transaction results. Consequently, participants in OB0 markets submitted an average of 5.79 orders per trading period, compared to 4.38 (OB1) and 3.74 (OB2). However, the number of transactions resulting from these orders does not differ significantly between the three types of markets (1.65, 1.76, 1.42).

The differences in individual order placement strategies must have some impact on the market as a whole. Not surprisingly, the bid-ask spread is significantly larger at the beginning of a trading period in the intransparent OB0 markets. The liquidity of the market, as measured by the closeness of the bid-ask spread, increases when transaction uncertainty is reduced either by observations of past transactions or by order book information.

By affecting the order flow as a whole, transparency also influences the price discovery process of the market. In a transparent market, changing opinions on the value of the stocks may be signalled without a transaction. Therefore, price movements between periods may be completed before the first transaction in a new trading period. This reduces the dispersion of transaction prices within trading periods, i.e. price changes which cannot be explained by new exogenous information (excess volatility). Excess volatility, as measured by the standard deviation of transaction prices within a period, is reduced from an average of 6.2 percent in OB0 markets to 4.6 percent in OB1 markets and 2.5 percent in OB2 markets.[34] However, the correlation between fundamental values and market prices does not differ systematically between the market types.

In general, the main difference is observed between markets which entirely lack order book information (OB0) and markets with bid-ask price information (OB1), while the incremental in-detail information increases the difference only slightly. In real markets with more heterogeneity between traders' endowments and order sizes, this incremental information on volumes and order limits on both sides of the bid-ask spread may be more important.

---

[33] OB2 does not seem to increase competitiveness further when compared to OB1. More detailed information may be used to signal "false" prices outside the bid-ask spread which is not possible in OB1 markets.

[34] Significant at $\alpha < 0.05$ (Kruskal-Wallis test).

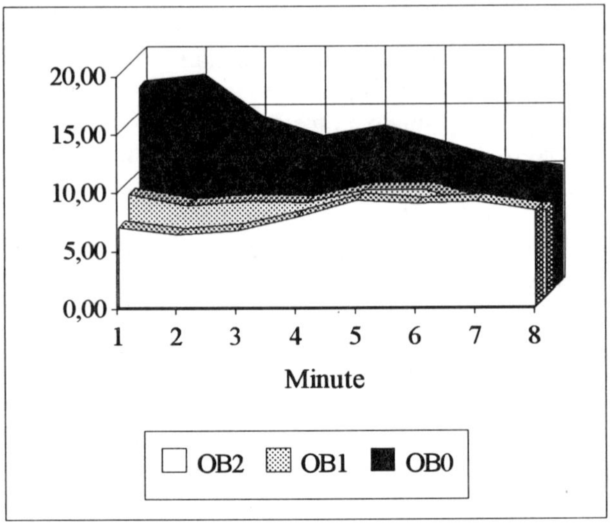

Figure 3: Development of bid-ask spreads during a trading period (percent)

Friedman (1991) finds a detrimental impact of order book transparency on the depth of continuous markets, whereas transparency reduces the bid-ask spread in our experiments. While other factors may contribute to this divergence of results, we conjecture that the difference in the distribution of fundamental information is the most important experimental variation. When the diversity of information with clear-cut implications dominates the strategic incentives for the market participants, transparency may reduce the liquidity of a market. When informational factors are less important, transparency may enhance the coordination function of the market. If, in the context of stock markets, "information" is interpreted as knowledge implying a forecast of future stock prices, there may be little reason to expect large differences in information. It may be contended that most theoretical models overstate the importance of informational diversity by assuming an exogenous revelation of some fundamental value in the near future.

However, a comparison of these results with an otherwise identical market in which traders have diverse information on fundamental factors will help to gain a better understanding of the factors that determine the relation between transparency and liquidity.

4. Conclusion

In the experiments, a small number of homogeneously informed and endowed traders deal in a small number of fairly abstract stocks for a short period. These simplifications must be borne in mind when interpreting the results and when drawing conclusions about more complex, real stock markets.

However, the close experimental observation of the factors driving the market process, and of their interaction, may increase the understanding of even more complex markets. In particular, the simplifications made are balanced to create a situation that is similar to more complex markets: individual agents pursue the goal of increasing their wealth, receive information on future stochastic payments and interact to determine market prices for the stocks generating these payments. Simplifications in the information structure and in the number of stocks are offset by the compressed time horizon.

Broadly speaking, in such experiments we may expect to observe cognitive patterns and heuristics and popular models of complex interdependent market processes that are similar to those which influence the behavior of investors and traders in the world's stock markets. And the way these patterns interact in our experimental model may reveal some important features of the way in which behavioral patterns are shaped by, and simultaneously determine, market dynamics in these markets.

We now plan to extend these experiments by introducing privileges for individual traders and by varying the market mechanism. The results will be combined with insights gained from different experimental designs, from empirical studies and from theoretical models. The objective is to find the questions that must be asked if decisions on the organization of a stock market are to enhance the subsequent performance of this market, and the ways to answer these questions for specific environments.

References

Camerer, C. D. (1992): The rationality of prices and volume in experimental markets, in: Organizational Behavior and Human Decision Processes 51, 237-272.

Cohen, K. J., Maier, S. F., Schwartz R. A. and Whitcomb, D. K. (1981): Transaction costs, order placement strategy, and existence of the bid-ask spread, in: Journal of Political Economy 89, 287-305.

Davis, D. and C. Holt (1992): Experimental economics. Princeton (Princeton University Press).

Ferris, S. P., Haugen, R. A. and Makhija, A. K. (1988): Predicting contemporary volume at differential price levels: evidence supporting the disposition effect, in: Journal of Finance 43, 677-697.

Friedman, D. (1991): How trading institutions affect financial market performance: some laboratory evidence. Working paper, University of California. Santa Cruz, forthcoming in Economic Inquiry.

Friedman, D. and S. Sunder (1994): Experimental methods: a primer for economists. Cambridge/UK-New York/USA (Cambridge University Press).

Gerke, W. (1992): Optimierung der Börsenstruktur, in: Arbeitsgemeinschaft der deutschen Wertpapierbörsen (ed.): Finanzmarkttheorie und Börsenstruktur. Frankfurt, 93-111.

Gerke, W. (1994): Lernen im Modell: Erfahrungen mit der experimentellen Computerbörse CAT, in: Albach, H. and P. Mertens (eds.): Hochschuldidaktik und Hochschulökonomie, Zeitschrift für Betriebswirtschaft, supplemental issue 2/94.

Gerke, W. and Bienert, H. (1993): Überprüfung des Dispositionseffektes und seiner Auswirkungen in computerisierten Börsenexperimenten, in: Bühler, W., H. Hax and R. Schmidt (eds.): Empirische Kapitalmarktforschung. Zeitschrift für betriebswirtschaftliche Forschung, special issue 31, 169-194.

Gerke, W. and Bienert, H. (1994): Computerisierte Börsenexperimente: Ein Beitrag zu einer Experimentellen Kapitalmarktforschung, in: Zeitschrift für Wirtschafts- und Sozialwissenschaften 114, 573-596.

Gerke, W., Bienert, H. and Schroeder-Wildberg, U. (1995): Orderbuchtransparenz bei homogenem Informationsangebot - eine experimentelle Untersuchung, in: Kredit und Kapital 28, 227-269.

Gerke, W., H. Bienert and M. Sun (1992): Experimentelle Kapitalmarktforschung am Beispiel des Dispositionseffektes. Working Paper (second, revised and extended version), Lehrstuhl für Bank- und Börsenwesen, University of Erlangen-Nuremberg.

Gerke, W., H. Garz and U. Schroeder-Wildberg (1994): The effects of market transparency on the efficiency of asset markets: some experimental results. Paper presented at the CEPR/ESF Network in Financial Markets conference on Market Microstructure in Konstanz, 25/26 March 1994.

Gerke, W. and U. Schroeder-Wildberg (1993): Das Verhalten an einer experimentellen Wertpapierbörse in Planwirtschaft und Marktwirtschaft, in: Gerke, W. (ed.): Zentrale Planwirtschaft am Ende - Marktwirtschaft in der Krise? Stuttgart (Schäffer-Poeschel), 375-397.

Glosten, L. R. and Milgrom, P. R. (1985): Bid, ask and transaction prices in a specialist market with heterogeneously informed traders, in: Journal of Financial Economics 14, 71-100.

Harris, L. E. (1990): Liquidity, trading rules, and electronic trading systems. Monograph series in finance and economics. Monograph 1990-4, New York University, Salomon Center.

Hey, J. D. (1991): Experiments in economics. Oxford/Cambridge (Blackwell).

Jamal, K. and Sunder, S. (1991): Money vs. gaming: effects of salient monetary payments in double oral auctions, in: Organizational Behavior and Human Decision Processes 49, 151-166.

Kachelmeier, S. and Shehata, M. (1992): Examining risk preferences under high monetary incentives: experimental evidence from the people's republic of China, in: American Economic Review 82, 1120-1141.

Kahneman, D. and Tversky, A. (1979): Prospect theory: an analysis of decision under risk, in: Econometrica 47, 263-291.

Keynes, J. M. (1936): The general theory of employment, interest and money. London (Macmillan and Co.), reprinted 1951.

Kyle, A. S. (1985): Continuous auctions and insider trading, in: Econometrica 53, 1315-1335.

Lakonishok, J. and Smidt, S. (1986): Value for winners and losers: taxation and other motives for stock trading, in: Journal of Finance 41, 951-974.

Marimon, R. and Sunder, S. (1993): Indeterminacy of equilibria in a hyperinflationary world: experimental evidence, in: Econometrica 61, 1073-1107.

Schachter, S., Ouellette, R., Whittle, B. and Gerin, W. (1987): Effects of trend and of profit or loss on the tendency to sell stock, in: Basic and Applied Social Psychology, Vol. 8, 259-271.

Schwartz, R. A. (1991): Reshaping the equity markets. New York (HarperBusiness).

Shefrin, H. and Statman, M. (1985): The disposition to sell winners too early and ride losers too long: theory and evidence, in: Journal of Finance 40, 777-792.

Shleifer, A. and Summers, L. H. (1990): The noise trader approach to finance, in: Journal of Economic Perspectives 4, No. 2, 19-33.

Smith, V. L. (1972): Experimental economics: induced value theory, in: American Economic Review 66, 274-279.

Smith, V. L. (1989): Theory, experiment and economics, in: Journal of Economic Perspectives 3, 151-169.

Smith, V. L. (1991): Experimental economics: behavioral lessons for microeconomic theory and policy, in: Smith, V. L. (ed.): Papers in experimental economics. Cambridge/Mass. (Cambridge University Press), 802-812.

Stanley, T. D. (1994): Silly bubbles and the insensitivity of rationality testing: An experimental illustration, in: Journal of Economic Psychology 15, 601-620.

Stoll, H. R. (1992): Principles of trading market structure, in: Journal of Financial Services Research 6, 75-107.

Sunder, S. (1992): Experimental asset markets: a survey. Working Paper No. 1992-19, Carnegie Mellon University. Pittsburgh, PA.

Tirole, J. (1985): Asset bubbles and overlapping generations, in: Econometrica 53, 1499-1528.

Tversky, A. and Kahneman, D. (1992): Advances in prospect theory: cumulative representation of uncertainty, in: Journal of Risk and Uncertainty 5, 297-323.

Weber, M. and C. D. Camerer (1991): The disposition effect in securities trading: an experimental analysis. Working Paper. Kiel/Chicago.

Designing an Experimental Stock Market

Jan P. Krahnen, Christian Rieck and Erik Theissen
University of Frankfurt

1. Introduction

Trading mechanisms on asset markets and their impact on the pricing and allocation of securities have always constituted focal points for scholars of financial economics. Standard theories such as the Capital Asset Pricing Model rely on specific assumptions concerning the functioning of the market mechanism and the behavior of market participants. The market mechanism is usually assumed to function in textbook fashion. Transaction costs and frictions, or incentives, inherent in the institutional design of the market are assumed away.

As a result of growing competition for transaction volume between different exchanges in North America, Europe and the Far East, the working principles of asset markets first came under scrutinity in the early eighties. An important area of research comprised the determinants of liquidity and the liquidity cost implicit in the prevailing bid-ask spread. In a related field of research, the relaxation of the assumption of symmetrically distributed information resulted in models of market processes that differentiated between the behavior of outsiders and insiders.

Market participants are usually modeled as rational, utility maximizing agents. However, empirically observed price "anomalies", and the bulk of experimental work in both economics and psychology, cast doubt on this assumption. In the field of finance, this has led to models which incorporate quasi-rational agents, often termed noise traders. The two developments just mentioned lead to the basic assumptions of this paper, namely, a market and its organizational (or micro-) structure matter in much the same way as the organizational (or internal-) structure of a firm is related to its performance; and, the behavior of market participants has to be examined using methods that go beyond the assumption of expected utility maximization.

If these assumptions hold, market outcomes in terms of prices and allocation are sub-optimal. Price fads, or bubbles, become a conceivable market outcome although arbitrage operations are, in principle, profitable. Furthermore, informational asymmetries may drive up liquidity premiums, leading to sub-optimally diversified portfolios.

Empirical research based on the above assumptions encounters a general problem. In most cases it is not possible to gain a sufficient degree of control over the relevant variables. Laboratory experimentation overcomes this problem. The experimental environment, including such dimensions as the information set, can be defined in a way that allows the direct testing of behavioral hypotheses. Typical trading mechanisms such as those implemented at the Frankfurt Stock Exchange or the New York Stock Exchange can be compared under `ceteris paribus′ conditions. This requires, however, a framework for experimental research that is flexible enough to allow the implementation of different designs whilst simultaneously holding all other variables constant. Together with a desire for "research efficiency" this calls for a computerized environment which has to meet several requirements. First, it has to represent the main characteristics of a stock market, namely, the trading of one or several claims among a number of individuals. Second, prices on the market have to be endogenous whereas the value of each asset is exogenous and stochastic. Third, different institutional forms of the market-clearing mechanism have to be permissible, notably the auction market (continuous and batched auction), and the dealer market (with competitive dealers or monopolist specialists). Fourth, single characteristics of the market institution should be variable, for example, the initial endowment of participants and their individual access to information about the fundamental value of the asset or the order book, to mention but a few.

The primary purpose of this paper is to describe the development of such an environment. The starting point was a series of market experiments conducted on a "paper-and-pencil" basis. They were designed to investigate questions about the informational efficiency of the market and the influence of the information structure, endowments, expectations and risk aversion on the market outcome. Experience gained from these experiments influenced the design of the software system which had to be developed. The choice of a particular experimental design, the extent to which the results of pilot studies influenced the laboratory set-up, and whether or not certain experimental results are robust, i.e. remain unchanged under minor variations of the design,[1] are therefore reported in greater detail below.

The paper is organized as follows. Section 2 describes the experimental design. Sections 3 to 5 report results on the informational efficiency of the

---

[1] See Roth (1994) for a discussion of methodological standards concerning the development of experimental designs.

experimental markets, the formation of expectations in the market, and the attempt to construct a reliable measure of risk aversion. Section 6 contains a description of the software system MAX and a preview of intended future experiments with this software tool. The conclusions in section 7 touch on methodological and empirical issues as well as directions for future research.

2. The experimental design

In our experimental asset markets subjects trade a risky security against money over a sequence of 14 rounds. The *fundamental value* (FV) of the asset is stochastic and its realizations evolve over time following a binomial process. The properties of the process, but not the initial value, are held constant across all experiments. Upward and downward movements of 7 percent in fundamental value occur with probabilities of 0.6 and 0,4, respectively, implying a drift of 1.4 percent per round or 19.8 percent over 14 rounds. Maximum and minimum terminal fundamental values are 240.99% (prob.= 0.131%) and 38.9% (prob.= 0.00066%) of the initial value respectively.[2] To render the alleged exogeneity of the FV-process credible, the upward or downward movement in every period was determined openly by drawing one ball from an urn containing six red (= up) and 4 white (= down) balls. In each round, one of the informed participants was selected to draw the ball. The fundamental-value process just described was chosen to fulfill two requirements: (a) it should be simple enough to allow participants to calculate the expectation of the fundamental value at the end of the experiment; and, (b) it should conform to "everyday experience" of price movements on the stock exchange. In our view, a binomial process with upward drift fulfills these requirements. Contrastingly, stationary replications of the same situation (as in Plott/Sunder 1982) or a fundamental value that declines to zero in the course of the experiment (as in Smith/Suchanek/Williams 1988) are not in accordance with what subjects know a priori about asset trading.

Subjects receive the full value in German Marks of their Round-14 portfolio after the termination of the experiment. The portfolio consists of the Round-14 money balance and the monetary equivalent of the stocks then held (valued at their period-14 fundamental value). Earnings ranged from DM 17.60 to DM 74.00, the average being DM 28.59 for an experiment lasting up to three hours.

Participants are asymmetrically endowed, yielding a 2 x 2 factorial design. Half the subjects start with a portfolio consisting of 100% cash, the others start with 100% securities. The initial money balance is approximately equal to the round-zero value of the securities endowment. Furthermore, subjects have different access to the fundamental-value information that is revealed every

---

2 The entire ex-ante distribution of Round 14 fundamental values is skewed to the right.

period. The fundamental-value process itself is common information. However, one half of all subjects, the "informed" participants, observe the initial value and the subsequent realizations of the process, whereas "uninformed" participants see neither the initial value nor the realizations. The latter therefore have to infer the fundamental value from public information comprising the past sequences of market prices and the transaction volumes. The presence of insiders in the market is common information.

In six out of the nine experiments reported here a call market institution was employed.[3] The call market mechanism was made the starting point of the analysis because it is widely employed for trading on German exchanges and because it has hitherto received little attention in experimental research.[4] In a call market, the transaction price is determined by a double-sided sealed-bid auction (*batched auction*, or *call market*) at the end of each round. Prices are volume-maximizing prices where, (i) in the case of rationing, priority is given to the limit price (highest buy/lowest sell order) and, subordinately, to order volume and, (ii) in the case of indifference,[5] priority is given to the lower price. Note that this is a schematic rule of price choice which may lead to extreme price fluctuations, provided that the indifference interval is large.[6] A typical trading round in a call market experiment consists of the following sequence:

1. Subjects place their orders, which may be a single purchase order, a single sale order, both, or none. In all cases (except "none"), they have to specify a limit price (maximum in case of purchase, minimum in case of sale) and the desired quantity. Orders are subject to a budget constraint since short sales of money, or securities, are not allowed.
2. Orders are collected and the market price is determined via the call market mechanism described above. The resulting market price and the transaction volume are communicated to all participants, supplemented by "short-cut information", identifying the "longer" market side,[7] if applicable.

---

[3] In two early call market experiments the number of trading periods was not announced in advance. Since the asset does not have a clearly defined fundamental value, we decided not to utilize these data.

[4] Notable exceptions are Smith/Williams/Bratton/Vannoni (1982), Van Boening (1991), Friedman (1993) and Van Boening/Williams/LaMaster (1993).

[5] Suppose there is only one order to buy at 230 and one order to sell at 220. In this case any price between 220 and 230 maximizes the trading volume. We refer to the range 220-230 as the *indifference interval*.

[6] *All* schematic rules face this problem, although a mean-value rule, for instance, may lower price variability. In real stock markets, the problem of indeterminacy arises mostly in thin markets. At the Frankfurt Stock Exchange, no schematic rule is said to exist. Rather, brokers ("Amtliche Kursmakler") claim to rely on "their feeling" to identify the equilibrium price in case of indeterminacy.

[7] Following the practice at the Frankfurt Stock Exchange "bG" ("bB") signifies that, at the market price, demand exceeds (falls short of) supply.

3. Individual balances of money and stocks are adjusted according to completed trades.
4. A new realization of the fundamental value process is observed by the informed participants (either up or down by 7 percent).
5. Participants write down their forecast of the next period's market price and of the expected Round-14 fundamental value (i.e. the value at which securities will ultimately be exchanged for cash). The quality of expectations is not rewarded separately in order to prevent any bias in recorded expectations stemming from an attempt by participants to diversify between portfolio performance and expectational performance.

The first four of the six call market experiments were run on a "paper-and-pencil" basis. The last two made use of an early version of the MAX software described in section 6. The design itself, however, remained unchanged.

Three additional experiments were conducted as computerized continuous double auctions, also using an early version of the MAX software system. Subjects can submit buy, or sell, orders (subject to the short selling restriction) at any time. A new order is required to narrow the market spread. The highest buy order and the lowest sell order are displayed to all participants. The subject who has entered the order remains anonymous in order to prevent the identification of insiders. Transactions occur whenever a participant completely, or partially, accepts the standing bid or the standing ask.

From time to time a subject erroneously entered a very unfavourable order (e.g. a sell order at a price of 1) which was immediately accepted by another trader. In such cases the corresponding transactions were eliminated from the data set.[8] In the present version of the software system, subjects have to confirm orders whenever the limit price is "far" away from recent transaction prices.

The results of the experimental investigation of informational efficiency (Krahnen/Rieck/Theissen 1994b, 1995), expectations formation (Krahnen/Rieck/Theissen 1994c), and risk attitudes (Krahnen/Rieck/Theissen 1994a, d) are reported in the following pages.

---

[8] We eliminated a total of 6 transactions. In all cases, the transaction price was less than 12% of the previous transaction price. It therefore seems safe to attribute these transactions to typing errors.

3. Informational efficiency of experimental markets

3.1 Deviations of prices from fundamental values

If all traders were risk neutral, the equilibrium price in period t would have to be equal to the mathematical expectation in period t of the final, i.e. Round-14, fundamental value. If traders were risk averse, prices would have to be below the fundamental value. The difference, $E_t(V_{14}) - P_t$, should decrease over time since the risk associated with the fundamental value process (in terms of variance) also decreases.

The experimental results are shown in Figures 1 and 2 which plot the relative mispricing

$$RM = \frac{E_t(V_{14}) - P_t}{E_t(V_{14})} \tag{1}$$

against periods for the call market experiments and the continuous double auction experiments, respectively.[9]

In most cases, prices tend to converge towards the fundamental value by period 14. During the course of the experiment, however, prices can deviate considerably from their equilibrium levels. The direction and magnitude of these deviations do not exhibit any clear pattern. This finding is in contrast to the experimental results of Smith/Suchanek/Williams (1988), who found a strong tendency for prices to be too high. As discussed in more detail in Krahnen/Rieck/Theissen (1994b), differences in the experimental design, and especially the different fundamental-value processes employed, might explain the different findings.

---

[9] The difference is divided by the expected fundamental value in order to make experiments comparable.

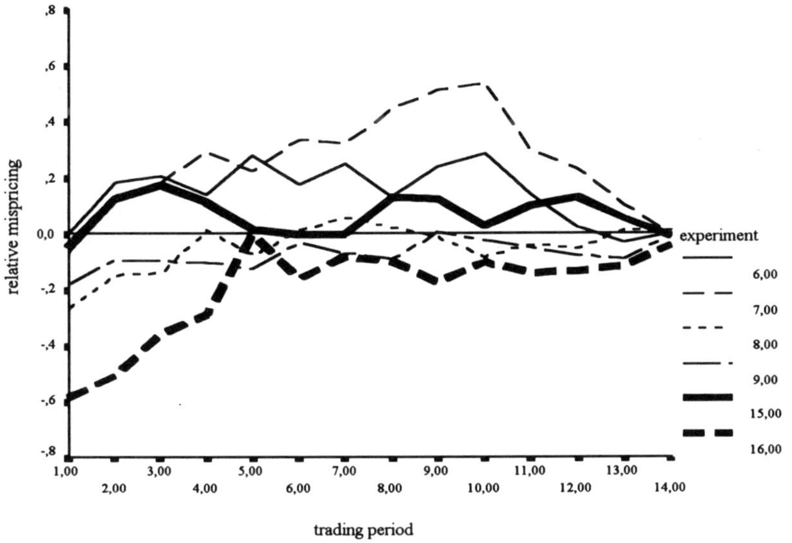

Figure 1: Relative mispricing in the call market experiments.

The lines show the relative mispricing for each of the six call market experiments. "Mispricing" is defined as the difference between the price in period t and the mathematical expected value in period t of the final (i.e. period-14) fundamental value. To obtain the *relative* mispricing, this variable is divided by the mathematical expected value in period t of the final fundamental value.

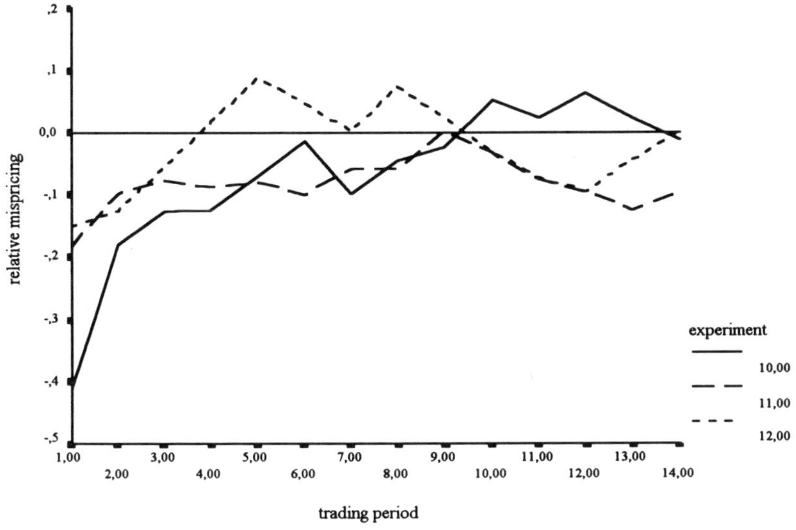

Figure 2: Relative mispricing in the continuous double auction experiments.

The lines plot the relative mispricing for each of the three continuous double auction experiments. "Mispricing" is defined as the difference between the price in period t and the mathematical expected value in period t of the final (i.e. period-14) fundamental value. To obtain the relative mispricing, this variable is divided by the mathematical expected value in period t of the final fundamental value.

Table 1 exhibits some summary statistics which measure the (in)efficiency of prices. The pricing errors, averaged over the 14 trading periods, range from 0.06 (i.e. 6% of the fundamental value) in experiment 12 to 0.26 in experiment 7. It is thus apparent that there is a considerable degree of inefficiency, which creates a potential for insider gains.

Table 1: Mean absolute difference between price and mathematical expectation of the fundamental value

---

This table shows the mean absolute difference (MAD) and the mean relative difference (MRD) for each of the nine experiments. The MAD measure is defined as

$$\mathrm{MAD} = \frac{1}{14} \sum_{i=1}^{14} \left| P_t - E_t(V_{14}) \right|. \tag{2}$$

This is the average (over the 14 trading periods) of the absolute value of the deviation between price and fundamental value ("mispricing"). The MRD measure is defined as

$$\mathrm{MRD} = \frac{1}{14} \sum_{t=1}^{14} \frac{\left| P_t - E_t(V_{14}) \right|}{E_t(V_{14})}. \tag{3}$$

It thus corrects the MAD measure for different fundamental value levels in the experiments. A value of 0.15 has to be interpreted as an average absolute deviation between price and fundamental value amounting to 15% of the fundamental value.

Exp.	6	7	8	9	10	11	12	15	16
MAD	82.45	95.97	18.84	27.52	47.56	32.75	30.38	36.31	94.05
MRD	0.15	0.26	0.07	0.07	0.09	0.08	0.06	0.08	0.20

3.2 Profitability of the insider position

The next step is to determine whether informed subjects were able to exploit their informational advantage. Table 2 shows the ratios of the average earnings of informed to those of uninformed participants. Averaged over all experiments, the insider position is advantageous. Informed participants' payoff is 6.1% higher than uninformed participants' income. As both the initial portfolio structure and the realization of the fundamental value process influence portfolio values, we also split the sample and give the figures for traders with cash-only and assets-only endowments separately. This analysis reveals that the insider advantage seems to be more pronounced for those insiders with an initial portfolio consisting only of cash. This result is, however, mainly due to the extreme result of experiment 15.

Both Table 1 and Table 2 reveal great differences between experiments. It is natural to relate the differences in pricing efficiency as measured by the MAD defined in Table 1 to those in the profitability of the insider position. The rank correlation coefficient is 0.5833 which is significant at the 10% level. Thus, it appears that insiders can take more advantage of their superior information when the market is less efficient.

Table 2: Ratio of average earnings of informed and uninformed participants.

The figures show the ratio of the average earnings of the informed to the uninformed participants for each experiment. Columns 3 and 4 contain the separate ratios for participants with a cash-only and an assets-only initial endowment respectively. The last row contains the (unweighted) averages over the nine experiments.

Experiment	all traders	cash-only	assets-only
6	1.029	0.979	1.057
7	1.141	1.100	1.153
8	0.996	0.987	1.007
9	0.972	0.996	0.961
10	1.032	1.027	1.066
11	1.008	1.041	1.001
12	1.060	1.110	1.015
15	1.274	1.427	1.175
16	1.037	1.179	0.935
average over all experiments	1.061	1.094	1.041

3.3 Effects of different endowment structures

As was noted earlier, half of the subjects in the experiments were endowed with a portfolio consisting entirely of cash while the portfolio of the other half consisted entirely of assets. We refer to these as the "cash-only group" and the "assets-only group", respectively.

Two questions concerning the structure of the endowments are of importance:

- How long does it take to balance the portfolios?
- Is there a systematic difference between the final portfolio structures of the cash-only and the assets-only groups?

Theory would suggest that subjects balance their portfolios, the target portfolio being determined by their respective degrees of risk aversion. As the subjects were randomly assigned to the endowment groups, there should not be systematic differences between the risk aversion of the groups. Therefore, one might expect the final portfolio structure of both groups to be equal. Table 3 demonstrates, however, that the data do not corroborate this hypothesis. There is clear evidence of an endowment effect. Subjects who start with an assets-only portfolio tend to end up with more assets than do subjects in the cash-only group.

There are two possible explanations for this finding. First, it is possible that the 14 trading periods are simply insufficient for portfolio balancing to be completed. However, this is obviously not the case. Portfolio balancing is terminated halfway through the experiment. The completion of rebalancing is measured as follows. Initially, those subjects who started with a portfolio of cash can only buy shares while the other group can only sell shares. In the subsequent periods, the traders of the cash-only group remain, on average, on the buying side whereas the assets-only group remains, on average, on the selling side. Portfolio balancing is deemed to be terminated when the subjects of the cash-only group *sell* assets on average for the first time. This happens between period 4 (in experiments 11 and 12) and period 9 (in experiment 7).

The finding reported in Table 3 must therefore be attributed to a genuine endowment effect. It is possible that the initial endowment serves as a reference point and that subjects are reluctant to move too far away from this point. In such a case, uninformed subjects might, as a consequence of the greater uncertainty imposed on them, be expected to be even more reluctant dramatically to change the composition of their portfolios. The figures in Table 4 are consistent with this hypothesis; the endowment effect seems to be more pronounced for uninformed subjects. The fact that the transaction volume is higher for informed subjects in 6 out of 9 experiments also (weakly) supports the hypothesis.

Table 3: Comparison of initial and terminal portfolio structure

This table shows the ratios of the final (after period 14) asset holdings of the assets-only group to the cash-only group. This ratio is shown for every experiment in column 2. Columns 3 and 4 contain this ratio calculated separately for the uninformed and the informed subjects, respectively. A value of 1.80 has to be interpreted as follows: final asset holdings of the assets-only group exceed those of the cash-only group by a factor of 1.8; e.g., subjects in the former group hold 18 shares on average while those in the latter group hold 10.

Experiment	all	uninformed	informed
6	1.80	2.29	1.34
7	1.29	1.30	1.26
8	0.94	1.08	0.80
9	1.37	2.67	1.00
10	2.49	2.82	2.27
11	1.64	16.0	1.23
12	1.25	0.81	1.74
15	1.41	1.42	1.33
16	1.73	1.89	1.57

3.4 Continuous double auction versus call market

Of the nine experiments included in our analysis, six were conducted using a call market institution while, in the three remaining experiments, a continuous double auction was employed. The fact that each experiment constitutes one observation precludes a detailed statistical analysis. The following commentary is therefore confined to a description of the data.

In market experiments with symmetric information, the continuous double auction institution achieves a faster convergence of prices to their equilibrium levels and higher allocative efficiency than does the call market (Smith/Williams/Bratton/Vannoni 1982). Friedman 1993 compared the two institutions in an asset-market setting with asymmetric information. He found that there were no significant differences between the informational efficiency of the call market and the continuous double auction. Allocational efficiency and trading volume were higher in the double auction whereas the call market provided greater market depth.[10]

Our results are summarized in Table 4. Trading volume is higher in the continuous double auction. The results concerning informational efficiency, however, are inconsistent with those of Friedman (1993). The efficiency of the continuous double auction, as measured by the MAD and MRD measures defined in Table 1 is higher than the efficiency of the call markets. This is remarkable since the number of participants was considerably higher in the call market experiments (29, on average, as compared to 11 for the continuous double auction experiments).

To the extent that it is permissible to draw conclusions from nine observations, our experiments suggest that the continuous double auction institution might be superior to the call market as far as volume and informational efficiency are concerned. Results on allocational efficiency cannot be presented since our design does not allow clear predictions about the allocation of assets. However, the high allocational efficiency of the continuous double auction institution has repeatedly been demonstrated and apparently does not even depend on trader rationality (Gode/Sunder 1993 a,b).

4. The role of expectations

4.1 Design of the experiment

It was conjectured that participants' behavior might be explained by their expectations. Prior to each trading period subjects were therefore asked to write down two types of expectations:

1. the market price they expected in the subsequent trading period; and,
2. the fundamental value they expected for the final trading period, i.e., period 14.

Participants were obliged to make forecasts, but their expectations were not remunerated, i.e., had no effect on their payoff. This procedure was chosen in order not to influence their behavior in the market with incentives other than those resulting from market behavior; it might otherwise have been worth their trying to influence the market price strategically.

---

[10] Depth is measured by the bid-ask spread. In the call market the spread is defined as the difference between the highest rejected bid and the lowest rejected ask.

Table 4: Comparison of Call Market and Double Auction

The table contains averages for the six call market experiments and the three double auction market experiments. MAD is the mean absolute difference between price P_t and the expectation in period t of the Round 14 fundamental value, $E_t(V_{14}) = V_t \cdot 1{,}014^{(14-t)}$. MRD is the mean of the normalized absolute difference between price P_t and the expectation in period t of the Round-14 fundamental value. Normalization is obtained by dividing by $E_t(V_{14})$ in order to make experiments comparable which have different starting values and different subsequent realizations of the fundamental value process. Insider advantage is the ratio of the average payoff to the informed participants to the average payoff to the uninformed participants.[11] Normalized trading volume is the average trading volume divided by the total number of shares outstanding.

	MAD	MRD	Insider Advantage	Normalized Volume
Call Market	59.19	0.138	1.056	0.07
Double Auction	36.90	0.077	1.033	0.22

Apart from hinting at subject behavior, the forecast questions were also intended to stimulate a thorough consideration of the participants' own decisions: the market price is the cut-off value for possible trading. For every participant intending to trade it is therefore essential to forecast the market price. The fundamental value in period 14 is also highly relevant, as it directly influences the participants' monetary payoff (via the valuation of the final portfolios).

Two aspects of expectations are reported below, namely, their accuracy and their influence on the market outcome. For a more comprehensive analysis of many other details reference is made to Krahnen/Rieck/Theissen (1994 b, c).

4.2 The accuracy of expectations

In the experiments, informed traders have access to all information which is necessary for calculating the expected value of the final fundamental value. In contrast, uninformed traders do not have any information about the fundamental value (not even the starting value in the first period). Hence, one obvious

[11] The values in Table 4 cannot be directly related to those in Table 3 because the number of participants differs across experiments.

hypothesis is the conjecture that the value forecasts of informed traders are more accurate than those of traders who are uninformed. Furthermore, informed traders should also be able to predict the next market price more accurately because they are always aware of the latest realization of the fundamental value.

Adopting the mean squared error summed over individuals as an appropriate measure (separately for each experimental session), informed groups are clearly better at forming fundamental-value expectations but apparently do not have an advantage in forming price expectations. This indicates either that they do not use their superior knowledge, or that the information incorporated in the fundamental value does not help them to predict the next period's price.

A second plausible hypothesis is that those traders who become active in one market period make better forecasts than inactive participants. To determine its validity, we calculated two measures, namely, *average expectations*, which are the simple arithmetic mean of all forecasts; and, *market expectations*, which are the average expectations of those subjects who actually submitted an order, weighted with the individual transaction size. To assess the accuracy of forecasts we further calculated the root mean squared error (RMSE) on the basis of these two measures for each experiment (Krahnen/Rieck/Theissen 1994 b).

The results show that in all but two sessions average expectations lead to a lower RMSE than market expectations. One possible explanation is that the trading volume of uninformed participants (who possess less information and can therefore be expected to form less precise forecasts) is higher than that of those who are informed. This is, however, not true. The transaction volume of uninformed traders is lower than that of informed traders in 6 of the 9 experiments. An alternative explanation is that the participants who actually trade in the market have a forecasting ability that is below average. It is possible that this effect is due to the fact that subjects with a higher estimation error are more likely to place orders.

4.3 Are expectations rational or adaptive?

We are particularly interested in the way expectations are formed and have therefore attempted to determine whether the data are compatible with rational expectations or with adaptive expectations.

The concept of *rational expectations* is based upon the assumption that agents utilize all available information in constructing their beliefs (Nash 1950, Muth 1961). Forecasts are confirmed by future realizations so that deviations between expectations and actual outcomes are random. Muth's theory also assumes that expectations correspond to the predictions of the relevant economic theory which is implicitly assumed to be known. With rational expectations, forecasts are unbiased and efficient estimators of true values. This hypothesis is testable in principle, even if the true underlying economic model is not known[12]. For this purpose we estimate, separately for each trial, the following two equations:

$$\begin{aligned} P_t &= \alpha_1 + \alpha_2 E_{i,t-1}(P_t) + \varepsilon_{i,t} \\ V_t &= \beta_1 + \beta_2 E_{i,t-1}(V_t) + \varepsilon_{i,t} \end{aligned} \tag{4}$$

P_t is the market price in period t, $E_{i,t-1}(.)$ are the expectations of agent i, formed in period t-1, V_t is the mathematical expectation of the fundamental value in the final round 14. Expectations are said to be unbiased if $(\alpha_1 ; \alpha_2) = (0;1)$, and $(\beta_1;\beta_2) = (0)$, respectively. This analysis was undertaken for each experimental session with all subjects, the latter being divided into "informed" and "uninformed" subgroups.

The hypothesis of unbiasedness must be rejected[13] in all trials, with the exception of M 15. The RE model has almost no explanatory power for the value expectations of uninformed subjects. For price expectations, the RE-model tends to do better in the case of informed subjects. However, the R-squared varies greatly between trials, a result which may be due to differences in the realized price path.

Expectations are called *adaptive* if a forecast is constructed by adding a fraction of the past forecasting error to the last period forecast. Hence, adaptive price expectations can be modeled as follows:

$$E_t(P_{t+1}) = E_{t-1}(P_t) + b\left[P_t - E_{t-1}(P_t)\right] \tag{5}$$

The coefficient b determines the weight of one's own expectational error in determining the next period's forecast. The adaptive expectation hypothesis (AEH) assumes b-values between 0 and 1. Hence, b specifies the fraction of past forecasting error that is believed to be permanent and therefore relevant for the formation of expectations. AEH can be tested via the following expression:

$$E_{i,t}(P_{t+1}) - E_{i,t-1}(P_t) = \alpha_1 + \alpha_2\left[P_t - E_{i,t-1}(P_t)\right] + \varepsilon_{i,t} \tag{6}$$

[12] As Smith/Suchanek/Williams (1988), pp. 1136-7 point out, it is the REH according to NASH which is being tested here.

[13] Rejection refers to two independent t-tests of the null hypotheses $\{\alpha_1 = 0,\ \alpha_2 = 1\}$ and $\beta_1 = 0,\ \beta_2 = 1\}$ at the 1%-level. The hypotheses (α_1, α_2) and $(\beta_1, \beta_2) = (0, 1)$ have not been simultaneously tested with an F-test. Our justification for this rests on the Bonferroni-inequality (see Sachs 1992, p. 39).

The relevant restrictions are $\alpha_1 = 0$ and $0 < \alpha_2 < 1$. In an analogous fashion it is possible to test the validity of the AEH with respect to value expectation. In that case it is necessary to differentiate between informed participants, who actually know past values, and uninformed participants. For the latter group we have substituted past prices for (unobservable) past values. The regression equation (for the informed) is:

$$E_{i,t-1}(V_t) - E_{i,t-2}(V_{t-1}) = \beta_1^I + \beta_2^I\left[V_{t-1} - E_{i,t-2}(V_{t-1})\right] + \varepsilon_{i,t} \quad (7)$$

In all cases the estimated coefficient is compatible with the AEH. The coefficient of 0.219 for the value expectations of the informed is quite small compared with previous investigations (Williams 1987, Smith/Suchanek/ Williams 1988). The reported R^2 (0.176) is also much smaller than in the other cases. This comes as no surprise, since the informed have no reason to form expectations according to the AEH. Due to their information advantage they are capable, at least in principle, of calculating the true fundamental value. For the uninformed, however, the AEH explains the data quite well. A more comprehensive analysis can be found in Krahnen/Rieck/Theissen (1994c).

4.4 Does it pay to be a good forecaster?

If subjects trade according to their expectations, i.e., if they buy when they perceive the asset to be underpriced and sell when they perceive it to be overpriced, good forecasters should, on average, earn higher profits. To test this hypothesis, the final value of the portfolio of all subjects was regressed on the root mean squared error (RMSE) of prices and values respectively (Krahnen/Rieck/Theissen 1994c, table 22).

Surprisingly, the expectational error, measured by RMSE, has no effect on personal wealth. In the regressions, the expectational errors of prices and values remain insignificant in all trials. On the other hand, both initial endowment and information status explain much of the variation in personal wealth within each trial: the respective dummy-coefficients are significant in most sessions. The initial endowment (only stocks or only cash) in particular has a strong influence on the final wealth.

It can therefore be concluded that forecasting accuracy did not pay in the sense of increasing expected terminal wealth. A possible explanation for this effect could be that subjects do not detect profitable deviations between price and value. As a means of examining the validity of this explanation, two indicators were defined, namely, *objective mispricing,* which denotes the difference between market price and "true" fundamental value in any given period, i.e., the expected value of the period 14 fundamental value, $OB_t = P_t - EFW_t$; and, *subjective mispricing* which is the difference between expected price and expected value, $SB_{i,t} = E_{i,t}P_{t+1} - EFW_{i,t}$.

The analysis shows that for uninformed subjects, subjective perception of mispricing has no "objective" foundation. For informed subjects, however, a significant relationship is found in 5 out of 6 cases. Nevertheless, the R-squared is small in all cases except one (M16).

To summarize: informed traders are aware of mispricing while those who are uninformed are not, but the former can hardly take advantage of their knowledge. The reason for this effect seems to be that subjects do not trade on their expectations. A close relation between individual expectations and behavior in the market could not in fact be found.

5. Risk attitude in market experiments

5.1 Approaches to risk attitude assesment

Experimental results might be partially explained by subject risk aversion. Therefore, it is worth considering ways of controlling for subjects' attitudes towards risk. Basically, there are two possible approaches: on the one hand to "induce" a certain risk attitude by means of the Roth/Malouf (1979) procedure (see also Berg/Daley/Dickhaut/O'Brien 1986) or, on the other, to "measure" the subjects' risk attitudes. Although the Roth/Malouf-types of risk attitude inducement are theoretically convincing, it has not yet been determined whether risk attitudes can be successfully induced[14]. Therefore we decided to use conventional monetary payoffs in our experiments (instead of lottery-transformed payoffs) and to measure each individual's risk attitude.

Measuring risk attitudes is one of the oldest tasks in experimental economics. As far as we are aware, the first attempt at risk attitude measurement was that of Mosteller/Nogee (1951). We used a modified version of the "certainty equivalent" (= CE) approach[15].

---

[14] See Radner/Schotter (1989), who present experimental evidence against the procedure.

[15] See Farquahr (1984). For a further discussion of methods for measuring risk attitudes see Krahnen/Rieck/Theissen (1994a).

5.2 Measuring risk attitudes by eliciting certainty equivalents with a Vickrey auction

We elicited the certainty equivalents for given lotteries and took these values as indicators of risk attitudes. Traditionally, certainty equivalents are elicited by presenting the subjects with a set of choices between lotteries and a safe payoff. This method has some disadvantages, the most important of which is that the financial incentive for telling the truth is low.

Using an incentive compatible auction (the Vickrey auction (Vickrey 1961)) and taking the bids as the individual certainty equivalents circumvented this problem. In this auction, n identical objects are auctioned to m bidders, $m > n$. The n bidders with the highest bids win the auction and receive one object each. The winners do not have to pay their own bid prices but only the price of the $n+1$ highest bid.

This "highest-rejected-bid, uniform-price, sealed-bid auction" has several advantages.

- A subject's bidding of his, or her, true valuation constitutes a *dominant strategy* so that truth telling is optimal, regardless of the assumed theory of behavior under risk, e.g., it is not necessary to assume the validity of the "subjective expected utility theory" in order to prove the incentive compatibility of the Vickrey auction mechanism.
- Every subject tenders a bid, as opposed to the English auction, which has essentially the same strategic properties, so that the experimenters can observe a value for each participant.
- The auction design is easy to explain and the auction itself is not very time-consuming.
- It has a structure similar to the call market institution.
- If a sufficiently large number of lottery tickets is auctioned, the probability of winning the auction is high and hence there is a strong incentive to tell the true value.

5.3 Is the certainty equivalent a reliable measure of risk attitude?

One pre-test lottery auction was conducted in conjunction with each of the market experiments and was followed by a post-test lottery auction in most sessions. The investigation concentrated on the reliability of the certainty equivalent (CE) mechanism. The objective was to explore the ability of the Vickrey auction mechanism to elicit meaningful estimates of individual risk attitudes.

In some sessions, a high proportion of subjects (up to 50% in one trial) tendered a higher bid for the pre- or post-test lottery that had the lower expected value. The coefficient of rank correlation between pre- and post-test bids averaged 0.58 which led to the conclusion that the reliability of the CE as a measure of risk attitude is quite low.

In searching for an explanation, this result could be attributed to the Vickrey auction mechanism and not to the interpretation of the CE as an indicator of risk attitude. To test this possibility, we conducted several Vickrey auctions in which safe money values, rather than lotteries, were auctioned. If subjects did not believe in the incentive compatibility, considerable deviations between bids and the values auctioned should have been observed. This was not the case, and we conclude that subjects accept the Vickrey mechanism.

The most promising candidate for explaining the low connection between pre- and post-test bids is the idea that subjects observe a noisy version of their own CE. This approach would explain the results without completely abandoning the concept of a stable utility function. To provide an estimate of the degree of noise necessary to explain our results we conducted some computer simulations. Under the assumptions made in these simulations, the standard deviation of the noise term must be about 60% of the variability of the "true" certainty equivalents in order to explain our experimental results. Thus, whilst it seems that the hypothesis of noisy certainty equivalents has some explanatory power, further investigations are apparently necessary.

6. A tool for computerized market experiments

One of the major objectives of this research project was to develop a flexible software tool to cope with the requirements described in the introduction. Experience with our early "paper and pencil" experiments influenced the design of the software system. We decided to have the program run under "Windows" because most students were trained in the use of this software.

Available software was not flexible enough to be adapted to all requirements. PLATO (Williams 1980) and MUDA (Plott/Gray 1990) did not support the call market institution at the time when our project started. All other asset-market programs of which we are aware serve as special purpose applications, for instance CAT (Gerke/Bienert 1991, Wendel 1995).

We therefore developed the software tool MAX (**Ma**rket e**X**periments) which has the features described hereafter[16].

---

[16] Further details can be found in Rieck/Schneider/Theissen/Wirth (1994).

Participants can trade assets freely among themselves and each asset can be traded on a single market, each of which has its own trading rules. The most important difference between markets is the auction mechanism, i.e., whether the call market or the continuous double auction is used. Apart from these differences many details can be freely adopted; for example, whether or not orders can be queued, whether orders must improve on the best standing offer, or whether one person can queue for more than one order.

One set of trading rules is called a *market prototype*. The screen on which the prototypes can be defined is shown in Figure 3.

With MAX it is possible to endow each participant with an individual and arbitrary number of different assets, one of which is money. The number of different assets is only restricted by the clarity of the participants' screens.

As the program uses Windows, participants can organize their screens according to their personal tastes. An example of a typical trader's screen display is depicted in Figure 4 which shows that each subject can observe his, or her, current portfolio on the right hand side of the screen. By clicking the respective buttons, subjects can accept the standing orders or insert an order to buy, or an offer to sell, the various assets. By clicking other buttons past prices become visible (if the participant has access to that information). In this example, three different assets are traded on three continuous double auction markets, which are represented by the rows on the left-hand side of the screen.

Each participant's information status can be varied widely. The experimenter can, for instance, choose whether or not a subject has access to the fundamental value or to the other participants' orders, i.e. whether the orderbook is open or closed for single subjects, whether subjects know the state of nature which determines dividends, or whether they can observe the identity of participants who have made a contract.

It is also possible in the case of each individual to allow, or prohibit, short selling. If a subject tries to retrieve information to which he has no access, or if he places a prohibited order, MAX rejects the operation.

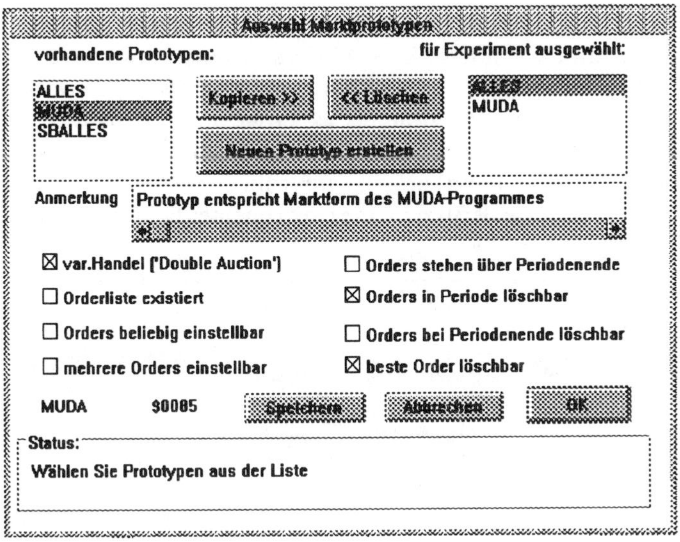

Figure 3: Screen for defining the market prototypes.

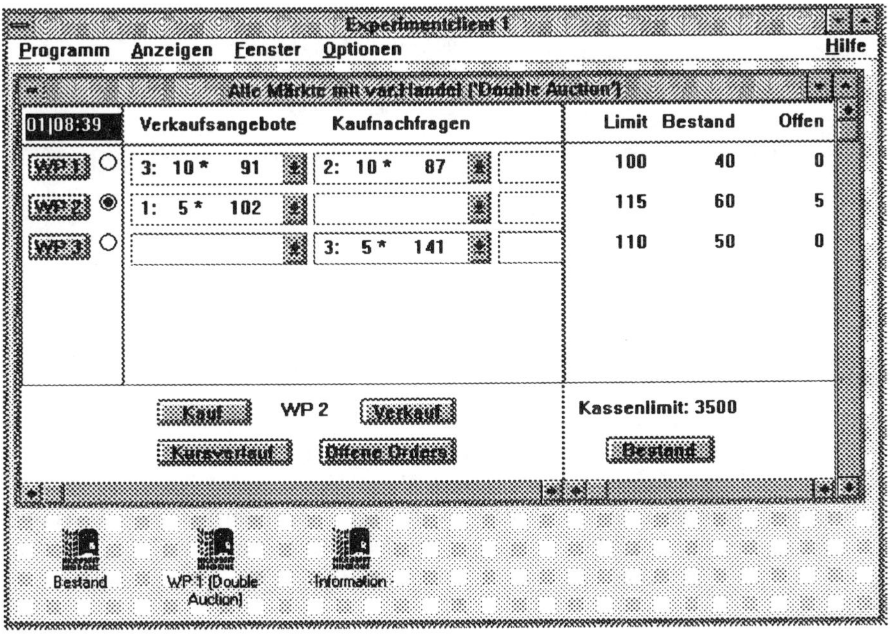

Figure 4: Typical trading screen.

Many experimental designs, e.g. factorial designs, require groups of subjects to work under the same conditions. In MAX it is therefore possible to define subject groups that are equally endowed and have equal access to information etc. It is also possible to send messages from the experimenter to individual subjects or to groups, and dividends can differ across different subject groups. Analogously to the market prototypes, these groups are called *participant prototypes.* The participant prototypes are defined by the experimenter before a session starts.

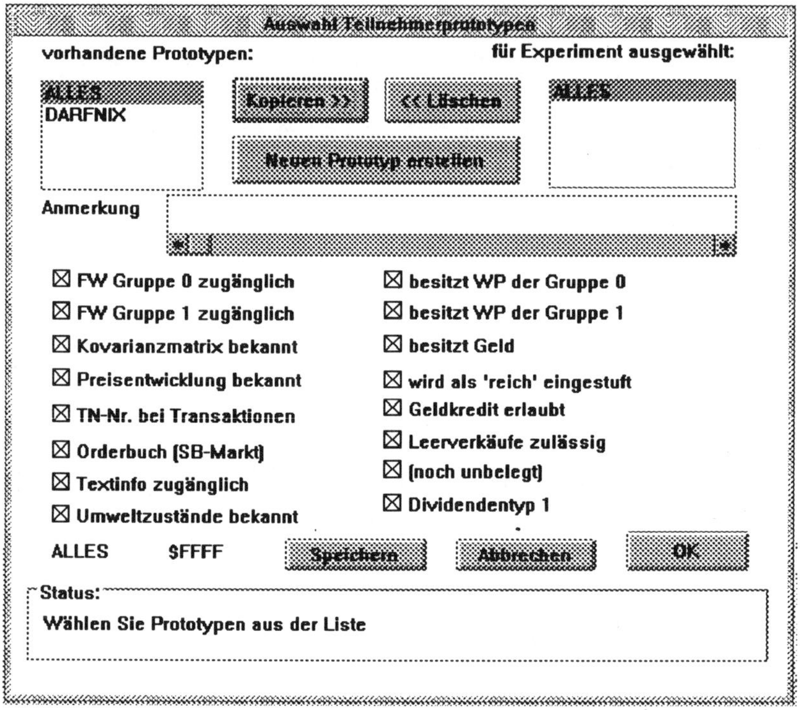

Figure 5: Screen for the definition of participant prototypes.

The whole software system is organized as a client-server relationship on a PC-net, with the experimenter's terminal as the server. The experimental environment (the design) is adjusted on the latter terminal whereas the trading takes place on the client PCs. All inputs to MAX are stored in a logfile on the server and can be exported to other data formats after the termination of the experiment.

In summary, the MAX software system provides flexible support to our research program by making it possible to choose freely from a wide set of institutional and environmental alternatives.

7. Conclusion

7.1 Methodological issues

Replication is at the heart of the process of learning from experimental work. As simple as this statement may seem, it is not easily put into practice if a dynamic market setting is to be modelled. In contrast to experiments concentrating on static, i.e. one-period decision-making, we have attempted to analyze human decision-making in a setting in which each period's individual endowment is inherited from the preceding period (multi-period condition). Hence the time series of informational innovations, i.e., the time series of fundamental values, has to be drawn from a given distribution, if credibility of the stochastic nature of information arrival is to be maintained. From the point of view of the experimenter, the exogeneity of the fundamental-value process is therefore necessary to ensure market-oriented, rather than strategically-oriented subject behavior (credibility-condition). The similarity of the fundamental-value process to everyday experiences is also required.

As far as we are aware, all investigations of decision-making under different market institutional arrangements that are reported in the literature violate at least one of these conditions. Either the stochastic process is not exogeneous (thereby inviting strategic behavior against the experimenter), or the individual endowments are reinitialized every period (thereby restricting the analysis to a series of one-period trials), or the fundamental value does not have the properties usually encountered in real life markets.

A basic dilemma is a feature of multi-period market modelling: fulfilment of the credibility condition hinders the exact replication of experimental trials. Therefore, establishing credibility as an experimenter comes at a considerable cost. If the value process underlying the market dynamics is not exactly replicated, a considerable amount of noise is added to the data. Not surprisingly, then, statistical tests of hypotheses relating to general behavioral patterns under a specific market institution will remain weak, and typically inconclusive.

One possible solution to this dilemma lies in a much greater number of replications so that identical time paths of the information process are realized by chance. In the model described above, the 14-round binomial information process has 2^{14} different paths. Therefore, limited budgets to pay subjects, not to mention (life-) time constraints, effectively rule out this solution.

On the same argument, experiments should concentrate on varying just one element from the array of institutional characteristics defining the market. For example, in the absence of a considerable increase in the number of replications, the design employed in our first experimental sessions (which are not reported in this paper) entailed too many degrees of freedom. Although differentiation of initial endowments among subjects may have its merits under one-period conditions, the trade-off between individual differentiation and statistical significance has to be recognised.

A final methodological observation concerns the introduction of subjects to the the rules of a specific experimental design. Typically, subjects are encouraged to practice their tasks before the recorded "true" session starts. Only after every participant has demonstrated a sufficient understanding of his task will the session begin. Note, however, that numerical values utilized during the practice period may significantly influence the behavior of subjects. This is especially true during the initial phase of the experiment and, in experiments with asymmetric information, for less informed participants. Hence, numerical examples have to be chosen with care, because they may tend to anchor the expectations of some subjects.

7.2 Empirical issues

As yet[17] true replications of experimental trials have not been carried out. The data gathered in sessions therefore display too much noise to allow an outright comparison of market institutions. Results reported in the preceding sections of this paper are concerned with four aspects, namely (i) the eliciting of subject's risk preferences, (ii) the measurement of short-term and longer-term expectations, (iii) the profitability of insider advantages, and (iv) the occurrence of price fads.

As regards individual behavior towards risk, the most surprising result is probably the large variation in individual risk measures over time. While the Vickrey auction-technique normatively elicits an unbiased estimate of a subject's risk preference, the evidence reported here supports a noisy certainty equivalent hypothesis. Accordingly, subjects "observe" their own risk preferences with a random error, so that individual bidding behavior is highly volatile over time, even if very similar lotteries are involved.

Modelling information innovations, i.e., the time series of fundamental values, as a binomial stochastic process with known transition probabilities allows a

[17] At the time of writing this paper the first phase (24 months) of the project, during which the market model has been developed and tested in an explorative way, is nearing completion. During the second phase (24 months), detailed comparisons between different organizational market mechanisms by means of replications are to be undertaken.

distinction between price and value expectations. Does the rational or the adaptive model provide a superior explanation of these expectations? Our data give a mixed impression. Informed subjects tend to form expectations rationally, whereas uninformed subjects clearly "prefer" to form expectations in an adaptive manner. There is little correlation between expectations and individual behavior, especially with respect to order placement and limit setting. Surprisingly, however, the longer-term expectations of uninformed subjects have a clear tendency to display overestimation, even in the final phase of the sessions.

Contrary to other experiments described in the literature, observed price paths display both over- and undervaluation in some, but not in all sessions. Positive and negative price fads indicate that deviations between price and value are not immediately competed away. In some sessions, the fad may persist for as long as 8 to 10 periods. Compared with market-models with a dividend design, the fundamental value process employed in our experiment does not bias mispricing in a particular direction.

Given the complex structure of our experimental design, it comes as no surprise that, although equipped with an informational advantage, insiders are, on average, not capable of earning higher returns. The ability of participants to exploit informational advantages seems to be rather limited and dependent on the market institution employed. Further research is needed here to derive behavioral, as well as institutional, conditions in which subjects can take advantage of early information.

7.3 Outlook and future research

The comparative analysis of market institutions may lead to improvements in the organizational structure of existing asset markets. Competition between exchanges has increased in the past decade, and the institutional structures of markets play an important role in this regard.

Experimental research offers the opportunity to study the specific attributes of such an institutional design under idealized ceteris paribus conditions. Although some work has already been done in this area,[18] much more remains to be accomplished. At least three areas deserve closer attention. First, a comparative study of auction and dealer markets seems to be of major importance. On an international level there is considerable competition between exchanges relying on market makers, e.g. the London Stock Exchange and the New York bond market, and exchanges relying on auctions (Frankfurt Stock Exchange or Tokyo

---

[18] The most recent survey of research on experimental asset markets is to be found in Sunder (1993). Another valuable source is Roth (1988).

bond market). However, a comparison of these market institutions with respect to their liquidity and their ability to digest new information on the grounds of "real world" empirical data is difficult to conduct, if not impossible. There are too many differences between these institutions to permit a reliable inference about any single organizational feature. In an experimental study the ambiguity of real world data can largely be avoided.

A second problem-area has to do with the trading system that is best suited to dealing with large orders, when there is private information in the market. Anecdotal evidence[19] suggests that continuous double auctions, the preferred clearing system for internationally traded big caps, may break down when the market expects the arrival of important information. There may be a case for rehabilitating the call market institution when information is asymmetrically distributed.

As a third problem-area investor decision-making remains an important research topic for experimental economists. Consider individual behavior towards risk. The results of our investigations on certainty equivalents need to be tested against new data. It may be necessary to abandon the understanding, common among economists, that people "have" a certain degree of risk aversion. People may utilize some sort of mental accounting[20] instead through which their resources are (mentally) allocated to separated funds. If so, a person would "have" several, and possibly different, degrees of risk aversion, one for each fund.

In closing, we recall Roth's (1994) methodological article, which harmonizes well with our own experience in the realm of experimental economics. On the preceding pages, therefore, we have not only surveyed two years of DFG-supported experimental work, but have also prepared the ground for a second, improved stage of research on the functioning of asset markets.

References

Berg, J.E., Daley, L.A., Dickhaut, J.W. and O'Brien, J.R. (1986): Controlling Preferences for Lotteries on Units of Experimental Exchange, in: Quarterly Journal of Economics 101, 281-306.

Farquhar, P. (1984): Utility Assessment Methods, in: Management Science 30, 1283-1300.

Friedman, D. (1993): How Trading Institutions Affect Financial Market Performance: Some Laboratory Evidence, in: Economic Inquiry 21, 410-435.

---

[19] Ketterer (1994) proposes to switch to a sealed-bid auction in situations of "infomation overflow".

[20] Thaler (1985) develops the idea of mental accounting.

Gerke, W. and Bienert, H. (1991): Experimentelle Kapitalmarktforschung an einer Computerbörse, in: Die Bank, 499-506.

Gode, D.K. and Sunder, S. (1993a): Allocative Efficiency of Markets With Zero-Intelligence Traders: Market as a Partial Substitute for Individual Rationality, in: Journal of Political Economy 101, 119-137.

Gode, D.K. and S. Sunder (1993b): Lower Bounds for Efficiency of Surplus Extraction in Double Auctions, in: Friedman, D. and J. Rust (eds.): The Double Auction Market. Reading, MA (Addison-Wesley).

Güth, W., J.P. Krahnen and C. Rieck (1992): Financial Markets With Asymmetric Information: An Experimental Study of Insider Advantages. Working Paper, University of Giessen .

Ketterer, J.A. (1994): Trading Systems in Electronic Markets. Working Paper MEFF, Barcelona.

Krahnen, J.P., C. Rieck and E. Theissen (1994a): Messung individueller Risiko-einstellungen. Working Paper, University of Giessen.

Krahnen, J.P., C. Rieck and E. Theissen (1994b): Price Fads in Experimental Markets. Working Paper, University of Giessen.

Krahnen, J.P., C. Rieck and E. Theissen (1994c): Price and Value Expectations in an Experimental Call Market. Working Paper, University of Giessen.

Krahnen, J.P., C. Rieck and E. Theissen (1994d): Inferring Risk Attitudes with Certainty Equivalents: Some Lessons from an Experimental Study. Working Paper, University of Giessen.

Krahnen, J.P., C. Rieck and E. Theissen (1995): Insider Trading and Portfolio Structure in Experimental Asset Markets. Working Paper, University of Giessen.

Mosteller, F. and Nogee, P. (1951): An Experimental Measurement of Utility, in: Journal of Political Economy 59, 371-404.

Muth, J.F. (1961): Rational Expectations and the Theory of Price Movements, in: Econometrica 29, 315-335.

Nash, J. (1950): The Bargaining Problem, in: Econometrica 18, 315-335

Plott, C. R. and Gray, P. (1990): The Multiple Unit Double Auction, in: Journal of Economic Behavior and Organization 13, 245-258.

Plott, C. R. and Sunder, S. 1982: Efficiency of Experimental Security Markets With Insider Information: An Application of Rational Expectations Models, in: Journal of Political Economy 90, 663-698.

Radner, R. and Schotter, A. (1989): The Sealed-Bid-Mechanism: An Experimental Study, in: Journal of Economic Theory 48, 179-220.

Rieck, C., M. Schneider, E. Theissen and A. Wirth (1994): Systemunterstützung von Kapitalmarktexperimenten. Working Paper, University of Giessen.

Rieck, C. and C. Syha (1992): An Experimental Investigation of the Psychology of Crashes. Working Paper IAREP/GEW-Conference 1992. Frankfurt.

Roth, A. (1988): Laboratory Experimentation in Economics: A Methodological Overview, in: The Economic Journal 98, 974-1031.

Roth, A.(1994): Lets Keep the Con out of Experimental Econ.: A Methodological Note, in: Empirical Economics 19, 279-289.

Roth, A.E. and Malouf, M.W.K. (1979): Game-Theoretic Models and the Role of Information in Bargaining, in: Psychological Review 86, 574-594.

Sachs, L. (1993): Angewandte Statistik, 7th ed. Berlin.

Smith, V.L., Suchanek, G.L. and Williams, A.W. (1988): Bubbles, Crashes and Endogenous Expectations in Experimental Spot Asset Markets, in: Econometrica 56, 1119-1159.

Smith, V.L., Williams, A.W., Bratton, W.K. and Vannoni, M.G. (1982): Competitive Market Institutions: Double-Auctions vs. Sealed Bid-Offer Auctions, in: American Economic Review 72, 58-77.

Sunder, S. (1993): Experimental Asset Markets: A Survey. Working Paper No. 1992-19, revised January 1993, Carnegie Mellon University. Pittsburgh.

Thaler, R.H. (1985): Mental Accounting and Consumer Choice, in: Marketing Science 4(3), 199-214.

Van Boening (1991): Call versus Continuos Auctions. Ann Arbor (UMI Dissertation Services).

Van Boening, M.V., Williams, A.W. and LaMaster, S. (1993): Price Bubbles and Crashes in Experimental Call Markets, in: Economic Letters 41, 179-185.

Vickrey, W. (1961): Counterspeculation, Auctions, and Competitive Sealed Tenders, in: Journal of Finance 16, 8-37.

Wendel, M. (1995): Spieler oder Spekulanten. University of Frankfurt (Diss.).

Williams, A.W. (1980): Computerized Double-Auction Markets: Some Initial Experimental Results, in: Journal of Business 53, 235-258.

Williams, A.W. (1987): The Formation of Price Forecasts in Experimental Markets, in: Journal of Money, Credit, and Banking 19, 1-18.

Private Investor Behavior in Germany: An Empirical Survey and Experimental Results

Andreas Oehler
University of Bamberg

1. Introduction

Most of the concepts of financial theory attempt to describe, to explain, and to forecast what is happening in financial markets. This research concentrates primarily on highly organized securities markets. Theoretical and empirical approaches to financial market research are interrelated because, on the one hand, the selection and the interpretation of variables in empirical examinations are being influenced by theoretical models, and on the other hand, empirical results initiate modifications in theoretical approaches. The majority of theoretical and empirical approaches in finance focus on a high aggregation level. In its assumptions and statements the individual behavioral patterns of investors are usually regarded as "black boxes". This is accomplished by analyzing the relation between firm specific and general economic information on the one hand and asset prices and turnovers in financial markets on the other, without really causally explaining what is occuring in the markets. Research and studies on the goals, the expectations, or the behavior of single market participants or groups of market participants is not extensive (Oehler 1995, pp. 1f., Bitz/Oehler 1993a, pp. 247f.).

The results of empirical examinations, which contradict rational behavior such as the propositions of the expected utility theory, have led to an intensive analysis of the behavior of market participants and the micro level of financial markets in the last few years. Typical concepts are the behavioral finance and the market microstructure approaches.[1]

The research project upon which this essay is based seeks to open the "black box" investor behavior and to explain the behavior of the participants in financial

[1] For a short overview about the so called anomalies, paradoxes and biases see Oehler (1992, pp. 97-124) and the literature quoted there. For the newer approaches in the financial market theory see, for example, the overview of Franke (1993, pp. 389-398) and the remarks of Krahnen (1993).

markets. The main focus of this study is an examination of the behavior of private investors in the stock market, some of its findings are valid for institutional investors. To accomplish the essay's objective, approaches in the fields of finance, financial markets, and behavioral economics were linked with concepts of empirical and experimental economic research to form a behavioral financial market-approach. A future consequence of the approach could be a normative, non-equilibrium model of private investor behavior, which differentiates between rational (i.e. goal-minded) and irrational behavioral patterns of private investors (Bitz/Oehler 1993a, pp. 250-252, Oehler 1995, pp. 22f. and pp. 55-61).

The breaking up of "black box" investor behavior is made possible, in the tradition of the empirical economic research, by conducting interviews with relevant people. In addition to causal explanation of investor behavior based on survey results, a further research method should be considered, namely the laboratory experiment, a technique rarely used in German empirical financial market research.

To realize the project's objective, two interdependent procedures were selected whose design and results are to be described in this paper:

- A written survey of private investors considering previous theoretical and empirical work was conducted. Private investor behavior is mainly illustrated by the real portfolio structure of financial assets (dependent variable).[2]
- In a parallel approach, experiments with either one-shot or with consecutive decisions were conducted in different variations. It was possible to use the same groups of subjects as in the written survey. The experimental research focuses on the extent to which private investors' portfolio decisions correspond to the theory of Markowitz and on the extent to which investors exhibit special behavioral patterns (positive feedback trading, negative feedback trading, disposition effect, loss aversion).

The paper is organized as follows. The next section contains a short description of the survey design and results. Section 3 documents the experimental procedures, the results of the diversification of risky portfolios, and the asymmetrical evaluation relative to a reference point such as the WTA-WTP disparity and the disposition effect.

---

[2] Financial investments in building societies and life insurance companies are not counted as financial assets here; see Oehler (1995, pp. 67 f.).

2. Survey design and results

2.1 Data

Empirical examinations of the behavior of individual investors based on a system of determinants are virtually unknown in the literature.[3] Therefore, the survey results contribute to basic research in this field. The main reason for using a questionnaire is to filter out an explanatory *structure* of the behavior of private investors. Correspondingly, overly detailed questions on a few essential factors have to be omitted because of limited financial resources. Deviating from normal practice in almost all empirical surveys in this field of research, special attention was given to a careful asking for the real portfolio structure of financial assets in DM-values. This procedure was chosen because the real portfolio structure represents the most important indicator of the behavior of private investors. After extensive pretests, the survey was carried out in the first half of 1992 with 822 students from University of Hagen.[4] In several attributes the sample strongly deviates from the student populations at conventional universities that have been analyzed in similar surveys.

- When the survey took place, over 80% of all participants were in full-time employment. 10% of the participants were self-employed or professional workers; 5% were housewives or "house-husbands". The others were employed as white-collar workers (65%), as civil servants (18%), or as workers (2%).
- The personal monthly net income of the respondents was approximately 3,000 DM and their personal financial assets averaged 43,200 DM. The comparable German population-wide average is approximately 31,200 DM. Additionally, the subjects revealed a higher percentage of stocks in their financial assets portfolio of 14% instead of 6%. The individuals can be characterized as being appropriate for an examination of the behavior of private investors because of their income, their wealth, and their knowledge of economic affairs. It is therefore expected that they have experience with different financial investments. The high percentage of stockholders in the sample constitutes an important advantage for experimental studies concerning stock market backgrounds (see section 3).
- The participants also differ in a few other attributes from the population in pre-1990 Germany. It can therefore be stated that the respondents are atypical of the total population with respect to sex (75% male instead of

[3] An overview of related research is given by Oehler (1995, pp. 150-153).

[4] The students at University of Hagen can take most of their courses at home, but most of the examinations take place in Hagen.

48%), age (more young investors, average age: 29), and education (usually "Abitur" or higher qualifications).

As already stated, an important part of the survey was to investigate the *real* financial asset portfolios of the respondents measured in DM-values. The procedure employed makes it possible to gain relatively undistorted information about portfolio structure. This is possible because control questions such as the possession of a single type of investment or the amount of net wealth were asked. As reported in the literature, such an investigation of financial variables is often rejected on the grounds that the number of subjects rejecting such questions or the questionnaire in its entirety would be too large. Such behavior could not be observed in the survey. The percentage of "missings" (no responses), regarding to the question on the amount of each investment type (in DM-values) is no higher than the percentage of missings in other questions in the questionnaire.[5]

2.2 Determinants of private investor behavior

The empirical examination differentiates two main categories of determinants:

- the *environment* of the investor and
- the *person* of the investor.

The personal attributes of the investor can be separated into two sub-categories:

- the personal *disposition* (emotional, motivational and cognitive factors) and
- the personal *situation* (age, sex, salary, education, job).

The determinants of the private investor's environment can also be separated into two spheres:

- the external information (general economic and firm specific information) and
- the social environment (influences of culture, reference groups, especially that of family).

Due to space limitations the following statements on the survey's results are reduced to a few determinants (Oehler 1995, pp. 62-118, Bitz/Oehler 1993a, pp. 259-273 and 1993b, pp. 375-405). As an example of the determinants' category "environment" the economic climate's influence on the portfolio structure of the

[5] The proportion of "missings" is about 5%. For more details on the procedure of the survey and on the subjects see Oehler (1995, pp. 153-157).

financial assets is discussed below. In the section on personal attributes of the investor, the author refers to some determinants of personal disposition and, moreover, introduces the survey results on motivation concerning investment decisions and risk attitudes.

2.3 Selected results

2.3.1 The influence of economic development on private investment decisions

Increasing doubts on the model of the "homo oeconomicus" as an economic subject[6] enforce considerations that the behavior of individuals depends on the specific individual situation and therefore differs inter- and intra-personally. This point of view was essentially initiated and advanced by Katona (1975). Katona's work has led, among other things, to the development of measurement concepts which would be able to estimate the influence of the course of the economy (e.g. labour market situation, inflationary conditions) on individual behavior. The large number of possible factors, that are difficult to operationalize together with the existing complex and reciprocal effects lead to a rejection of the direct measurement of the influences on economic subjects' behavior in favor of an indirect (indicatorial) measurement of individuals` expectations. One of the most common concepts of indirect measurement that is concerned with the effects and influences of economic development can be directly linked to the work of Katona, which has led, among other things, to the periodical examination of the "Index of Consumer Sentiment" (ICS).

An equivalent concept of investment behavior in this form does not exist. Nevertheless, many concepts of ICS-construction stemming from the general term "economic sentiment" can be used to explain the behavior of private investors. Thus, based on a paper by van Raaij/Gianotten (1990), subjects in our survey were given (reformulated) questions on the "investor sentiment". The main focus in this part of the survey is the assessment of the economic situation in Germany in the preceding and in the following 12 months as well as an estimation of whether they will be able to invest money in the next 12 months.[7] The relationship between subjects' situation assessments (past and future) and their investment expectations is documented in Table 1.

---

[6] I.e. a subject with the ability to calculate all necessary information in unlimited speed so that he is able to maximize his utility in the sense of substantial rationality.

[7] "Preceding" and "following" refers to the time of answering the questionnaire.

Table 1: Estimation of future money investment taking account of assessments of the past and future economic situation

Assessment of economic trend...	Estimation of whether money can be invested in the next 12 months (% of subjects)	
	more likely yes	more likely no
for the last 12 months		
better	89% ***	11% ***
worse	79% ***	21% ***
for the next 12 months		
better	87% ***	13% ***
worse	81% ***	19% ***
Average	83%	17%

t-tests: ***: $\alpha = 0.01$
(regarding to the difference between "better" and "worse").

- The data show that on average more than 80% of all respondents believed that they could invest money in the next 12 months, given their assesment of the economic situation (although one can see a limited influence of the determinant). The majority of subjects who assessed the last 12 months (top half of Table 1) or the forthcoming 12 months (lower half of Table 1) positively, believed that they would invest in the latter period.
- An additional analysis shows that there is a significant positive relation between the amount of money being invested per year (last calendar year) and investors′ estimation of their ability to invest money in the future. Investors who perceive investment opportunities in the next 12 months had much higher levels of investment in the previous calendar year.
- In general it is obvious that worse economic situation causes lower income increases and a decreased propensity to save. The results show, as expected, that investors spend more money on financial assets during periods in which they perceive a positive economic trend.

A further question raised here that has not been systematically analyzed in the literature is concerned with the relationship between the structure of individuals′ portfolios and the expectation of a positive or negative future economic trend. The survey results with respect to this question are summarized in Table 2.

Table 2: Assessment of economic situation, investors' future money investment and structure of financial assets portfolio

Kind of investment	Future economic situation		Future money investment		Average
	+[a]	-[b]	+[a]	-[b]	
Savings deposits	34	37	33***	50***	36
Time deposits	16	18	18**	12**	17
Bonds	21*	25*	25***	18***	23
Stocks	19***	11***	15*	11*	14
Investment certificates	10	9	9	9	10

a: Better; more likely yes. t-tests: ***: $\alpha = 0.01$; **: $\alpha = 0.05$; *: $\alpha = 0.10$ b:Worse; more likely no (regarding "+" and "-"). Totals are not equal to 100% because of rounding.

The columns of the table correspond to both indicators for assessing the future economic situation. The data reveal that private investors who are optimistic about future economic situation as a whole include a significantly higher percentage of stocks in their financial assets portfolios than do pessimistic investors. A similar result obtains with respect to future possibility of money investment. Private investors who, given their assessment of future economic trend, expect that they would not invest money, hold significantly higher (lower) proportions in savings deposits (securities).

2.3.2 On the motivation for private investment decisions

Possible investment motives were elicited by means of a question consisting of ten items measured on a scale from 1 (= "unimportant") to 5 (= "very important"). Ten items were selected after a series of pretests and literature analysis. The survey results were subjected to a factor analysis, and five categories of motives were identified:

- Increase in wealth.
- Personal provisions (for example retirement pensions, unemployment insurance).
- Future income.
- Family provisions (for example reserves for emergencies, for the education of children).
- Savings for large outlays (for example for long vacation trips and durable consumer goods).

It is assumed that the evaluation of the motives′ importance is reflected in the portfolio structure of financial assets held by investors. It can therefore be predicted that investors' savings and provisions motives will be satisfied by savings deposits, whereas the considerable importance of wealth and income motives will be corrclated with investments in securities. Table 3 shows the survey results for this topic.

Table 3: Importance of the five motives and portfolio structure of financial assets

Kind of investment	Percentages of the financial assets portfolio and importance of motive categories										
	verm		vorsei		eink		vorsfa		anscha		Av
	-	+	-	+	-	+	-	+	-	+	
Savings deposits	41	32***	36	46***	39	31***	34	40*	31	37	36
Time deposits	18	17	18	17	17	18	17	15	21	18	17
Bonds	21	25*	23	18	23	24	23	26	24	25	23
Stocks	10	17***	12	13	10	19***	17	10***	14	12	14
Investment certificates	10	13	10	9	12	9**	10	11	10	8	10

t-tests: ***: $\alpha = 0.01$; **: $\alpha = 0.05$; *: $\alpha = 0.10$.
Totals are not equal to 100% because of rounding.
- = unimportant
+ = important

verm = increase of wealth
vorsei = personal provisions
eink = increase of income
vorsfa = family provisions
anscha = savings for large investments

The five categories of motives are listed in the columns of Table 3. The rows represent the five different kinds of investments. For the sake of clarity every five point-scale is divided into two parts. The numbers 1 to 3 (marked with "-") whilst 4 and 5 (marked with "+") are adjacent to each other. Minus means unimportant, plus means important. The assumption regarding the influence of the motives on the portfolio composition can now be defined more exactly and is partially verifiable:

- Investors who ascribe particular importance to assets and income motives hold an above-average proportion of stocks in their financial asset portfolios. Compared to the average, savings deposits, are slightly underrepresented in their portfolios.
- Individual investors who emphasize family provisions and/or their own provisions are primarily invested in savings deposits. Compared to the average investments in securities are underrepresented. The deviations from the average are clearly greater in the case of personal provisions than in the case of family provisions.

2.3.3 Absolute and relative risk aversion

The following analyses of the empirical data use the concept of risk aversion stemming from the research of Arrow and Pratt (Arrow 1971, pp. 92-96 and Pratt 1964, pp. 122f.).[8] Adopting this concept generally a distinction can be made between two different points of view. Although there is consensus on the assumption that most of the investors have a decreasing absolute risk aversion, there are some differences concerning relative risk aversion:

- Arrow (1971, p. 96), Pratt (1964, pp. 134-135) and a few authors of later papers (e. g. Siegel/Hoban 1982) postulate an increasing relative risk aversion for most decision makers.
- Cohn/Lewellen/Lease/Schlarbaum (1975) and other authors (e.g. Lampman 1962, Morin/Suarez 1983) conclude that the majority of investors reveal decreasing relative risk aversion.

The postulate of increasing relative risk aversion can be classified as an assumption of "neo-classical" financial theory. "The justification for this, however, is often one of convenience rather than belief about descriptive accuracy" (Elton/Gruber 1991, p. 199). Although risk aversion is defined intra-personally the present study uses cross-sectional data[9] to analyze investors' absolute and relative risk aversion. As regards the financial assets portfolio, investments in securities are classified as risky, while investments in bank-accounts are assumed to be riskfree. Whilst it is self-evident that no form of investment is completely riskfree, short-term government bonds are not considered to be risky investments. The analysis of Pearson's correlation coefficients between the whole value of the portfolio and the single proportions of each asset reveal a decreasing absolute and relative risk aversion (Table 4).

The positive correlation coefficients for the securities in the middle column of Table 4 shows that there is, as expected, both a decreasing absolute risk aversion (increasing absolute amount which is invested with increasing wealth) and a decreasing relative risk aversion (right hand column of Table 4). The coefficients of the relative percentages of risky securities are significantly positive and the coefficient for the safe savings deposits is significantly negative. Thus, the relative percentage of investments in securities increases with increasing wealth while the proportion of savings deposits decreases. Decreasing risk aversion can also be demonstrated by reference to the portfolio structure of financial assets as a function of the amount of wealth. The data in Table 5 show that the percentage of savings deposits clearly decreases (from 52% to 14%) and the percentage of

[8] A detailed discussion of the concept of absolute and relative risk aversion relating to this research project is presented in: Oehler 1995, pp. 104-113 and pp. 168-171, Bitz/Oehler 1993b, pp. 398-401.

[9] Further measurement problems are discussed by Oehler (1995, pp. 112f.).

investments in securities increases considerably (from 28% to 53%) with increasing wealth.

Table 4: Correlations between each kind of investment and wealth in absolute and relative values

Kind of investment	Pearson's correlation coefficients in relation to the financial assets portfolio (wealth)	
	in absolute values	in relative values
Savings deposits	0.42***	-0.20***
Time deposits	0.39***	0.03
Bonds	0.84***	0.14***
Stocks	0.83***	0.09***
Investment certificates	0.60***	-0.02

t-tests: ***: $\alpha = 0.01$; (2-tailed)

Table 5: Volume of wealth and structure of financial assets portfolio

Kind of investment	Percentage of each investment and wealth[a] (thousand DM)						
	< 20	20 - 40	40 - 60	60 - 80	80 - 100	≥ 100	Average
Savings deposits	52	27	18	17	20	14	36
Time deposits	11	21	27	28	23	24	17
Bonds	16	29	34	25	33	35	23
Stocks	12	13	15	19	21	18	14
Investment certificates	10	10	6	11	3	9	10

a: Sample sizes for each column (from left to right): 327, 155, 84, 40, 19, 50. 148 cases were excluded from the analysis because of "missings" in one or more variable ("listwise deletion"). Totals are not equal to 100% in each column because of rounding.

3. Experimental results

3.1 The diversification of risky portfolios

Experiments with one-shot decisions were developed to answer the question of whether private investors' decisions reflect the Markowitz approach to portfolio theory and, in particular, whether they take the correlations among risky investments into consideration.

- Subjects could hypothetically invest in five stocks and one safe low-interest security in each decision situation.
- At the beginning of the experiments, each subject was endowed with a hypothetical 50,000 DM (about 32,000 $).
- All participants received the price sequences of the last seven periods and a short run price forecast for the end of the current period as basic information for each risky alternative.The investment decisions were made in this eighth period.
- In general, all participants received written instructions about the stock market and a description of the experimental design two weeks before the experimental sessions.

The experiments were performed primarily to obtain important basic information on subjects′ behavior, without disturbance through consecutive decisions. The study considers order sizes, portfolio structure, and the use of information on price forecasts and correlations. The participants in these one shot-experiments were the same as those of the survey. 779 of the total 822 persons who were tested in the survey participated. The experimental design consists of two different types. The investors′ behavior is measured by their buy orders. The two designs differ only in that additional data was given on the correlations between the risky investment alternatives in the second experiment.

At the beginning of each period, every subject makes his investment decision under uncertainty with respect to the future price development. There is no uncertainty with regard to order execution because subjects receive the prices of the last period as fixed purchase prices. The price forecast is given as an interval. The upper (lower) end is calculated by taking the price of the last period (period 7) increased (lowered) by the standard deviation of the whole price sequence (including period 8 for which the price is known to the experimenter). This calculation is not revealed to the subjects, but the general instructions inform them that the price of period 8 can be expected to be within the forecast interval with a probability of 70%. The participants entered their orders on prepared forms.

Taking account of the author′s pretests and other studies (Oehler 1992, p. 107), changes in investor behavior to result from using correlation information would not be expected. Also, the experimental results in the studies of Kroll/Levy/Rapoport (1988) and Weber/Camerer (1992) do not depict investor behavior as in Markowitz′s portfolio theory. To be on the safe side, the correlation information (concerning the future development of the risky alternatives) was revealed in the study′s experiments in both a numerical and in a verbal form.[10]

---

[10]For example: correlation coefficient for two shares is 0.9: „the prices of the two shares will develop very similarly in the current period".

To facilitate an assessment of investors' portfolio behavior the expected values and the standard deviations of the participants' portfolios were calculated in the same manner for both investment situations, i.e. in type 1-experiments, in which correlation information was not given, the calculation embodies the correlations although the subjects did not know them at the time. Nevertheless the connections between the alternatives in the given price sequences were easily recognizable. The additional explicit correlation information was primarily intended to be used for diversification. Assuming an active use of correlation information, one can delineate three groups of Markowitz investors:

- a group which increases the expected value of their portfolios at a fixed standard deviation
- a group which lowers the standard deviation at a fixed expected value of their portfolios
- a group which increases the expected value and lowers the standard deviation of their portfolios.

Complete data for all experimental situations is available for 675 subjects. 98 of them are characterized in the sense of the three defined groups as being "diversifiers". The hypothesis of low use of correlation information can be rejected at least for this group.

Looking at the structure of risky portfolios before and after the arrival of the correlation information, it can be observed that investors tend to behave like "diversifiers" who are first stimulated by additional and explicit correlation information. After receiving the correlations the subjects of this group should be able to combine a portfolio which is somewhat closer to the efficient frontier and the tangential portfolio (optimal portfolio). Contrastingly, the other investors attained such a portfolio structure without the knowledge of the explicit correlation information (Table 6). In the light of these results, the "diversifiers" can now be better characterized as "latecomers" who could not, or would not, use the implicit correlation information documented in the price sequences (charts) without any additional information. Approximately 5% of the "latecomers" structured portfolios with negative expected values in the type 1-experiment (without correlation information).[11] An additional analysis of the "latecomers" using data from the survey reveals that the real volume of their financial assets lies approximately 12% below the average, and that the percentage of savings deposits in the real financial assets portfolio lies 4% above the average of the other individuals. The "late" use of the correlation information by this group of investors could be explained by their limited experience regarding investments in securities.

---

[11] Similar results are presented by Weber/Camerer (1992, p.144).

Table 6: Risky portfolios structured by "latecomers" and other subjects before and after receiving correlation information

Stocks	Portfolio structure (%) "Latecomers"		Others		Optimal portfolio
	before	after	before	after	
1	5.4	1.5	2.0	1.6	0.0
2	2.5	2.0	0.6	1.4	0.0
3	13.0	11.1	7.0	6.8	10.0
4	22.3	6.6	6.4	11.1	0.0
5	56.8	78.7	84.1	79.1	90.0
μ	9.55	13.59	14.38	13.48	14.80
σ	4.57	3.91	4.17	4.47	2.90

The final analysis examines how many investors can get close to the efficient frontier of the risky investments. After all, 46% of the test persons lie at the efficient frontier.[12] The common feature of these investors is that they hold a slightly higher percentage of stocks in their real financial assets portfolio, namely, 10% above average. This may imply that a little more experience with investments in stocks results in a "better" diversification of experimental portfolios.

Summarizing, the majority of the individual investors do not, or cannot, make a portfolio decision in the manner predicted by the portfolio theory of Markowitz. An essential reason for this seems to lie in the incorrect use of correlation information. Another explanation could be that private investors do not understand standard deviation as a measure of risk. The results of an extensive final questionnaire suggest that there is a considerable divergence between the knowledge acquired during one's studies, e.g. the basics of portfolio theory and financial markets, and its transfer into a (simplified) reality.

3.2 Asymmetric evaluation relative to a reference point

3.2.1 Experimental design and data

The experiments described below were also run with students from Hagen University. All of the subjects had taken courses in banking and finance as a part

[12]The results from Weber/Camerer (1992, p. 144) and Kroll/Levy/Rapoport (1988) are even worse.

of a major course of study. As already stated each subject received additional information on the functioning of stock markets and the consequences of buy and sell orders together with detailed written instructions thereon. In total 845 persons participated in the experiments (see also Oehler 1994, pp. 945-954). A further 443 subjects were used in pilot studies in related experiments. The subjects could hypothetically invest in five stocks and in one riskfree low-interest security in each of eleven investment periods. The buy and sell orders were placed after (before) the current prices were announced in experiments I and II (in type III) by mail. The calculation of the five stock prices (the fixing) occured independently of investors′ orders. Thus, prices were not determined by trading. Short sales and borrowing were not allowed, and the subjects were endowed with 50,000 DM at the beginning of the experiment. The stocks were given artificial names to avoid associations with actual listed stocks. The experiment was run using a questionnaire. A period was defined as one week. Because of postal delivery time, the actual decision time of each subject is about two days. Each participant received a form for recording transactions and the related consequences (inventory changes, cash, stock holdings with book values). The price information at the beginning of each period for type I and type II experiments (at the end of each period in case of type III experiment) expressed new information about previous price movements. The order execution for experiments I and II was known with certainty, because the actual prices were used at the same time as the settlement prices (the charts of the price sequences are available from the author).

At the beginning of an experiment, the subjects received a price forecast for each stock. These were given as an interval from a point in time after the end of an experimental session (approximately 3 months from the beginning). Each interval, unknown to the subjects, was calculated by adding (subtracting) the standard deviation of the whole price sequence (from the past to the end of the experiment) to (from) the last price of the price history for the upper value (for the lower value) of the interval. To prevent an identity of interval′s expected value with the last historical price, the boundaries were raised by 3% each. The subjects were told in the instructions that the realized prices of the forecast period could be expected to be within the interval with a probability of 70%. This design applied to the above mentioned three types. In type I, correlation information on the stocks was not given until the middle of the experiment, while in types II and III it was provided at the beginning. In type III investors did not receive the current prices until the end of the period, and were not therefore given any transaction prices in advance. This type was performed for the WTA-WTP disparity examination. The differential timing of correlation information was intended to facilitate the analysis of portfolio behavior (see above). Variations I and II were used to elucidate a possible disposition effect. In type I, 261 subjects participated, while in types II and III respectively 279 and 305 subjects participated.

3.2.2 Asymmetrical evaluation relative to a reference point and endowment effect

Theoretical considerations

One of the best known, most discussed and most frequently tested modifications of the expected utility theory is the "prospect theory" of Kahneman and Tversky (1979). One of the main issues is the assertion that comparable profits and losses are evaluated differently with regard to a reference-point and "... losses are weighted substantially more than objectively commensurate gains in the evaluation of prospect and trades ..." (Kahneman/Knetsch/Thaler 1990, p. 2), i.e., decision makers are risk averse in the domain of gains and risk prone in the domain of losses (reflection effect). Earlier work by Staw (1976, p. 27), which has not been extensively deliberated in the literature, elaborates this phenomenon and places it in the context of investment decisions. "... [W]ithin investment decision contexts, negative consequences may actually cause decision makers to increase the commitment of resources and undergo the risk of further negative consequences."

The relevance of the prospect theory's reflection effect is examined in the following sections in the context of investment decisions in the stock market. Some related studies such as those by Shefrin/Statman (1985) and Weber/Camerer (1991) illustrate the relevance of an asymmetrical evaluation relative to a reference point in the context of investment decisions. The starting points for the analyses were the ideas and empirical examinations of Thaler (1990) who argues that a good increases in value to an individual when it becomes part of his endowment. Thaler called this phenomenon the "endowment effect". Kahneman/Knetsch/Thaler (1990, p. 2) characterize this bias of the EU-theory as an expression of the asymmetrical valuation of profits and losses in relation to a reference point. One consequence of such "biased" evaluations by decision makers is the so-called disparity between an individual´s maximum willingness to pay (WTP) for a good and an individual´s minimum willingness to accept (WTA) an offer to sell it (identical risks). Following Shefrin/Statman (1985), a second consequence of asymmetrical evaluation in the context of investment decisions can be characterized as the "disposition effect". Investors quickly sell shares that have risen to a price above the reference-point ("winners") and sell shares that have fallen to a price below the reference-point ("losers") with a time-lag. This behavior is called the "reluctance to sell at a loss" (Kahneman/Knetsch/Thaler 1990, p. 1339 and p. 1345).

WTA-WTP Disparity

In order to analyze the difference between the willingness to pay and the price for compensation in the behavior of private investors, three hypotheses are stated.

H1: The price limits of sell orders (WTA) lie above the price limits of buy orders (WTP).

H2: The disparity is stronger in investment situations when prices declined in former periods than in investment situations with rising prices.

Hypothesis 1 reflects the endowment effect, whereas hypothesis 2 refers to the valuation of profits and losses. Both hypotheses are explicitly based on an inter-personal examination. Because the WTA-WTP disparity characterizes an intra-personal phenomenon, the author's analysis goes beyond average investor behavior. Thus, the experimental technique is supplemented with a disaggregated examination which can be defined as an intra-personal analysis for comparing each subject in terms of two decision points in time.

H3: The WTA-WTP-disparity can also be regarded as an intra-personal phenomenon. This means that investors state significantly higher sell order prices compared to the relevant buy order prices at an earlier point in time.

The results of the experiment-type III were used to analyze the three hypotheses. The results pertaining to hypotheses 1 and 2 demonstrate the following:

- On average all participants reveal a considerable difference between willingness to pay and the price for compensation demanded. The inter-personal WTA/WTP-ratio is about 1.2 for each of the five stocks. Hypothesis 1 cannot be rejected. This result is not unassailable because the ratio values in related studies are higher. Kahneman/Knetsch/Thaler (1990, p. 1327) quoted intra-personal ratio values between 1.4 and 16.5.
- The results document a stronger disparity for periods of falling rather than rising prices for each kind of stock. Hypothesis 2 can also not be rejected.

A disparity coefficient v is calculated for each investor j to analyze his intra-personal difference between willingness to pay and willingness to accept. This coefficient relates to investor j's total number of orders and the difference between the number of sell orders with a limit exceeding the (relevant) former buy order limit and such sell orders as have limits below the (relevant) former buy limit.[13]

$$v_j = 1/I * \sum_{i=1}^{I} (A_{i+} - A_{i-}) / (A_{i+} + A_{i-}) \quad (1)$$

where, i = kind of share, i=1,...,I; j = investor; A_{i+} = number of orders with limit to sell > limit to buy; A_{i-} = number of orders with limit to sell < limit to buy; and $1 \geq v \geq -1$, which means, for example, the closer a positive v lies to 1 for an investor, the more clearly the endowment effect appears in form of the WTA-WTP-disparity. Table 7 shows the distribution of the coefficient v vis à vis three possible investors′ groups (on average). The average value of v for investors who reveal the bias is almost +1. This group represents approximately three quarters of the participants. Approximately 25% of the investors do not reveal the defined disparity, and in this group, there are 5% for whom the disparity coefficient is exactly 0 together with 20% for whom an inverse disparity is observed. The average of all investors is significantly different from zero at a significance level of $\alpha = 0.01$ (2-tailed t-test). The results of the analysis of individual behavior support the third hypothesis. It should be emphasised that the measurement procedure derived here is limited because of a particular problem: The measure v is defined intertemporally, but the intra-personal WTA-WTP disparity is postulated for a point in time. So, it is possible that the result partially measures income effects (see Kahneman/Knetsch/Thaler 1990, p. 1326).

Table 7: Intra-personal disparity

Coefficient	Experiment III	
	Value of v^a	Percentage of subjects (%)
> 0	0.91	74.1
= 0	0	5.2
< 0	-0.78	20.7
Average	$+0.52^b$ (+7.60)	

a: Average of each group; b: $\alpha = 0.01$ (2-tailed t-test).

[13]If one additionally adjusts v for the price trend (between the period the buy order is submitted and the period the sell order is stated) by summing up the price differences, the results will be even stronger.

Disposition effect in stock trading

It is necessary to differentiate between two reference-points with which profits and losses can be evaluated for the research on the "disposition effect" in the context of individuals′ decisions[14]: The (original) purchase price and the last available past price, i.e. the price which is the result of the price changes since the purchase of a stock. Stocks whose current price lies above (under) the reference price are also known as winners (losers). The two following hypotheses can be defined using the basic assumptions of section 3.2.2.1:

H1: Investors submit more sell orders, and sell more stocks, when the current price is above the last period price than when the current price is below the last available past price.

H2: Investors state more sell orders, and sell more stocks, when the current price is above the purchase price than when the current price is below the purchase price.

For an analysis of both hypotheses the data from experiments type I and II with consecutive decisions are used. In those experiments the current stocks′ prices were calculated independently of the participants' actions and were given at the beginning of each period (see above section 3.2.1). Because the respective numbers of winner and loser periods are quite different, all results are standardized. Therefore the experimental data, e.g. the number of sales, was divided by the number of periods. The results of both experiment types I and II (in total 540 investors who participate regularly in all periods) are very similar: The results of experiment type II are therefore not reproduced here.

a) The disposition effect with the last available price as a reference point

This section contains a brief summary of the examination of investors as a whole followed by an outline of the analysis of individual behavior using the same procedure as for the eliciting the WTA-WTP disparity. Table 8 presents the results of the number of sales for both decision situations, winners and losers. The decision situations are differentiated, in the left hand column of the table. The symbols "--" and "+-" are investment situations with losing stocks whose current prices are below the last period price. The two sub-groups can be differentiated by reference to a negative or a positive price change prior to the last negative price change. The other two sub-groups "++" and "-+" are defined analogously. The data in Table 8 clearly show a distinct reluctance to sell losers,

---

[14]Profits (losses) are the positive (negative) difference between the reference price and the actual (market) price. See Weber/Camerer (1991) for related work.

namely, a proportion of 1:2 compared to the winners. A very similar result, namely, 38%:62% instead of 35%:65% also emerges when an additional past period is used. For example, instead of "++" and "-+" for winners, consider "+++", "-++" and "--+" periods. The experimental results for the number of shares sold are very similar. Summarizing the aggregate results clearly shows the endowment effect in the form of a reluctance to sell losers. Hypothesis 1 cannot be rejected.

Table 8: Number of sell orders per period regarding winner and loser periods

Winner/Loser	Experiment I	
	Sales per period	%
- -	11.7	13
+ -	19.7	22
Σ Loser	14.9	35
+ +	30.9	38
- +	22.5	27
Σ Winner	28.1	65

Standardized.

Individual investor behavior is next examined prior to an analysis of the disposition effect with the purchase price as a reference point. The coefficient z for each investor j is computed as the difference between the number of sales of winners and losers in relation to the total number of sales:

$$z_j = (V_{j+} - V_{j-}) / (V_{j+} + V_{j-}) \quad (2)$$

where, V_{j+} = number of sales of participant j for winners; V_{j-} = number of sales of subjects j for losers and therefore $1 \geq z_j \geq -1$, i.e. the closer a positive z_j lies to 1 for an investor, the more clearly he reveals his "loss aversion" (reluctance to sell at a loss). Table 9 shows the average value of z for three groups of investors. The average of z for those subjects who exhibit a loss aversion ($z_j>0$) amounts to 0.68. Two thirds of the investors belong to this group. The data corroborate the results of related studies by Kahneman et al. (1990, pp. 1338f.) and Weber/Camerer (1991, p. 18), which report a value of 0.30 from a similar coefficient. These authors also report that not all subjects exhibit the endowment effect.

Table 9: Coefficient z for measurement of the disposition effect in single case analysis

Coefficient	Experiment I	
	Value of z[a]	Percentage of subjects (%)
> 0	0.68	67.5
= 0	0	0.0
< 0	-0.55	32.5
Average	+0.29[b] (+6.30)	

a: Average of each group; b: $\alpha = 0.01$ (2-tailed t-test)

b) The disposition effect with the purchase price as a reference point

An analysis of the disposition effect with the purchase price as a reference-point encounters problems, because during the consecutive decision periods no unique purchase price exists. Applying the techniques of accounting, "first-in, first-out" (fifo) or "last-in, first-out" (lifo) methods are used. A moving average method could also be used. All three procedures were used in this analysis. Because the respective results are not greatly disparate, only the results of the lifo method are presented here.

Table 10: Experimental results on the disposition effect with the purchase price as a reference point

Stocks	Shares sold per period		
	Winner	Loser	= [a]
1 shares	609	150	0
%	80	20	0
2 shares	791	512	173
%	54	35	11
3 shares	1463	645	255
%	62	27	11
4 shares	322	241	0
%	57	43	0
5 shares	138	31	0
%	82	18	0
Average shares	607	327	223
%	52	28	20

a: Neither a winner nor loser period.
Standardized.

Table 10 documents the experimental results for each kind of stock and on average. Introducing the purchase price as a reference point also reveals a reluctance to sell at a loss. These results are valid for all stocks and on average. Hence, hypothesis 2 cannot be rejected. The experimental analyses on the disposition effect can be completed with results from the final questionnaire. The subjects were asked to describe how they use the information given in the experiment. The item "use of past price movements" (price changes) received the highest rating.[15] A second question asked for a description of the individual strategies and thoughts during the experiment. 15% of the investors explicitly named actions which raise the presumption that they used the purchase price as a reference point (e.g. "lowering the aquisition price").

4. Conclusion

The results of the research project on the behavior of private investors suggest the following:

- A complex "web" of determinants influence investment behavior, but a closed concept cannot yet be formulated. Nevertheless, further research on the determinants of investor behavior may facilitate the development of a complete descriptive model.
- The experimental results reveal strong evidence of the existence of biases in decision behavior, particularly in stockholders' behavior. The risk aversion analyzed in the survey data can, in principle, be observed in the experimental test of diversification behavior. However, the subjects act contrary to the axioms of the (S)EU-theory in revealing an asymmetrical valuation relating to a reference point.

The extent to which (S)EU-theory and further developments thereof can explain decision behavior remains an open question. For example, do decision makers really use probability distributions for different states of nature or coefficients of such distributions, e.g. the expected value and the standard deviation? Or, do the theoretically oriented concepts of most researchers in this field restrict the creative potential for the eliciting of alternative explanations about decision behavior?

The results of this project have stimulated further initiatives in this field, including work on theoretical and methodological problems, and in response of the necessity of both empirical and experimental methods in particular:

[15] The study uses a 6-point-scale from 1 (= "not at all") to 6 (= "very strong").

- Decision criteria and their weights in single and group decisions concerned with financial investments.
- Operationalization and measurement of risks perceived by subjects in investment decisions.
- Analysis of the portfolio structure of stock owners.
- Characteristics of stock owners.
- Economic analysis of the behavior of insiders (costs and benefits, advantages and disadvantages).
- Structure and flow of information and decision processes of institutional investors (banks, insurance companies, investment funds, large non-financial enterprises).

In future research it will be interesting to deal with more intensive analyses of investor behavior. Research on financial markets would benefit from disaggregated and carefully performed examinations using surveys and experiments, e.g., intensive studies on biases in decision making, herding by institutional investors, or the relationship between a market's microstructure and the market participants' behavior seem worthwhile. Such work would help explain investors' behavior and price movements in financial markets.

References

Arrow, K.J. (1971): Essays in the Theory of Risk-Bearing. Amsterdam/London (North Holland).

Bitz, M. and Oehler, A. (1993a): Überlegungen zu einer verhaltenswissenschaftlich fundierten Kapitalmarktforschung - ein Erklärungsansatz zum Anlegerverhalten, Teil I, in: Kredit und Kapital 26, 246 - 273.

Bitz, M. and Oehler, A. (1993b): Überlegungen zu einer verhaltenswissenschaftlich fundierten Kapitalmarktforschung - ein Erklärungsansatz zum Anlegerverhalten, Teil II, in: Kredit und Kapital 26, 375 - 416.

Cohn, R.A., Lewellen, W.C., Lease, R.C. and Schlarbaum, G.G. (1975): Individual Investor Risk Aversion, in: Journal of Finance 30, 605 - 620.

Elton, E.J. and M.J. Gruber (1991): Modern Portfolio Theory and Investment Analysis. 4th ed. New York (John Wiley).

Franke, G. (1993): Neuere Entwicklungen auf dem Gebiet der Finanzmarkttheorie, in: Wirtschaftswissenschaftliches Studium 22, 389 - 398.

Kahneman, D. and Tversky, A. (1979), Prospect Theory: An Analysis of Decision under Risk, in: Econometrica 47, 263 - 291.

Kahneman, D., Knetsch, J.L. and Thaler, R.H. (1990): Experimental Tests of the Endowment Effect and the Coase Theorem, in: Journal of Political Economy 98, 1325 - 1348.

Katona, G. (1975): Psychological Economics. New York (John Wiley).

Krahnen, J.P. (1993): Finanzwirtschaftslehre zwischen Markt und Institution. Ein Essay, in: Die Betriebswirtschaft 53, 793 - 806.

Kroll, Y., Levy H. and Rapoport, A. (1988): Experimental Tests of the Mean-Variance Model for Portfolio Selection, in: Organizational Behavior and Human Decision Processes 42, 388 - 410.

Lampman, R. (1962): Share of Top Wealth-Holders in National Wealth 1922-1956. Princeton (Princeton University Press).

Morin, R.A. and Suarez, A.F. (1983): Risk Aversion Revisited, in: Journal of Finance 38, 1201 - 1216.

Oehler, A. (1992): "Anomalien", "Irrationalitäten" oder "Biases" der Erwartungsnutzentheorie und ihre Relevanz für Finanzmärkte, in: Zeitschrift für Bankrecht und Bankwirtschaft 4, 97 - 124.

Oehler, A. (1994): Verhaltensmuster individueller Anleger - eine experimentelle Studie, in: Zeitschrift für betriebswirtschaftliche Forschung 46, 939 - 958.

Oehler, A. (1995), Die Erklärung des Verhaltens privater Anleger - Theoretischer Ansatz und empirische Analysen. Stuttgart (Poeschel).

Pratt, J.W. (1964): Risk Aversion in the Small and in the Large, in: Econometrica 32, 122 - 136.

Raaij, W.F. van and Gianotten, H.J. (1990): Consumer Confidence, Expenditure, Saving, and Credit, in: Journal of Economic Psychology 11, 269 - 290.

Shefrin, H.M. and Statman, M. (1985): The Disposition to Sell Winners too Early and Ride Losers too Long: Theory and Evidence, in: Journal of Finance 40, 777 - 792.

Siegel, F.W. and Hoban, J.P. (1982): Relative Risk Aversion Revisited, in: Review of Economics and Statistics 64, 481 - 487.

Staw, B.M. (1976): Knee-Deep in the Big Muddy, in: Organizational Behavior and Human Performance 27, 27 - 44.

Thaler, R.H. (1990): Anomalies: Saving, Fungibility, and Mental Accounts, in: Journal of Economic Perspectives 4, 193 - 205.

Weber, M. and C. Camerer (1991): The Disposition Effect in Securities Trading: An Experimental Analysis. Manuskripte aus den Instituten für Betriebswirtschaftslehre der Universität Kiel, No. 276. University of Kiel.

Weber, M. and Camerer, C. (1992): Ein Experiment zum Anlegerverhalten, in: Zeitschrift für betriebswirtschaftliche Forschung 44, 131 - 148.

Market Structure and Bid-Ask Spread

Hartmut Schmidt, Peter Iversen and Kai Treske
University of Hamburg

1. Introduction

From a national perspective, the global competition in financial services requires operationally efficient securities markets. Improvements in operational efficiency allow for lower transaction costs to investors and add to the competitiveness of national securities markets. Increasing competition has reduced the commission component of transaction costs and, as a result, there is a keen interest of market organizers in market structures that achieve the lowest possible bid-ask spreads and thus reduce the cost of immediacy. Much research has thus been focussed on the relative spread sizes of dealer markets and auction markets. But there is little evidence at the international level and, except for a study by Haller/Stoll (1989), no related empirical work has been done on the German market. The purpose of the present study is to shed additional light on this issue by comparing bid-ask spreads for a matched sample of U.S. and German stocks and by relating any spread differences to differences in market structure.

This paper provides a summary of the results. In a way it is also a survey on how the study proceeded, because the results are closely linked to the rapid development of the German markets during the period under investigation. Space limitations preclude a survey of the related literature and detailed descriptions of floor trading, of the methodology and of the data used.[1]

2. The German stock market and the cost of immediacy

Currently, stocks are traded on eight floor exchanges and on the electronic trading system IBIS (*Integriertes Börsenhandels- und Informationssystem*). On the floors, listed stocks are allocated to specialists. These specialists run a batch auction to start

---

[1] For this information, the reader is referred to Schmidt/Iversen (1992), Schmidt, Iversen/Treske (1993), Iversen (1994), Booth/Iversen/Sarkar/Schmidt/Young (1994) and to Schmidt/Oesterhelweg/Treske (1995).

the continuous trading of active stocks, a batch auction around noon and, possibly, a third batch auction at the end of the trading session. Inactive stocks are traded only once a day through a batch auction at noon. On the automated trading system IBIS, banks, specialists (*Kursmakler*) and floor brokers (*Freimakler*) quote bids and offers and are thus considered to be market makers. Trading is anonymous and can best be described as an open book continuous auction at individual prices. Both market makers and investors having limit orders on the IBIS book are competing potential counterparties on the non-initiating side of the market.

It is frequently claimed that the liquidity of German equities is poor because of the structure of the German stock market. Many have maintained that regional exchanges are detrimental to the liquidity and international competitiveness of the German equity markets. Consequently, there is a steady flow of proposals for change, including proposals to replace the agency auction system with a multiple market maker system. Whether the liquidity of the German equity market is likely to improve for active or inactive stocks under a multiple market maker system is, from a German perspective, an important, timely and open question.

In our view, the answer to this question requires a realistic picture of the current liquidity situation and strong empirical clues to guide microstructure experiments in a direction which will improve, or transform, the current auction regime. This paper is a first step and concentrates on analyzing the liquidity situation. For the investor, an important, if not the most important, aspect of liquidity is the bid-ask spread because it is generally considered a good proxy for the cost of immediacy. Therefore, we focus on this liquidity measure. So far, there has been at best anecdotal evidence of the allegedly poor liquidity of the German equity market. Research supporting this allegation has not been forthcoming. On the contrary, Haller/Stoll (1989), in a seminal effort to estimate implied spreads for German stocks, using Roll's pioneering estimation procedure and continuous trading data for a 4-week period, could not find an implied spread significantly different from zero for German stocks actively traded on the Frankfurt Stock Exchange. Schmidt/Iversen (1990) duplicated this study for an extended period of 15 months and arrived at the same result.

However, in addition to estimated implied spreads, liquidity should also be measured by actual quoted spreads and market spreads. Unfortunately, the relevant data are still not available for German floor trading. But data from electronic quotation and trading systems do allow insights beyond those of Haller/Stoll (1989). Moreover, the location of transaction prices on the floor relative to the midpoint of the spread of electronic quotation systems for the same stocks can be used to judge the liquidity of both trading floors and electronic trading systems. During the course of this project, for which a preliminary funding application was filed in 1988, electronic quotation systems were established in Germany. These gradually improved the data situation and influenced project direction and progress.

3. Electronic systems for equities

Since 1987 the major German banks have pursued a strategy of "replacing the middlemen with the computer" in order to save hundreds of million marks in floor commissions. They established an automated futures and options exchange, the *Deutsche Terminbörse* (DTB), that is run without specialists and floor brokers. At the same time, they moved to scale down the role played by specialists and floor brokers in the spot market. To achieve this, the banks decided to have much longer trading hours on the DTB than on the floors of the spot market. Moreover, they installed an electronic interbank spot market system, with trading hours matching those of the DTB, to provide for an underlying spot market before and after exchange hours. As might have been expected, this *Inter-Banken-Informations-System*, abreviated IBIS, from which they were initially excluded, caused specialists to respond with a system of their own called MATIS (*Makler-Tele-Informations-System*).

3.1 IBIS

Originally, IBIS was a quotation and settlement support system, which is usually referred to as IBIS I. It operated from December 1, 1989 to April 4, 1991. Trading hours were 8:30 a.m. to 5 p.m., whereas the floors are open from 10:30 a.m.[2] to 1:30 p.m. Originally, participating banks could enter quotes or limit orders for all 14 stocks underlying DTB options. Since May 1990 all 30 stocks included in the DAX (*Deutscher Aktienindex*) and since September 1990 a number of actively traded government bonds have also entered the system. Quotes proved to be firm, even though market making is voluntary and unregulated. The actual trading was by phone and, immediately thereafter, the trade data had to be entered by both parties via their IBIS terminals into the settlement system. Within minutes the compared trade data were ready to be processed, together with trade data flowing from the floors to the DWZ (*Deutsche Wertpapierdaten-Zentrale*), the German securities clearing service.

IBIS II, in contrast, which has been in operation since April 5, 1991, is an automated trading system. Legally, it was initially a segment of the Frankfurt Exchange. Later, it became part of all other German stock exchanges. As a result, all exchange members, including the floor brokers and specialists, may now participate in IBIS trading. A controversial consequence of this is that the "*Courtage*", a floor brokerage (six hundredths of one percent of the consideration for shares), may be charged by specialists or floor brokers, if they advertise this brokerage with their quotes on the IBIS screen. To reflect these developments, the name of IBIS was changed from *Inter-Banken-Informations-System* to *Integriertes Börsenhandels- und Informations-System*.

---

[2] 11:30 a.m. until January 1990.

If banks or specialists enter clients′ orders, such public orders may meet even though the bulk of bids and offers is quoted by members who act like market makers. In principle, bids and offers are executed under a regime of best price and (time) priority. The bid or offer that is hit determines the price. A trade is consummated when a member keys in that he accepts the highest ranking bid (or offer) in full or, alternatively, any part thereof which constitutes a round lot. Trades larger than the size at the best bid, or offer, price are effected by two or more transactions, unless the member chooses to accept a single lower ranking bid, or offer, that is large enough. The minimum size of bids, or offers, is one round lot, which, except for Allianz (100 shares), was 500 shares until March 13, 1992. Since than it has been 100 shares for 15 other less actively traded DAX stocks as well. Once a transaction is consummated, trade data are automatically transmitted to the German securities clearing service DWZ. This, along with electronic trading, increased the speed of transacting dramatically and is considered to be the most important feature of IBIS II. IBIS I never captured more then a few percent of German share volume. IBIS II, however, attracted much more trading right from its start. If viewed as an exchange of its own, it has grown to be second only to Frankfurt.

3.2 MATIS

From December 15, 1989 to December 1, 1992 the federal association of specialists operated MATIS through Reuters. It was an off-hours quotation system that encompassed 60 securities including the 30 stocks underlying the DAX index, government bonds and warrants. The minimum quote size for stocks was 250 shares, though the specialists were prepared to trade 500 or 1000 shares at their quoted prices. Quotes were firm and the specialists would accept any exchange member as counterparty who, by trading, incurred an obligation to pay *Courtage*. Specialists were under no obligation to maintain quotes while the system operated. Contrary to IBIS, the system closed down during floor trading hours. For settlement the specialists used the regular DWZ facilities. MATIS enjoyed a market share larger than IBIS I, but it fell back after IBIS II was introduced.

3.3 SEAQ International

SEAQ International is a quotation system operated by the International Stock Exchange, London, since June 1985. It complements SEAQ, the quotation system for domestic securities. As of September 30, 1991, 32 German stocks were quoted on SEAQ International.[3] According to Davis (1993), most trading of German stocks outside Germany is concentrated on SEAQ International, which reports a volume equivalent to about 11 percent of the trading inside Germany. Quotes are firm if there

[3] Stock Exchange Quarterly, Autumn 1991, p. 48 and 49.

are more than two market makers. Market makers are required to maintain quotes in the system during the mandatory quote period[4] for at least minimum marketable quantities. These minimum quote sizes for German stocks are generally 500 or 1000 shares. A market maker quoting in larger size must be prepared to deal at the displayed price up to and including this larger size (Rule 336.2b).[5]

3.4 NASDAQ/NMS

NASDAQ is a multiple market maker system operated by the National Association of Security Dealers since 1971. NMS stands for the NASDAQ segment in which the largest U.S. OTC stocks are traded. Unlike the German and U.S. exchanges, which share a strong agency element and allow public orders to meet, market spreads on NASDAQ by design reflect market maker quotes. This marked difference in market structure, the substantial number and size of the companies that have chosen NASDAQ/NMS as the primary market place for their shares, and the considerable data availability make NASDAQ/NMS the obvious choice in an international study that focusses on the impact of market structure on the bid-ask spread.

NASD registered market makers are required to maintain quotes throughout the trading day from 9:30 a.m. to 4 p.m. for the issues in which they are registered to trade. These quotes must be good for at least 1,000 shares and are displayed on the level 2 service screen along with the names of the related market makers. This service is commonly used by the trading desks of securities firms and institutional investors. Accordingly, there are as many quotes on the NASDAQ screen as there are market makers and the number of these quotes is essentially constant throughout the trading day. A market maker who fails to maintain a quote is prohibited from entering such quotes for the following 20 business days. Traditionally, transactions are executed by a telephone call to the market maker advertising the highest bid or lowest ask quote, or to a market maker who might match or exceed this quote.

---

[4] As of September 1, 1991, the mandatory quote period for German stocks was 9:45 a.m. to 3:30 p.m. London time.

[5] However, he may refuse to deal less than the minimum marketable quantity at this price (Rule 336.2c).

4. Spreads of German stocks

4.1 Implied spreads on the floor

As already stated, the course of the project was very much influenced by data availability. At the outset, there was only one way to obtain bid-ask spreads for stocks of German companies, namely, estimation based on transaction prices. Later, with substantial differences in scope and attendant information (such as quote size and quote deletion time), quotes became available from the MATIS, IBIS and SEAQ systems. Unfortunately, for floor trading, the data situation only improved in late 1994. However, floor trading quotes are still not recorded in Germany, and it is necessary to estimate the bid-ask spread with transaction data. Roll´s (1984) estimation procedure is used for a comparison of the spreads at the Frankfurt and the Hamburg exchanges (Iversen 1994, pp. 115-153). The sample consists of the 30 stocks that make up the DAX Index.

Spreads on the Frankfurt floor were estimated for 33 months from 1989 to 1991. The average spread was 0.082 percent, which is significantly different from zero (t-statistic: 8.14). There is a tendency for less actively traded stocks to have higher spreads. For the Hamburg exchange, data were available for only 8 months. The average spread was 0.0496 percent (t-statistic: 1.82). Since spreads vary over time, only the results for the same months were compared and no significant difference was found (t-statistic: 1.17). These results suggest that bid-ask spreads on different German floors are much the same and that the spread levels (less than 0.1 percent) are very low by international standards.

4.2 Quoted spreads and market spreads on the electronic systems IBIS, MATIS and SEAQ International

Quoted and market spreads were calculated from the data generated by these electronic systems. Factors determining the spread were also analyzed (Iversen 1994, pp. 192-204). Thirdly, the intraday pattern of the market spread was established (Schmidt/Iversen 1991, 1992, Iversen 1994, pp. 176-183, 228-238) and, finally, the spreads on different systems were compared (Schmidt/Iversen 1991, 1992, Iversen 1994, pp. 246-266).

The data cover identical securities that are traded on the three systems. The German banks, through which most of the business in German equities flows, have access to each of the three systems. Therefore, the bid-ask spreads observed on these systems should provide a reliable measure of the liquidity of the German equity market and only negligible, if any, system-to-system differences in bid-ask spreads are to be expected.

Bid-ask spreads can be measured in a number of ways. Implied spreads as used by Haller/Stoll (1989) are derived from transaction prices. Alternatively, the highest bid and lowest ask in the market at the close are widely used spread measures. However, these closing spreads are misleading if during most of the trading session higher or lower spreads prevail. A spread measure that improves on implied spreads and closing spreads should be based either on all quotes entered into a system (quoted spreads or individual dealer spreads) or on the highest bids and lowest asks that were observed at various points throughout the trading day (inside or market spreads).[6]

Obviously, the mean quoted spread observed for a stock should be larger than its mean market spread. Even if a market spread at any one time reflects the quote of only one member, there are simultaneous quotes of other members, which are wider than the market spread and enter the calculation of the mean quoted spread. These quotes, however, are disregarded for market spread calculations. Quoted spreads may be particularly inflated in a system in which some dealers quote who do not want to deal. On SEAQ International, because quoting is mandatory, larger mean quoted spreads are to be expected than on the German systems. Between the German systems, MATIS should have larger quoted spreads than IBIS II where quotes are anonymous. A strategy of inviting phone calls by having a quote on the screen and a reputation to deal with the calling party inside that quote is not feasible on IBIS II.[7] Observed quoted spreads are reported in Table 1.

---

6 For market spreads slightly differing modes of calculation had to be used due to data restrictions. For a survey and discussion of related measures see Stoll (1991).

7 Alternatively, the hypothesis that IBIS quotes are tighter than MATIS quotes could be supported by information related arguments. First, universal banks, contrary to specialists, tend to have ready access to company inside information. Therefore, one might expect that the banks can afford to deal at lower spreads due to a lower adverse information cost component. Second, the banks, particularly the larger ones, see and direct substantial parts of the order flow before it is, if at all, reflected in the specialists' books, which have become very thin on the exchanges outside Frankfurt.

Table 1: Overall means of quoted spreads on electronic systems for German equities 1991 in percent[8]

	February	March	April	May	June	July
IBIS	1.05 (IBIS I)	1.01 (IBIS I)	0.92 (IBIS II)	0.91 (IBIS II)		
MATIS	0.78	0.76	0.63	0.56		
SEAQ				1.25	1.25	1.29

Contrary to expectation, the IBIS overall mean is higher than the MATIS overall mean. In both systems, there is a strong negative relationship between the volume of individual stocks and the corresponding mean quoted spread (R^2 = 0.82 for IBIS II and 0.84 for MATIS in a logarithmic regression). The regressions also suggest that MATIS, in addition to offering the lower spreads, was equally well suited for the provision of liquidity services in all 30 stocks. In other words, IBIS did not seem to have a comparative advantage in the most active securities. We tested whether the difference between MATIS and IBIS is significant by introducing a dummy variable. The difference proved to be significant (t-statistic: 5.75) and, according to the regression equation, the IBIS mean spreads are 1.29 times the MATIS mean spreads. This outcome appears to be inconsistent with the belief that anonymous IBIS market makers quote more narrowly than the specialists on MATIS.

In interpreting these results, the regional concentration of the IBIS quotes may be a factor. Since about 94 percent of IBIS quotes originated in Frankfurt and Munich, whereas the MATIS quotes were fairly evenly distributed over German financial centers, this concentration may indicate that most IBIS quotes were entered by major German banks, headquartered in Frankfurt or in Munich, which sponsor IBIS. In other words, probably a mere handful of major banks quoted on IBIS and this may have influenced spreads early in 1991.

The SEAQ International spreads are not easily compared with those of the German systems. The last mean quoted spreads for a full month on the German systems are

[8] Intraday data were kindly provided by the *Bundesverband der Kursmakler* through Reuters, by the DWZ, and by the International Stock Exchange in London. IBIS I data cover the period February 14 through March 31, 1991. IBIS II data are available for the period April 5 to May 31, 1991. MATIS data contain quotes entered February 1 through May 31, 1991. The MATIS spreads are adjusted for the "courtage" by adding 0.12 percent. In contrast to the IBIS and MATIS data, which cover all 30 stocks underlying the DAX, data for SEAQ International were made available on 6 stocks for the period May 24 to July 31, 1991.

available for May, the earliest full month spreads for SEAQ are for June. Because the SEAQ mean spreads (Table 1) were remarkably stable over time, a comparison of these May and June spreads appears to be justified. For each stock, for which the results of both systems are available, the mean quoted spreads on SEAQ were, as expected, higher than on IBIS.

The results for market spreads on the three systems are presented in Table 2.

Table 2: Overall means of market spreads on electronic systems for German equities 1 1991 in percent[9]

	April	May	June	July
IBIS II	0.76	0.75		
MATIS	0.41	0.36		
SEAQ		0.63	0.65	0.64

The means of market spreads are lower than the corresponding means for quoted spreads, which is in line with expectations. The most relevant determinant for both quoted and market spreads was found to be trading activity measured by DM volume. Stocks subject to option trading on the DTB seem to have smaller spreads than other stocks.

Another relevant determinant of spreads is the time of the day. This is documented by McInish/Wood (1992) for NYSE stocks, by Pagano/Roell (1990) for French stocks, by Lüdecke/Schlag (1992) for derivatives of German stocks and by the related studies of Finnerty/Park (1988) and Cheung/Ng (1990). Different shapes of the intraday pattern of market spreads have been found. McInish/Wood (1992) find a reverse J-shape, Pagano/Roell (1990) a U-shape and Lüdecke/Schlag (1992) a W-pattern. Obviously, any stable pattern is of interest to investors. They may want to shift their trades to those times of the day at which the spreads tend to be relatively low.

On MATIS, a U-shaped pattern was found in both sessions - the before and after floor hours. The trading activity is concentrated around the middle of each trading session, a fact which adds further support to the thesis that trading activity is the most important determinant of the spread. On IBIS, we again find U-shaped market spread patterns during the time before and the time after floor hours, and a third U-pattern in between, when the floors are open. As on MATIS there is a corresponding intraday pattern of trading volume. The market spread pattern on SEAQ shows relatively low spreads prevailing from 9:30 a.m. to 12:30 p.m. London time, which lends additional

[9] For data and methodology see Table 1.

support to the notion that spreads decrease until the middle of the trading session and increase thereafter. This mid-session effect has been observed by McInish/Wood (1992), and it may also be reflected in the MATIS morning-session and afternoon-session lows.

If one views, in contrast, the 9:30 to 12:30 section of the London pattern (Figure 1) with specific reference to the fact that the main markets for the underlying stocks are located in Germany, it strikes that this period exactly matches German floor trading hours. Apparently, there is a home-market effect. A substantial number of potential SEAQ International users are likely to have ready access to German exchanges. This suggests that the competitive pressure of bids and asks on the eight German trading floors is an explaining factor[10] and that the home-market effect reinforces the mid-session effect. It also suggests that the unrestricted access of competing potential counterparties, which is the key characteristic of agency auction markets such as the German floors, is the major source of competitive pressure. For the sample of "cross listed" stocks in Figure 1 this pressure of the agency auction market appears to be conveyed into the pure multiple market maker system SEAQ International. Consequently, any attempt to obtain insights into market structure influences on the bid-ask spread should preferably be focussed on the spreads of matched samples of stocks with different home markets, and not on a sample of cross-listed stocks.

Figure 1: Intraday pattern of SEAQ International market spreads, May 24 to July 31, 1991

[10] This is in line with the findings of Pagano/Roell (1990, p. 104) who show that SEAQ spreads for French stocks are low while the Bourse is open.

4.3 Effective spreads: cost of immediacy on the floor and on the computer

The electronic quotation and trading systems provide a data base that is superior to floor data. However, the spreads on these systems may not be representative of the German markets, since most of the trading is still concentrated on the floors. In order to compare the cost of immediacy on IBIS II and on the floors, it is necessary to focus on the same type of spread at the same point of time. The effective cost of immediacy (for two opposite transactions) on IBIS II is expressed by the market spread because, due to system design, it is not possible on IBIS II to deal inside the market spread. Viewed differently, this effective cost of immediacy, or effective spread at a point in time, may be restated as the difference between the price of a buy trade minus the midquote (ask-side transaction) plus midquote minus price of a sale (bid-side transaction). To determine the effective spread, timestamped information is needed on midquote (midpoint of the market spread) and on price and direction of the trades.

On the floor, transactions may be priced inside or outside the IBIS market spread that prevails at this time. To determine the effective spread it is, as for IBIS, assumed that on average the spread straddles the equilibrium price symmetrically and that a price above (below) midquote indicates that the trade was initiated by a buyer (seller). A similar approach was recently employed by Lee (1993). Thus, the difference between the IBIS midquote and the floor transaction price measures the effective cost of immediacy on the floor. This difference doubled yields the effective floor spread. For the stocks which make up the DAX index, the mean effective floor spread was lower than the corresponding mean market spread on IBIS based on observations at the same points in time. At the end of 1991 the effective spread on the Hamburg floor exchange was 0.45 percent on average and, in contrast, 0.83 percent on IBIS. About two thirds of all floor transactions were priced inside the IBIS market spread. For less actively traded stocks, as can be seen in Figure 2, the cost of immediacy advantage of the floor was pronounced. Even for the most actively traded stocks the effective spread was considerably lower on the floor. More recently, an analysis based on November and December 1994 data covering all eight floors yielded similar results (Schmidt/Oesterhelweg/Treske 1995).[11]

---

[11] Inspite of the narrower spreads and contrary to intuition, the floors have lost market share to IBIS. This floor paradox closely parallels the MATIS paradox, which is discussed in Schmidt and Iversen (1992).

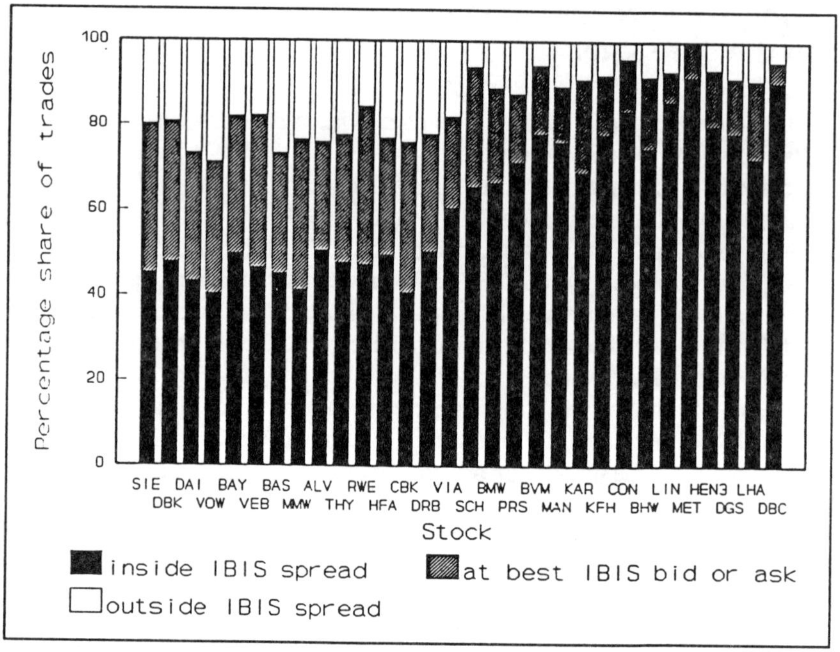

Figure 2: Percentage share of trades inside, at or outside the IBIS market spread, November and December 1991.

5. Market structure and competing potential counterparties

5.1 German markets versus NASDAQ

A dealer market is one in which the public buys and sells to a dealer. In an agency market, public investors transact with each other without the intervention of a dealer. The basic feature of an *auction* market is the exposure of an executable order to a number of competing potential counterparties such as limit orders on the book or dealers present on the floor. In dealer markets, as long as there is more than a single dealer, an executable order is also exposed to competing potential counterparties as manifested by competing bids and offers on the screen. Thus, it is useful to distinguish between *dealer auction* markets and *agency auction* markets. The terms *quote driven* and *order driven* point to the dominant sources of competing potential counterparties. NASDAQ, with its multiple market makers, is by original design a dealer auction market. The German market is a hybrid with strong agency and strong dealer components. On a continuum that extends from a dealer auction market to an agency auction market, the German markets, including IBIS, should properly be placed in a position much closer to the agency auction market than to NASDAQ.

The question addressed in this paper is whether the larger agency component of the German stock market affects the bid-ask spread. Since the bid-ask spread reflects the price of immediacy service, it is likely to narrow as the number of those explicitly or implicitly offering this service, i.e., the number of competing potential counterparties, increases. The NASDAQ registration and quote maintenance requirements result in a rather stable, yet not necessarily large, number of market makers in each stock. However, on the German stock market there is a keen, but less stable, dealer involvement and, possibly, an even more volatile number of public investors competing through limit orders. This unrestricted access of all suppliers of immediacy service to the German market, which leads to the higher volatility in the number of competing potential counterparties, may not equally affect the bid-ask spread of high and low volume stocks. Nevertheless, the level of interest that investors and dealers have shown in the most active stocks, though unstable over time, appears to be sufficient to hypothesize that unrestricted access of all suppliers of immediacy narrows the market spread of these stocks. Therefore, it is expected that the market spreads of active German stocks are lower than those of comparable NASDAQ stocks. In contrast, if an intraday perspective is taken, the expectation is that the difference between the spread level on NASDAQ and that on the German stock market widens as the number of competing potential counterparties increases. This latter expectation is based on the assumption that the intraday number of suppliers of immediacy tends to vary in Germany but not on NASDAQ (Booth/Iversen/Sarkar/Schmidt/Young 1995).

On the Frankfurt floor the overall mean implied spread for 1990 and 1991 is 0.10 percent. Applying the same estimation method to transaction prices of NASDAQ stocks resulted in wider implied spreads, with the average spread being 0.80 percent. As shown in Figure 3, all monthly means are positive and greater than those of the German stocks.

The average market spread of a sample of matched German and NASDAQ/NMS stocks was found to be 0.82 percent on IBIS and 1.07 percent on NASDAQ. Whereas the intraday pattern of IBIS market spreads shows a U-shape during each of the three phases - before, during and after floor hours - the intraday pattern for NASDAQ is nearly constant over time, though less smooth. The narrowing of IBIS spreads within each phase and the increasing divergence from the NASDAQ spread level should, according to hypothesis, reflect the unrestricted access of the suppliers of immediacy service in the German market. While the number of suppliers of immediacy on NASDAQ is, at least in principle, constant and equal to the number of registered market makers, this figure may vary intraday on IBIS. Therefore, the intraday pattern of the number of parties having bids and asks in the IBIS system was analyzed.

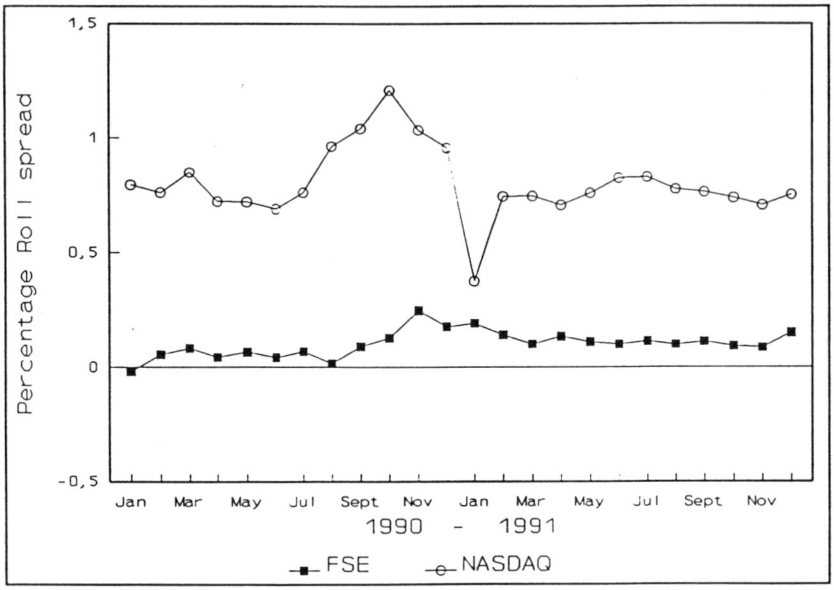

Figure 3: Implied spreads on the Frankfurt Stock Exchange and on NASDAQ, January 1990 to December 1991

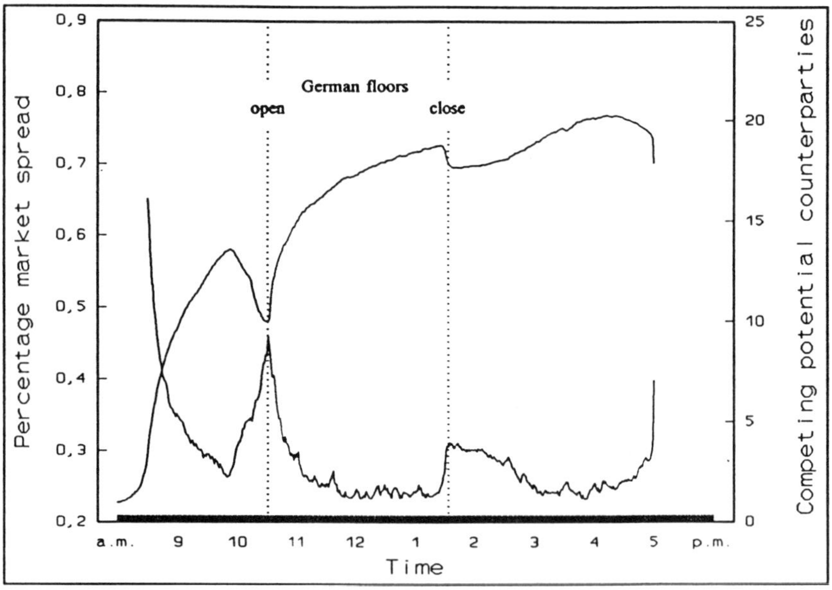

Figure 4: Intraday pattern of IBIS market spreads and potential competing counterparties per stock, November and December 1991

A decline in market spreads in the course of the day corresponds closely to an increase in the number of competing potential counterparties. On IBIS, the monthly average number of competing potential counterparties is positively correlated with the mean market spreads for different stocks. The market spread is likely to narrow as the number of those offering immediacy, the number of competing potential counterparties, increases. Registration and quote maintenance requirements on NASDAQ constrain this number. In an agency auction market, such as the German stock market, the number of competing potential counterparties is unrestricted and, as hypothesized, is associated with lower market spreads.

5.2 Single price batch auctions

So far, the focus has been on two-party prices. In some securities markets investors can choose to deal either individually at two-party prices or collectively at multi-party prices. Collective prices are established in single price batch auctions. The spatial and temporal consolidation of batch auctions provides for a substantial number of competing potential counterparties. Therefore, the times for which batch auctions are scheduled should be attractive trading points and draw considerable investor interest. Batch auction trading should be relatively more attractive than continuous trading at individual prices in case of stocks with wide bid-ask spreads. On the German floors, there are batch auctions at the opening, at noon and at the close. The average percentage shares of batch auction volume (ABAS) in total daily volume[12] of the 40 stocks traded on IBIS were regressed on the IBIS market spreads. The results are significant and consistent with expectations. They are shown in Figure 5.

6. Summary and conclusions

The goal of this project was to shed additional light on how market structure influences the cost of immediacy, a cost generally measured by bid-ask spreads. For a number of reasons, quoted spreads and even market spreads, as this study demonstrates, may be less desirable measures than effective spreads. Implied spreads are generally affected by estimation problems but appear to be reliable if based on a substantial number of prices per trading day.

---

[12] Total volume is total floor volume as reported on the basis of the BOSS-CUBE activity on eight floors. The IBIS spreads and the effective spreads on the floors are closely correlated (R^2 = 0,96).

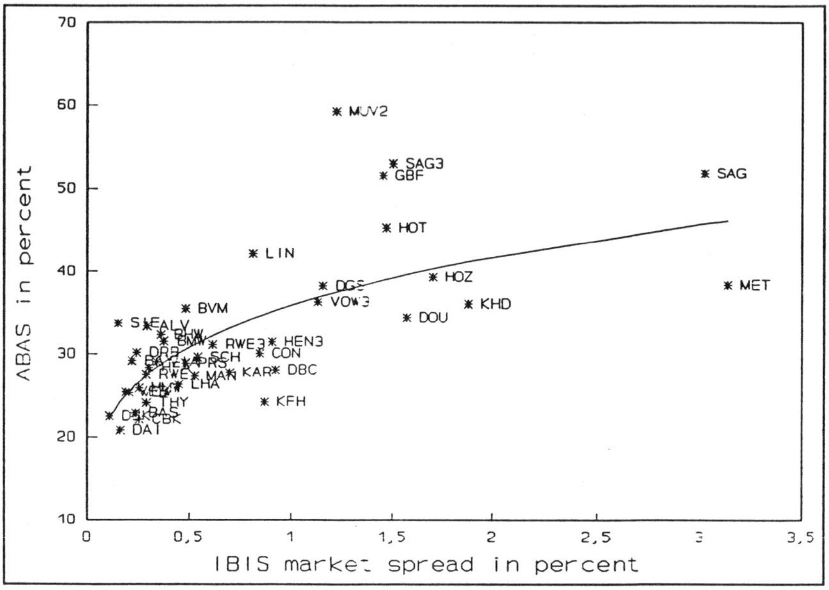

Figure 5: Average batch auction share and IBIS market spread November and December 1994

In a dealer auction market the cost of immediacy is expected to be higher than in an agency auction market. The evidence found for NASDAQ, a dealer auction market, and for the German markets, is consistent with this hypothesis. For a matched sample of the 30 most active stocks on NASDAQ/NMS and on the German markets, implied spreads and market spreads were found to be higher on NASDAQ. Due to data restrictions, effective spreads could not be obtained. However, Lee (1993) reports little activity inside the NASDAQ market spread. In contrast, this study finds evidence that, on average, the prices of floor trades of German stocks are located far inside the IBIS market spread, which was compared with the market spread of the NASDAQ/NMS sample. This outcome is consistent with the substantial difference found for implied spreads.

The driving force behind the intraday spread pattern on IBIS is the unrestricted access of competing potential counterparties. In contrast, during the course of a trading day the number of competing potential counterparties on NASDAQ is stable, and the market spread seems to be unaffected by the number of market makers. This result is in line with NASDAQ related arguments that are currently the subject of public debate in the U.S. In response, the NASD has announced that it will implement the *Aqcess* system later in 1995. This system will allow limit orders of up to 3000 shares to compete with market maker quotes on the NASDAQ screen. On the market structure continuum, this development moves NASDAQ toward an agency auction market, although it is aimed at retail investors only. Viewed from a German perspective, our results advise against moving in the opposite direction. The so-called fragmented German market is shown to be surprisingly competitive and integrated. The bid-ask spreads for the most active equities appear to at least match the international standard. On all floors, investors trade, on average, inside the IBIS bid-ask spread. SEAQ trading accounts only for a small share in volume. Investors respond sensibly to the cost of immediacy. They seem to direct their orders to batch auctions to avoid the cost of immediacy, particularly in the case of stocks with wider spreads.

This project focussed on the most active stocks. For these stocks, the unrestricted access of suppliers of immediacy that is the distinctive feature of agency auction markets appears to reduce transaction costs. The question of which market structure is most suitable for lower volume stocks can, by and large, be tackled along the lines applied in this project. Unfortunately, sufficient data on less active German stocks are not available. It has been asserted that for less active stocks dealer auction markets, or even monopoly dealer markets, lead to lower transaction costs than agency auction markets. This hypothesis must be left to future research.

References

Booth, G. G., P. Iversen, S. K. Sarkar, H. Schmidt and A. Young (1994): Market Structure and Bid-Ask Spreads vs. the German Stock Market. Working Paper, Institut für Geld- und Kapitalverkehr, University of Hamburg.

Cheung, Y.-W. and Ng, L.K. (1990): The Dynamics of S&P 500 Index and S&P 500 Futures Intraday Price Volatilities, in: The Review of Futures Markets 9, 458-486.

Davis, R. (1993): London Trading in German Equities, in: Stock Exchange Quarterly With Quality of Markets Review, 11-16.

Finnerty, J. E. and Park, H.Y. (1988): Intraday Return and Volatility Patterns in the Stock Market: Futures versus Spot, in: Advances in Futures and Options Research 3, 301-317.

Haller, A. and Stoll, H. R. (1989): Market Structure and Transaction Costs: Implied Spreads in the German Stock Market, in: Journal of Banking and Finance 13, 697-708.

Iversen, P. (1994): Geld-Brief-Spannen deutscher Standardwerte. Wiesbaden (Gabler).

Lee, C. M. C. (1993): Market Integration and Price Execution for NYSE-Listed Securities, in: Journal of Finance 48, 1009-1038.

Lüdecke, T. and Schlag, C. (1992): Die Marktstruktur der Deutschen Terminbörse: Eine empirische Analyse der Bid-Ask Spreads, in: Zeitschrift für betriebswirtschaftliche Forschung 44, 323-346.

McInish, T. H. and Wood, R. A. (1992): An Analysis of Intraday Patterns in Bid/Ask Spreads for NYSE Stocks, in: Journal of Finance 47, 753-764.

Roll, R. (1984): A Simple Implicit Measure of the Effective Bid-Ask Spread in an Efficient Market, in: Journal of Finance 39, 1127-1139.

Schmidt, H. and P. Iversen (1990): Kursermittlungsprinzip und Transaktionskosten. Working Paper, Institut für Geld- und Kapitalverkehr, University of Hamburg.

Schmidt, H. and Iversen, P. (1991): Geld-Brief-Spannen deutscher Standardwerte in IBIS und MATIS, in: Zeitschrift für Bankrecht und Bankwirtschaft 3, 209-226.

Schmidt, H. and Iversen, P. (1992): Automating German Equity Trading: Bid Ask Spreads on Competing Systems, in: Journal of Financial Services Research 6, 373-397.

Schmidt, H., Iversen, P. and Treske K. (1993): Parkett oder Computer?, in: Zeitschrift für Bankrecht und Bankwirtschaft 5, 209-221.

Schmidt, H., O. Oesterhelweg and K. Treske (1995): Investor Acceptance of Call Market Trading in Germany, in: Schwartz, R. A. (ed.): Electronic Call Market Trading. New York University, Salomon Center.

Stoll, H. R. (1993): Equity Trading Costs in-the-large and in-the-small, in: Journal of Portfolio Management 19, 41-50.

Statutory Induced Switching into a New Market

Hartmut Schmidt and Torsten Schrader
University of Hamburg

1. Introduction

In the early eighties declining equity ratios and a decreasing number of exchange traded corporations led to discussions about more efficient equity financing in Germany. Proposals to promote the public equity capital raising of small and medium size firms focussed on: 1. Reducing the requirements of the German Stock Corporation Act to allow more small firms to become stock corporations (AG), which is a listing requirement. 2. Creating tax incentives to induce firms to change from other legal entities into stock corporations. 3. Introducing possibilities for the trading of non-stock corporations' equity. 4. Restructuring the segments of the organized capital market. At first, proposals for changing the stock exchange organization and trading were viewed as being inadequate to satisfy the objectives. But successful new segments at other European exchanges centered the German discussion on the question of how the market structure should be changed to create more incentives for firms to go public and have their shares traded on a stock exchange.

The lack of a well functioning secondary market for the equity of small and medium size stock corporations was attributed to regulations for the official and non-official segments leading to market intransparencies for both issuers and investors. Stock trading took place in three segments. The official segment, the "Amtlicher Handel" (Official Market), which imposed the most stringent requirements on corporations in terms of size and compulsory disclosure and granted the best investor protection against transaction risks. A non-official segment, the "Geregelter Freiverkehr", was not part of the exchanges although trading in that segment took place within the exchanges; prices were not official and investors appeared less protected against transaction risks. The second non-official trading segment was the "Ungeregelter Freiverkehr", which was also located on the floors.

An expert commission at the Federal Ministry of Finance suggested a new segment that would be integrated into the exchanges and which would impose less stringent requirements on corporations than those of the Amtlicher Handel thus opening the door for smaller size firms. The segment should nevertheless grant investors more transaction risk protection than the Geregelter Freiverkehr. The German Bundestag and Bundesrat implemented this idea in the "Börsenzulassungs-Gesetz" (Exchange Listing Act), which was passed on December 16, 1986. The new segment, the "Geregelter Markt" (Regulated Market) has been in operation since May 1987. It was assumed that establishing a fourth segment would not lead to more market transparency, so the Geregelter Freiverkehr was closed down one year later on April 30, 1988. Based on the new § 78 of the Stock Exchange Act, the Ungeregelter Freiverkehr was transformed into a new segment called the "Freiverkehr" (Free Market). During the preceding one-year period firms in the Geregelter "Freiverkehr" had to choose between a listing on the more regulated Geregelter Markt and an inclusion (Einbeziehung) into the less regulated Freiverkehr.

1.1 Listing on the Geregelter Markt

Since the transfer to the Geregelter Markt merely required a letter to the exchange and implied no extra expense, most of the corporations listed on the Geregelter Freiverkehr chose to be listed on the Geregelter Markt. Additionally, many German initial public offerings came to be listed in this segment. Of the 60 initial public offerings in a four-year period prior to the establishing of the new segment, 37 were listed in the Amtlicher Handel and 23 in the Geregelter Freiverkehr. The number of initial public offerings in the following four years grew to a total of 103, of which 39 were listed in the Amtlicher Handel and 64 on the Geregelter Markt. The new segment thus attracted a higher share of new companies than had the Geregelter Freiverkehr.

As the objective was to create a trading segment for the stocks of small and medium size firms it is useful to look at the average issue volume of the newly listed firms.

Except for 1983, the average issue volumes in the Geregelter Markt and the Geregelter Freiverkehr were substantially lower than those of the Amtlicher Handel. The relatively high average issue volumes in the Geregelter Markt might raise doubt as to whether the new market actually serves smaller companies. The absence of a commonly accepted definition of the term "small and medium size firm" leaves room for different interpretations.

Table 1: New listings in a four year period before and after the establishing of the Geregelter Markt1

Year / Segment	1983	1984	1985	1986	1987	1988	1989	1990	1991
Amtlicher Handel	5	11	7	14	9	3	8	10	9
Geregelter Markt					10	11	16	17	10
Geregelter Freiverkehr	2	9	4	8					

Table 2: Average issue volume in millions of DM

Year / Segment	1983	1984	1985	1986	1987	1988	1989	1990	1991
Amtlicher Handel	9.5	28.2	39.5	55.7	20.8	15.6	28.2	76.5	58.9
Geregelter Markt					9.8	5.4	8.6	26.1	36.8
Geregelter Freiverkehr	8.9	2.8	8.3	4.2					

1.2 Objectives of the empirical study

The main differences between the old Geregelter Freiverkehr and the new Geregelter Markt from the issuer's perspective are the more elaborate reporting requirements and therefore higher costs. From the investor's perspective, the new segment might have reduced transaction risks because the pricing process is now supervised by an exchange commission and investors are entitled, as in the official market, to order execution, price limits permitting.

Reduced transaction costs for investors at given security risk levels should lead to lower gross yield requirements, and corporations should be able to reduce their equity costs by raising new equity capital at higher prices. A clear-cut comment on the benefits arising from the Geregelter Markt is almost impossible because

[1] A four year period is chosen because data prior to 1983 are incompatible. At the end of February 1995, shares of 832 German firms were traded in organized segments; 539 (64.8%) corporations were listed in the Amtlicher Handel, 171 (20.6%) in the Geregelter Markt and 122 (14.6%) in the Freiverkehr.

there is no simple analytic solution to the question of how the different cost effects balance out. To elucidate this question it is necessary to undertake empirical analysis.[2]

2. Empirical studies

In analyzing investor reactions it is useful to distinguish between the economic impact of an event and the impact of its announcement (Malatesta/Thompson 1985). The reaction depends on the type of event and its anticipation. The economic effect equals the firm's value if the event occurs minus its value if that event is perpetually absent.

When events happen unexpectedly the economic and the announcement effect appear together. If an anticipated event will happen at an indeterminate point in time, its announcement is valuable because it reduces uncertainty. The impact of the announcement equals the firm's value after the announcement minus the firm's value before the announcement. This has important implications for analyzing the economic impact of statutory actions. To ascertain their economic impact one can focus on the announcement day. The announcement effect is much easier to determine, but it is smaller than the economic effect.

The investor reactions to the announcement of a changeover, and to market segment switching, are tested by analyzing trading volume performance and by analyzing stock price performance. Looking purely at the total number of corporations could lead to wrong interpretations of the changeover effects as market, industry and individual influences might also affect the results. To adjust for market factors, the usual event study methodology is used (Brown/Warner 1980, 1985). To monitor industry influences, the market adjusted price developments of corresponding corporations (industry, size, trading volume, risk) listed on the upper segment, the Amtlicher Handel, are examined. To exclude individual influences, a subgroup of changeover firms is formed for which no other company announcements within a period of 50 trading days before and after the changeover can be found.

2.1 Trading volume analysis

In examining investor reactions to market switching by analysis of changes in trading volume, three different measures are used: the number of trades, the number of shares traded and the number of shares per trade. The event period

[2] Fourteen firms chose to be listed in the Freiverkehr. A too small number to expect reasonable test results.

covers ten weeks before and after the changeover. The investigation is based on averaged weekly data. The data are standardized to the week in which the changeover took place.

Figure 1 shows how the changeover affected the trading volume (measured in number of trades) for the group that comprises all switching firms in comparison with the whole market (trades reported from all eight German stock exchanges). Figure 2 gives an overview over the group of changeover firms for which no company information was published during the period.

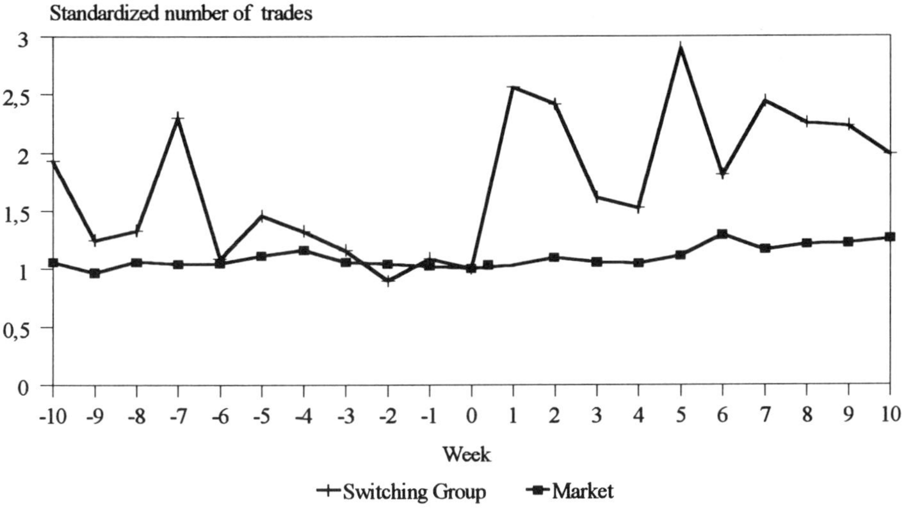

Figure 1: Number of trades in relation to the week of the market switching for the full sample

Figures 1 and 2 both show that the number of trades after the changeover increased. This supports the notion that investors react positively to a changeover. Similar results were obtained for the other two measures. Comparing the development of the market with the changeover firms gives a first indication of the investor reaction but does not describe the economic effect of the market switching. This leads to the analysis of market returns.

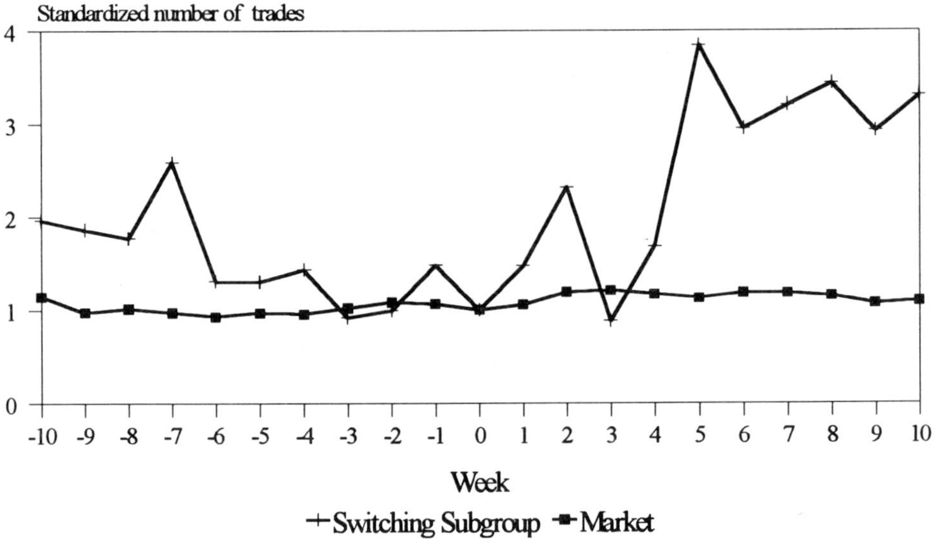

Figure 2: Number of trades in relation to the week of the market switching for the subsample of stocks unaffected by company news

2.2 Return analysis

How investors react to specific events can be examined by looking for abnormal returns, which can be characterized as the difference between expected returns and actual returns:

$$AR_{jt} = r_{jt} - E\left(\tilde{r}_{jt}\right) \tag{1}$$

where AR_{jt} = abnormal return of stock j at time t

r_{jt} = actual return of stock j at time t

$E(\tilde{r}_{jt})$ = expected return for stock j at time t.

The trading volume study showed that some of the switching stocks were not traded daily. The problem of thin trading and parameter estimation has been addressed in literature (e.g. Scholes/Williams 1977, Dimson/Marsh 1983, Cohen/Hawawini/Maier/Schwartz/Whitcomb 1983). To improve the parameter estimation of the market model the trade-to-trade-model of Dimson/Marsh (1983) is used:

$$\tilde{r}^{s}_{jk} = \frac{\tilde{r}_{jk}}{\sqrt{\tilde{d}_k}} = \frac{\alpha_j}{\sqrt{\tilde{d}_k}} + \frac{\beta_j \tilde{r}_{mk}}{\sqrt{\tilde{d}_k}} + \tilde{\varepsilon}_{jk} \qquad (2)$$

where $\tilde{r}^{s}_{jk}$ = standardized return of stock j during time interval k

$\tilde{r}_{mk}$ = return of the market index m during time interval k

$\tilde{d}_k$ = number of days between successive tradings

$\tilde{\varepsilon}_{jk}$ = disturbance term for return changes that cannot be explained by changes in the index return.

We test cumulative abnormal returns for significance. Corrado (1989) proposed a non-parametric test which yields less influenced results than parametric tests when there is event day clustering.[3]

An obvious first hypothesis is that market switching affects all stocks in the same way. But as investors might have reacted differently to varying constellations of the switching firms, it might also be useful to distinguish between different influences. Therefore, the overall group is divided into subgroups to test for different investor reactions. These groups are high versus low trading volume firms, early switchers versus late switchers and a group of high versus a group of low earning firms. These definitions relate to the period before the firms switched to the Geregelter Markt. The results are briefly summarized in the remainder of this section.

2.2.1 The period before the announcement

Figure 3 shows the cumulative abnormal returns of the switching firms in the 50 trading days before the changeover. Whereas parallel curves for the control group firms and the switchers might have been postulated, Figure 3 shows that the switchers enjoyed strong abnormal returns. On the day of the announcement (t_0) the cumulative abnormal return for the switchers (6.44%) is nearly double that of the control group (3.75%). The abnormal return on the announcement day for the changeover firms is 0.69%, which is significant at the 0.05 level. This can be interpreted as positive investor reaction. It is therefore interesting to note that the control group also shows a positive abnormal return of 0.33%, which is significant at the 0.1 level.

[3] Event day clustering plays an important role when statuatory influences affect stock prices. A further discussion on how prices could have been affected in these circumstances, can be found in Schrader (1993).

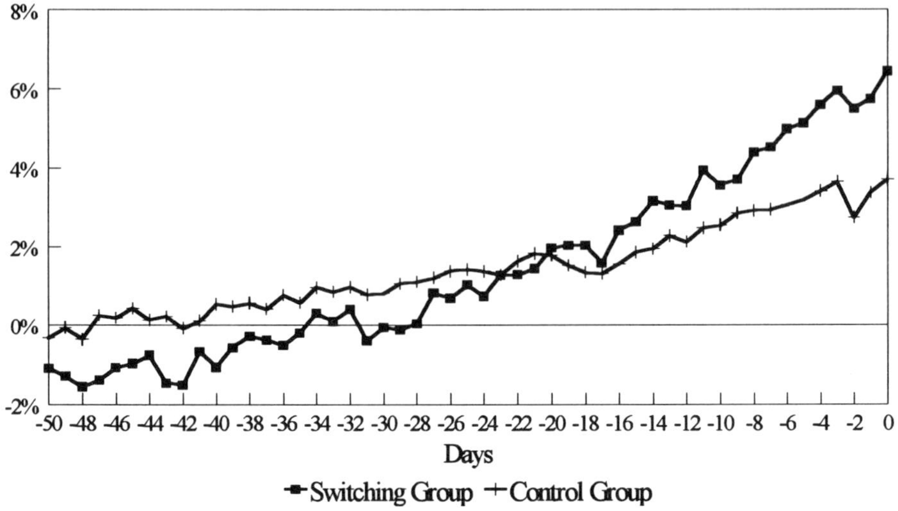

Figure 3: Cumulative abnormal returns 50 days before the market switching for the full sample

The subgroup of switching firms for which no company information was released produces a different picture (Figure 4). The cumulative abnormal returns are negative and reach their low shortly before the switching was announced. The control group earned positive cumulative abnormal returns. Positive abnormal returns for the switchers were found two days before (significant), and on the day before, the announcement (not significant). The different curves for the overall group and the subset of switchers suggest positive information releases by some corporations.

Comparing the results for the overall group of switchers with those of the subgroup suggests that the first clear indication for a (positive) investor reaction manifests itself when market switching is announced. This is consistent with efficient market theory.

2.2.2 The period between the announcement and the actual changeover

Table 3 shows that the period between announcement and actual switching was up to nine days.

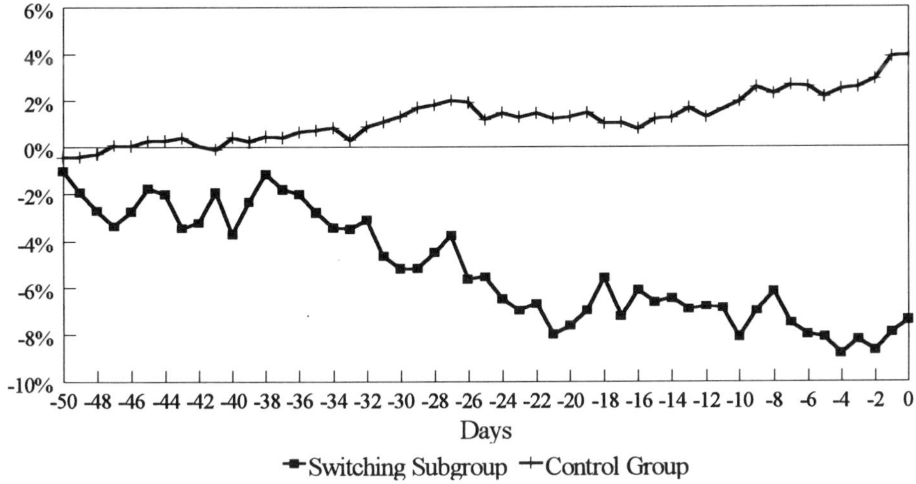

Figure 4: Cumulative abnormal returns 50 days before the market switching for the subsample of stocks unaffected by company news

The average daily abnormal return for the overall group of switchers is 0.63%. For the subgroup it is 0.37%. For the control groups the average daily abnormal returns are -0.43% and 0.01 respectively. This suggests that there was a positive impact between the announcement and the changeover.

The findings are not consistent with the semi-strong form of the efficient market theory. The explanation could be that the announcement was not disseminated to the whole market but at first made only on the listing exchange's floor.

2.2.3 The period after the market switching

The abnormal returns of the switchers are positive and significant at the 0.05 level on the switching day (0.89%) and on the following day (1.31%). Positive and significant (0.05 level) abnormal returns (0.27%) were also found for the control group on the switching day. The cumulative abnormal returns suggest that the switchers enjoyed a better performance during the following five days and then came into line with the control group.

Table 3: The period between announcement and changeover

Number of days between the announcement and the actual switch	Number of Corporations *)
0	23 (5)
1	18 (7)
2	4 (2)
3	13 (5)
4	2 (0)
5	1 (0)
9	1 (1)

*) Data in brackets relate to firms with no other information release.

For the subgroup of switching firms, increasing cumulative abnormal returns were found for the seven days after switching. Thereafter, the curve moves in line with the curve of the control group.

A positive investor reaction prevails after the market switching. Investors who might have received delayed notice of the switching could still have reacted positively. This is not consistent with efficient market theory.

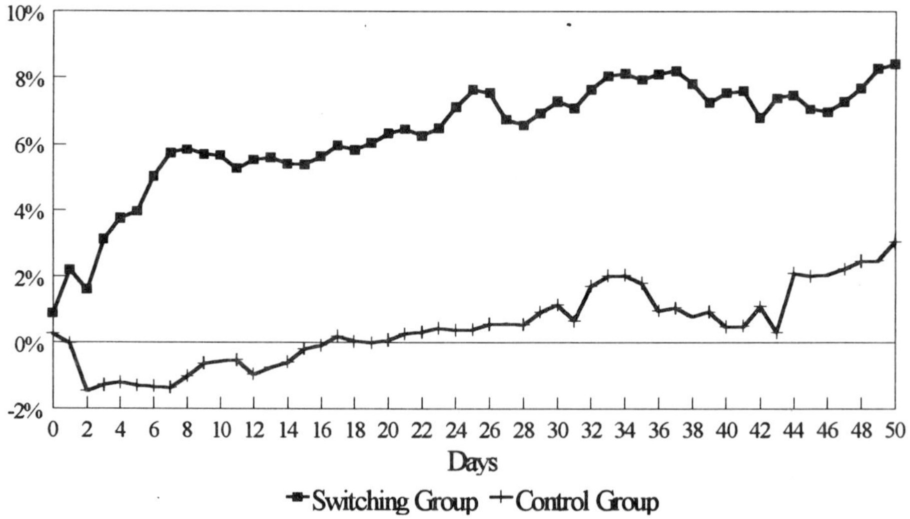

Figure 5: Cumulative abnormal returns 50 days after the market switching for the full sample

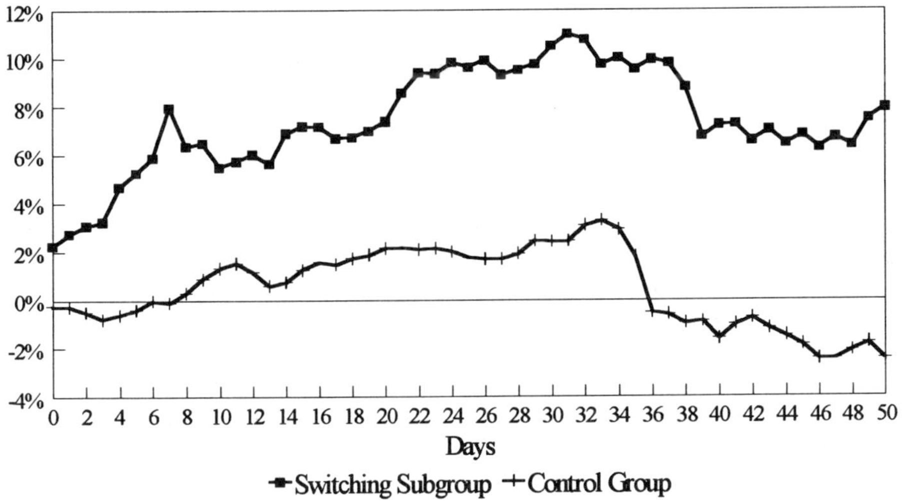

Figure 6: Cumulative abnormal returns 50 days after the market switching for the subsample unaffected by company news

2.3 Results when the market switchers are classified by volume, earnings or time of changeover

The results of the abnormal return tests when the switching firms are classified by trading volume, earnings performance and date of market switching are reported only briefly hereafter.

Because the pricing process in the Geregelter Markt is supervised by an exchange committee, it might be argued that investors face a lower trading risk in that segment. The risk reducing effect should be stronger for inactively traded stocks. The market switchers are therefore divided into firms "frequently traded" and "less frequently traded" in the year before the changeover announcement. The test results support the notion of a stronger positive reaction in the case of less frequently traded firms.

To test whether the changeover signals management expectations of higher, or more stable, earnings, the swithers were devided into high and low performers (Grammatikos/Papaioannou 1986). Performance is measured as the relative change in annual earnings over the period of seven years before the changeover divided by the standard deviation of annual earnings. The empirical analysis does not support a signaling hypothesis of statutory induced market switching.

The period within which firms could change market segments was one year. During the first four months 33 firms switched and, during the last four months, 22 firms transferred to the Geregelter Markt. Two contrary hypotheses can be proposed. On the one hand, investors could have learned from the increasing stock prices of the early switchers so that for late switchers no positive abnormal returns should be expected. On the other hand, investors could not be sure whether a company would transfer to the Geregelter Markt or not. The announcement reduced the probability of a no-listing outcome, which should be higher for firms that belong to the group of late switchers. The results support the thesis that switching at the end of the period was more valuable than at the beginning.

3. Summary

This paper analyzed the performance of stocks that became listed on the Geregelter Markt after this stock exchange segment was instituted by the 1986 Amendments to the German Stock Exchange Act. The new market attracted a substantial number of companies that were previously traded on the Geregelter Freiverkehr. This changeover was associated with higher trading volumes and positive abnormal returns. The results are consistent with the notion that investors expected the Geregelter Markt to reduce their transaction costs to an extent that exceed the costs of the additional disclosure requirements that were imposed by the Amendments on entrants to the market.

References

Börsensachverständigenkommission (1983): Vorschläge der Börsensachverständigenkommission beim Bundesfinanzministerium zur Erleichterung des Zugangs von Unternehmen zur Börse durch Schaffung eines neuen Marktes. Berlin.

Börsenzulassungs-Gesetz (1986): Gesetz zur Einführung eines neuen Marktabschnitts an den Wertpapierbörsen und zur Durchführung der Richtlinien des Rates der Europäischen Gemeinschaften vom 5. März 1979, vom 17. März 1980 und vom 15. Februar 1982 zur Koordinierung börsenrechtlicher Vorschriften (Börsenzulassungs-Gesetz), December 16th 1986, Bundesgesetzblatt 1986, part I 68, 2478-2484.

Brown, S.J. and Warner, J.B. (1980): Measuring Security Price Performance, in: Journal of Financial Economics 8, 205-258.

Brown, S.J. and Warner, J.B. (1985): Using Daily Stock Returns, in: Journal of Financial Economics 14, 3-31.

Bundesminister für Wirtschaft (1984): Stellungnahme zur Verbesserung der Eigenkapitalausstattung der Unternehmen, in: Zeitschrift für Wirtschaftsrecht und Insolvenzpraxis 5, 116-121.

Claussen, C.P. (1984): Plädoyer für den Freiverkehr, in: Zeitschrift für das gesamte Kreditwesen 37, 706-713.

Claussen, C.P. (1985): Zur rechtlichen Fundierung des geregelten Freiverkehrs, in: Lutter, M., H.J. Mertens and P. Ulmer (eds.), Festschrift für Walter Stimpel. Berlin (de Gruyter), 1049-1064.

Cohen, K.J., Hawawini, G.A., Maier, S.F., Schwartz, R.A. and Whitcomb, D.K. (1983): Estimating and Adjusting for the Intervalling-Effect Bias in Beta, in: Management Science 29, 135-148.

Corrado, C.J. (1989): A Nonparametric Test for Abnormal Security-Price Performance in Event Studies, in: Journal of Financial Economics 23, 385-395.

Dimson, E. and Marsh, P. (1983): The Stability of UK Risk Measures and the Problem of Thin Trading, in: Journal of Finance 38, 753-783.

Giersch, H. and H. Schmidt (1986): Offene Märkte für Beteiligungskapital: USA-Großbritannien-Bundesrepublik Deutschland, Vorstand der Baden-Württembergischen Wertpapierbörse zu Stuttgart (eds.). Stuttgart.

Grammatikos, T. and Papaioannou, G.J. (1986): The Informational Value of Listing on the New York Stock Exchange, in: Financial Review 21, 485-499.

Herdt, H.K., E. Padberg and D. Walther (1988): Der Gang an die Börse. Frankfurt/Main (Börsen-Zeitung).

Kommission "Zweiter Börsenmarkt" (1987): Börsenzugang für kleine und mittlere Unternehmen, Ministerium für Wirtschaft, Mittelstand und Technologie Baden-Württemberg (eds.). Stuttgart.

Krämer, W. and H. Sonnberger (1986): The Linear Regression Model under Test. Heidelberg (Physica).

Kümpel, S. (1986): Börsenrechtliche Fragen bei Schaffung des geregelten Marktes, in: Hofmann, P., U. Meyer-Cording and H. Wiedemann (eds.), Festschrift für Klemens Pleyer. Köln (Carl Heymanns), 59-76.

Malatesta, P.H. and Thompson, R. (1985): Partially Anticipated Events, in: Journal of Financial Economics 14, 237-250.

Schmidt, H. (1981): Mehr Unternehmen an die Börse durch differenzierte Marktorganisation, in: Jahresbericht der Hanseatischen Wertpapierbörse Hamburg, 4-17.

Schmidt, H. (1984): Special Market Segments for Small Company Shares: Capital Raising Mechanism and Exit Route for Investors in New Technology Based Firms. Brussels/ Luxembourg (Office for Offical Publications of the European Communities).

Schmidt, H. (1986): Causes of Change and Innovation in the Mix of Financial Instruments: The new Emphasis on Small Company External Equity Financing and its Impact on Capital Market Structure, in: Fair, D.E. (ed.), Shifting Frontiers in Financial Markets. Dordrecht/Boston (Martinus Nijhoff Publishers), 65-78.

Schmidt, H. (1988): Wertpapierbörsen. München (Vahlen).

Schmidt, H. and Schrader, T. (1993): Kurseffekte beim Wechsel in den geregelten Markt, in: Bühler, W., Hax, H., R. Schmidt (eds.): Empirische Kapitalmarktforschung. Zeitschrift für betriebswirtschaftliche Forschung, special issue 31, 227-255.

Scholes, M. and Williams, J. (1977): Estimating Betas from Nonsynchronous Data, in: Journal of Financial Economics 5, 309-327.

Schrader, T. (1993): Geregelter Markt und geregelter Freiverkehr, Wiesbaden (Gabler).

Schwark, E. (1976): Börsengesetz. München (C.H. Beck).
Schwarze, H.-J. (1983): Märkte und Nebenmärkte, in: Jahresbericht der Frankfurter Wertpapierbörse, 33-36.
Sharpe, W.F. (1963): A Simplified Model for Portfolio Analysis, in: Management Science 9, 277-293.
von Rosen, R. (1987): Geregelter Markt unter Erfolgszwang, in: Börsen-Zeitung 63, 5.

B Information and Capital Market

Financial Market Indicators and Real Capital Investment in Germany

Wolfgang Gebauer, Klaus J.W. Schmidt and Dirk Veestraeten
University of Frankfurt/Main

1. Introduction

There is a continuing divide between monetary macrotheory and practical policy analysis. More than half a century ago, Hawtrey (1932) coined the expression 'art of central banking' to characterize this situation. Modern writers like Goodhart (1991), Issing (1993) or Niehans (1978) have reemphasized this view. The situation implies a challenge to economists who try to build an analytical foundation of central bank policy. The core of such an attempted foundation consists of theoretical and empirical knowledge concerning the transmission process of monetary policy actions, via financial markets, into the real sector of the economy. In particular, a century-old central question pertains to the (Wicksellian) relation between changes in nominal interest rates and real capital investment.

The following contribution concentrates on one specific issue within this broad Wicksellian theme. We tackle the question of how financial market indicators of central bank policy actions can explain the developments of aggregate real capital formation by German firms during the last twenty years. Our approach is predominantly empirical, as we try to arrive at explicit conclusions for central bank policy.

1.1 On the relevance of Tobin's q

In order to get from art to science, we start by following a theoretically simple and empirically testable line of reasoning, which leads from Wicksell via Keynes to Myrdal and Tobin, and according to which the aggregate accumulation of real capital is determined by an interest rate ratio, i.e., by the expected rate of return on physical capital relative to the financial cost of capital. If capital costs are determined by the interest rate policy of central banks, the conventional hypothesis of an inverse relation between capital market interest rates and aggregate accumulation of real capital, respectively economic activity, follows accordingly.

However simple the theoretical outline may be, the empirical examination is difficult. The expected marginal rate of return on physical capital[1] is not a measurable magnitude. Tobin (1969) and Brainard/Tobin (1968) took this objection into account - as did Myrdal (1931, 1933)[2] - and suggested an operational reformulation, which defines the 'q-ratio' as a relation between market value and replacement costs of physical capital. With the help of the DFG data base and additional data research, we constructed new quarterly time series of Tobin's q and Myrdal's Q for Germany. In our opinion, these time series approximate the theoretical variable in a more reliable way than the existing statistical approximations published hitherto - assuming that an explicit consideration of taxes can be disregarded on statistical grounds.

It could perhaps have been predicted that no monocausal explanation of aggregate investment in physical capital assets would be uncovered, even if our q-ratio could be accurately calculated. Shortcomings of the q-concept itself, aspects of the term structure of interest rates as well as the potential relevance of additional variables representing return and cost aspects (output, prices, wages) have to be taken into account. One particular result of our efforts to approximate Tobin's q is worth emphasizing: the time series shows a distinct break in the mid-1980s, which leads to the conjecture that its former explanatory power for real capital investment has strongly declined ever since.

This hypothesis is based on two observations:

(1) The time series behaviour of q is dominated by the development of the market value of equity capital, that is, by the development of share prices, and

(2) since the mid-1980s, volatility of share prices has considerably increased.

We therefore assume that since the mid-1980s share prices no longer mainly reflect the present values of the future returns on quoted companies' physical capital, but more closely represent the changing influence of primarily financial events, policies and expectations (e.g. yield and risk expectations, financial crises etc.). But if stock market value is increasingly separated from its underlying (real capital) basis, a variable like Tobin's q, reflecting prices quoted in that market, will inevitably lose its former role as an indicator of real economic activity. Thus,

---

[1] 'Marginal efficiency of capital' in Keynes (1936).

[2] As stressed by Schmidt (1995) the basic ideas behind the q-theory can be traced back to Myrdal (1931, 1933).

in the last decade, Tobin's q appears to have 'degenerated' into a modified share price index, i.e., become largely detached from the real sector.

1.2 Term structure of interest rates and macro model

Since it can now be assumed *a priori* that, as a single indicator, Tobin's q no longer satisfactorily explains real capital investment, we investigated the term structure of interest rates as a further potential determinant of real investment and production decisions. The term structure has gained increasing importance in the course of the project, not only because of the diminished explanatory power of Tobin's q, but also as the result of two closely connected recent developments:

(1) In recent empirical studies, the predictive power of the term structure of interest rates with respect to real economic activity proved to be exceptional. Using a 'congruent model', Schmidt (1993) demonstrated the remarkable ability of the term structure of interest rates to predict the business cycle in Germany. Thus, it may also be assumed that the term structure of interest rates will be a good predictor of investment in physical capital as investment constitutes a major component of business cycle development.

(2) In the course of our project, we have placed increasing emphasis on the LSE-methodology of time series analysis. This obviates the conventional procedure of first postulating a 'suitable' theoretical model, the implications of which can then be tested empirically. Using the 'general-to-specific' modelling approach made it possible to postulate *a priori* financial and real variables as potential determinants of physical capital investment and, thereafter, to test their relative empirical significance step by step. In particular this methodology also allows a direct statistical comparison of the explanatory power of rival empirical models.

Section 3 reports empirical analyses of three rival explanations of physical capital investment, namely Tobin's q (q-only model), the term structure of interest rates (spread model) and a macroeconomic model, which explicitly captures financial, production and return dimensions (macro model). The macro model postulates the conventional point of view, namely that investment in physical capital depends positively on expected returns, approximated by real production and its price component, and negatively on cost elements, approximated by the prices of capital goods and the nominal long-term capital market interest rate. The latter stands for the cost of external finance and/or the opportunity cost of financial investment. These three approaches were tested empirically and compared within the LSE-methodological framework.

2. Data

The endogenous variable to be modelled is the aggregate investment spending of the private sector[3] denoted by the accumulation quota (ACQ). This concept is defined as the relation between gross investment at current prices and the total net capital stock of the private sector at replacement prices.[4] The latter is valued at the beginning of the quarter. ACQ can be considered as a real variable as the price dimensions in the numerator and denumerator cancel each other out.

The vector of independent variables consists of short- and long-term interest rates, the interest rate spread, Euro-USD interest rates, price indices, real GNP and Tobin's q. German short-term interest rates (RS) are represented by three-months money market rates and long-term interest rates (RL) are assumed to be adequately approximated by yields on long-term public bonds. The term structure of interest rates (spread) is operationalized as the difference between RL and RS (SPREAD). Euro-USD interest rates (RUS) represent three-months maturities. The price index characterizing cost effects is the index of investment good prices as reported for domestic sales (PI). The GNP deflator (P) stands for the index reflecting output price development. We use real GNP data (Y) which are not seasonally adjusted because Ericsson/Hendry/Tran (1993) have demonstrated the destructive effects of seasonal adjustment on the cointegration properties.

The q-variable (q) is calculated for West German nonfinancial quoted firms and represents average q excluding tax components. This strategy reflects the empirical insignificance of the theoretical superiority of the (differential tax-adjusted) marginal q proposed by Hayashi (1982) over average q.[5] In contrast to the majority of empirical studies, we explicitly adjust for the increasing significance of financial investment in total corporate investment - a development which creates an increasing wedge between the market value of the corporation and the market value of physical capital. Accordingly, q is defined as 'the sum of the market value of equity capital *plus* the book value of long-term debt *minus* the book value of financial capital', *divided by* 'the beginning-of-the-period replacement value of the net physical capital stock (plant, equipment and

---

[3] The notion of the private sector in this study comprises the corporate sector after exclusion of the house renting sector.

[4] Quarterly data on gross and net investment were kindly provided by the Deutsche Bundesbank. Yearly data on the net capital stock of the private sector were taken from Statistisches Bundesamt (1991, 1992). Quarterly figures were obtained by relating these time series to the quarterly development of net investment.

[5] Further evidence is given by Abel/Blanchard (1986) and Fazzari/Hubbard/Petersen (1988). Sensenbrenner (1991) uses average q in his study of investment behaviour in six OECD countries including West Germany. Funke (1992) is not able to detect significant differences between regression models for West Germany based on average q and marginal q allowing for differential tax effects.

inventories)'.[6] The book values of the individual components of the physical capital stock - with the exception of inventories - were transformed into their replacement values by using factors for plant and equipment for the entire private sector that were computed from data published by the Statistisches Bundesamt (1991, 1992). Quarterly values for long-term debt, financial capital, plant, equipment and inventories were obtained from the corresponding annual data via multiplicative interpolation using the quarterly development of net investment.[7]

Tobin's q and the development of the stock price index for the nonfinancial private sector are depicted in Figure 1. As mentioned above, the time series properties of Tobin's q appear to be dominated by the development of the market value of equity, as approximated by the stock price index for nonfinancial firms.[8] Moreover, visual analysis of Figure 1 shows a remarkable upward shift in the time series for Tobin's q from 1983-1984 onwards.

Consequently, empirical analysis can be assumed to detect a structural break in the explanatory properties of the q-model of investment as a result of the stock market boom of the mid-1980s in conjunction with the slow increase in the physical capital stock. This structural break is detrimental to the former explanatory power of the q-variable as is shown below.

---

[6] The subtraction of the financial component, however, turned out to be immaterial for the empirical results reported in section 3 as was shown in our analysis of potential mismeasurement in the construction of the q-variable.

[7] The yearly transformation ratios were considered to follow the quarterly development of price indices for plant and investment goods, respectively. Alternative methods of deriving quarterly values produced insignificant changes of the explanatory power of the q-model of investment.

[8] The graphic representation of the development of the individual components of Tobin's q - keeping in mind their relative weight - confirms this conjecture (see Gebauer/Schmidt/Veestraeten 1994). Empirical analysis corrobates this argument as the regression properties of the rough q-approximation constructed as the relation between the market value of equity and the replacement value of the physical capital stock shows an extremely high correlation of 0.9915 with the time series in figure 1. and delivers qualitatively identical regression results as the q-only model investigated below.

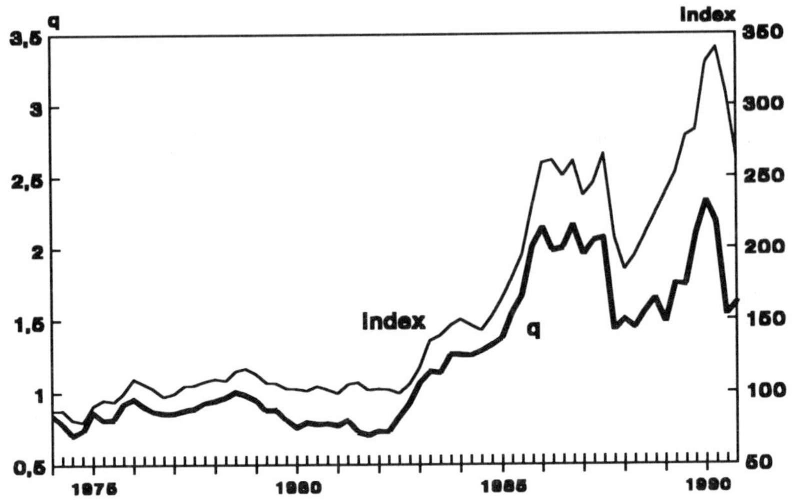

Figure 1: Tobin's q and the development of the stock price index for West German nonfinancial firms (31.12.1980 = 100, source: Statistisches Bundesamt).

3. Empirical models

3.1 Methodological remarks

Our empirical analysis is based on the LSE-approach.[9] It can be contrasted with the traditional 'text-book approach' to econometrics, namely, the 'measurement' of operationalized theoretical models which have been previously derived in a hypothetico-deductive manner. According to the LSE-approach, an empirical model should be a simple but adequate characterization of the unknown data-generation process (DGP).

The empirical model is derived from the DGP by the successive marginalization (of irrelevant variables), conditioning (the categorization of relevant variables as exogenous or 'given' and endogenous or 'modelled'

[9] A textbook presentation is given by Banerjee/Dolado/Galbraith/Hendry (1993), Charemza/Deadman (1992) and Spanos (1986). Methodological considerations appear in Hendry (1993), Hendry/Ericsson (1991) and Gilbert (1987).

variables) and simplification (by imposing testable restrictions). The stationarity properties are considered explicitly, as most macroeconomic time series appear to be integrated of order 1 or I(1).

Table 1: The information-congruent model: criteria, types of information and tests.

Congruency criteria	**Type of information**	**Relevant tests**
Data coherency ('white noise innovation errors')	Relative past of the data	AR 1-n F, ARCH n F (of order n), normality χ^2, Xi^2 F, RESET F
Valid conditioning ('weak exogeneity')	Relative present of the data	(Implicit)
Parameter constancy	Relative future of the data	Chow F, RLS-coefficient estimates and t-values, 1↑ Chows, N↑ Chows, N↓ Chows
Data admissibility	Measurement system of the data	(Enforced by logarithmic transformation)
Theory-consistency	Economic theory ('a priori')	Plausibility of the 'static long-run solution', WALD test χ^2, unit root t-tests
Encompassing	Rival models	Joint model F

We employ the general-to-specific modelling strategy using OLS. Starting from a rather general autoregressive distributed-lag (ADL)-model of the variables in (log-)levels, we (1) delete insignificant lags, (2) compute the static long-run solution, (3) test for cointegration of the I(1) level variables in the static long-run solution and (4) reparameterize the ADL-model to an error correction model imposing the static long-run solution via an error correction term (ECM). Finally, we test whether the resulting model satisfies the requirements of information congruency, i.e., whether all available types of information have been used efficiently in such a way that the remaining model characterizes the DGP as 'good' as possible. In particular, we test for the criteria of information congruency reported in Table 1 using the tests offered by Doornik/Hendry's

(1994) PcGive Professional 8.0. With the exception of q and interest rates, all variables are expressed as natural logarithms.

3.2 The q-only model

In this subsection, it is investigated whether an empirical model with q as the only explanatory variable is able to characterize the DGP of aggregate investment spending. Although the LSE-approach does *not* prescribe the *a priori* marginalization of all other variables on the grounds of irrelevance, we do so in order to examine the explanatory power of the monocausal q-theory of investment. Figure 2 shows the time series behaviour of ACQ, i.e., the variable to be modelled. The upper part contains the original level values of that variable, whereas the lower part shows the quarterly differenced logarithms of ACQ, i.e. the approximate annual rates of change, as well as the level values of q.[10]

As is clearly apparent, ACQ displays a seasonal pattern which, for example, can be eliminated by the seasonal difference operator as in the lower part of Figure 2. As necessary, seasonal dummy variables are also used to model the seasonal component of ACQ. It is already visually evident that the rather tight comovement of $\Delta_4 acq$ and q breaks down around 1984; from 1984 onwards, q rises sharply on average and does not return to its theoretical equilibrium value of 1. Although investment activity in the second half of the 1970s behaves in roughly the same way as in the second half of the 1980s, q is much higher in the latter period. For 1975(1) to 1983(4) the mean value of q equals 0.89, whereas it amounts to 1.73 for 1984(1) to 1990(4). For the same periods, the correlation coefficient between q and $\Delta_4 acq$ declines from 0.55 to 0.39.

These descriptive findings are confirmed by formal analysis. Anticipating and emphasizing the main result; it is not possible to establish a stable q-only model over the entire sample period (until 1990). Moreover, the empirical analysis shows a structural break in the first quarter of 1984. The results are therefore presented as follows. First, it is shown that a well-defined q-only model can be formulated for the period 1975 to 1983. Second, by means of recursive parameter estimates and associated Chow-tests it is demonstrated that the (previously) stable model breaks down if the sample period is extended to data beyond 1983.[11]

---

[10] With the exception of q, lower-case variables indicate natural logarithms of the original variables (upper-case notation), i.e., $x_t = \ln X_t$.

[11] Hoshi/Kashyap (1990) obtain qualitatively similar results for Japan, even though their sample period ends in March 1987 and hence does not contain the stock market crashes of 1987 and 1990.

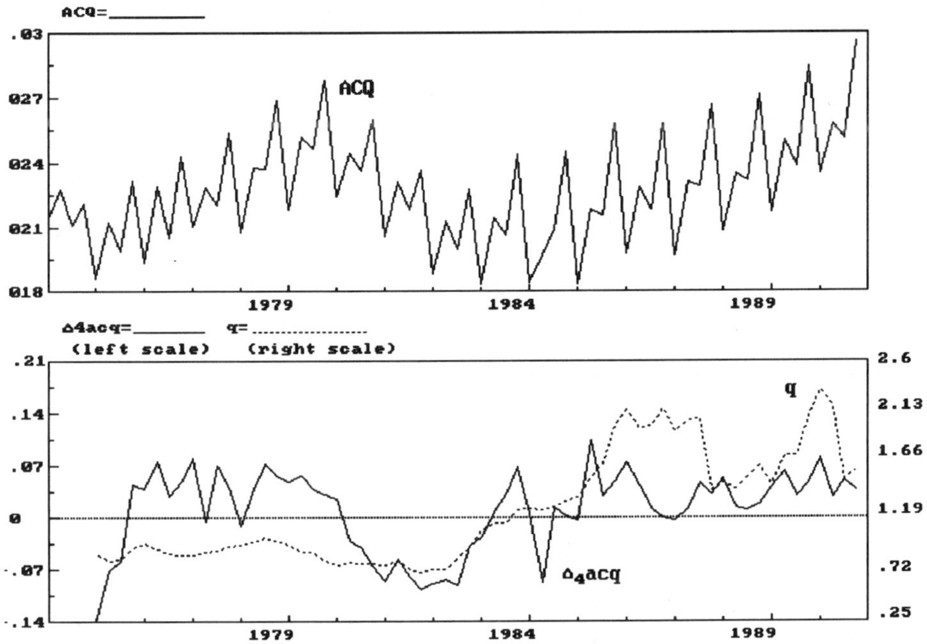

Figure 2: Accumulation quota: levels (upper part) and annual rates of change versus q in levels (lower part).

The static long-run solution of the ultimately selected and statistically valid ADL(4,4)-model - i.e., a model of acq being conditioned on a constant, its own lagged values up to the fourth lag, the contemporary and lagged values of Tobin's q (up to the fourth lag also), and three S(easonal dummy variables) - is given by equation (1) for the period 1975(1) to 1983(4).

acq = -4.46 + 1.49 q - 2.44 S(easonal) (1)
(SE) (0.21) (0.43) (0.84)

T=1975(1)-1983(4), WALD test $\chi^2(2) = 12.303$ [0.0021]**,
Unit root t-test(acq) = -3.30

The WALD test χ^2-statistic indicates joint significance of all estimated long-run parameters, each of which greatly exceeds its asymptotic S(tandard) E(rror). Furthermore, a lack of cointegration between q and acq can be rejected.[12] The

[12] Throughout this paper, the degrees of freedom are reported in parentheses after the distributional form of the tests (either F or χ^2). The error probability of rejecting the null

long-run semi-elasticity of the accumulation quota with respect to q amounts to 1.49, which appears to be consistent with economic theory.

However, extending the sample period to 1975(1) - 1990(4) yields unfavourable outcomes from the point of view of the q-only model:

$$acq = -1.76 + 0.22\, q - 8.99\, S(easonal) \qquad (2)$$
$$(SE) \quad (2.40) \quad (0.30) \quad (10.53)$$

T=1975(1)-1990(4), WALD test $\chi^2(2) = 0.73063$ [0.6940],
Unit root t-test(acq) = -0.86

Hence, as a statistical generating mechanism the general ADL-model and its static long-run solution do not represent a sound statistical basis for the general-to-specific modelling sequence when the entire sample period is considered.

Consequently, we only use the short period to derive an error correction model describing the dynamic adjustment of investment behaviour to q. The model finally chosen is presented as equation (3). ECMq is the error correction term or 'equilibrium error' derived from (1), which imposes the static long-run solution of the levels on the dynamic model in differences. R^2 is the unadjusted coefficient of determination, followed by the (residual) s(tandard error), the D(urbin-) W(atson statistic), and the diagnostic tests for information congruency presented in subsection 3.1.

$$\Delta_4 acq_t = 0.93\Delta_3 acq_{t-1} - 0.19 ECMq_{t-1} - 0.25\Delta_2 q_{t-2} - 0.29 S_t + 0.43 S_{t-1} - 0.15 S_{t-2} \qquad (3)$$
$$(SE) \quad (0.06) \quad (0.015) \quad (0.05) \quad (0.02) \quad (0.03) \quad (0.01)$$

T=1975(1)-1985(2) less 6 forecasts, $R^2 = 0.90$, s = 0.021, DW = 2.76, AR 1-4 F(4,26) = 2.2996 [0.0857], ARCH 4 F(4,22) = 1.6081 [0.2077], Normality $\chi^2(2) = 0.3694$ [0.8313], Xi^2 F(9,20) = 0.7563 [0.6561], Xi*Xj F(21,8) = 0.4048 [0.9437], RESET F (1,29) = 1.5855 [0.2180], Chow F(6,30) = 19.306 [0.0000]**

Despite the Chow F test referring to the forecast period 1984(1) to 1985(2), no test rejects the desirable null hypothesis. The structural break in 1984 becomes even more visible when the parameters of (3) are estimated recursively using RLS ('recursive least squares') and the sample period is successively extended to 1990. Figure 3 shows selected results.

---

hypothesis is given in brackets after the test results. Significant outcomes are marked by * for 5% and ** for 1% error probability, respectively.

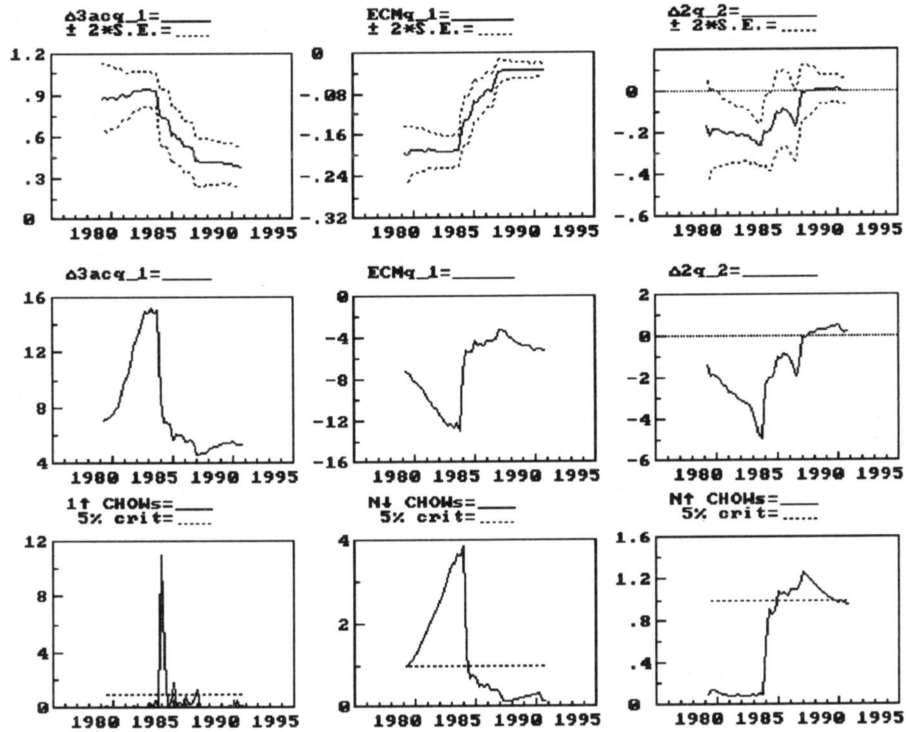

Figure 3: q-only error correction model, T=1975(1)-1990(4), selected results from recursive least squares estimates.

The graphs in the first row of Figure 3 display the point estimates for the coefficients of Δ_3acq_{t-1}, $ECMq_{t-1}$, and Δ_2q_{t-2} together with their 95% confidence bands. Ideally, the point estimates should represent a flat line within converging confidence bands as time increases. The second row shows the corresponding recursive t-values. Ideal, absolute values would increase with time. The third row reports various Chow-test graphs. The 1↑ Chow tests whether the parameters of the model estimated until time t are stable compared with time t-1. The N↓ Chow compares the parameters of the model estimated until time t with the estimates for the final sample period - here 1975(1) to 1990(4). Finally, the N↑ Chow compares the parameters of the model estimated up to time t with the estimates for the initial sample period - here 1975(1) to 1980(1). All test statistics are divided by their respective critical values (here with 5% error probability). Consequently, a test statistic above the critical line of 1 indicates rejection of the null hypothesis of parameter constancy. The structural break in 1984 is readily apparent in all graphs. Thus, the q-only model cannot serve as an adequate characterization of the DGP of investment behaviour over the entire sample period. How then can the DGP be adequately characterized? This question is examined in the next subsection which contains a congruent model of aggregate investment.

3.3 The macro model

The poor performance of the q-only model reinforces the need of a good model of aggregate investment behaviour which is stable over the entire sample period. Taking into account theoretical preconsiderations concerning macroeconomic determinants of investment as, for instance, in Catinat/Cawley/Ilzkovitz/ Italianer/Mors (1987), it is suggested that aggregate investment should be modelled as a function of real output and output prices (variables dealing with the returns to aggregate capital utilization) as well as long-term interest rates - as a proxy for capital and/or opportunity costs - and input prices (cost side variables).[13] Hereafter this model is described as the 'macro model'. The respective variables have been discussed in some detail in Section 2. Equation (4) represents the static long-run solution of the corresponding statistically valid ADL(4,4,4,4,4)-model.

$$\underset{(SE)}{acq} = \underset{(3.61)}{-1.29} - \underset{(0.60)}{1.78\,RL} + \underset{(0.29)}{1.75\,y} + \underset{(0.58)}{1.64\,p} - \underset{(0.60)}{2.86\,pi} \qquad (4)$$

T=1975(1) to 1990(4), WALD test $\chi^2(4)$ = 141.52 [0.0000] **, unit root t-test(acq)=-5.86**

The test statistics confirm the statistical significance of the long-run parameters and cointegration of the variables involved.[14] Congruous with theory, the return side variables y (real output) and p (output prices) enter the static long-run solution with positive elasticities, whereas the cost side variables RL (long-term interest rate) and pi (investment good prices) have negative long-run (semi-) elasticities. Thus, equation (4) is well-defined and consistent with theory.

---

[13] We also considered the three-months money market rate, indices of orders received, labour costs, and various money stock and credit aggregates as further potential determinants of investment. All of these variables could be marginalized as being 'irrelevant' in the LSE-sense of this notion.

[14] As five I(1)-variables enter the static long-run solution, it is not certain *a priori* whether this cointegrating relation is unique. Therefore, we tested for uniqueness using Johansen's trace and maximum eigenvalue tests in the version adjusted for degrees of freedom as available in PcFiml 8.0. We found evidence of exactly one cointegration vector.

$$\Delta_4 acq_t = \underset{(0.05)}{0.88}\, \Delta_3 acq_{t-1} - \underset{(0.07)}{0.71}\, ECM_{t-1} - \underset{(0.08)}{0.68}\, \Delta y_{t-1} + \underset{(0.71)}{1.49}\, \Delta pi_t - \underset{(0.54)}{1.39}\, \Delta RL_{t-3}$$

(SE)

$$+ \underset{(0.08)}{1.41}\, \Delta(y+p)_t - \underset{(0.22)}{1.29}\Delta_3 p_{t-1} \qquad (5)$$

T=1975(1)-1990(4) less 6 forecasts, R^2 = 0.90, s = 0.019, DW = 2.12, AR 1-4 F(4,47) = 0.6176 [0.6522], ARCH 4 F(4,43) = 0.4542 [0.7688], Normality $\chi^2(2)$ = 3.2166 [0.2002], Xi^2 F(14,36) = 0.7239 [0.7369], Xi*Xj F(35,15) = 0.7606 [0.7547], RESET F (1,50) = 1.8468 [0.1803], Chow F(6,51) = 1.6166 [0.1616]

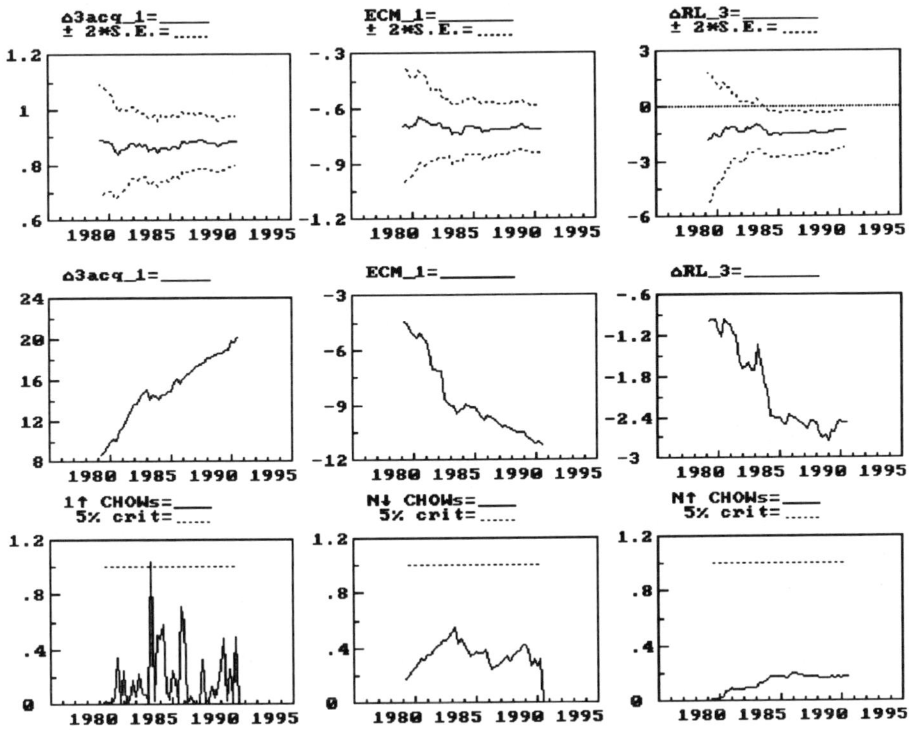

Figure 4: Macro error correction model, T=1975(1)-1990(4), selected results from recursive least squares estimates.

The dynamic adjustment is described by the error correction model (5). As above, ECM is the error correction mechanism derived from the static long-run solution (4) and describes the difference between the actual and equilibrium values of acq as implied by equation (4). The feedback effect of 0.71 suggests a rather rapid adjustment towards equilibrium, as more than two thirds of the lagged equilibrium error are eliminated in the actual period. The diagnostic tests presented below equation (5) are exactly the same as for model (3). No test rejects the desirable null hypothesis at conventional levels of significance.

Figure 4 illustrates the stability of the model over the entire sample period using the same tools as in Figure 3. Despite the very marginal 5% border line rejection of the 1↑ Chow test in 1983(1), no further test rejects parameter constancy.[15] The point estimates and t-values of the coefficients reported here (of $\Delta_3 acq_{t-1}$, ECM_{t-1}, and ΔRL_{t-3}) serve as an example and are absolutely comparable with the behaviour of the other coefficients not shown here due to space limitations. The near ideal behaviour, especially in comparison with the coefficients of the q-only model given in Figure 3, is noteworthy.

Being a well-defined and stable model, the macro model provides an adequate characterization of the DGP of investment behaviour. Moreover, it should be able to encompass rival models - here in particular, the q-only model - in order to satisfy all criteria of information congruency. The test results are as follows:

H_0: q-only model encompasses macro model (1975-1983):
Joint model $F(6,24)=4.42$ [0.0038]**,
H_0: Macro model encompasses q-only model (1975-1983):
Joint model $F(5,24)=3.30$ [0.0209]*,
H_0: q-only model encompasses macro model (1975-1990):
Joint model $F(6,46)=35.4$ [0.0000]**,
H_0: Macro model encompasses q-only model (1975-1990):
Joint model $F(5,46)=0.23$ [0.9476].

With a 1% error probability the macro model encompasses the q-only model in both periods considered here, but not *vice versa*. With a 5% error probability, however, the q-only model also encompasses the macro model in 1975-1983, the period before the q-only model broke down. Hence, until 1983 the q-only model has some power to explain investment over and above that of the macro model. Afterwards, however, the q-only model is completely dominated by the macro model.

[15] With 1% error probability the 1↑ Chow test would be clearly insignificant in 1983(1), as well. Because an error probability of 5% means that the true null hypothesis is rejected in 5 out of hundred cases (here: in 2.15 of 43 cases), we are not inclined to consider that particular undesirable test result for 1983(1) as clear evidence against parameter constancy - especially when we take the other very favourable test results into account.

3.4 Macro model and spread model

In the modern literature, e.g., Estrella/Hardouvelis (1991), Plosser/Rouwenhorst (1994), Ragnitz (1994), Schmidt (1993), Harvey (1991), Jaeger (1992), Krämer/Langfeld (1993) and Wizman (1992) various successful attempts are reported with respect to the use of the spread, i.e., the difference between long- and short-term interest rates, as a predictor of real economic activity. Taking into consideration the rather tight comovement of aggregate investment and real economic activity in general, e.g. for the period 1975(1)-1989(2) the correlation coefficient between $\Delta_4$acq and Δ_4 amounts to 0.78, roughly the same predictive ability of the spread model with respect to aggregate investment might also be expected.

This conjecture is confirmed both by descriptive statistics and empirical analysis. For the period 1975(1)-1990(4) the correlation coefficient between $\Delta_4$acq, the *actual* annual rate of change of the accumulation quota, and $SPREAD_{t-5}$, i.e., the difference between yields to maturity of public bonds and three-months money market rates *lagged 5 quarters*, equals 0.7. Equation (6) represents our formal empirical spread model in which investment behaviour in five quarters is predicted using the contemporary spread as unique variable:

$$\Delta_4 acq_t = \underset{(0.007)}{-0.01} + \underset{(0.33)}{2.57}\, SPREAD_{t-5} - \underset{(12.35)}{27.82}\, SPREAD^2_{t-5} \qquad (6)$$
(SE)

T=1975(1)-1990(4) less 6 forecasts, R^2=0.53, s = 0.038, DW = 1.24, AR 1-4 F(4,51) = 3.6373 [0.0111]*, ARCH 4 F(4,47) = 0.6166 [0.6528], Normality $\chi^2(2)$ = 1.7431 [0.4183], Xi^2 F(3,51) = 0.7420 [0.5320], Xi*Xj F(4,50) = 0.6127 [0.6554], RESET F (1,54) = 0.8723 [0.3545], Chow F(6,55) = 1.2481 [0.2966]

Following Konishi/Ramey/Granger (1993), spread models of this type can be considered as a special case of models which use the equilibrium error of a subsystem - here the spread as the error correction term of a term structure relation - to predict real economic activity. By analogy with, e.g. Hendry/Ericsson (1991), we additionally introduce the square of the spread, in order to allow the predictions to vary nonlinearly with the extent of term structure disequilibrium, as this kind of nonlinearity can remarkably improve the diagnostic test results compared with those of a purely linear spread model (sole exception: AR 1-4 F).

As is demonstrated below, the spread model (6) is a useful forecasting model of aggregate investment behaviour. It is therefore quite surprising that the spread is not even an implicit explanatory variable in the macro model. As already stated above, the three-months money market rate was marginalized as being 'irrelevant' in an early stage of the general-to-specific modelling sequence. This step was totally correct; if $SPREAD_{t-5}$ is added as an additional explanatory variable to the macro model (5), it proves to be insignificant (estimated coefficient = 0.097, t-value = 0.464). However, with a correlation coefficient of 0.697, it is individually more highly correlated with $\Delta_4$acq then are all other explanatory variables (followed by -0.410 for Δpi; the remainder are approximately 0.3 (absolute value) or less). Encompassing tests yield further unambiguous results in favour of the macro model:

H_0: Spread model encompasses macro model: Joint model F(7,48)=25.6 [0.0000]**,
H_0: Macro model encompasses spread model: Joint model F(3,48)=0.22 [0.8805].

Hence, given the explanatory power of the variables in the macro model, the lagged spread does not contain additional information, although it appears to be a good predictor. How can those seemingly contradictory findings be reconciled? We suggest that the spread is a variable which contains condensed information summarizing early expectations regarding the future development of such variables as (long-term) interest rates (Fama 1976, 1990, Hardouvelis 1988, 1994, or Sinkey 1973), prices (Frankel/Lown 1991, Jorion/Mishkin 1991, Mishkin 1990a,b, 1991, or Robertson 1992), or real economic activity (see references mentioned above). All these variables constitute the (contemporary or less than 5 quarters lagged) explanatory variables of the macro model. If this is the case, it is not surprising that the macro model, which uses the realizations of those variables as determinants to explain aggregate investment, performs better than the spread model, which uses only one variable summarizing expectations about the determinants. Although the spread does not have additional explanatory power in respect of aggregate investment, i.e. the information contained in the realizations completely substitutes the exploitable information from the expectations summary measure, the spread can be used as a predictor at an early stage if expectations are not systematically wrong. The predictive ability of the spread model is confirmed by the following artificial regression of the fitted values of the macro model (FITmacro) on a constant and the fitted values of the spread model (FITspread).

FITmacro =	0.00023 +	0.9736 FITspread	(7)
(SE)	(0.0047)	(0.1158)	

T=1975(1)-1990(4) less 6 forecasts, R^2 = 0.56, s = 0.035, DW = 1.22, AR 1-4 F(4,52) = 2.5014 [0.0535], ARCH 4 F(4,48) = 1.2989 [0.2838], Normality $\chi^2(2)$ = 5.5978 [0.0609], Xi^2 F(2,53) = 0.1176 [0.8893], Xi*Xj F(2,53) = 0.1176 [0.8893], RESET F (1,55) = 1.1590 [0.2864], Chow F(6,56) = 0.7785 [0.5902]

The constant differs only insignificantly from 0 and the slope coefficient differs insignificantly from 1. The residuals do not appear to have any systematic structure. Thus, forecasts of the spread model (FITspread), which are available five quarters before the fitted values of the macro model, on average correctly anticipate aggregate investment behaviour as explained by the macro model (FITmacro). Although the explanation of aggregate investment spending solely relies on the previously developed macro model, the spread model provides an early and useful prospective view of the near future.

4. Conclusions

4.1 Summary of empirical results

Our empirical results may be condensed into three propositions:

(1) The q-model loses its explanatory power after 1983. This result corresponds with the evidence of a structural break in the q-time series. The behaviour of German equity prices since the mid-1980s suggests that they have lost contact with their underlying 'real basis' of aggregate investment in physical capital by German business firms.

(2) The macro model turns out to be a well-specified and stable characterization of physical capital investment. The quantitatively crucial determinants of investment behaviour in the observation period are clearly well represented by our four explanatory variables. The static long-run solution shows that gross investment per unit of physical capital (measured as 'accumulation quota' ACQ, i.e., by the ratio of gross investment to the net capital stock in actual replacement prices) is:

- positively related to aggregate production y and the price level p, with theory-consistent elasticities exceeding 1, and
- negatively related to the price index of investment goods pi and the cost of external financing, or opportunity cost, as approximated by the long-term capital market interest rate RL:

$$acq = -1.3 + 1.8y + 1.6p - 2.9pi - 1.8RL \qquad (8)$$

The capital market interest rate RL has a semi-elasticity of -1.8, which, multiplied by the arithmetic mean of the long-term interest rate of 7.4 %, corresponds to a 'full' (average) interest rate elasticity of the accumulation quota of -0.13 for the time period 1975 to 1990.

(3) Within the given specification of the macro model, the term structure of interest rates does *not* provide additional explanatory power. This is at first sight astonishing, bearing in mind:

- that the interest rate spread, lagged 5 quarters, is not only positively correlated with the annual rate of change in the accumulation rate ($\Delta_4$acq), but also shows the highest (pairwise) correlation with $\Delta_4$acq relative to the explanatory variables of the macro model; and,
- that as the sole determinant in a forecast model of the accumulation quota, the spread offers good results.

In order to find an explanation, the relative information loss in the spread model as caused by its lag structure has to be considered (see Table 2).

Table 2: Forecast model versus explanatory model.

Spread model		**Macro model**
Term structure of interest rates in t - 5		
↓		
Approximates relevant *expectations* of prices, production and interest rates in t-5	→	Observed actual development of prices, production and interest rates in t, t - 1, ...
↓		↓
Forecasts investment in t		Explains investment in t

The spread forecast model solely uses information embodied in the term structure of interest rates available at time t-5. On the other hand, the macro model contains the actual explanatory variables as well as those with a time lag of less than five quarters. Given corresponding evidence in the literature, it can be argued that the term structure reflects the *expected* development of real income (y), overall prices (p, pi) and the capital market interest rate (RL) in the next year, i.e., exactly those expected variables whose realizations are specified as explanatory variables in the macro model. Therefore, adding the term structure of interest rates to the macro model cannot provide further explanatory power, as actual data already have replaced the (historical) expectations and forecasts. However, this reasoning does not preclude the term structure from providing correct forecasts of future investment.

4.2 Policy implications

The term structure of interest rates was approximated as a 'spread' variable - i.e., as the difference between the long-term interest rate level in the capital market and the short-term money market interest rate. The latter can be characterized as the operational target of central bank policy. It is an exogenous variable under the direct control of the monetary authorities. Assuming that, as indicated by our spread and macro models, actual term structure variations are systematically related to future macroeconomic development,[16] this implies in principle a 'transmission channel' for interest rate policy effects into the real sector of the economy as follows:

money market interest rate → capital market interest rate → investment in real capital.

The usual objection to this hypothesis is that the 'crucial' variable, the 'capital market interest rate', does not systematically depend on the money market interest rate, so that the effects of interest rate policy implemented by the central bank, and therefore its responsibility for the level of economic activity, cannot be so readily captured in a longer-term perspective relevant for monetary policy.

In a previous empirical study, however, we have investigated the determinants of the capital market interest rate. The results indicated that the capital market interest rate in Germany is systematically determined by the money market interest rate; in a long-run state of equilibrium, a change of the money market rate of 1 percentage point implies a variation of the capital market interest rate of 0.36 percentage points.[17] Put another way; in the long run, the term structure of interest rates (the spread) is inversely related to the level of the short-term money market rate. This statement is confirmed by descriptive evidence, according to

---

[16] See also Schmidt (1993). 'Macroeconomic' here can be seen as representing annual rates of change of investment in physical capital and/or of macroeconomic output; both variables are closely correlated ($r = +0.8$).

[17] The only additional explanatory variable for Germany is the three-months Eurodollar interest rate which has a relatively small impact. In particular, we obtained the following OLS-results for the cointegrating regression over the period 1967(1)-1994(11):

$$RL_t = 0.05 + 0.36RS_t + 0.08RUS_t + ECM_t \ .$$

R^2=0.67, DW=0.07. The $ADF_{12}(ECM)$=-3.60 test statistic indicates stationarity of the ECM, i.e., cointegration of RL, RS and RUS at the 5% level of significance (crit. value =-3.36, taken from MacKinnon (1991)). The corresponding error correction model, however, displays a rather low feedback effect (0.043) indicating slow adjustment towards equilibrium. For an application of this empirical strategy on selected European countries see Gebauer/Müller/Schmidt/Thiel/Worms (1994).

which the German yield curve becomes flatter or even inverted in times of restrictive monetary policy, i.e., of increasing money market interest rates, and *vice versa* in times of expansionary policy.

Formulated in whatever way: The systematic relationship between short- and long-term interest rates yields a forceful and simple long-run channel to transmit the effects of central bank policy actions into the real sector of the economy (as empirically underpinned in our macro model). This interest rate linkage suggests a term structure policy approach as an alternative concept for central bank policy making. After all, such a policy design appears to be well-founded by our evidence. Of course, there is still a need for the 'art of central banking': The 'art' will be to apply this new concept in practice in a credible way.

References

Abel, A. B. and Blanchard, O. J. (1986): The Present Value of Profits and Cyclical Movements in Investment, in: Econometrica 54, 249-273.

Banerjee, A., J. Dolado, J. W. Galbraith and D. F. Hendry (1993): Co-Integration, Error-Correction, and the Econometric Analysis of Non-Stationary Data. Oxford (Oxford University Press).

Brainard, W. C., and Tobin, J. (1968): Pitfalls in Financial Model Building, in: American Economic Review Papers and Proceedings 58, 99-122.

Catinat, M., Cawley, R., Ilzkovitz, F., Italianer, A. and Mors, M. (1987): The Determinants of Investment, in: European Economy 31, 5-60.

Charemza, W. W., and D. F. Deadman (1992): New Directions in Econometric Practice - General to Specific Modelling, Cointegration and Vector Autoregression. Aldershot (Edward Elgar).

Doornik, J. A., and D. F. Hendry (1994): PcGive Professional 8.0 (PcGive 8.0 - An Interactive Econometric Modelling System, and PcFiml 8.0 - Interactive Econometric Modelling of Dynamic Systems). Oxford (International Thomson Publishing).

Ericsson, N. R., D. F. Hendry and T. Hong-Anh (1993): Cointegration, Seasonality, Encompassing, and the Demand for Money in the United Kingdom, Board of Governors of the Federal Reserve System. International Finance Discussion Paper No. 457, October.

Estrella, A. and Hardouvelis, G. A. (1991): The Term Structure as a Predictor of Real Economic Activity, in: Journal of Finance 46, 555-576.

Fama, E. F. (1976): Forward Rates as Predictors of Future Spot Rates, in: Journal of Financial Economics 3, 361-377.

Fama, E. F. (1990): Term-Structure Forecasts of Interest Rates, Inflation and Real Returns, in: Journal of Monetary Economics 25, 59-76.

Fazzari, S. M., Hubbard, R. G. and Petersen, B. C. (1988): Financing Constraints and Corporate Investment, in: Brookings Papers on Economic Activity 1, 141-206.

Frankel, J. A. and Lown, C. S. (1991): An Indicator of Future Inflation Extracted from the Steepness of the Interest Rate Yield Curve Along its Entire Length, in: Quarterly Journal of Economics 109, 517-530.

Funke, M. (1992): Tobin's Q und die Investitionsentwicklung in den Wirtschaftszweigen des Unternehmenssektors in der Bundesrepublik Deutschland. Berlin (Duncker & Humblot).

Gebauer, W., M. Müller, K. J. W. Schmidt, M. Thiel and A. Worms (1994): Determinants of Long-Term Interest Rates in Selected European Countries, in: Johnson, C. and S. Collignon (eds.): The Monetary Economics of Europe - Causes of the EMS Crisis. London (Pinter Publishers), 189-226.

Gebauer, W., K. J. W. Schmidt and D. Veestraeten (1994): Kapitalmarktindikatoren und Investitionen in Sachkapital - Eine empirische Analyse, Geld-Währung-Kapitalmarkt Working Paper No. 37, University of Frankfurt, November; Also available as: Beiträge zur Theorie der Finanzmärkte No. 11, Institut für Kapitalmarktforschung. Frankfurt, December.

Gilbert, C. L. (1986): Professor Hendry's Econometric Methodology, in: Oxford Bulletin of Economics and Statistics 48, 283-307. Reprint in: Granger, C. W. J. (ed.): Modelling Economic Series. Oxford 1990 (Oxford University Press), 279-303.

Goodhart, C. (1991): The Conduct of Monetary Policy, in: Green, C.J. and D.T. Llewellyn (eds.): Surveys in Monetary Economics, Volume 1: Monetary Theory and Policy. Oxford (Blackwell Publishers), 263-323.

Hardouvelis, G. A. (1988): The Predictive Power of the Term Structure during Recent Monetary Regimes, in: Journal of Finance 43, 339-356.

Hardouvelis, G. A. (1994): The Term Structure Spread and Future Changes in Long and Short Rates in the G7 Countries: Is There a Puzzle?, in: Journal of Monetary Economics 33, 255-283.

Harvey, C. R. (1991): Interest Rate Based Forecasts of German Economic Growth, in: Weltwirtschaftliches Archiv 127, 701-718.

Hawtrey, R.G. (1932): The Art of Central Banking. London (Longmans, Green & Co.).

Hayashi, F. (1982): Tobin's Marginal q and Average q: A Neoclassical Interpretation, in: Econometrica 50, 213-224.

Hendry, D. F. (1993): Econometrics: Alchemy or Science?. Oxford (Blackwell Publishers).

Hendry, D. F. and Ericsson, N. R. (1991): An Econometric Analysis of U.K. Money Demand in Monetary Trends in the United States and the United Kingdom by Milton Friedman and Anna J. Schwartz, in: American Economic Review 81, 8-38.

Hoshi, T. and Kashyap, A. (1990): Evidence on q and Investment for Japanese Firms, in: Journal of the Japanese and International Economies 4, 371-400.

Issing, O. (1993): Central Bank Policy-Goals and Reality, in: Arestis, P. (ed.): Money and Banking - Issues for the Twenty-First Century. Basingstoke (MacMillan Press Ltd).

Jaeger, A. (1992): Zinssätze als vorauseilende Indikatoren der Konjunkturentwicklung, in: Monatsberichte des Österreichischen Instituts für Wirtschaftsforschung 65, 286-290.

Jorion, P. and Mishkin, F. S. (1991): A Multicountry Comparison of Term-Structure Forecasts at Long Horizons, in: Journal of Financial Economics 29, 59-80.

Keynes, J. M. (1936): The General Theory of Employment, Interest and Money. London (MacMillan & Co Ltd).

Konishi, T., V. A. Ramey and C. W. J. Granger (1993): Stochastic Trends and Short-Run Relationships Between Financial Variables and Real Activity. NBER Working Paper No. 4275, February.

Krämer, J. W. and E. Langfeldt (1993): Die Zinsdifferenz als Frühindikator für die westdeutsche Konjunktur, in: Die Weltwirtschaft, 34-42.

MacKinnon, J. G. (1991): Critical Values for Cointegration Tests, in: Engle, R.F. and C. W. J. Granger (eds.) (1991): Long-Run Economic Relationships - Readings in Cointegration. Oxford (Oxford University Press), 267-276.

Mishkin, F. S. (1990a): What Does the Term Structure Tell Us about Future Inflation?, in: Journal of Monetary Economics 25, 77-96.

Mishkin, F. S. (1990b): The Information in the Longer Maturity Term Structure about Future Inflation, in: Quarterly Journal of Economics 105, 815-828.

Mishkin, F. S. (1991): A Multi-Country Study of the Information in the Shorter Maturity Term Structure about Future Inflation, in: Journal of International Money and Finance 10, 2-22.

Myrdal, G. (1931): Om penningteoretisk jämvikt. En studie över den "normala räntan" i Wicksells penninglära, in: Ekonomisk Tidskrift 33, 191-302.

Myrdal, G. (1933): Der Gleichgewichtsbegriff als Instrument der geldpolitischen Analyse, in: Hayek, F. A. (eds.): Beiträge zur Geldtheorie. Vienna (Julius Springer), 361 - 487.

Niehans, J. (1978): The Theory of Money. Baltimore (Johns Hopkins University Press).

Plosser, C. I. and Rouwenhorst, K. G. (1994): International Term Structures and Real Economic Growth, in: Journal of Monetary Economics 33, 133-155.

Ragnitz, J. (1994): Zinsstruktur und Wirtschaftswachstum, in: Kredit und Kapital 27, 11-29.

Robertson, D. (1992): Term Structure Forecasts of Inflation, in: Economic Journal 102, 1083-1093.

Schmidt, K. J. W. (1993): Die Zinsstruktur als Prognoseinstrument der realwirtschaftlichen Entwicklung, in: Bühler, W., H. Hax and R. Schmidt (eds.): Empirische Kapitalmarktforschung. Zeitschrift für betriebswirtschaftliche Forschung, special issue 31, 257-285.

Schmidt, K. J. W. (1995): Tobins q? - Myrdals Q! Ein Fallbeispiel für den Wert von Fremdsprachenkenntnissen, forthcoming in Kredit und Kapital. Also available as: Geld-Währung-Kapitalmarkt. Working Paper No. 35, University of Frankfurt, June 1994.

Sensenbrenner, G. (1991): Aggregate Investment, the Stock Market, and the Q-Model. Robust Results for six OECD Countries, in: European Economic Review 35, 769-832.

Sinkey, J. F. Jr. (1973): The Term Structure of Interest Rates - A Time-Series Test of the Kane Expected-Change Model of Interest Rate Forecasting, in: Journal of Money, Credit, and Banking 5, 192-200.

Spanos, A. (1986): Statistical Foundations of Econometric Modelling. Cambridge (Cambridge University Press).

Statistisches Bundesamt (1991): Vermögensrechnung 1950 bis 1991, in: series 18: Volkswirtschaftliche Gesamtrechnungen, issue S. 17, 106-125.

Statistisches Bundesamt (1992): Konten und Standardtabellen, in: series 18: Volkswirtschaftliche Gesamtrechnungen, issue 1.3, 275-279.

Tobin, J. (1969): A General Equilibrium Approach to Monetary Theory, in: Journal of Money, Credit, and Banking 1, 15-29.

Wizman, T. A. (1992): Evidence from Tests of the Relation Between Interest-Rate Spreads and Economic Activity. Federal Reserve Bank of New York Research Paper No. 9203, February.

Financial Reporting and the Stock Market in Germany

Hans Peter Möller and Erich Keller
University of Aachen

1. Introduction

Research on the relationship between financial reporting and the stock market has hitherto been undertaken on a much smaller scale in Germany than in the USA. One reason for this is that in Germany there is nothing comparable to the US Conceptual Framework for financial reporting. Another reason is the absence of financial statement or stock market data bases like those of the Compustat and Crisp systems. Nevertheless a considerable, accumulating volume of research that has also been summarized in overviews can be mentioned (Coenenberg/Möller/Schmidt 1984, Möller 1993, Coenenberg/Haller 1993). Most of this work is devoted to the question of whether financial reporting has an impact on such basic stock market parameters as prices or returns. Research on the manner in which the stock market influences financial reporting, is however conspicuous by its virtual absence.

The aim of this article is to describe the topics and results of the most recent research on the relationship between financial reporting and the stock market. To help understand the topics, dimensions and difficulties inherent in this research, brief comments about financial reporting in Germany and the German stock market, are made in section 2. The subsequent sections deal with a review of the latest work on the information content of financial statements for shareholders (section 3) and a description of the work examining the value-relevance of German accounting data for investors (section 4).

2. Financial reporting in Germany

As a consequence of the Roman law basis of the German legal system, (codified law which is intended to regulate conflicts by the application of abstract rules) accounting and reporting regulations, hereafter called GAAP, are statutorily prescribed. The special Code which regulates financial reporting by all types of enterprises is the Commercial Code.[1] GAAP differ with respect to firm size, industry and form of business organisation. This has not always been the case. Prior to 1986 different GAAP were codified in statutes regulating individual legal forms of business organisation or specific industries. Thus, before 1986, the GAAP for a Gesellschaft mit beschränkter Haftung (GmbH), i.e. private limited company, were found in the GmbH-Gesetz whereas the GAAP for an Aktiengesellschaft (AG), i.e. public limited company, were prescribed in the Aktiengesetz[2]. Basic elements of financial reporting by banks and insurance companies of all legal forms have only recently been incorporated into the Commercial Code. Formerly they were to be found in (company form) specific statutes, in rulings of the minister of Justice and in the Kreditwesengesetz and the Versicherungsaufsichtsgesetz respectively.

The financial report of a German joint stock company - a separate legal entity mainly represented by AG and GmbH companies - comprises its balance sheet, income statement and notes (to both statements) as a legal, rather than economic entity. Those three collectively constitute a single unit which is supplemented with a statement of affairs (Lagebericht). The latter statement contains reviews of past performance, post balance sheet events, future prospects and research and development.

A parent company in the form of a joint stock company (AG or GmbH) is required to publish legal entity accounts and group accounts. The latter are solely intended to provide additional (unspecified) information and do not satisfy such other functions as profit measurement, profit distribution and the computation of taxable earnings. Group accounts do not therefore replace the financial reports of constituent group companies. A group financial report only closely resembles that of the ultimate parent company when it consolidates the financial reports of all group subsidiary companies, each of which is directly, or indirectly, wholly-owned by the parent company. In all other cases the equity and earnings in a group financial report differ from those of the parent company viewed as an economic entity. In such cases the earnings and equity of the parent company and economic entity can only be derived with additional calculations from the group accounts.

Relevant for accounting-related empirical research on the German stock market are only those GAAP as must be complied with by companies whose

---

[1] Details of German GAAP in English can be found Brooks/Mertin (1986) and Ordelheide/Pfaff (1994).

[2] Gesellschaften mit beschränkter Haftung differ from Aktiengesellschaften in some respects, the most important of which for capital market research seem to be the rights of the stockholders. In contrast to the stockholders of an AG those of a GmbH are allowed to inspect the accounts of the company, but their shares may only be sold by a special notarised agreement and may not be traded at a stock exchange.

shares are or may be, listed on a stock exchange. As German Law allows the shares only of AG companies to be traded on a stock exchange, only the GAAP regulating AG companies are relevant in the present context. These GAAP have evolved over time with amendments in 1937, 1959, 1965, 1985 and 1990. The change in 1959 mainly altered the form of the income statement, that of 1965 reduced management's influence on the valuation of assets and introduced financial reporting for groups by prescribing consolidation procedures for group accounts. However, banks and insurance companies, especially those in the legal form of an AG, were unaffected by the 1965 legislation. By virtue of special regulations, in the Kreditwesengesetz and Versicherungsaufsichtsgesetz, they still enjoy an almost unbounded discretion in the valuation of assets which may be recorded at values below historic cost. Changes in valuation need not be disclosed, either in the balance sheet or in the income statement nor in the notes. The 1985 change reflected the EU harmonization directives for industrial companies. A new form and an extension of the notes to the accounts as well as new consolidation procedures were introduced. The 1990 change relates to banks and insurance companies and enacted slightly new valuation rules for these companies which formally, though not materially, restrict their discretion.

The foregoing GAAP overview shows that empirical research on financial reporting in Germany has to cope with different subsets of data which in themselves are quite homogeneous e.g. those for 1967-85, but which differ from one GAAP regime to the next. Whilst current financial reporting by industrial companies defined as separate legal entities does not differ significantly from financial reporting in the period between 1965 and 1985, material changes in group accounting have occured. Group reports regulated by the 1965 Code differ from those prescribed under the 1985 regime in that consolidation procedures have changed, and also because a drift from domestic to global consolidation has complicated comparisons of old and new data. Furthermore, since 1965 the financial reports of banks and insurance companies have not been comparable with those of industrial firms.

The equity of all AG companies consists of two elements, namely Grundkapital and the Rücklagen. The Grundkapital is the amount of equity which may not be withdrawn by the owners without the consent of its lenders. If a company has issued shares with a par value - the normal case in Germany - its Grundkapital corresponds to the sum of the par values of those shares. The Rücklagen represent retained earnings plus share premia gained from new issues. The minimal par value of a share has recently been reduced from 50 DM to 5 DM.

Although there is a fluctuating population of approximate by only 2,000 AG companies in Germany, they constitute an important sector of the economy. Measured on an unconsolidated basis, their sales make up about 20 % of all

German sales. The shares of about one third to one fourth of these companies are listed at one, or more, of the German stock exchanges. A few are also listed on foreign stock exchanges, expecially in London. Many of these corporations have capital stakes in each other. Although the stocks of all companies whose shares are listed on a stock exchange, may be traded, trading volumes are large only in the case of a subgroup of about 150 of listed firms. The largest of the companies in this subset are included in several published indices of which the DAX-Index is the smallest. There are eight stock exchanges in Germany, of which Frankfurt has become the most important. Small orders of all types of shares, as well as large orders of infrequently traded shares, are traded on the floor on the basis of a pricing system that aims at clearing the market at a certain point in time. Large orders of frequently traded shares are processed by a computerbased trading system which facilitates continuous trading during the opening hours of the stock exchange.

Although the legal rights which characterise AG can vary quite considerably from one AG to the next, the owers of almost all traded shares enjoy very similar rights, the economically most important of which is the owner's right to vote at the shareholders' meeting. Shares without voting rights are often endowed with other rights and therefore called Vorzugsaktien, as opposed to the ordinary shares the so - called Stammaktien. The majority of companies has issued shares with voting rights. Most of these are bearer instruments with a dividend entitlement and the right to participate in company assets on cessation of operations.

In the empirical research contemplated here, it is important to identify the properties of the shares in question to obviate influences on the results that are not under investigation. In addition, shares normally entitle the holder exclusively to participate in rights issues. Shareholders can, however, sell their rights if they do not wish to participate in a new issue. Rights issues are therefore normally accompanied by the trading of rights letters. Empirical research using market-based returns thus needs to account for the sales of rights letters and/or the value of shares acquired in a rights issue.

As yet there is no institution in Germany that acts like the SEC in the US to project the interests of shareholders and even auditors are far from attesting a fair presentation of the economic position of the company when they attest compliance with legal and corporate constitutionaly requirements. A first glance at the process generating GAAP identifies executive directors and auditors as the main lobbying groups rather than investors or shareholders.

3. Capital market oriented research on the information content of German financial statements for shareholders

One of the approaches used to investigate the relationship between financial reporting and the stock market consists of measuring the information content of financial statements for shareholders. This approach follows the ideas of Ball/Brown (Ball/Brown 1968). It infers the information content of financial statement by references to share price reaction to new information that is provided by the disclosure of a financial statement. The problems inherent in this approach have been comprehensively described (Lev 1989) and result form the facts that (1) in the real world there are influences on share prices other than the disclosure of a financial statement and (2) that it is hard to define the new information that is contained in a financial statement. The basic approach by Ball/Brown has enjoyed frequent use and, to some extent, has been adjusted to overcome these problems - at least partially. Assuming there are no measurement problems and that the market reacts instantaneously to relevant information (information efficieny of the market), the degree of market reaction to the financial statement release on this information's degree of relevance. Again assuming the absence of measurement problems, and that the information in question is undoubtedly relevant, the information efficiency the market can be inferred accordingly. The first type of inference is the one that is used for the information content issue. The market reaction to the disclosure is regarded as a measure of information content since it reflects the hypothetical advantage (disadvantage) that a shareholder might have realized (avoided) had he known the financial statement information in advance of its disclosure. This information content is supposed to measure the hypothetical value of the (new) information provided by financial statements. It is hypothetical because such a value cannot be realised if a semi-strong efficient market obtains.

The concept of information content is applied in the data analysis of most of the German capital market oriented accounting research. One line of research utilises data for industrial firms, whereas another is concerned with banks. Using the data of companies (as legal entities as opposed to groups) together with ordinary share data, early papers support the idea that positive information leads, on average, to positive market reactions and that earnings have information content (Brandi 1977). Consistent with this idea is also the result that the information content of financial reports differs with respect to a company's attitude towards disclosure. Thus the reports of companies that only disclose a minimum as seldom as possible have greater information content than those of companies which frankly and frequently disclose very much more (Berndsen 1979). Other variables of industrial firms that have been examined for information content are: degree of earnings management, effect of notes disclosing changes in the basis of earnings measurement and ownership structure, i.e., owner-controlled firms versus manager-controlled firms (Coenenberg 1993, pp. 702-715).

Further extensions of this research are inter-country GAAP evaluations and assessments of alternative statutory disclosure requirements, e.g., the effects on industrial companies of changes in disclosure regulations resulting from the 1965 Aktiengesetz (Coenenberg/Möller 1979). The latter results clearly reveal that the restriction of management's discretion in measuring earnings and equity, that was induced by the 1965 change, causes an increase in information content. A similar line of research was undertaken, soon after the 1988 Börsengesetz (Stock Exchange Code) had imposed the regular disclosure of interim reports on companies listed on German stock exchanges (Keller/Möller 1993). As that research also contributed to the empirical capital market research project, it is described in more detail.

The regular disclosure, prior to 1988, of interim reports by about 50 companies facilitates a comparison of the information content of their annual financial reports with those of companies that had not disclosed interim reports. The interim report research includes all comparable German companies with fiscal years ending after the beginning of 1974 and before the end of 1986, whose ordinary shares were listed on a stock exchange. This time interval was chosen because of data restrictions and also for comparability reasons. Prior to 1974, stock prices were not available on a daily basis and for fiscal years after 1987 comparability might have been reduced by the statutory change in GAAP resulting from the 1985 Bilanzrichtliniengesetz (Financial Reporting Act). Furthermore, company financial reports were excluded from that sample when their information content seemed to lack comparability because of special influences or restrictions. Thus all cases characterised by any one of the five following conditions were rxcluded: (1) A relatively short listing period within the period of investigation. Such companies were excluded to obviate the effects on information content either of initial public offerings or events leading to a withdrawal from the stock exchange. (2) Control of the company by another company or person or small group of persons documented either by contract or by majority shareholdings. If more than 75 % (or 80 %) of the company's equity was owned by one (or several) persons in any individual year, that year's financial report was excluded. In both these cases it can be assumed that the financial report is of little importance to these majority shareholders because they can generally directly access information about their companies via their board representatives. (3) Important survival events within an individual year. Excluding the financial reports of such years obviates the effects of mergers, bankruptcy, acquisitions or control agreements etc. on the information content of annual financial reports and also immunises interim reports from such influences. (4) Extremely high or low market returns within a very short time interval. Thus, financial reports were excluded when the daily market return exceeded 20 % or when the market-adjusted return had halved or doubled within the six months of the abnormal performance tracking. The reason for this exclusion is the fear that unrecorded special events overwhelm the interim reporting issue. (5) Non-availability of the financial report. A few cases were excluded because financial reports were no longer available.

The adoption of these criteria in a sample of 1557 financial reports, of which 804 were for companies that had disclosed at least one interim report and 753 for companies without any interim reporting.

Using abnormal performance indices it is shown that the information content of annual financial reports in the case of companies not disclosing interim reports is significantly higher than that of the annual reports of companies which publish interim reports. For companies without interim reporting it is the change in earnings and not the change in dividends which causes share price adjustments whereas, in the absence of interim reporting, the latter are mainly attributable to dividend changes. If the interim reports reflect aspects of the economic position of the firm this result is quite intuitive. Thus, whilst earnings are known, or can be anticipated from interim reports, the dividend information reflects the new information contained in the financial report. These results hold for alternative ways of computing abnormal performance indices, i.e., variations in the modelling of abnormal returns and in the modelling of investors' expectations. It can therefore be concluded that whilst the introduction of interim reporting by listed companies may have imposed an expensive duty upon them it is also beneficial to investors in that it provides additional information to the market.

The second line of research on the information content of financial reports concerns GAAP for banks (Keller 1992, Keller/Möller 1992). On the one hand their accounting has to comply with very detailed prescriptions and comparability is assured by detailed regulations promulgated by the Bundesaufsichtsamt für das Kreditwesen. On the other hand most functions of their financial reporting are hampered by the discretion management may exercise with respect to an (undisclosed) definition of earnings. Contrary to the views of banks themselves, the literature is unanimous that the valuation of accounts receivables and securities, i.e. the bulk of bank assets, is entirely misleading because they may be disclosed at any value between zero and historic cost allregedly to take account of the general risks of banking operations. Management is thereby able to reduce earnings as long as these assets are valued above zero and to increase earnings as long as they are valued below historic cost. The adverse effect of this discretion is compounded by the right to missclassify four items in the income statement. Amounts written off accounts receivable may be classified as amounts written off securities and vice versa. A similar misclassification is also permissible on the revenue side. In addition, the deduction of these two expense items from each of the corresponding earnings items and vice versa, is also admissible so that an external analyst is unable to detect the amount of earnings management a bank has undertaken in any given year. The 1990 statutory changes in GAAP do not affect the discretions just described because, although formally restricted to 4 % of the sum of accounts receivable and securities, the earnings of banks seldom exceed 1 % of the latter sum.

The admissibility of such extreme discretion seems to negate the stewardship function of financial reporting and induces investors to attribute very low information content to the earnings disclosed by banks. Whether this is so, has been investigated empirically as a contribution to the capital market empirical research project (Keller/Möller 1992). From a comparison of bank GAAP with industrial GAAP it can be hypothethized (1) that the information content of the financial reports of banks should be much lower than that of industrial firms and (2) that the earnings level of banks cannot contribute much to the information content of their financial reports. If investors use a bank's financial report, then figures other than earnings should be relevant, for example, estimated cash-flows or profit before such items as those that facilitate earnings management.

Neither of these hypotheses could be rejected on the basis of an empirical analysis of the same 1,557 (industrial) financial reports, that were used for the interim reporting study described above, supplemented with 168 financial reports of banks. The total information content of financial statements - measured by the advantage to an investor with perfect knowledge of the future - was much lower for banks than for industrial firms. Furthermore, the information content of the earnings and dividend figures of financial reports - measured by the advantage to an investor with imperfect knowledge of the future who relies on either earnings or dividends - is, in the case of banks, far lower than in the case of industrial firms. Measuring the information content of the financial reports of banks by reference to earnings before items that facilitate earnings management, as opposed to earnings disclosed, greatly increases information content. This result suggests that investors are aware of possible misrepresentation in the financial reports of banks and try to overcome it by circumventing the misclassified items.

An interesting aspect of the development of German GAAP is that prior to the enacting of the 1965 Aktiengesetz, industrial firms and banks were subject to similar statutory accounting provisions. The 1965 Act greatly reduced the discretion enjoyed by industrial firms but not that of banks. This situation allows a general analysis of the effects of different degrees of discretion on the information content of the financial reports of companies. This analysis has also been undertaken within the framework of the capital market empirical research project (Keller/Möller 1995). The results of that research clearly imply that the shareholders of banks suffer a considerable information disadvantage compared to the shareholders of industrial firms. A society that aims at the optimal allocation of its capital and wishes to compete internationally for resources should draw the appropriate conclusions from such results.

4. Capital market oriented research on the value-relevance of German financial statements

Research on the value-relevance of financial statements analyses the correlation between market measures and accounting numbers. It can readily be shown that the market returns of a share should correlate with the corresponding earnings per share; and, that the market value of equity should correlate with the corresponding book value

Analyses of market returns and accounting earnings are based on the assumption that a firm's earnings level (and not merely the unexpected component of its earnings) is value-relevant. From a long-term perspective, earnings represent the only possible explanation for changes in the market value of a firm's equity[3]. This approach reflects the idea that events and actions, other than cash transfers between a firm and its equity holders, influence the book value of a firm's equity and the market value of its shares. Differences between a firm's equity book and market values, i.e. unrecorded goodwill due to the missing recognition of future earnings and between periodic changes in book and market values, will only occur, if investors evaluations of value-relevant events and actions with respect to returns and market values deviate from accounting valuations. Such deviations may arise if the consequences of those events and actions are incomplete and are in some degree uncertain. Hence, the difference between the changes in the market and book values of equity will be smaller, the longer the underlying time period. This reasoning reflects the fact that the effect of incomplete value-relevant events and actions decreases with longer time periods. Adopting this approach, the value-relevance of accounting information, especially that of earnings, can be described by the degree of correlation between a firm's earnings (adjusted for dividends net of capital contributions) and the change in its stock market value. The value-relevance of the book value of equity can be described by the degree of correlation between the corresponding book and market values of equity.

To compare firms of different size, it is necessary to standardize market value changes and earnings - usually by the beginning-of-period market value. If, during the time-interval during which market value changes are to be measured, there are cash flows between a company and its owners, the market value changes of different companies will not be comparable - notwithstanding the standardising corrective - should there be inter-company differences in the level

---

[3] A more detailed treatment can be found in Easton/Harris/Ohlson (1992).

and timing of these cash flows. The latter differences can however be accommodated with a further corrective. It is merely necessary to assume that the cash flows took place at the beginning, or end, rather than during the returns interval and, giving effect to such an assumption, to draw the appropriate financial-mathematical conclusion. Here it is assumed that all cash flows took place at the end of the returns interval.

Proceeding from the latter assumption: both earnings and market values need to be adjusted. Earnings must be revised upwards because such intra-window distributions could have been used to generate higher earnings had they first been distributed at the end of the returns interval. Capital contributions from shareholders (capital increases) necessitate downward revisions to earnings. This is because a (marginal) constituent of the latter is attributable to the intra-window capital contributions; and, had such contributions first been received at the end of the returns window, this marginal constituent would not have been generated. If the change in market value is to express the benefits derived by owners from their investments, market value differences also need to be corrected in respect of intra-window dividends and capital contributions. The difference would have been greater in the absence of dividends because such payments cause market values to decline by a similar amount. Conversely, the difference would have been lower had capital, causing a commensurate increase in market values, not been contributed by shareholders. The assumption that these cash flows took place later than they actually occured necessitates an assumption about the interim returns there on, or about their opportunity costs, as the case may be.

The earnings corrective implicit in the foregoing line of reasoning is equally as difficult to measure as is the market value corrective. The two can however be estimated and, as in capital budgeting, can be expressed in terms of the market interest rate. As regards intra-window dividend payments, this implies, for example, that earnings should be increased by the interest-income, which would have been earned from the investment of that dividend from its payment date until the end of the returns interval. The market value change corrective comprises the hypothetical compound interest received on dividends from their payment dates until the end of the returns interval, together with the hypothetical (compound) interest payable on capital increases from their payment dates until the end of the returns interval.

Viewed formally the research approach lies in the ascertaining and analysis of the correlation between two variables in a cross-sectional linear model about shares and companies. As regards the analysis of returns between time-points 0 and T, the dependent variable is in principle an investor's achieved return and the independent variable is the change in equity book value attributable to earnings:

$$y_T = a + bx_T + u_T$$

Unexplained factors are reflected in u_T. The dependent variable y_T for each firm is given by

$$y_T = \frac{M_T - M_0 + FVS_T}{M_0}$$

and the independent variable x_T by

$$x_T = \frac{\sum_{t=0}^{T} E_T + FVT_T}{M_0}$$

where

M_0, M_T	represent the market value of the firm at time-points 0 and T.
E_t	stands for earnings for the time interval t-1 to t.
FVS_T	ist the corrective applicable to the change in market value
FVF_T	is the corrective applicable to earnings in respect of cash flows between a company and ists shareholders in the returns interval from 0 to T

It seems to be reasonable to assume, that investors are not accurately informed about many firm value-relevant events and actions prior to the publication of the annual financial statements. They first learn the aggregate financial consequences on the publication of the earnings number. Since the publication of the financial statements reflects a time lag from the end of the fiscal year, the dates 0 and T must refer to the publication date and not to the financial year-end.

Let i be the interest rate for compounding calculations and d_t the cash flow, i.e. dividends net of capital contributions during the time period between t-1 and t. The following formulae can therefore be used to adjust for the cash flow timing differences of individual firms:

$$FVS_T = d_1(1+i)^{T-1} + d_2(1+i)^{T-2} + \ldots + d_{T-1}(1+i) + d_T$$

$$FVT_T = d_1(1+i)^{T-1} - d_1 + d_2(1+i)^{T-2} - d_2 + \ldots + d_{T-1}(1+i) - d_{T-1}$$

It is to be expected that the correlation between y_T and x_T will become stronger as the length of the event window between 0 and T increases because of the increasing effect of completed value-relevant events on aggregate earnings

$$\sum_{t=0}^{T} E_T$$

Events and actions which are incomplete become increasingly meaningless. The degreee of correlation can be interpreted as an indicator of the relevance of the accounting earnings information for investors since it indicates the strength of the association between financial statement earnings information and market returns. In such a setting the difference between the market and book values of equity can be explained by future earnings that have not yet been recognised by the accounting system. Consequently, the degree to which the book value of equity explains its corresponding market value can be regarded as a measure of the appropriateness of financial reporting from an investor or shareholder standpoint.

An empirical investigation of the correlation between the market and the book value of equity has to solve the problem of matching the book value disclosed in a financial statement with the market value on a specific day. While cash flows between a company and its shareholders should be known to shareholders, they are unaware of the earnings element of the book value of equity as long as it has not been disclosed. When financial statements are disclosed, investors learn about past earnings, but, at that time, a large amount of the new earnings has already been generated. The amount of these new earnings is, however, unknown to shareholders.

The concept of value-relevance offers a model with a much stronger link between accounting and the stock market than does the concept of information content. Within the empirical research project on the German capital market the value relevance concept has been used to evaluate German financial reporting in comparison with U.S. financial reporting (Harris/Lang/Möller 1994). The motivation for this kind of research is that, at least in Great Britain and in the US, German stock market investment is perceived to be abnormally risky. This perception seems to be attributable to: (1) weak competition between equity and debt holders, (2) the possibility of a flow of information from boards to major shareholders and banks; and, (3) the supposedly greater conservatism and earnings management potential of German financial reporting. An analysis of 1084 financial statements of German companies and a similar number of U.S. companies suggests that there is little to choose between the value-relevance of German and U.S. reports. German accounting earnings and equity book values could, in almost all data subsets, explain nearly as much of the German market returns and market prices as could U.S. accounting earnings and equity book values in respect of US market returns and market prices. The analysis reflected comparisons of different subsets of German data, namely, data for the periods prior to, and after, the 1985 change in the statutory GAAP provisions differentiating between companies disclosing only a "legal entity" financial report and those supplementing the latter with a group report. It seems that, in the case of "legal entity" reports, the EU harmonization changes in German GAAP do not contribute to its power to explain market values. However, in the case of the "economic entity" data that were constructed from group accounts, there is a clear difference between the results for the pre- and post-1985 GAAP regimes. The conservatism of the German GAAP clearly influences the size of earnings response coefficients and of the book value multiplier; its effect on the degree of total association is, however, low.

5. Conclusion

Financial reporting in Germany and the German stock market differ significantly from their English and US counterparts. These differences often lead foreign investors and researchers to conclude that investments in the German stock market are riskier than in other markets. However, statistical analysis reveals that German financial reports do have information content. The results also show that the development of German GAAP has progressively given effect to the interests of investors. A comparison of German GAAP and investor-orientied GAAP like those of the US, demonstrates a high potential for increasing the information content of German financial reports. Judging from value-relevance research German investors seem however to understand German financial reporting: There is little difference between the value-relevance of German und US financial reporting.

References

Ball, R. and Brown, P. (1968): An empirical evaluation of accounting income numbers, in: Journal of Accounting Research 6, 159-178.

Berndsen, H. P. (1979): Unternehmenspublizität. Augsburg (Diss.).

Brandi, E. H. (1977): Informationswirkungen der Jahresabschlußveröffentlichungen auf Entscheidungen am Aktienmarkt. Augsburg (Diss.).

Brooks, J. and D. Mertin (1986): New German accounting legislation: synoptic translation with introduction. Düsseldorf (IDW).

Coenenberg, A. G. and A. Haller (1993): Empirische Forschung, in: Chmielewicz, K., and M. Schweitzer (eds.), Handwörterbuch des Rechnungswesens, 4th ed., Stuttgart (Schäffer-Poeschel), 506-517.

Coenenberg, A. G. (1994): Jahresabschluß und Jahresabschlußanalyse, 14th ed. Landsberg/Lech (Moderne Industrie).

Coenenberg, A. G. and Möller, H. P. (1979): Entscheidungswirkungen von Jahresabschlußinformationen vor und nach der Aktienrechtsreform von 1965, in: Betriebswirtschaftliche Forschung und Praxis 31, 438-454.

Coenenberg, A. G., Möller, H. P. and F. Schmidt (1984): Empirical research in financial accounting in Germany, Austria and Switzerland: A review, in: Hopwood, A. G. and H. Schreuder (eds.): European contributions to accounting research. Amsterdam (Free University Press), 61-81.

Easton, P.D., Harris, T.S. and Ohlson, J.A. (1992): Aggregate accounting earnings can explain most of security returns: The case of long return intervals, in: Journal of Accounting and Economics , 119-142.

Harris, T.S, Lang, M. and Möller, H.P. (1994): The value relevance of German accounting measures: An empirical analysis, in: Journal of Accounting Research 32, 187-209.

Keller, E. (1992): Entscheidungswirkungen von Bankbilanzen am Aktienmarkt. Heidelberg (Physica-Verlag).

Keller. E. and Möller, H. P. (1992): Einstufung von Bankbilanzen am Kapitalmarkt infolge von § 26a KWG, in: Zeitschrift für Bankrecht und Bankwirtschaft 4, 169-183.

Keller, E. and Möller, H. P. (1993): Die Auswirkungen der Zwischenberichterstattung auf den Informationswert von Jahresabschlüssen am Kapitalmarkt, in: Bühler, W., Hax, H., and R. Schmidt (eds.): Empirische Kapitalmarktforschung. Zeitschrift für betriebswirtschaftliche Forschung, special issue 31, 35-60.

Keller, E. and Möller, H. P.(1995): Zur Diskussion der bankspezifischen Bewertungssonderrechte des § 340f HGB - Lehren aus der Aktienrechtsreform von 1965 zum Informationsgehalt von Jahresabschlüssen mit "großen" und "kleinen" Bewertungswahlrechten, forthcoming.

Lev, B. (1989), On the usefulness of earnings and earnings research: Lessons and directions from two decades of empirical research, in: Journal of Accounting Research 27, 153-201.

Möller, H. P. (1993): Bilanzforschung, empirische, in: Wittmann, W., Köhler, R., Küpper, H.-U., and K. v. Wysocki (eds.): Handwörterbuch der Betriebswirtschaft, 5th ed., Stuttgart (Schäffer-Poeschel), 510-526.

Ordelheide, D. and D. Pfaff (1994): European financial reporting: Germany. London (Routledge).

C Risk and Return

An Investigation into the Number of Factors Generating German Stock Returns

Otto L. Adelberger and Gerd Lockert
University of Essen

1. Motivation for this research

Notwithstanding its alleged deficiencies, the capital asset pricing model (CAPM), the original version of which is attributable to Sharpe (1964), Lintner (1965), and Mossin (1966), probably still constitutes the most important theoretical approach to the (capital market) valuation of risky securities. The high degree of acceptance that was initially enjoyed by the CAPM in the literature of financial economics has suffered considerable erosion with the effluxion of time. Preeminent causes of this reappraisal are the relative weak empirical content of some of its underlying assumptions (see, for instance, Ross 1977, p. 190 and Möller 1986, pp. 88-91), accumulating empirical evidence that is inconsistent with its main implications (see e.g. Banz 1981, Winkelmann 1984, Lehmann/Modest 1988, Fama/French 1992, Warfsmann 1993), and fundamental doubts about the testability of the CAPM. Apropos of the latter issue, Roll's well-known paper (see Roll 1977), which questions the practical testability of the CAPM because the "true" market portfolio is unobservable, deserves special emphasis.

In an attempt to surmount the latter problems, Ross (1976, 1977) expressly formulated his arbitrage pricing theory (APT) as an alternative to the CAPM (see Ross 1976, p. 341). Now regarded by some authors as the paramount approach to the valuation of risky securities, the APT is the main focus of the study which is reported hereafter. The distinction between systematic and non-systematic risk, which is a fundamental feature of the CAPM, also characterizes the APT. In accordance with the exact APT valuation equation, and analogous with the CAPM security market line, only systematic risk is relevant to the relative pricing of risky capital assets. In contrast to the CAPM, the APT is based on the notion that systematic risk is attributable to k factors by assuming a linear factor model.[1]

---

[1] The following arguments deal exclusively with the linear APT; as regards non-linear APT see especially Bansal/Viswanathan 1993.

However, the APT specifies neither the identity of these factors nor their exact number.

The APT has already been the subject of extensive United States (US) empirical research. The results of those tests which, rather than prespecifying the systematic factors, apply factor analytic methods to estimate the factor betas are mainly consistent with the APT valuation hypothesis. However, they do not yet permit a definitive conclusion about its general validity. Thus, Roll/Ross (1980), Brown/Weinstein (1983), Chen (1983), Cho (1984), Lehmann/Modest (1988), and Shukla/Trzcinka (1990) do not reject the APT, whereas the results of Reinganum (1981), Dhrymes/Friend/Gultekin/Gultekin (1985a,b), Cho/Taylor (1987), and Gultekin/Gultekin (1987) do not corroborate the APT. Furthermore, as yet, the number of reported comprehensive APT tests based on German stock market data is severely limited (see Winkelmann 1984, Frantzmann 1989, Nowak 1994, Sauer 1994). This research deficit seems to justify further empirical investigations of the APT using German stock market data since definitive insights into the German market price establishing process can hardly be inferred from the mixed and inconclusive results of reported US studies.

A further difficulty lies in the fact that the various APT investigations have not revealed an unequivocal number of systematic factors.[2] The "true" number of factors is therefore still unknown (see also Wei 1988, p. 883 or Robin/Shukla 1991, p. 65 for similar statements) and must be determined empirically by resort to econometric procedures.[3] It follows from the identification problem of (exploratory) factor analysis that the number of factors whose risk premia are individually significantly different from zero does not provide clues about the appropriate number of systematic factors (see Dhrymes/Friend/Gultekin (1984), pp. 326-330 and Franke (1984), p. 113). This number must therefore be specified prior to the testing of the APT valuation equation. Furthermore, it must be emphasized that the "validity" of an APT test also generally depends upon the accuracy of the estimate of the number of factors. Finally, the "correct" determination of the number of factors is essential for an appropriate judgement about the practical applicability of the APT. Thus, the estimation of the number of factors is a crucial aspect of this research and the empirical specification of the factor model assumption is the key element of this paper. The research reported here stems from a project that is supported by the German Research Foundation

---

[2] Also the economic interpretation of the systematic factors seems to be a task of the empirical APT research which has not yet yielded satisfactory results (see e.g. Chan/Chen/Hsieh 1985, Chen/Roll/Ross 1986, Burmeister/McElroy 1988, McElroy/Burmeister 1988, and Nowak 1994).

[3] Similar statements are given by Wei (1988, p. 883), Robin/Shukla (1991, p. 65).

(Deutsche Forschungsgemeinschaft) as part of a comprehensive scientific program devoted to "empirical capital market research".[4]

The remainder of this paper is organized as follows. Following an overview of the major research contributions to the APT, the second part reports the numbers of factors identified in studies based on German stock market data. The foundations of our own empirical investigation are outlined in the third part. We first describe the essential properties of the selected data and, thereafter, outline the approaches taken in determining the relevant number of factors. Estimates of the number of factors for different data samples are contained in part 4. The fifth and final part summarizes the main findings and offers a judgement about the feasibility of a decision on the number of factors to be selected.

2. Overview of the APT and some empirical findings for the German stock market

The original version of the APT rests on comparatively weak assumptions. Firstly, it is assumed that the p securities under consideration are traded on a frictionless and perfectly competitive (infinite) capital market in which no asymptotic arbitrage opportunities exist. Secondly, investors are assumed to believe homogeneously that the single period random returns on capital assets, r_i $(i = 1, ..., p)$, are generated by a linear k-factor model (see Ross 1976, p. 347):

$$r = E(r) + Bf + e \, . \qquad (1)$$

In equation (1), r denotes the $p \times 1$ vector of r_i, E(r) is the $p \times 1$ vector containing the expected returns, B is the $p \times k$ matrix of sensitivity coefficients b_{ij} (b_{ij} represents the sensitivity of r_i to fluctuations in factor j), f denotes the $k \times 1$ vector of systematic (or common) factors f_j, and e is the $p \times 1$ vector of security-specific disturbance terms e_i. Furthermore, the following assumptions are made:

$$\text{rank}(B) = k \, , \quad k << p \, , \qquad (2a)$$

$$E(f) = 0 \, , \quad E(ff') = I \, , \quad E(fe') = 0 \, , \quad E(e) = 0 \, , \qquad (2b)$$

[4] Interim results from this project were presented to the 5th and 7th colloquium of the previously-mentioned research program; see Adelberger/Lockert (1992) and Adelberger/Lockert (1993). Prof. Dr. Gerd Ronning, Universität Tübingen, to whom the authors wish to express their sincerest thanks for many valuable suggestions and advice on econometric matters, refereed both papers.

$$E(ee') = \text{diag}[\text{Var}(e_1) \ldots \text{Var}(e_p)], \quad \text{with} \quad \text{Var}(e_i) \leq d < \infty \quad \text{for all i.} \qquad (2c)$$

The variable e_i is intended to reflect the reason for the non-systematic, diversifiable risk of security i, whereas the systematic, non-diversifiable risk is attributed to the k factors f_j. The condition (2c) characterizes the so-called exact (or strict) factor model. As already mentioned, the "content" of the systematic factors is not determined within the APT nor is the exact number of factors quantified.

The fundamental result of the "traditional" APT is that there exist coefficients λ_j (j = 0, 1, ..., k) such that the expected return on the majority of capital assets can be expressed as (see Ross 1976 and Huberman 1982):

$$E(r_i) \approx \lambda_0 + \lambda_1 b_{i1} + \ldots + \lambda_k b_{ik}. \qquad (3)$$

This valuation hypothesis is, however, only testable in principle, because the underlying relation

$$\lim_{p \to \infty} \sum_{i=1}^{p} (E(r_i) - \lambda_0 - \lambda_1 b_{i1} - \ldots - \lambda_k b_{ik})^2 \leq V < \infty \qquad (4)$$

represents a mathematical tautology for any large finite set of securities, and only such a set can be used in an empirical test (see Shanken 1982, p. 1132, 1992, p. 1570).

The APT has been modified and extended in various theoretical papers. As has been demonstrated first and foremost by Chamberlain/Rothschild (1983) (see e.g. Stambaugh 1983, Ingersoll 1984, Reisman 1988, 1992), inequality (4) can also be derived by replacing the assumption of an exact factor model with the more general premise of an approximate factor structure which itself permits correlated disturbance terms. The necessary and sufficient condition for the existence of an approximate k-factor structure is that the k largest eigenvalues of the covariance matrix of security returns increase without bound and that the remaining eigenvalues are uniformly bounded from above as p approaches infinity (see Chamberlain/Rothschild 1983, p. 1284). Other APT extensions, as may be subsumed under the so-called "equilibrium-APT" and which in most cases postulate a finite capital market, lead to more precise valuation hypotheses (see e.g. Dybvig 1983, Grinblatt/Titman 1983, Connor 1984). The assumptions from which these hypotheses are derived are, however, significantly more restrictive than the assumptions of the "traditional" APT. The exact APT valuation equation represents a practically testable expression and ought therefore to be chosen as the basis for empirical tests of the validity of the APT (see Dybvig/Ross 1985, p. 1184).

The assumption that the process generating security returns can be described by a linear k-factor model may be regarded as the main common property of the various, otherwise rather diverse, APT models. Several empirical APT studies which are mainly, or even exclusively, intended to determine the "true" number of systematic factors[5] have been reported in the literature (see Kryzanowski/To 1983, Dhrymes/Friend/Gultekin 1984, Diacogiannis 1986, Trzcinka 1986, Ehrhardt 1987, Conway/Reinganum 1988, Chatterjee/Pari 1990, and Connor/Korajczyk 1993). Except for Diacogiannis 1986, Kryzanowski/To 1983 who also use samples of stocks that are traded on the Toronto Stock Exchange, these studies are all based on US stock market data. Additionally, the estimation of the number of factors is in most cases an important step in the design of those APT tests which do not prespecify the systematic factors. Estimates of the number of factors identified in these studies (which often lie in the range of 1 to 10) cannot be discussed in detail here. We provide a brief overview hereafter of the relevant results of the APT research projects which investigate the German stock market. Table 1 indicates that the estimated values for k deviate significantly from each other mainly with respect to criterion/test. This is one reason for recommending that the determination of the number of factors should not be based on a single test or criterion only. Here we identify the factor structure in security returns by resorting to a heuristic procedure and the application of several standard tests.

3. Data and methodology

3.1 Data

The essential properties of the data used in this study and the main results of the empirical examination of different basic assumptions may be summarized as follows:

---

[5] The question of the "true" number of factors is also a focal point of the theoretical work of Brown (1989).

Table 1: Number of factors generating German stock returns: prior empirical research

Investigation	Data	Estimates of the number of factors (k)	Specified value of k
Winkelmann (1984)	1/1971-12/1981 93 stocks monthly returns	scree test: 1 or 3 Kaiser-Dickman test: 21 Bartlett test: 51	$1 \leq k \leq 8$
Peters (1987)	1/1975-3/1985 21 stocks daily returns	Kaiser-Dickman test: 2-5 likelihood ratio test: 5-8	------
Frantzmann (1989)	1/1980-12/1985 20 portfolios of 5 stocks each, daily ret.	likelihood ratio test: 2-7 criterion of Schwarz: (predominantly) 1	k = 1, 2
Müller (1992)	1/1972-12/1985 120 stocks weekly returns	scree test: 2-4; Kaiser-Dickman test: > 10 Bartlett test: > 10 likelihood ratio test: > 10	$2 \leq k \leq 6$
Verleger (1993)	2/1973-1/1991 75 stocks daily, monthly returns	scree test: 5 (monthly ret.: 11); Kaiser-D. test: 10 (16); likelihood ratio test: > 30 (> 30) Akaike criterion: 27 (11); Schwarz crit.: 8 (1)	k = 5, 10
Sauer (1994)	1/1970-12/1989 162-200 stocks weekly returns	likelihood ratio test: > 15 criterion of Schwarz: (predominantly) 1	k = 1, 2, 4, 8

(1) The empirical investigation is based on the returns of 134 domestic common stocks listed on the Frankfurt Stock Exchange. The time series of security returns were obtained from the Deutsche Finanzdatenbank (DFDB).[6] The sample covers the 15-year period from May 1976 to April 1991. The stringent selection of usable stock data was intended to preclude thinly-traded shares.

(2) Whilst the results of change point estimation and/or tests for detecting change points frequently confirm the stationarity assumption, several time series revealed change points which needed special attention. The overall data segmentation resulted in three sub-samples:

I. 5/1976-4/1991, 67 stocks;
II. 1/1982-4/1991, 86 stocks;
III. 1/1988-4/1991, 134 stocks.

Whereas both weekly and monthly returns were computed for sub-samples I and II, the analysis of sub-sample III is restricted to weekly returns because in this case the number of observations facilitating monthly measured returns would have been too small.

(3) The assumption of serial independence (randomness) is satisfied by the majority of the stock return time series and may therefore be maintained as a working hypothesis.

(4) Our tests for departures from normality provide substantial evidence of multivariate non-normality of weekly returns. Monthly rates of return violate the normal distribution assumption markedly less often; however, these rates of return can only be regarded to a limited degree as being normally distributed.

3.2 Eigenvalue size and eigenvalue trace tests

The approximate factor model is the appropriate point of departure for a natural approach to the determination of the unknown number of APT risk factors. This approach has, contrary to alternative methods and tests, a solid theoretical foundation. Its practical implementation is, however, of a heuristic nature. It should be recalled that the approximate k-factor model is principally distinguished from the strict factor model through the substitution of condition (2c) with the condition that exactly k eigenvalues of the population covariance matrix of security returns increase without bound as p tends to infinity, whereas

---

[6] We are grateful to the "Institut für Entscheidungstheorie und Unternehmensforschung" of the Universität Karlsruhe (TH) for the "frictionless" handling of our data requirements.

the remaining eigenvalues are uniformly bounded from above. If the rates of return in question are effectively being generated by an approximate factor model, the number of factors can be estimated from the number of such eigenvalues of the sample covariance matrix of security returns as appear to be unbounded from above.

A so-called nested sequence of sample covariance matrices of standardized stock returns, whose elements are characterized by the property that the ith matrix constitutes the upper left-hand submatrix of the i+1st matrix (see Chamberlain/Rothschild 1983, p. 1285), is constructed for each of the sub-samples. In calculating the first (smallest) matrix in each case, the rates of return of 25 randomly selected stocks are used. The larger matrices result from increasing the number of included stocks (p) successively by about 10 percent, where the additional securities are also randomly chosen. The computation of the last (largest) matrix is always based on the returns of all stocks included in the sub-sample.[7] It is presumed that the sequences of matrices constructed in this way approximate the nested sequence of population covariance matrices to a sufficiently accurate degree. The sequences considered comprise 11 (sub-sample I), 13 (sub-sample II), and 18 $p \times p$ matrices (sub-sample III). The respective eigenvalues are calculated for each of the matrices of these sequences. Information about the number of exploding eigenvalues is provided by two linear regression models (see Trzcinka 1986, pp. 352-353) which need to be estimated for each of the sequences.[8] Initially, for $j = 1, \ldots, 25$ we estimate the regression

$$L_j = a_j + b_j p + u_j \qquad (p = 25, 28, 31, \ldots), \tag{5}$$

where L_j denotes the jth eigenvalue (of the set of eigenvalues of the pertaining $p \times p$ matrix sorted in decreasing order). The estimated slope coefficients of those k eigenvalues which increase without bound (as p tends to infinity) should be positive and significantly different from zero. Secondly, for $k = 1, \ldots, 25$ we estimate the regression

$$T_k = a_k + c_k p + u_k \qquad (p = 25, 28, 31, \ldots), \tag{6}$$

where the dependent variable, T_k, is given by

[7] For instance, the complete sequence for the sub-sample III is p = 25, 28, 31, 34, ..., 108, 119, and 134.

[8] For this purpose the OLS method is always applied; testing the significance of the regression coefficients is done without exception by resort to conventional t-tests.

$$T_k = \sum_{j=1}^{k} \frac{L_j}{p} 100 \ . \tag{7}$$

T_k thus denotes the sum of the first k eigenvalues as a percentage of the trace of the related $p \times p$ matrix. According to Trzcinka (1986), the exploding eigenvalues' percentage of trace should not decrease as the number of stocks increases. From this property it follows that for the "true" number of factors there should not be a negative slope coefficient which differs significantly from zero.

3.3 Standard tests

To determine the unknown number of factors, resort can be made to, among others, the Kaiser-Dickman test, the scree test, and the likelihood ratio test, a test frequently used in empirical APT research. It should be noted that the latter test involves the testing of a sequence of hypotheses in which each is dependent on the rejection of all predecessors. The probability that the number of factors determined by the sequential process is larger than the "true" value cannot exceed the nominal level of significance.[9] However, the multiple level of significance of the sequential procedure is not known (see Kosfeld 1986, p. 140). It therefore seems to be necessary and important to resort also to the sequentially rejective Bonferroni test which was presented by Kosfeld (1986).[10] In the sequentially rejective Bonferroni test the preselected levels of significance, α (k), are not set equal to α for all the tests of the null hypotheses denoted by $H_0(k)$, k = (0,) 1, 2, ..., p-1. Instead they are defined by

$$\alpha(k) = \frac{\alpha}{p-k} \ , \tag{8}$$

where α (now) represents the multiple level of significance of the multiple testing procedure. Additionally two model selection criteria are employed, namely, the Akaike and Schwarz criteria. Their use is especially recommended by Jobson (1988) for samples that are small in terms of time series observations. In view of the problems that have been demonstrated by Shanken (1982) in using transformed securities for the (factor) analysis, the data for the relevant computations are consistently not portfolio rates of return but returns of individual stocks.

---

9 The predetermined level is equal to α in each of the single tests.

10 This multiple test procedure was developed by Holm (1979).

In interpreting the results of these studies the likelihood ratio test requirement of a multivariate normal distribution of the observed variables must first be taken into account. Pronounced departures from normality (which predominate in the present case) cause the testing procedure usually to overstate the correct number of common factors (see e.g. Jöreskog/Sörbom 1982, p. 408). Because the likelihood ratio test differs from the sequentially rejective Bonferroni test only with respect to the chosen level of significance, the latter testing device is also based on the assumption of normally distributed data. Strictly speaking, even the scree test implies the assumption of a normal distribution of the analyzed variables (see Ost 1984, pp. 603-604). Secondly, it should be noted that the likelihood ratio test is strictly only valid in the presence of an exact factor model. This test tends to identify too many factors when asset returns follow an approximate, rather than exact, factor structure (see Connor/Korajczyk 1993, p. 1264).

4. Empirical results

4.1 Eigenvalue size and eigenvalue trace tests

The principal results obtained from regression equations (5) and (6) are reported in this section.

- Irrespective of the sequence (sub-sample) examined, the estimated slope parameters of the regression of L_j on p (i. e., equation (5)) for j = 1, ..., 25 are positive and significantly different from zero even at the 0.1 % level. However, the first eigenvalue in each sequence increases at a distinctly higher rate in relation to p than do the other eigenvalues. Accordingly, $\hat{b}_1$ ranges from 0.3 to 0.4216, whereas estimated values for the slope parameter b_2 all lie between 0.0203 and 0.0441. The coefficient $\hat{b}_2$, on the other hand, is always larger than the estimated value for b_3 , which is greater than the estimated value of b_4 in all sequences. On the other hand, the estimated slope parameters of the other eigenvalues, which, without exception, are smaller than $\hat{b}_4$, do not take on an unambiguous pattern of relative magnitudes. Furthermore, it should be noted that there are only slight differences between some of the $\hat{b}_4$ to $\hat{b}_{25}$ coefficients. In particular the estimated regression lines for eigenvalues L_{10} to L_{25} are generally very close to parallel.
- Irrespective of the sequence (sub-sample) examined, the estimated slope parameters of the regression of T_k on p (i. e., equation (6)) for k = 4, ..., 25 are negative and significantly different from zero even at the 0.1 % level. On

the other hand, the estimates for c_1 and c_2 for both sequences of sub-sample II are positive. Furthermore, $\hat{c}_3$ is always negative, but in both cases not significantly different from zero at the 5 % level. The sequence which is based on the weekly rates of return of sub-sample I also yields a positive estimate of c_1. Although the estimated value of c_1 for the monthly returns of this sequence is negative, it does not, however, differ significantly from zero at the 5 % significance level. Solely in case of the sub-sample III sequence one finds throughout negative slope coefficients which are significantly different from zero at the 1 % level. However, a scrutinizing analysis of the pattern of T_k values leads in this case to the conclusion that the first (largest) eigenvalue's percentage of trace for $p > 31$ remains largely constant. Table 2 displays selected slope parameters of the regressions (6) which are estimated for the underlying sub-samples.

Table 2: Estimated slopes from regression (6) using different nested sequences

	Weekly returns			Monthly returns	
Dependent variable	I. 5/1976-4/1991	II. 1/1982-4/1991	III. 1/1988-4/1991	I. 5/1976-4/1991	II. 1/1982-4/1991
T_1 [a)]	0.0114• [b)]	0.0542	-0.0272***	-0.0036•	0.0232**
T_2	-0.0308**	0.0230**	-0.0493	-0.0627	0.0025•
T_3	-0.0781	-0.0118•	-0.0723	-0.0970	-0.0124•
T_4	-0.1238	-0.0435	-0.0958	-0.1246	-0.0399
T_5	-0.1638	-0.0788	-0.1178	-0.1545	-0.0643
T_{10}	-0.3463	-0.2330	-0.2045	-0.2714	-0.1627
T_{15}	-0.4855	-0.3422	-0.2608	-0.3495	-0.2338
T_{20}	-0.5916	-0.4347	-0.2934	-0.3769	-0.2623
T_{25}	-0.6372	-0.4953	-0.3017	-0.3726	-0.2646

The results of the regressions that have been run resemble in principle the empirical findings obtained by Trzcinka (1986) in a comparable study of the US stock market. Broadly speaking it can be said that the return-generating process may be partly described by a one-factor model. Several results, however, are also compatible with a set of low-dimensional multi-factor models of which a three-factor structure obviously is of the greatest importance.

a) T_k represents the sum of the k largest eigenvalues as a percentage of trace of the $p \times p$ return covariance matrix. The independent variable for the first sub-sample is 25, 28, 31, 34, 37, 41, 45, 50, 55, 61, and 67 while the independent variable for the second (third) sub-sample is 25, ..., 67, 74, and 86 (25, ..., 67, 74, 81, 89, 98, 108, 119, and 134).

b) Nearly all slope estimates are significant at the 0.1 % level (t-test). Values for which this is not true have been marked accordingly (• means not significant at the 5 % level, ** significant at the 5 % level, *** significant at the 1 % level).

4.2 Standard tests

Estimated values for the number of factors which are ascertained from the conventional criteria and tests are reported in Table 3. As this table shows, some estimated values differ markedly with respect to the applied criterion/test and differentiated by underlying sub-sample (as well as by the returns measurement interval). The majority of these tests indicates, however, that a comparatively large number of common factors should be selected. Thus, between 13 and 36 factors should be selected in accordance with the Kaiser-Dickman test, whereas both the likelihood ratio test and the sequentially rejective Bonferroni test point to factor numbers lying between 12 and 19 and 9 and 15, respectively, at the 5 % level. In accordance with the Akaike criterion 7 to 15 factors are required. A small number of factors results only from the scree test or from the application of the Schwarz criterion. Unlike the other criteria and tests, the scree test does not yield a unique estimated value for any of the sub-samples. Whilst there always exists a pronounced scree cut-off point after the first eigenvalue, a second scree cut-off point can be identified for all sub-samples (frequently after the third eigenvalue).[11] It is also apparent that in applying the likelihood ratio test to the monthly returns of sub-sample II in particular, a rather lower number of factors is estimated than in the case of the weekly returns of those securities. In that, as already mentioned, the likelihood ratio test tends to overstate the appropriate

[11] Cattell (1966, p. 267) conjectures that "double screes" (or "split-scree cases", respectively) carry a rather high probability of occurence: ".., the single scree line may well turn out to be the exception."

number of factors when there are marked departures from the normal distribution, these findings can be partially explained by the fact that the normal distribution assumption is violated considerably less frequently in respect of the monthly returns of sub-sample II than in the case of weekly returns for this sub-sample.

In some of the APT studies (see, e. g., Dhrymes/Friend/Gultekin/Gultekin 1985a,b, Cho/Taylor 1987) it became apparent that the estimated value for k via the likelihood ratio test depends positively on the sample size which, in the given context, is equal to the number of time points at which the rates of return are being observed. As the time period of sub-sample II is completely contained within that of sub-sample I, and because the time period of sub-sample II also contains that of sub-sample III, it can be concluded that the present data are fundamentally suitable for the analysis in question.[12] However, the potential influence of the different numbers of stocks on the factor number estimates has yet to be excluded. To this end, the constituent stocks of sub-samples II and III are reduced to those 67 stocks constituting sub-sample I. Thus, as the sub-samples have equal returns measurement intervals, they differ only in respect of the length of the time period. It can be concluded that the factor numbers that are estimated by means of the likelihood ratio test depend positively on the number of time series observations in the data base adopted. For example, at the 5 % significance level, 16 factors are to be extracted for the weekly returns of sub-sample I (769 observations), whereas the estimated numbers of factors for sub-sample II (479 weekly rates of return) and sub-sample III (169 weekly rates of return) amount to only 14 and 10, respectively. The estimated number of factors also depends positively on the number of time series observations when it is determined by means of the sequentially rejective Bonferroni test. On the other hand, the estimated numbers of factors which are obtained from the other criteria and tests seem to be largely independent of the number of time series observations.

To conclude this section, it is questioned whether the number of factors estimated by standard criteria and tests depends on the number of stocks. For this purpose one can refer to the already constructed sequences of sample covariance matrices which are properly characterized by the fact that the stocks, which are the elements for the calculation of the ith matrix, are also a subset of those stocks which are used for the computation of the i+1st matrix. For illustrative purposes the sequence of sub-sample III is considered in detail. Table 4 shows the number of factor estimates which are yielded by the selected conventional criteria and tests for the corresponding matrices. The number of factors which result from the application of the scree test and the Schwarz criterion seems to be independent of

---

12 Possibly the dependence to be tested is already manifest in the above mentioned impact of the returns measurement interval on the number of factors determined by the likelihood ratio test.

the number of stocks analyzed. For the remaining criteria and tests, however, a positive dependence of the estimated number of factors on the number of stocks can be reported. Accordingly, the number of factors determined via the Kaiser-Dickman test rises monotonically with the number of stocks.[13] Also the estimated values for k which result from the likelihood ratio test, the sequentially rejective Bonferroni test and from the criterion of Akaike increase with the number of stocks being factor-analyzed. For example, applying the likelihood ratio test to a group of 25 stocks, merely 3 factors are extracted at the 5 % level of significance, whereas in the case of a 119 stocks sub-set even the hypothesis that 11 factors are sufficient should be rejected at the 5 % significance level. Similar findings have been reported for the US stock market in particular.[14] For example, Dhrymes/Friend/Gultekin (1984) who used the likelihood ratio test and chose the 5 % level report three factors for a group of 30 stocks, whereas when dealing with a group which contained 90 stocks they discovered 9 factors. The comparable pairs of values (number of stocks, number of factors) for sub-sample III are (31, 4) and (89, 9).

5. Summary and conclusions

The findings of the present study on the determination of the number of APT risk factors for the German stock market may be summarized as follows:

(1) The analysis of the behaviour of the sample eigenvalues of the return covariance matrix, which is based on the assumption of an approximate factor structure, partly indicates that the returns on the securities in question are generated by a one-factor model. However, at least for some of the sub-samples, results are obtained which suggest that the return-generating process may be adequately characterized by specific multi-factor models of a low order (in particular by a three-factor model).

(2) Virtually the same may be said about the number of factors resulting from the application of the scree test and of the Schwarz criterion, respectively. However, other standard criteria and tests indicate uniformly that a relative large number of factors is needed. Estimated values for k often differ quite considerably relative to the applied criterion or test. Moreover, differences in the results as between the individual sub-samples are comparatively pronounced.

---

[13] With respect to the Kaiser-Dickman test Cattell (1966, p. 248) notes that it stops factoring too late for large values of p.

[14] Raveh (1985) points out that positive dependencies of the estimated number of factors on the number of variables under study have also been found in applying factor analysis in social science and predominantly psychological investigations.

Table 3: Number of factors for different sub-samples: standard tests

Sub-sample	Kaiser-Dick-man test	Scree test	Likelihood ratio test α = 0.01	Likelihood ratio test α = 0.05	Sequent. rejective Bonferroni-test α = 0.01	Sequent. rejective Bonferroni-test α = 0.05	Criteri-on of Akaike	Criterion of Schwarz
weekly returns								
I. 5/1976-4/1991 (p = 67)	13	1 (or 5)	16	16	14	15	15	5
II. 1/1982-4/1991 (p = 86)	17	1 (or 4)	16	17	14	15	13	5
III. 1/1988-4/1991 (p = 134)	36	1 (or 3)	17	19	14	15	7	1
monthly returns								
I. 5/1976-4/1991 (p = 67)	13	1 (or 3)	14	15	12	13	8	5
II. 1/1982-4/1991 (p = 86)	18	1 (or 3)	11	12	9	9	8	2

(3) In particular the number of factors detected by the likelihood ratio test seems to depend positively both on the number of time series observations and on the group size of the stocks subjected to factor analysis. These relations are partially observable in several reported APT studies which utilize US stock market data.

Table 4: Number of factors and number of stocks: standard tests (1/1988-4/1991, weekly returns, nested sequence)

Group size	Kaiser-Dick-man test	Scree test	Likelihood-ratio test α = 0.01	Likelihood-ratio test α = 0.05	Sequent. rejective Bonferroni-test α = 0.01	Sequent. rejective Bonferroni-test α = 0.05	Criterion of Akaike	Criterion of Schwarz
p = 25	6	1 (or 4)	3	3	2	2	3	2
p = 28	7	1 (or 4)	3	4	2	3	3	2
p = 31	8	1 (or 3)	4	4	3	3	3	2
p = 34	8	1 (or 3)	4	4	3	3	3	2
p = 37	9	1 (or 5)	5	6	3	4	3	2
p = 41	10	1 (or 3)	5	6	4	4	4	1
p = 45	12	1 (or 2)	5	6	3	4	4	1
p = 50	14	1 (or 2)	5	6	3	4	4	1
p = 55	15	1 (or 3)	6	7	4	5	4	1
p = 61	16	1 (or 3)	6	6	4	5	5	1
p = 67	19	1 (or 3)	7	8	6	6	6	1
p = 74	21	1 (or 3)	6	7	5	6	6	1
p = 81	22	1 (or 3)	8	9	6	7	6	1
p = 89	24	1 (or 3)	8	9	6	6	5	1
p = 98	26	1 (or 3)	8	9	7	7	6	1
p = 108	29	1 (or 4)	8	9	7	7	7	1
p = 119	33	1 (or 3)	10	12	8	9	6	1
p = 134	36	1 (or 3)	17	19	14	15	7	1

In view of the results obtained in this study, which are clearly dependent on the methods of analysis employed, a convincing unambiguous statement about the number of systematic factors generating German stock returns cannot be made. Especially because of the frequent absence of the normal distribution attribute of the stock returns in question, it can be presumed that several of the conventional criteria and tests will tend to fit too many factors so that the specification of the return-generating process will mainly reflect the outcome of the eigenvalue analysis of the given problem. However, the findings of our studies involving standard criteria and tests should be taken as evidence that the extraction of only one factor is entirely inadequate. Furthermore, it has to be emphasized that the APT starts from a unique, and therefore also sample-independent, number of systematic factors. Hence, differently specifying the number of factors by reference to different sub-samples of the totality of available data is an approach that must be rejected.

By and large it seems appropriate to use 3 factors in our tests of the APT. In addition a five-factor model was estimated for each of all the sub-samples. This factor structure is supported by some of the results that are reported in part 4. Furthermore, in addition to its specific function in the present study, a five-factor model can be regarded as the "standard specification" of the return-generating process because of its frequent utilization in empirical APT research.[15] To conclude the evaluation of our findings, we refer to the time series fit of the estimated factor models by reporting the proportion of the total variation explained by the systematic factors in cases in which the maximum likelihood method is applied. Whereas we can explain about half of the total variance of monthly stock returns with three- and five-factor structures, the explanatory power rates between 35 and about 40 percent for weekly rates of return.

References

Adelberger, O. L. and Lockert, G. (1992): Überprüfung der Gültigkeit der Arbitrage Pricing Theory: Grundlagen und erste empirische Ergebnisse, Working Paper, Fachgebiet Finanzwirtschaft, University of Essen.

Adelberger, O. L. and Lockert, G. (1993): Empirische Ergebnisse zur Anzahl und Bewertung der APT-Risikofaktoren am deutschen Aktienmarkt. Working Paper, Fachgebiet Finanzwirtschaft, University of Essen.

---

[15] Similar arguments are found in Dhrymes/Friend/Gultekin/Gultekin (1985a, p. 78). A five-factor model is applied, e. g., in the APT studies by Roll/Ross (1980), Chen (1983), and Dhrymes/Friend/Gultekin/Gultekin (1985a), using it as the one and only specification of the return-generating process. Besides these, also Reinganum (1981), Brown/Weinstein (1983), Lehmann/Modest (1988), Robin/Shukla (1991), and Müller (1992), among others, partly base their APT tests on a five-factor version.

Bansal, R. and Viswanathan, S. (1993): No Arbitrage and Arbitrage Pricing: A New Approach, in: Journal of Finance 48, 1231-1262.

Banz, R. W. (1981): The Relationship between Return and Market Value of Common Stocks, in: Journal of Financial Economics 9, 3-18.

Brown, S. J. (1989): The Number of Factors in Security Returns, in: Journal of Finance 44, 1247-1262.

Brown, S. J. and Weinstein, M. I. (1983): A New Approach to Testing Asset Pricing Models: The Bilinear Paradigm, in: Journal of Finance 38, 711-743.

Burmeister, E. and McElroy, M. B. (1988): Joint Estimation of Factor Sensitivities and Risk Premia for the Arbitrage Pricing Theory, in: Journal of Finance 43, 721-733.

Cattell, R. B. (1966): The Scree Test for the Number of Factors, in: Multivariate Behavioral Research 1, 245-276.

Chamberlain, G. and Rothschild, M. (1983): Arbitrage, Factor Structure, and Mean-Variance Analysis on Large Asset Markets, in: Econometrica 51, 1281-1304.

Chan, K. C., Chen, N.-f., and Hsieh, D. A. (1985): An Exploratory Investigation of the Firm Size Effect, in: Journal of Financial Economics 14, 451-471.

Chatterjee, S. and Pari, R. A. (1990): Bootstrapping the Number of Factors in the Arbitrage Pricing Theory, in: Journal of Financial Research 13, 15-21.

Chen, N.-f. (1983): Some Empirical Tests of the Theory of Arbitrage Pricing, in: Journal of Finance 38, 1193-1414.

Chen, N.-f., Roll, R., and Ross, S. A. (1986): Economic Forces and the Stock Market, in: Journal of Business 59, 383-403.

Cho, D. C. (1984): On Testing the Arbitrage Pricing Theory: Inter-Battery Factor Analysis, in: Journal of Finance 39, 1485-1502.

Cho, D. C. and Taylor, W. M. (1987): The Seasonal Stability of the Factor Structure of Stock Returns, in: Journal of Finance 42, 1195-1211.

Connor, G. (1984): A Unified Beta Pricing Theory, in: Journal of Economic Theory 34, 13-31.

Connor, G. and Korajczyk, R. A. (1993): A Test for the Number of Factors in an Approximate Factor Model, in: Journal of Finance 48, 1263-1291.

Conway, D. A. and Reinganum, M. R. (1988): Stable Factors in Security Returns: Identification Using Cross-Validation, in: Journal of Business and Economic Statistics 6, 1-15.

Dhrymes, P. J., Friend, I., and Gultekin, N. B. (1984): A Critical Reexamination of the Empirical Evidence on the Arbitrage Pricing Theory, in: Journal of Finance 39, 323-346.

Dhrymes, P. J., Friend, I., Gultekin, N. B., and Gultekin, M. N. (1985a): An Empirical Examination of the Implications of Arbitrage Pricing Theory, in: Journal of Banking and Finance 9, 73-99.

Dhrymes, P. J., Friend, I., Gultekin, M. N., and Gultekin, N. B. (1985b): New Tests of the APT and Their Implications, in: Journal of Finance 40, 659-674.

Diacogiannis, G. P. (1986): Arbitrage Pricing Model: A Critical Examination of Its Empirical Applicability for the London Stock Exchange, in: Journal of Business Finance and Accounting 13, 489-504.

Dybvig, P. H. (1983): An Explicit Bound on Individual Assets' Deviations from APT Pricing in a Finite Economy, in: Journal of Financial Economics 12, 483-496.

Dybvig, P. H. and Ross, S. A. (1985): Yes, the APT is Testable, in: Journal of Finance 40, 1173-1188.

Ehrhardt, M. C. (1987): Arbitrage Pricing Models: The Sufficient Number of Factors and Equilibrium Conditions, in: Journal of Financial Research 10, 111-120.

Fama, E. F. and French, K. R. (1992): The Cross-Section of Expected Stock Returns, in: Journal of Finance 47, 427-465.

Franke, G. (1984): On Tests of the Arbitrage Pricing Theory, in: OR Spektrum 6, 109-117.

Frantzmann, H.-J. (1989): Saisonalitäten und Bewertung am deutschen Aktien- und Rentenmarkt. Frankfurt/Main (Fritz Knapp).

Grinblatt, M. and Titman, S. (1983): Factor Pricing in a Finite Economy, in: Journal of Financial Economics 12, 497-507.

Gultekin, M. N. and Gultekin, N. B. (1987): Stock Return Anomalies and the Tests of the APT, in: Journal of Finance 42, 1213-1224.

Holm, S. (1979): A Simple Sequentially Rejective Multiple Test Procedure, in: Scandinavian Journal of Statistics 6, 65-70.

Huberman, G. (1982): A Simple Approach to Arbitrage Pricing Theory, in: Journal of Economic Theory 28, 183-191.

Ingersoll, J. E., Jr. (1984): Some Results in the Theory of Arbitrage Pricing, in: Journal of Finance 39, 1021-1039.

Jobson, J. D. (1988): Comment, in: Journal of Business and Economic Statistics 6, 16-20.

Jöreskog, K. G. and Sörbom, D. (1982): Recent Developments in Structural Equation Modeling, in: Journal of Marketing Research 19, 404-416.

Kosfeld, R. (1986): Theoretische und numerische Aspekte in der Maximum-Likelihood-Faktorenanalyse. Frankfurt/Main-New York (Campus).

Kryzanowski, L. and To, M. C. (1983): General Factor Models and the Structure of Security Returns, in: Journal of Financial and Quantitative Analysis 18, 31-52.

Lehmann, B. N. and Modest, D. M. (1988): The Empirical Foundations of the Arbitrage Pricing Theory, in: Journal of Financial Economics 21, 213-254.

Lintner, J. (1965): The Valuation of Risk Assets and the Selection of Risky Investments in Stock Portfolios and Capital Budgets, in: Review of Economics and Statistics 47, 13-37.

McElroy, M. B. and Burmeister, E. (1988): Arbitrage Pricing Theory as a Restricted Nonlinear Multivariate Regression Model: Iterated Nonlinear Seemingly Unrelated Regression Estimates, in: Journal of Business and Economic Statistics 6, 29-42.

Möller, H. P. (1986): Bilanzkennzahlen und Ertragsrisiken des Kapitalmarktes: Eine empirische Untersuchung des Ertragsrisiko-Informationsgehaltes von Bilanzkennzahlen deutscher Aktiengesellschaften. Stuttgart (C. E. Poeschel).

Mossin, J. (1966): Equilibrium in a Capital Asset Market, in: Econometrica 34, 768-783.

Müller, W. (1992): Bilanzinformation und Aktienbewertung: Eine theoretische und empirische Überprüfung der Entscheidungsrelevanz von Jahresabschlußinformationen für die Preisbildung deutscher Aktien. Frankfurt/Main (Fritz Knapp).

Nowak, T. (1994): Faktormodelle in der Kapitalmarkttheorie. Köln (Botermann & Botermann).

Ost, F. (1984): Faktorenanalyse, in: Fahrmeir, L. and A. Hamerle (eds.): Multivariate statistische Verfahren. Berlin-New York (Walter de Gruyter), 575-662.

Peters, H.-W. (1987): Kapitalmarkttheorie und Aktienmarktanalyse. Frankfurt/Main-Bern-New York-Paris (Peter Lang).

Raveh, A. (1985): A Note on Factor Analysis and Arbitrage Pricing Theory, in: Journal of Banking and Finance 9, 317-321.

Reinganum, M. R. (1981): The Arbitrage Pricing Theory: Some Empirical Results, in: Journal of Finance 36, 313-321.

Reisman, H. (1988): A General Approach to the Arbitrage Pricing Theory (APT), in: Econometrica 56, 473-476.

Reisman, H. (1992): Reference Variables, Factor Structure, and the Approximate Multibeta Representation, in: Journal of Finance 47, 1303-1314.

Robin, A. and Shukla, R. (1991): The Magnitude of Pricing Errors in the Arbitrage Pricing Theory, in: Journal of Financial Research 14, 65-82.

Roll, R. (1977): A Critique of the Asset Pricing Theory's Tests: Part I: On Past and Potential Testability of the Theory, in: Journal of Financial Economics 4, 129-176.

Roll, R. and Ross, S. A. (1980): An Empirical Investigation of the Arbitrage Pricing Theory, in: The Journal of Finance 35, 1073-1103.

Ross, S. A. (1976): The Arbitrage Theory of Capital Asset Pricing, in: Journal of Economic Theory 13, 341-360.

Ross, S. A. (1977): Return, Risk, and Arbitrage, in: Friend, I. and J. L. Bicksler (eds.): Risk and Return in Finance, Vol. 1. Cambridge/Mass. (Ballinger), 189-218.

Sauer, A. (1994): Faktormodelle und Bewertung am deutschen Aktienmarkt. Frankfurt/Main (Fritz Knapp).

Shanken, J. (1982): The Arbitrage Pricing Theory: Is It Testable?, in: Journal of Finance 37, 1129-1140.

Shanken, J. (1992): The Current State of the Arbitrage Pricing Theory, in: Journal of Finance 47, 1569-1574.

Sharpe, W. F. (1964): Capital Asset Prices: A Theory of Market Equilibrium under Conditions of Risk, in: Journal of Finance 19, 425-442.

Shukla, R. and Trzcinka, C. (1990): Sequential Tests of the Arbitrage Pricing Theory: A Comparison of Principal Components and Maximum Likelihood Factors, in: Journal of Finance 45, 1541-1564.

Stambaugh, R. F. (1983): Arbitrage Pricing with Information, in: Journal of Financial Economics 12, 357-369.

Trzcinka, C. (1986): On the Number of Factors in the Arbitrage Pricing Model, in: Journal of Finance 41, 347-368.

Verleger, A. (1993): Risikostrukturen am deutschen Aktienmarkt. Münster-Hamburg (Lit-Verlag).

Warfsmann, J. (1993): Das Capital Asset Pricing Model in Deutschland: Univariate und multivariate Tests für den Kapitalmarkt. Wiesbaden (Deutscher Universitäts-Verlag).

Wei, K. C. J. (1988): An Asset-Pricing Theory Unifying the CAPM and APT, in: Journal of Finance 43, 881-892.

Winkelmann, M. (1984): Aktienbewertung in Deutschland. Königstein/Ts. (Anton Hain).

The German Equity Market: Risk, Return, and Liquidity

Hermann Göppl, Torsten Lüdecke, Christian Schlag and Heinrich Schütz
University of Karlsruhe

1. Introduction

Within the international research community knowledge about German capital markets is not widespread. This may be due to the absence of a central data base and the fact that empirical results in German journals cannot be easily accessed by the English speaking majority. However, data bases on stocks, bonds, warrants and all derivative products of the German options and futures exchange are now available to researchers.

In this article we provide some more general characteristics of the German stock market. Following a description of the stock data base and market organization, we focus on the liquidity of the German stock market, the risk-return relationship and the pricing anomalies.

2. The German stock market

There are eight stock exchanges in Germany with the Frankfurt Stock Exchange (FSE) as the largest, representing approximately 75 percent of the national total trading volume. The second largest is Dusseldorf with a share of 10 percent, thus leaving only a small percentage to the other stock markets which, ordered by volume, are Munich, Hamburg, Stuttgart, Berlin, Hanover and Bremen. The 40 most liquid stocks are also traded on the Integriertes Börsenhandels- und Informationssystem (IBIS), which was finally introduced in April 1991. IBIS is part of the FSE and accounts for about 30 percent of the total trading volume in these stocks.

The market capitalization of domestic companies in Germany was DM 728,74 billions at the end of 1994 (Deutsche Börse AG 1994). At the same time, 417[1]

---

[1] Because different types of shares can be issued simultaneously the number of shares always exceeds the number of companies

domestic and 344 foreign companies were listed in Frankfurt. Despite the number of foreign listings, the volume of trading in foreign stocks accounts for only 2 percent of total volume.

Stock option trading is concentrated at the electronic exchange, the Deutsche Terminbörse (DTB) in Frankfurt. Currently the DTB offers 20 stock options, and options, futures and futures options on the Deutscher Aktienindex (DAX), a performance index of 30 stocks. Besides the DTB there is also a dying options segment at the FSE.

The FSE has 238 member firms: 68 domestic and 69 foreign banks, 41 Kursmakler and 60 Freimakler. Participation in IBIS is either possible exclusively or in connection with membership of one of the floor exchanges. Currently 12 Freimakler are exclusively admitted for trading on IBIS. Trading hours on the floor-based exchanges are from 10:30 to 13:30. Trading hours on IBIS are from 8:00 to 17:00, which matches the trading hours at the DTB. Off-exchange trading among banks and institutional investors is possible at any time between 8:00 and 17:00. Direct trades and exchange trades are immediately entered into the host of the Deutsche Wertpapier-Datenzentrale (DWZ) for settlement purposes.

There are three market segments, the Amtlicher Handel, Geregelter Markt and Freiverkehr. The first segment is subdivided into the continuous market and the periodic market. The determination of prices is based on auction principles. The segments differ in terms of listing requirements and legal oversight. The major stocks are listed in the Amtlicher Handel and trade continuously.

3. Data

The data for the empirical research are drawn from the Deutsche Finanzdatenbank (DFDB). The DFDB contains daily data for all German stocks, warrants and options traded at the Frankfurt Stock Exchange (FSE). Price and volume data for stocks and warrants are available from 1974. Daily stock prices are also accessible for the period from 1960 to 1973 for a sample of 100 stocks. Prices for the remaining stocks exist on an end-of-month basis. In addition to the price data, the DFDB contains the data necessary for adjusting prices in respect of dividends, capital alterations and stock splits. Daily prices from the floor-based options market at the FSE exist since April 1983. Furthermore, several indexes for the German stock market are available, among them is the Deutsche Aktien-Forschungsindex (DAFOX), which was especially constructed for research purposes (Göppl/Schütz 1993). A detailed description of the DFDB is given in Bühler/Göppl/Möller (1993).

Beyond the DFDB data the University of Karlsruhe has several other datasets available. These cover daily prices and volumes for all stocks and warrants traded on one of the seven regional exchanges, daily bid prices of investment funds, and daily price and volume data for a sample of bonds issued by the Bund, Bahn, Post or Treuhand.[2] All data series commence in 1974, except for the volume data of the regional exchanges, which start in April 1990. Transaction data comprising time-stamped prices and volume from IBIS and DTB were recently added to the database. Data from the DTB are available for all derivative products for the period since trading began.

All data are derived from official German capital market sources. Price and volume data are provided by the Deutsche Wertpapier-Datenzentrale (DWZ) and the Deutsche Terminbörse (DTB). Since January 1990 and January 1994, respectively, both the DWZ and DTB have been under the roof of the Deutsche Börse AG. Information necessary for price adjustments is provided by Wertpapier-Mitteilungen (WM).

4. Stock market liquidity

To investigate the liquidity of the German stock market we use a sample of 508 common and preferred stocks traded at the FSE in the period from January, 2, 1987 to December 30, 1994. To be qualified for inclusion in the analysis by year a stock must be traded for at least 220 days in the particular year.

The literature is replete with alternative measures of liquidity which is an elusive concept (Bernstein 1987). Here we use the daily number of shares traded as a proxy for liquidity. The analysis is done by year and by market segment. The tendency of trading to concentrate on certain stocks is also examined by reference to three samples of stocks, namely the DTB, DAX and DAX100 samples. The DTB sample contains 15 stocks (16 stocks in 1994) admitted for options trading at the DTB; the DAX sample contains 30 and the DAX100 sample comprises 100 stocks. All stocks in the samples trade in the first segment, the Amtlicher Handel.

First, we compute the total number of shares traded annually in the sampling period. To show how total trading volume is distributed across market segments and samples, the corresponding volumes are expressed as a percentage of total volume in a particular year. Second, liquidity in each year is analyzed on a daily basis.

---

[2] The maturities of these bonds, which are guaranteed by the Federal Government, range from 5 to 30 years.

Descriptive statistics for liquidity measured on a yearly basis are shown in Table 1. From 1987 to 1994, the number of shares traded increased by more than 300 percent, while the number of stocks increased by approximately 35 percent. With the exeception of 1991, there was a strong growth of stock trading in every year. The largest jump, about 56 percent, was in 1989, which was partly driven by the German reunification (Grisvold 1995).

Stock market liquidity is heavily concentrated in the first segment (Amtlicher Handel) and within this segment in the continuous market, while the periodic market only captures a very low percentage of the total trading volume. Continuous trading in the first segment is about 97 percent of overall trading, leaving only a small percentage to the periodic markets in the first, second and third segments.

Periodic trading has generally lost ground to the continuous market since 1990. Within the periodic markets the second tier has regained some of its attraction in recent years. In particular in 1994, its share outgrew the periodic market in the first segment. The market shares of the three samples given in Table 1 provide some insight into these developments. As can be seen, trading is heavily concentrated in the upper 16 (DTB-sample) and 30 (DAX-sample) stocks. The stocks not included in the DAX100 sample account on average for less than 10 percent of the total trading volume. However, the numbers are not stable over time. During the hausse period from 1988 to 1990 the traded volume of smaller stocks, as indicated by the ΔDAX100 and residual market shares, tended to increase. In later years this trend was reversed and the residual market share in particular decreased substantially.

This may be due to the opening of the DTB in the spring of 1990, which is reflected in the growing market share of the DTB- and DAX-samples. In the last two years there was a slight recovery in the trading volumes of stocks outside the DAX-sample.

In Table 2, trading volume is ordered by the daily number of shares traded in every year of the sampling period. The numbers confirm a strong concentration of trades (i.e. liquidity) in the last decile. Over time the liquidity of this group of stocks nearly tripled. The relative improvement in other quantiles is remarkable, too, but low in absolute terms.

Table 1: Number of shares traded by year and market segment

	1987	1988	1989	1990	1991	1992	1993	1994
Total[a]	810.48	991.81	1546.34	1983.45	1858.97	2055.86	2761.92	2662.41
	(344)	(360)	(372)	(401)	(428)	(445)	(451)	(465)
Percentage of yearly volume by market segment[b]								
1.1	96.97	96.97	95.39	98.07	98.77	98.79	98.80	98.10
	(129)	(138)	(144)	(153)	(160)	(165)	(168)	(174)
1.2	2.56	2.25	3.85	1.22	0.71	0.70	0.64	0.61
	(121)	(125)	(126)	(138)	(146)	(145)	(145)	(146)
2	0.33	0.37	0.46	0.39	0.35	0.39	0.47	1.15
	(27)	(33)	(40)	(44)	(55)	(68)	(73)	(78)
3	0.21	0.36	0.30	0.33	0.17	0.13	0.10	0.14
	(67)	(64)	(62)	(66)	(67)	(67)	(65)	(67)
Percentage of yearly volume by index samples[c]								
DTB	62.92	60.72	55.16	65.60	68.12	71.74	67.91	65.13
ΔDAX	15.85	14.19	15.73	14.05	15.13	14.25	15.37	15.75
ΔDAX100	14.00	14.27	16.19	12.74	11.51	9.06	10.32	11.21
Residual	7.23	10.82	12.92	7.61	5.24	5.05	6.40	7.91

[a]Number of shares × 1.000.000.

[b]The number of stocks qualifying for the sample in the respective year is given in parentheses. The numbers on the left refer to the market segments: 1.1 denotes the Amtlicher Handel/continuous trading, 1.2 denotes the Amtlicher Handel/periodic trading, 2 denotes the Geregelter Markt, and 3 denotes the Freiverkehr.

[c]ΔDAX is the share of the DAX sample minus the percentage of the DTB sample. ΔDAX100 is the share of the DAX100 sample minus the percentage of the DAX sample. The residual share is 100-DTB-ΔDAX-ΔDAX100.

5. The relationship between risk and return

This section contains an analysis of the risk and return behaviour of the German stocks using the Deutsche Aktien-Forschungsindex DAFOX (German Stock Price Research Index). The DAFOX is a capital-weighted performance index comprising all German stocks which are traded in the Amtlicher Handel on the FSE. It is important to emphasize that, in contrast to many indices, the DAFOX is a total return index, including dividends and the proceeds of rights issues. German investors receive a 30 percent tax credit with their dividends (before 1994: 36 percent), which is deductible from personal income tax. This tax credit is (also in the case of the DAX) not included in the index, which therefore allows for a 30 percent personal tax rate.

Table 2: Daily average number of shares traded by decile and year

Decile	1987	1988	1989	1990	1991	1992	1993	1994
1	2	2	12	4	3	2	3	2
2	10	9	48	24	14	16	18	19
3	24	28	113	66	49	54	72	69
4	71	96	263	180	152	138	244	236
5	209	277	620	468	338	302	491	457
6	555	713	1331	1082	650	619	938	805
7	1366	1374	2847	2092	1465	1422	1970	1854
8	3627	3389	5874	4403	3092	3356	5103	4508
9	10272	10325	16936	14075	9316	8116	13392	13404
10	78850	94014	139374	173585	159403	168352	221322	207932

5.1 Risk and return

The overall risk-return relation in the German market is described by the DAFOX and further analyzed by two subindices, the DAFOX-BC and the DAFOX-SC[3]. Descriptive statistics are given in Table 3. Annual returns are computed from continuously compounded monthly returns and expressed in percent. The sampling period (1/1974 - 12/1994) is divided into three subperiods (1974 - 1980, 1981 - 1987, 1988 - 1994). Table 3 shows that blue chips earned the highest return over the whole period, whereas small caps earned 0.83 percent less. The blue chips were also more profitable than the small caps in the second and the third subperiods. Only in the years 1974 to 1980 were the small caps able slightly to outperform the market as a whole.

Mean returns are lower in the first and higher in the second and third subperiod than on average. The same applies to the volatilities: They are above average in the second and third subperiods and lower in the first subperiod. Overall, mean returns move in the same direction as volatilities. A closer look at the numbers reveals that this return-volatility-relationship does not hold in the first subperiod. The mean return of the small-cap-index is slightly greater and its volatility smaller than the corresponding values.

---

[3] The DAFOX-BC (*Blue Chips*) and the DAFOX-SC (*Small Caps*) are subsamples of the DAFOX. The DAFOX-BC consists of all German stocks traded in the *continuous* market of the Amtlicher Handel at the FSE and the DAFOX-SC includes only stocks traded in the *periodic* market of the first segment. Both subsamples are treated as separate indices. The DAFOX is a non-linear combination of the subindices, since variations in and between the subsamples occur even within one year.

Table 3: Statistics of DAFOX-indices for the whole sample period and three subperiods

Index	Mean	Volatility[a]	Skewness	Kurtosis
		January 1974 to December 1994		
DAFOX	9.65	16.49	-0.91	4.20
DAFOX-BC	9.81	17.15	-0.84	3.74
DAFOX-SC	8.98	15.36	-0.77	4.67
		January 1974 to December 1980		
DAFOX	6.72	11.73	0.06	0.63
DAFOX-BC	6.85	12.48	0.07	0.58
DAFOX-SC	6.83	11.10	0.38	0.97
		January 1981 to December 1987		
DAFOX	11.85	19.55	-1.16	4.54
DAFOX-BC	12.06	20.02	-1.07	4.01
DAFOX-SC	10.91	19.30	-1.20	4.86
		January 1988 to December 1994		
DAFOX	10.31	17.35	-0.88	2.79
DAFOX-BC	10.53	18.23	-0.87	2.83
DAFOX-SC	9.19	14.74	-0.28	1.44

[a]Volatility is calculated by multiplying the standard deviation of monthly returns by the square root of 12.

Over the whole period, the distributions of the three index returns are not symmetric but skewed to the left. The kurtosis values imply fat-tailed return distributions. The periodic differences in these statistics indicate that the distributions are unstable over time.

5.2 Risk premia

Risk premia are calculated as the mean excess return on the stock market, i.e. as the mean difference between market returns and the riskless interest rate. The DAFOX-returns serve as different proxies for the market returns and Frankfurt interbank rates are identified as riskless rates. The annualized risk premia are then calculated from the monthly differences as mentioned before. Table 4 exhibits their means and standard deviations (in parentheses) for the different periods.

Table 4: Risk premia of the DAFOX-indices for the whole sample period and three subperiods

Index	1/74 - 12/94	1/74-12/80	1/81-12/87	1/88-12/94
DAFOX	3.33 (16.52)	1.06 (11.78)	5.58 (19.54)	3.36 (17.42)
DAFOX-BC	3.52 (17.18)	1.19 (12.53)	5.79 (20.01)	3.58 (18.30)
DAFOX-SC	2.68 (15.39)	1.17 (11.15)	4.64 (19.30)	2.24 (14.81)

Over the whole period risk premia are positive for the DAFOX and both subindices. Blue chips earned a risk premium which was 0.19 higher than that of the DAFOX and 0.84 higher than the small cap-premium. Small caps had a premium 0.65 below the DAFOX. As also indicated by Table 3, higher volatilities (as risk proxies) earn higher risk premia, again with the exception of the DAFOX-SC in the first period.

Figure 1 reveals high variations in risk premia over time. Ten out of twenty-one years exhibit negative premia. Hence, the positive risk premia in all subperiods are partially due to the choice of the sampling subperiods. A different subdivision of the sampling period could also produce subperiods with negative risk premia.

As already observed, investors in German equities always receive (on average) a premium for risk. Attempts to explain this risk premium by reference to the CAPM or to the APT provided at best mixed results. Whereas Winkelmann (1984) rejects the validity of the CAPM, Frantzmann (1989) finds a significant positive relation between mean returns and market (beta) risk. But as in Müller (1992), this result holds only in bull markets. Idiosyncratic risk is also compensated but does not increase the explanatory power of the cross-sectional regression.

Table 5 shows the mean annual returns and betas of 12 industry groups for the period 1974 to 1994. The industry groups correspond to the classification of the Statistische Bundesamt and the DAFOX is used as a market index. The cross-sectional regression yields $\gamma_0 = 4.63$ percent and $\gamma_1 = 4.48$ percent with $R^2 = 0.16$.

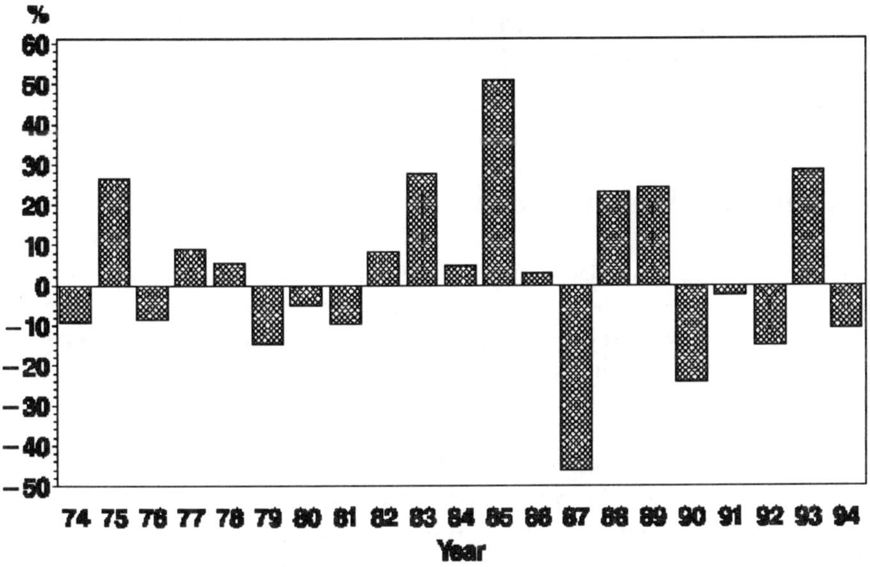

Figure 1: Risk premia of the DAFOX

Tests of the APT by Frantzmann and Müller give results similar to those of the CAPM tests. Whereas bull markets appear to be characterized by significant risk premia, the null hypothesis of zero risk premia cannot be rejected in the case of bear markets. Sauer (1994) does not find significant premia for systematic risk, so that no exact factor valuation model exists.

Table 5: Mean annnual returns and betas of industry groups

Industry	Mean return (percentage p.a.)	beta
Chemicals/Pharmaceutical	9.97	0.89
Electrical	8.08	1.10
Utilities/Energy/Coal	10.14	0.63
Banking/Insurance	10.60	1.13
Vehicles/Machinery	9.81	1.18
Steel/Metals	8.81	1.03
Construction/Building/Material	9.89	0.86
Retail	5.67	0.87
Consumer Goods/Leisure	6.60	0.71
Transportation	7.59	0.87
Holdings	11.89	1.08
Others	6.32	0.80

6. The intervalling effect and other anomalies in the German stock market

6.1 Anomalies revisited

Empirical studies have detected a number of anomalies in stock returns, i.e. systematic patterns in returns with respect to calendar time or certain firm characteristics. The most prominent of these regularities are the turn-of-the-week (or Monday) effect, the turn-of-the-year (or January) effect and the size (or small firm) effect.[4]

The turn-of-the-week effect was discovered by French (1980) and also reported by Gibbons/Hess (1981) who find that Monday returns are systematically lower than returns on any other day of the week. Banz (1981) analyzes the relationship between the market value of the equity of a firm and the average return on its stocks. He shows that the stocks of firms with small equity market values have significantly higher average returns than the stocks of larger firms. The January anomaly was first detected by Keim (1983). He investigates the behaviour of the size anomaly across the different months of the year and finds that the return differences are signifiantly larger in January than in any of the other eleven months.

Frantzmann (1989) provides a detailed study of seasonalities in the German stock market. He finds that in the period 1970 to 1980 Friday returns were significantly positive and higher than those on any other day of the week whereas Monday and/or Tuesday returns were not significantly different from zero. These results hold for all months. Chang/Pinegar/Ravichandran (1993) show, that the Monday effect that is apparently observable on the German market disappears, when the test statistics are adjusted for potential heteroskedasticity. The turn-of-the-year-effect exists for the whole period, too. Whereas January shows the highest returns, May exhibits significantly negative returns. In addition, a turn-of-the-month-effect can be found.

Studies on a size effect in Germany were conducted by Stehle (1992) and by Schlag/Wohlschieß (1992). Whereas Stehle finds some evidence of a size effect in Germany, especially in January, Schlag/Wohschieß obtain very low *t*-statistics for size as an explanatory variable for mean returns. Sauer (1994) is also unable to detect a size related anomaly for stock returns in Germany.

---

[4] Other anomalies are, for example, the dividend-yield effect and the price-earnings effect.

6.2 Overreaction

The overreaction hypothesis stipulates that extreme stock price movements in one direction are followed by movements in the opposite direction. The reaction will be the greater, the more extreme is the initial price movement. Empirical results mainly reported by DeBondt/Thaler (1985, 1987) for the U.S. have been criticized in the literature for several reasons. The main arguments are that overreaction is due to size or to changing risk over time.

In a comprehensive investigation Meyer (1994) takes into account most of the criticisms of previous studies. For the period 1961 to 1990 he generally finds an overreaction effect for the German stock market. The results are strong and more significant for longer formation and test periods. The effect holds for market and for risk adjusted returns. It can be explained neither by size nor by a risk change in the investigation period. It is nevertheless unclear whether a contrarian investment strategy including transaction and information costs would prove profitable.

6.3 Underpricing

Another anomaly in the German stock market is the underpricing of initial public offerings (IPOs). Different studies (Göppl/Sauer (1990a, 1990b), Ljungqvist (1995) and Uhlir (1989)) estimate an average initial (adjusted) return between 10.2 and 28 percent, depending on sample size and period. Since 1988 initial returns have dropped significantly. In the long run German IPOs underperformed relative to the market.

6.4 The intervalling effect

The intervalling-effect bias in the estimated coefficient for the systematic risk of a stock was first analyzed and empirically documented by Cohen/Hawawini/Maier/ Schwartz/Whitcomb (CHMSW) (1983a, 1983b) for the U.S. market. Frantzmann (1990) reports the first results on this issue in respect of the German market. He finds that the (equally weighted) average β coefficient for the stocks in his sample almost monotonically increases with the length of the return interval. Schlag (1994) groups the stocks in his sample by reference to their market capitalizations and trading volumes. He detects that the direction of the monotonic relationship between the estimate for β and the length of the return interval is exactly opposite for small and large stocks, and that this result also holds for the liquidity classification. Consistent with the results for the U.S. market it can be observed that the estimated β decreases with the return interval for large stocks, and that it increases for small stocks. There is one important difference, however. Whereas in the U.S. smaller stocks tend to have a higher β, just the opposite is true for Germany. Consequently, the difference in estimated systematic risk between highly capitalized stocks and small firms tends to increase with increasing return intervals in the U.S., but the gap narrows in Germany.

This is also confirmed by the results of the following study. The sample consisted of all stocks traded on the Frankfurt Stock Exchange which had no more than two missing daily return observations during the period from January 1987 to December 1993. These stocks were grouped into ten size deciles in accordance with their equity market values on December 31, 1986. The β coefficients were then estimated using a technique suggested by Corhay (1992) for intervals of 1, 5, 10, 20, 30, 60 and 120 trading days. The DAFOX was used as the market index, and the regressions were performed using OLS.

Table 6 shows some descriptive statistics for the equity market values in the ten groups.

Table 6: Market value of equity for size deciles[a]

Decile	Mean	Minimum	Maximum
1	12,988	3,225	23,895
2	40,978	24,000	58,740
3	75,532	58,800	95,000
4	132,651	96,000	184,000
5	249,968	191,400	343,000
6	485,515	377,513	624,800
7	885,243	689,005	1,090,000
8	1,343,623	1,092,000	1,648,800
9	2,610,362	1,739,500	3,881,200
10	15,188,526	3,882,760	52,172,102

[a]Measured in thousands of DEM on Dec. 31, 1986.

It is interesting to note that the increase in mean market value is rather slow from deciles 1 to 9. In decile 10, however, the mean market value is about six times as large as in decile 9. Furthermore, the average firm in decile 10 has a market capitalization that is about three times as large as the sum of the market values of the representative firms in all of the other nine groups. These statistics clearly show that the German market capitalization is heavily concentrated in a few very large stocks. Sauer (1994) provides further evidence on this issue.

Table 7 shows summarises the estimated systematic risk coefficients. The entries represent the average β for the respective size decile for the given return interval. It may first be noted that decile 10 has the largest coefficient for each return interval. Furthermore, it is the only decile with β coefficients larger than one. Decile 6 differs from the other groups in that it violates the monotonicity of β with respect to size for each return interval.

Referencing to the main point of interest, namely the monotonic relationship between systematic risk and β this study confirms the results of Schlag (1994). For small stocks we observe a steady increase in β with increasing return intervals. In deciles 1 to 9 there is only one violation of this monotonicity, i.e. in group 9, where the average β is slightly lower for an interval of 120 days than it is for 60 days. In decile 10 there is not such a strict pattern of monotonicity, although the tendency for β to decrease with the length of the return interval is clearly noticeable, especially in the range from one to 30 days. In addition, the β for 120 days has the lowest estimate across all intervals in this class.

Table 7: Mean β for size deciles for various return intervals[a]

	Return Interval (Trading Days)						
Decile	1	5	10	20	30	60	120
1	0.1625	0.2502	0.3133	0.4092	0.4848	0.5958	0.6239
2	0.2244	0.3086	0.3560	0.4304	0.4786	0.5411	0.6047
3	0.2529	0.3868	0.4358	0.4838	0.5013	0.5627	0.6162
4	0.3695	0.4760	0.5397	0.5931	0.6214	0.6711	0.6987
5	0.5132	0.5911	0.6171	0.6774	0.6970	0.7263	0.7688
6	0.7342	0.7533	0.7824	0.8323	0.8542	0.8869	0.9699
7	0.6103	0.6905	0.7292	0.8007	0.8331	0.8645	0.9088
8	0.7000	0.7050	0.7308	0.7680	0.7929	0.8258	0.8631
9	0.9221	0.9416	0.9568	0.9645	0.9663	0.9786	0.9760
10	1.1631	1.1328	1.1161	1.0986	1.0980	1.1017	1.0768

[a] β computed as in Corhay (1992).
Values in the table are mean values for the respective size decile.
Regression method: OLS.

It is also interesting to note that, as described above, the deviation between the estimated β coefficients for small and large stocks decreases with increasing return periods. For daily returns the difference between the extreme deciles is more than 1.0 with a value of 0.1625 for the smallest and 1.1631 for the largest stocks. For an interval of 120 days the distance is just 0.4529, i.e. less than half of what is observed for daily returns.

7. Summary

We have shown that the German stock market which is part of the international equity market, exhibits most of the results and problems reported in the literature. The valuation process is not yet clear and research is still in progress. No mention was made of the empirical analysis of accounting information. An excellent overview of this area of research can be found in Müller (1992).

References

Banz, R.W. (1981): The Relationship Between Return and Market Value of Common Stocks, in: Journal of Financial Economics 9, 3-18.

Bernstein, P.L. (1987): Liquidity, Stock Markets, and Market Maker, in: Financial Management, Summer, 54-62.

Bühler, W., H. Göppl, Möller, H.-P. et al. (1993): Die Deutsche Finanzdatenbank (DFDB), in: Bühler, W., Hax, H., and R. Schmidt (eds.), Empirische Kapitalmarktforschung, Zeitschrift für betriebswirtschaftliche Forschung, special issue 31, 287-331.

Chang, E.C., M.J. Pinegar and Ravichandran, R. (1993): International Evidence on the Robustness of the Day-of-the-Week Effect, in: Journal of Financial and Quantitative Analysis 28, 497-513.

Cohen, K.J., G.A. Hawawini, S.F. Maier, R.A. Schwartz and Whitcomb, D.K. (1983a): Friction in the Trading Process and the Estimation of Systematic Risk, in: Journal of Financial Economics 12, 263-287.

Cohen, K.J., G.A. Hawawini, S.F. Maier, R.A. Schwartz and Whitcomb, D.K. (1983b): Estimating and Adjusting for the Intervalling-Effect Bias in Beta, in: Management Science 29, 135-148.

Corhay, A. (1993): The Intervalling Effect Bias in Beta: A Note, in: Journal of Banking and Finance 16, 61-73.

DeBondt, W.F.M. and Thaler, R.H. (1985): Does the Stock Market Overreact?, in: Journal of Finance 40, 793-805.

DeBondt, W.F.M. and Thaler, R.H. (1987): Further Evidence on Investor Overrreaction and Stock Market Seasonality, in: Journal of Finance 42, 557-581.

Deutsche Börse AG (1994): Frankfurter Monatsstatistik für Dezember 1994. Frankfurt.

Frantzmann, H.-J. (1989): Saisonalitäten und Bewertung am deutschen Aktien- und Rentenmarkt. Frankfurt (Fritz Knapp).

Frantzmann, H.-J. (1990): Zur Messung des Marktrisikos deutscher Aktien, in: Zeitschrift für betriebswirtschaftliche Forschung 42, 67-83.

French, K.F. (1980): Stock Returns and the Weekend Effect, in: Journal of Financial Economics 8, 55-69.

Gibbons, M. and Hess, P. (1981): Day of the Week Effects and Asset Returns, in: Journal of Business 54, 579-96.

Göppl, H. and A. Sauer (1990a): Die Bewertung von Börsenneulingen: Einige empirische Ergebnisse, in: Ahlert, D., K.P. Franz und H. Göppl (eds.): Finanz- und Rechnungswesen als Führungsinstrument. Wiesbaden (Gabler).

Göppl, H. and A. Sauer (1990b): Die Bewertung von Börsenneulingen am deutschen Aktienmarkt: Eine empirische Notiz, in: Heilmann, W.R., Eichhorn, W., Franke, G., Göppl, H., Heilmann, W.-R., Ketterer, K.-H., Kloten, N., Meier-Preschany, M., Schwebler, R., and A. Zink (eds.): Geld, Banken und Versicherungen. Vol. 1. Karlsruhe (VVW).

Göppl, H. and H. Schütz (1993): The Design and Implementation of a German Stock Price Research Index (Deutscher Aktien-Forschungsindex DAFOX), in: Diewert, D.E., Spremann, K., and F. Stehling (eds.): Mathematical Modelling in Economics Essays in Honor of Wolfgang Eichhorn. Berlin (Springer), 506-519.

Grisvold, D.R. (1995): German Reunification: Analysis of its Impact on German Equities. Chicago (Diss.).

Keim, D. (1983): Size-Related Anomalies and Stock Return Seasonality - Further Empirical Evidence, in: Journal of Financial Economics 12, 13-32.

Ljungqvist, A.P. (1995): The Effect of Market Conditions on the Underpricing of German Initial Public Offerings, Working Paper, Oxford School of Management.

Meyer, B. (1994): Der Overreaction-Effekt am deutschen Aktienmarkt. Frankfurt (Fritz Knapp).

Müller, W. (1992): Bilanzinformation und Aktienbewertung. Frankfurt (Fritz Knapp).

Sauer, A. (1994): Faktormodelle und Bewertung am deutschen Aktienmarkt. Frankfurt (Fritz Knapp).

Schlag, C. and V. Wohlschieß (1992): Is β dead ? - Results for the German Stock Market, Discussionpaper No. 178, Institut für Entscheidungstheorie und Unternehmensforschung, University of Karlsruhe (TH).

Schlag, C. (1994): Neues zum Intervalling-Effekt am deutschen Aktienmarkt, in: Kredit und Kapital 27, 437-460.

Stehle, R. (1992): The Size Effect in the German Stock Market, Working Paper, University of Augsburg.

Uhlir, H. (1989): Der Gang an die Börse und das Underpricing Phänomen, in: Zeitschrift für Bankrecht und Bankwirtschaft 1, 2-16.

Winkelmann, M. (1984): Aktienbewertung in Deutschland. Königstein (Anton Hain).

Estimation and Prediction of Systematic Risk with Market-Based and Accounting-Based Data for German Shares

Bernd Rudolph and Peter Zimmermann
University of Munich

1. Introduction

As a measure of systematic risk, beta is used in numerous methods and tools of portfolio management and security analysis. The beta-concept is also germane to the control of portfolio risk and to the valuation of risky assets and investments. Recent empirical findings have revived doubts about the validity of the capital asset pricing model (CAPM) which is the theoretical foundation of the beta concept. While academic discussion (Fama/French 1992, Black 1993) continues to question the CAPM, beta applications nevertheless persist. An accurate estimation, or prediction, of beta is crucial to the reliability of these applications.

Beta estimates obtained from the market model regression do not appear to be stable over time. Therefore, historical or market-based beta forecasts derived from previous stock and index returns do not provide reliable predictions of systematic risk. Shifts in the systematic risk of a firm are caused by changes in macroeconomic and industry factors and by changes in the sensitivity of the company's returns thereto. The latter may also be attributable to strategic adaptions of the firm's investment policies to changes in macroeconomic and industry factors. Accounting data are thought to contain information on this sensitivity. It should therefore be reasonable to employ accounting risk measures for predicting systematic risk. Empirical studies of US stocks report significant associations between accounting numbers and beta as well as a superior predictive ability of accounting-based (fundamental) beta predictions compared with market-based predictions (Beaver/Kettler/Scholes 1970, Rosenberg/Marathe 1975, Eskew 1979, Lee/Newbold/Finnerty/Chu 1986).[1] Studies of this problem-area using German stocks have yielded ambiguous results which partly conflict with findings for the US market and theoretical propositions (Möller 1988, Bauer 1992, Steiner/Bauer 1992, Steiner/Beiker/Bauer 1993, Müller 1992, Pfennig 1993).

---

[1] Elgers (1980), however, failed to find an advantage of accounting-based forecasts.

The purpose of this paper is to evaluate the accuracy of market-based and accounting-based predictions of systematic risk. The analysis has been extended in three ways compared with previous work. 1. It examines the influence of the estimation procedure of historical beta on the association between accounting variables and systematic risk. 2. It explores the impact of infrequent trading on this relation and on beta prediction. For this purpose a number of correction procedures for non-synchronous trading are analyzed. 3. A special focus is given to the lag between the publication of accounting data and the beta estimation period.

The next section describes the database and the accounting ratios selected for this study, summarizes estimation, adjustment and forecast procedures, and presents the measure of forecast error employed in this research. Section 3 contains the empirical results. The final section provides a summary of the findings.

2. Data and methodology

2.1 The database

The empirical investigation reported in this paper is based on stock price and accounting data for a sample of 160 German non-financial firms for the period of 1968 to 1991.[2] The companies were listed on the Frankfurt Stock Exchange for at least five years during this period. To qualify for inclusion in the sample the companies were required to have disclosed a 10 million DM minimum book value of equity capital in five consecutive annual financial statements. Daily share prices with price notation, indicating whether prices are based on trading or not, are available since 1974. As proxies for the market index five German stock indices are used, namely, the Deutscher Aktien Forschungs-Index (DAFOX), the Deutscher Aktienindex (DAX), the Index of the Frankfurt Stock Exchange, the Commerzbank-Index and the FAZ-Index.

[2] The data were kindly supplied by the Deutsche Finanzmarkt-Datenbank. The data files provide stock prices, balance sheets and income statements for more than 250 German companies. The remaining firms which are excluded from our study are characterized to a great extent by infrequent trading. We cannot report the results for all periods in this paper. For further details see Zimmermann (1993, 1994).

2.2 Market-based beta estimation

Beta coefficients are obtained from market model regressions using ordinary least squares (OLS) for successive, non-overlapping periods of one, three, and six years. Stock prices, the DAFOX, and the DAX (since 1987)[3] are corrected for dividends and capital adjustments. Returns are computed continuously for different return intervals.

Hawawini (1980, pp. 140-143) shows that, under the standard independence assumptions of the market model, beta computed with continuous returns is invariant to the length of the return interval. This does not hold when shares are traded infrequently because of frictions in the adjustment of prices to new information. As a consequence, stock prices are non-synchronously generated with the index. Under these conditions, beta coefficients estimated with short-term returns are downward-biased for shares which suffer from infrequent trading, while OLS betas for frequently traded stocks overestimate true betas. Thus, OLS betas for infrequently traded securities increase as the return interval is extended (positive intervalling effect), and betas for stocks which are not subject to thin trading are a decreasing function of the return interval (negative intervalling effect).[4]

Scholes/Williams (1977), Dimson (1979), Marsh (1979), and Cohen/ Hawawini/Maier/Schwartz/Whitcomb (1983a, b) developed methods to correct for the intervalling effect. The procedure explored by Marsh (1979, p. 849) is an OLS estimation using only prices from trading days. The aggregated coefficient procedure adopted by Dimson (1979, p. 203) computes lead and lag betas[5] in a multiple regression of the stock return on a number of lead and lag returns of the index. The Dimson estimator of beta is the sum of the estimated beta coefficients of this multiple regression. By contrast, lead and lagged coefficients for the methods of Scholes/Williams (1977) and Cohen Cohen/Hawawini/Maier/ Schwartz/Whitcomb (1983b) are obtained from single regressions. The formula for the corrected beta estimator is computed as follows:[6]

---

3 The other indices are only corrected for dividends or capital adjustments.

4 This intervalling effect has also been discovered for the German stock market by Frantzmann (1990), Schlag (1994), and Zimmermann (1993).

5 A lag-one-beta, for example, is computed in a linear regression with the stock return of today as the dependent variable and the index return of the previous day as the independent variable.

6 The Scholes/Williams (1977, p. 317) procedure uses exactly one lead and one lag, while the generalization of Cohen/Hawawini/Maier/Schwartz/Whitcomb (1983b, pp. 269-270) allows for more leads and lags.

$$\beta_{i,SW} = \frac{\beta_i + \sum_{k=1}^{K} \beta_{i,k} + \sum_{l=1}^{L} \beta_{i,l}}{1 + \sum_{k=1}^{K} corr(r_{M,t}, r_{M,t+k}) + \sum_{l=1}^{L} corr(r_{M,t}, r_{M,t-l})}, \tag{1}$$

where β_i is the contemporaneous OLS estimator for the *i*th stock estimated with daily returns, $\beta_{i,k}$ is the lead beta for a k period lead of the index return, $\beta_{i,l}$ is the lag beta for a *l* period lag of the index return, $corr(r_{M,t}, \ldots)$ are the *k*-lead or *l*-lag autocorrelations of the market index returns r_M. It can be shown that OLS betas that are biased by the intervalling effect converge asymptotically to the unobservable true betas as the return interval *L* is increased to infinity (Cohen/Hawawini/Maier/Schwartz/Whitcomb 1983b, p. 271). This implies an extremely long estimation period. In practice estimation intervals are limited by the available data set and by the possibility of structural changes. Cohen/Hawawini/Maier/Schwartz/Whitcomb (1983a, p.138) proposed a procedure for estimating an asymptotic beta for a stock *i* by regressing OLS betas computed with different return intervals *L* on an appropriate function of *L*

$$\beta_{i,L} = \gamma_{0,i} + \gamma_{1,i} \cdot f(L) + e_i, \tag{2}$$

where the regression coefficient $\gamma_{0,i}$ is the estimator for an asymptotic beta. The function $f(L)$ must be specified experimentally by searching for the function with the best linear fit for the average of the cross-section of stocks. A negative (positive) $\gamma_{l,i}$ coefficient indicates a positive (negative) intervalling effect for security *i*. Cohen/Hawawini/Maier/Schwartz/Whitcomb (1983a, p. 139) developed another estimator (inferred asymptotic estimator), which is calculated in a third step using $\gamma_{l,i}$ from the above regression.

2.3 Market-based beta predictions

Market-based, or historical, forecasts of systematic risk can be obtained by a naive prediction in which the beta estimation of the previous period is used as the predictor of the beta of the succeeding period. Blume (1971, p. 8) reports a tendency for beta coefficients from successive periods to be mean reverting. The autoregressive adjustment methods of Blume (1971) and Vasicek (1973) utilize the autoregressive tendency to improve the accuracy of beta forecasts. The adjusting equation of the Blume (1971, p. 8) procedure is estimated from the cross-sectional regression

$$\beta_{i,t} = a + b \cdot \beta_{i,t-1} \tag{3}$$

of the betas of period t on the coefficients of period t-1. Beta of period t-1 is then replaced by period t beta to predict the beta of period t+1. The Bayesian correction proposed by Vasicek (1973, p. 1236) uses the cross-sectional beta information of the previous period:

$$\beta_{i,t+1} = \frac{\dfrac{\overline{\beta}_{i,t}}{\text{var}(\beta_{i,t})} + \dfrac{\beta_{i,t}}{s_{\beta}^{2}}}{\dfrac{1}{\text{var}(\beta_{i,t})} + \dfrac{1}{s_{\beta}^{2}}}, \tag{4}$$

where $\beta_{i,t+1}$ is the mean of the posterior distribution of beta for stock i which serves as the beta forecast. s_{β}^{2} represents the variance of the OLS regression coefficient $\beta_{i,t}$, $\overline{\beta}_{i,t}$ is the cross-sectional mean of beta for period t, and $\text{var}(\beta_{i,t})$ is the variance of the cross-section of betas.[7]

2.4 Accounting variables and fundamental beta predictions

The relationship between systematic risk and (fundamental) accounting variables has been explored in a considerable number of theoretical and empirical studies. Theoretically, a positive association with beta can be formulated for financial leverage, operating leverage, accounting beta, and earnings variability (see Bowman 1979, 1981, Callahan/Mohr 1989). According to the CAPM, systematic risk is not related to any other accounting number. Beaver/Kettler/ Scholes (1970) and other researchers confirm the empirical significance of these determinants of the systematic risk of U.S. stocks. Furthermore, these studies also uncovered significant interactions between beta and other accounting variables, e.g. dividend yield, size, growth or market to book ratio. Empirical findings about the fundamental determinants of the systematic risk of German stocks are not wholly consistent with U.S. empiricism and received theory (see Möller 1988, Bauer 1992, Müller 1992, Steiner/Bauer 1992, Steiner/Beiker/ Bauer 1993, Pfennig 1993). The most important variable seems to be size which reveals an inexplicable positive association with beta. Other accounting variables show unstable or insignificant relations, or theoretically incorrect signs.

---

[7] Several other autoregressive methods are discussed in the literature which can be conceived as simplifications of the two basic methods (see Reilly/Wright 1979, pp. 64-65).

Nevertheless, Bauer (1992) and associated studies find fundamental predictions of beta to be superior to market-based forecasts.[8]

The theoretical considerations emphasized in previous studies and the empirical results reported therein are the basis of our choice of accounting variables. Here, we report only the regression results for the most important variables.[9] Accounting ratios were classified in groups representing different risk elements and determinants of beta. Financial risk is measured by financial leverage and debt to total capital ratio, both computed with the book and market values of equity, respectively. Accounting betas, or regression coefficients as variables for operating leverage proposed and employed in previous studies (see Beaver/Manegold 1975, Mandelker/Rhee 1984, pp. 50-51, Chung 1989, pp. 348-349)[10], have not been used because the problems resulting from small samples and instability seem to be too serious. Instead we apply the "plant and equipment to total capital (valued at book value) ratio", which showed a significant relation to systematic risk in previous studies (see Möller 1988, Bauer 1992) for German stocks, and the "tangible fixed assets to sales ratio" to represent operating leverage.[11] Size is measured by the natural logarithms of nominal capital and by book and market value of equity, growth by percentage change of market value of equity, and dividend policy by dividend yield. The market to book ratio of equity, which may be interpreted as a proxy for monopoly power (see Conine 1983, pp. 177-179), was also included in the regressions. The strong relationships between size variables and betas presumably result from size being a proxy variable for liquidity in stock trading. The percentage ratio of prices resulting from trades against all prices in a year and the percentage of non-zero-returns of all returns in a year were adopted as measures of trading liquidity.

The common procedure for predicting systematic risk with fundamental variables is a regression of historical beta on accounting ratios which serve as instrumental variables. Removing the error term from the cross-sectional multiple regression function yields the corrected, fundamental beta which is used as the predicted beta for the next period. This instrumental variables approach tries to correct measurement errors in historical betas.[12] If the beta estimation period and the fiscal year are coterminous (lag 0), a fundamental prediction

---

[8] Müller (1992), who employs a less extensive set of accounting variables rejects this finding.

[9] Detailed results including further accounting variables are presented in Zimmermann (1994).

[10] Furthermore, because of the short time-series of annual reports these variables cannot be used to predict systematic risk. For the same reasons variances of accounting variables were not employed.

[11] Both variables should have a positive relationship to beta, because higher values indicate higher fixed costs and hence a higher degree of operating leverage.

[12] The application of the instrumental variables approach to fundamental beta prediction is described in Beaver/Kettler/Scholes (1970, pp. 671-672).

usually is impossible, because the relevant accounting data are not published. A time lag of at least 6 months between fiscal year-end and the end of the beta estimation period has to be considered.[13]

Shifts in a company's systematic risk are caused by changes in macroeconomic and industry factors and changes in the sensitivity of the company's earnings to these factors (see Rosenberg/Guy 1976). Accounting ratios may describe these sensitivities and thus could be conceived as determinants of beta. Assuming that cross-sectional interactions between fundamental variables and beta expressed by the coefficients of a multiple regression are stable, it could be useful to insert accounting ratios obtained from subsequent annual reports in the estimated function. This method requires a time lag of 18 months between the fiscal year-end of the period, from which the accounting ratios are taken to estimate the regression, and the end of the beta estimation period. Therefore, the relationships are estimated for lags of 0, 6, 12 and 18 months. Alternatively, predicted accounting ratios could be used to forecast beta. In that case, the change in systematic risk would be predicted by changes in accounting ratios.

2.5 Measuring the accuracy of beta forecasts

The forecast error of beta predictors can be evaluated by mean squared error (see Mincer/Zarnowitz 1969, p. 11, Klemkosky/Martin 1975, pp. 1123-1124).

$$\mathrm{MSE} = \frac{1}{n} \cdot \sum_{i=1}^{n} \left(\beta_{a,i} - \beta_{p,i}\right)^2 \tag{5}$$

and its analytical decomposition

$$\begin{aligned} \mathrm{MSE} &= \left(\bar{b}_a - \bar{b}_p\right)^2 + (1-b) \cdot \mathrm{var}(b_p) + \left(1-R^2\right) \cdot \mathrm{var}(b_a) \\ &= \text{bias} + \text{inefficiency} + \text{random disturbance} \end{aligned} \tag{6}$$

where $\beta_{p,i}$ is the predicted and $\beta_{a,i}$ is the realized beta of security i, $\bar{\beta}_a$ and $\bar{\beta}_p$ are the cross-sectional means of the predicted and realized betas,

[13] Whereas the financial year-end of most German companies is 31st December, some of those included in the sample have other financial year-ends. In this paper statements for financial years ending between June 30th and May 31st (in the following year) are grouped in the same fiscal period and December 31st is definded as their common balance sheet date. German companies are required to publish their annual reports within 6 months of their financial year-ends. It is assumed here that the accounting data for the companies in our sample are available on June 30th of the following year.

respectively, and var(.) are the cross-sectional variances of these betas. b represents the slope coefficient of the regression of the realized betas on the predicted betas, and R^2 is the coefficient of determination for this regression. For perfect forecasts the MSE equals zero. The random disturbance component is that part of the forecast error which cannot be explained. The prediction is biased when the average prediction differs from the average realization. The second term of (6) is the inefficiency component of the MSE which indicates whether the forecast tends to overestimate high betas and to underestimate low beta values. The autoregressive tendency of beta causes the inefficiency component to be non-zero. The inefficiency component can also be expressed as (see Lee/Newbold/Finnerty/Chu 1986, p.53):

$$\text{inefficiency} = \left(\text{var}(\beta_p) - R \cdot \text{var}(\beta_a)\right)^2. \qquad (7)$$

Since the correlation R between forecasts and realizations will not be perfect, the inefficiency component will be lower, if the predicted betas will have a lower variance than the realized betas.

3. Empirical results

3.1 Intervalling effect and adjustment techniques

Analyzing the influences of the return interval and the index on beta, the latter was estimated for periods of 6 and 3 years with different return intervals L as listed in Table 1. For example, computing 4 day interval returns means that there are 4 possible time-series beginning with the first, second, third, and fourth day of the period. The market model was estimated for all possible time-series. The 40-day-beta of a stock, for example, is thus computed as the average of 40 beta estimates.14 Betas were computed in the same way for all intervals. Table 1 displays the equally weigthed, cross-sectional averages of the L-day-betas for the estimation period 1980-1985 computed with the returns of the 5 indices.15 It is apparent that an intervalling effect is also present in the case of German stocks. The positive effect for the stock average results from the infrequently traded

---

[14] This procedure was proposed by Corhay (1992, p. 64) and was recently applied by Schlag (1994) to German data.

[15] The tables for the other 6-year- and 3-year-periods have been omitted, but the results are similar. Further details are presented in Zimmermann (1993).

shares in the sample.16 The amount of the positive intervalling effect of these stocks is greater than the amount of the negative effect for the frequently traded stocks. The value of the beta estimator also depends on the index used as proxy for the market portfolio. Indices which incorporate a greater number of stocks, like the DAFOX and the index of the Frankfurt Stock Exchange (FWB), yield higher values of beta.17

Table 1: Average betas estimated with different return intervals and indices for the period 1980-1985

L	COX	DAX	DAFOX	FAZ	FWB
1	.496	.439	.614	.528	.622
2	.539	.501	.643	.567	.676
3	.561	.528	.655	.588	.680
4	.575	.549	.665	.602	.686
6	.596	.577	.682	.624	.693
8	.609	.602	.695	.640	.701
10	.623	.625	.705	.655	.709
12	.639	.642	.722	.671	.723
14	.651	.657	.733	.685	.732
16	.661	.669	.742	.696	.742
20	.683	.695	.761	.718	.757
25	.696	.711	.770	.731	.770
30	.709	.729	.781	.744	.781
35	.714	.739	.785	.752	.786
40	.714	.744	.787	.754	.785

L = length of return interval, COX = Commerzbank Index, DAX = Deutscher Aktienindex, DAFOX = Deutscher Aktien Forschungsindex, FAZ = FAZ-Index, FWB = Index of the Frankfurt Stock Exchange (Index der Frankfurter Wertpapierbörse).

The adjustment procedures for the intervalling effect which have been described in section 2.2 are tested only for a sub-sample of 95 stocks and only with FAZ-Index returns as independent variables.[18] If the adjustment methods

[16] If the beta coefficients are weighted with market values, the cross-sectional averages would be around one and an intervalling effect would not be observable. The beta estimators for most of the infrequently traded stocks are low, insignificant, and sometimes negative.

[17] Although the averages of the beta coefficients estimated with DAFOX and FWB returns seem to be equal for longer return intervals, the single OLS estimators for the stocks differ slightly.

[18] Results are presented in detail in Zimmermann (1993).

adequately correct for the intervalling effect, the resultant beta estimates of infrequently traded stocks should be higher than for betas estimated from daily or weekly returns. For frequently traded stocks the corrected betas should be lower. This can be observed in general in respect of the procedures of Scholes/Williams (1977), Dimson (1979), and Cohen/Hawawini/Maier/ Schwartz/Whitcomb (1983b). The higher the number of leads and lags incorporated in these procedures, the higher is the cross-sectional average of betas in the majority of periods. But serious exceptions to this rule have to be reported for greater numbers of leads and lags. Since only the coefficients of the lag-one-betas are significant for the majority of the infrequently traded stocks, it seems reasonable to apply these methods only in the case of using just one lag and perhaps one lead.[19] Beta coefficients computed with weekly returns seem to produce a similar correction. The procedure of Cohen/Hawawini/Maier/ Schwartz/Whitcomb (1983a) showed the greatest deviations from unadjusted daily, or weekly, betas in generating extreme and implausible values of the asymptotic beta estimator $\gamma_{0,i}$ for some of the stocks.[20] Trade-to-trade betas differ only slightly from OLS betas computed with daily returns. None of the adjustment techniques seems to be able to correct systematically and reliably the betas of all stocks. The practical usefulness of these methods thus appears to be questionable.

3.2 The association between beta and accounting numbers

In order to examine the relationships between historical beta and accounting variables, correlations and adjusted coefficients of determination R^2 were estimated in cross-sectional, single regressions for different non-overlapping

---

[19] With this number of leads and lags the Cohen/Hawawini/Maier/Schwartz/Whitcomb (1983b) procedure is on a par with the procedure proposed by Scholes/Williams (1977). The differences between the Dimson (1979) estimator and the Scholes/Williams (1977) estimator using one lead and lag are extremly small.

[20] The best linear fit on average of all stocks was found for the function $f(L) = L^{-n}$. The average R^2 for the second step regression is between 0.15 and 0.43 depending on the length and location of the estimation period. The sign of the $\gamma_{1,i}$ coefficients is in most cases as expected, but for some stocks it changes from period to period. Thus the use of one function for all stocks seems to be problematic. The coefficients of the third step regression turned out not to be stable over time, therefore an application of the third step brings no simplification as supposed by Cohen/Hawawini/Maier/Schwartz/Whitcomb (1983a). For further details see Pfennig (1993, pp. 13-20), and Zimmermann (1993, pp. 47-50).

periods, for different estimation procedures[21] of historical beta, and for different time lags. In all cases the results appear to be similar. Table 2 contains the average and maximum adjusted R^2, the number of significant relations (F-test, $\alpha = 0.05$), and the sign of the association between accounting ratios and beta, estimated for annual estimation periods from 1974 to 1991 with lag 0 using weekly returns (computed from Wednesday to Wednesday). The correlations are, except for the size variables, very weak and, in most periods, not significant.[22] The signs of the relations appear to be unstable and are inconsistent with theoretical principles. The greatest explanatory power is observed for the two trading liquidity variables which are listed in the two last rows of Table 2. The size variables seem to proxy for trading liquidity. The correlations between size and liquidity variables range from 0.25 to more than 0.5.

Table 2: Relations between accounting variables and beta for one-year periods from 1974 to 1991

Variable	Avg. R^2	Max. R^2	F-test[1)]	Sign[2)]
Financial leverage (book value)	.0091	.0297	1	
Financial leverage (market value)	.0131	.0518	3	+
Debt to total capital (book value)	.0099	.0363	2	-
Debt to total capital (market value)	.0094	.0423	3	+
Plant and equipment to total capital	.0259	.0996	7	-
Tangible fixed assets to sales	.0160	.0581	3	--
ln(nominal capital)	.1639	.3206	18	++
ln(book value of capital)	.1491	.2871	17	++
ln(market value of capital)	.1302	.2424	16	++
Growth of market value of capital	.0643	.2941	8	+
Dividend yield	.0112	.0363	3	+
Market to book ratio	.0246	.1136	7	-
Percentage of trading prices	.3299	.4631	18	++
Percentage of non-zero returns	.4070	.5547	18	++

1) number of significant relations ($\alpha = 0.05$).

2) ++ (--) positive (negative) sign in all periods, + (-) positive negative) signs in most periods.

---

[21] The betas used for the following statistics have been computed with the DAFOX as market proxy, because the DAFOX returns employed in the market model regression generate the highest R^2 compared to the other indices.

[22] For the accounting ratios not listed in Table 2 the relations are by no means stronger (see Zimmermann 1994). The findings of this study are largely consistent with previos results for German shares.

Using daily returns for beta estimations or different Scholes/Williams (1977) estimators leads to higher correlations for liquidity and size variables.[23] This could be explained by the greater estimation bias for beta caused by the intervalling effect. It also could be interpreted as an indication that the adjustment techniques cannot effectively correct for the intervalling effect. The results for the other variables are similar to betas computed with weekly returns. Similar results occur, when systematic risk is estimated with monthly returns for 3-year periods and the accounting numbers are computed as the averages of three successive financial statements. For a sub-sample of liquid stocks, which have more than 80% trading prices per period, the trading liquidity still has the greatest explanatory power, but it is nearly 20% weaker than for the whole sample. Computing the single regressions for lags of 6, 12 and 18 months no systematic differences for the fundamental relationships with systematic risk between the lags can be observed.

To estimate a fundamental prediction rule stepwise regression was initially employed.[24] The adjusted R^2 varies between 10% and almost 60% for different periods and lags. The variables selected by the stepwise procedure differ from period to period. A size variable has been included in the regression for nearly every period. A stable prediction rule cannot be estimated with this method. Therefore, several prediction functions with fixed independent variables were tested for every period. The highest adjusted R^2 and subsequently the best predictions were obtained from functions containing a size variable together with the "plant and equipment to total capital ratio". Selecting the other variables at will does not cause basic differences in the results. None of the different combinations of variables has superior explanatory or predictive power in every period. On average the best results were attained with a function of the logarithm of the nominal capital, the "plant and equipment to total capital ratio", the debt to total capital (market value), the dividend yield, the growth of market value of equity, and the market to book ratio as independent (instrumental) variables. Table 3 displays the standardized regression coefficients, the adjusted R^2 and the significance level for the multiple regression function, where as the dependent variable historical beta was computed with weekly returns.[25] The F-test of the regression indicates highly significant relations for every period but, apart from nominal capital and "plant and equipment to total capital", the regression coefficients for the variables are insignificant or have unstable signs.

---

[23] The maximum adjusted R^2 for percentage of non-zero returns is 67% with an average of 56%. The results are presented in detail in Zimmermann (1994).

[24] The probabilities of F to enter and to remove a variable were set at 5% and 10% respectively. To reduce the estimation bias caused by collinearity of the independent variables the accepted tolerance was set at 0.8.

[25] Since a lag of 6 months is necessary to ensure that accounting data is published, this lag has been employed for the following computations.

The signs of the significant variables are inconsistent with theoretical propositions about their interaction with systematic risk.

Table 3: Standardized regression coefficients for the prediction rule using a lag of 6 months and weekly returns for beta estimation

Fiscal period	ln(nominal capital)	Plant and equipment to total capital	Debt to total capital (market value)	Dividend yield	Growth of market value of capital	Market to book ratio	Adj. R^2
1974	.446***	-.225***	.199**	.073	-.460***	-.026	.308***
1975	.464***	-.137**	.065	-.011	.260***	.003	.326***
1976	.606***	-.189**	.180**	.030	.003	-.074	.362***
1977	.429***	-.279***	.182**	.179**	.248***	-.003	.271***
1978	.372***	-.369***	.209**	.126	.270***	.034	.253***
1979	.373***	-.258***	.119	.074	-.264***	-.057	.269***
1980	.394***	-.184**	.190**	-.022	-.179**	.047	.204***
1981	.297***	-.109	-.005	.135	.142	.102	.126***
1982	.388***	-.395***	.153*	.002	.060	-.129	.241***
1983	.398***	-.362***	.007	-.006	.212***	-.105	.278***
1984	.441***	-.275***	.107	.059	.024	-.039	.216***
1985	.443***	-.088	-.014	-.083	.250***	-.003	.293***
1986	.509***	-.197**	-.005	-.016	-.002	.124	.253***
1987	.307***	-.016	-.086	-.044	-.466***	-.113	.363***
1988	.483***	-.113	-.083	-.001	.211***	-.170**	.292***
1989	.494***	-.125*	.050	.002	.362***	.033	.332***
1990	.385***	-.218***	.174**	-.018	-.111	-.060	.259***

* $\alpha = 0.1$ (t-test or F-test), ** $\alpha = 0.05$, *** $\alpha = 0.01$.

3.3 Market-based and accounting-based beta predictions

The return interval not only influences the value of the beta estimator, it also has an impact on the stability of the beta coefficient, which can be measured by the mean squared error (MSE) of the naive forecasts. Table 4 displays the MSE and its components for the naive forecasts estimated with daily and weekly returns for annual, non-overlapping periods. Betas computed from shorter return intervals appear to be more stable.[26] The regression tendency of beta, indicated by the value of the inefficiency component of the MSE, is also lower for shorter return intervals.

Table 4: Mean squared errors of naive historical forecasts

End of prediction period	Naive beta forecasts							
	With daily returns				With weekly returns			
	MSE	Bias	Ineffic.	Random	MSE	Bias	Ineffic.	Random
7606	.09409	.00235	.00099	.09076	.27354	.04245	.03579	.19530
7706	.06120	.00082	.00271	.05767	.16240	.00066	.01415	.14759
7806	.14156	.01695	.00931	.11530	.27033	.01638	.07647	.17748
7906	.14657	.00030	.03617	.11011	.32607	.00103	.07824	.24680
8006	.09377	.00231	.00529	.08616	.27027	.00396	.11645	.14986
8106	.08738	.00121	.00447	.08170	.28872	.00137	.02202	.26533
8206	.14500	.01543	.01479	.11479	.48169	.00772	.16442	.30955
8306	.16251	.02057	.04035	.10160	.37049	.00128	.19603	.17319
8406	.07606	.01830	.00681	.05095	.22517	.02385	.03997	.16135
8506	.07736	.00264	.01177	.06296	.23877	.00039	.05328	.18510
8606	.07603	.00667	.00918	.06018	.19773	.01097	.08908	.09768
8706	.04480	.00093	.00456	.03931	.10370	.00063	.01853	.08454
8806	.06038	.00856	.00044	.05138	.14364	.02246	.01296	.10822
8906	.06807	.00176	.00702	.05929	.19174	.01403	.02479	.15292
9006	.16743	.05802	.00447	.10493	.20498	.01296	.05136	.14066
9106	.11871	.02523	.02095	.07253	.13084	.00672	.02968	.09444

As expected, autoregressive adjustment procedures improve the beta forecasts compared with naive predictions. Table 5 indicates that the MSEs of the Blume and the Bayes predictors computed from weekly returns are lower than for the naive forecasts in most periods. For this sample, the Bayes adjustment is superior to the Blume forecasts in every period.[27] The autoregressive methods in

[26] Weekly returns were computed from Wednesday to Wednesday. The MSE for the average of 5 betas estimated from all 5 possible weekly returns is lower than for betas estimated from single weekly returns, but it is not as low as for betas from daily returns. The stability of the Scholes/Williams (1977), and the Cohen/Hawawini/Maier/Schwartz/ Whitcomb (1983b) estimators is similar to the stability of betas computed with single weekly returns. Betas of frequently traded stocks are more stable than the betas of the whole sample. For further details see Zimmermann (1993, 1994).

[27] For a sample of 95 stocks employing index returns of the FAZ index, which was used in Zimmermann (1993), the Bayes adjustment proved to be superior in most of the periods. The improvement of the forecast for betas computed from daily returns induced

particular reduce the inefficiency component of the MSE, because they generate beta predictors which have a lower cross-sectional variance compared with the naive forecasts. As mentioned above, inefficiency is reduced when the predictors have lower variances than those of the realized betas. The coefficients of the Blume regression (3) are significant for most of the periods, but they are not stable. This, and the additional incorporation of the estimation error by the Bayes procedure, are the reasons for the inferiority of the Blume adjustment compared with the Bayes prediction.

Table 5: Mean squared errors of autoregressive methods

End of prediction period	Autoregressive forecast methods							
	Blume predictor				Bayes predictor			
	MSE	Bias	Ineffic.	Random	MSE	Bias	Ineffic.	Random
7606	-	-	-	-	.23239	.03888	.00342	.19009
7706	.16065	.01124	.00181	.14759	.14469	.00023	.00001	.14446
7806	.25611	.01854	.06010	.17748	.21672	.01181	.02429	.18062
7906	.26950	.00190	.02080	.24680	.26287	.00061	.01730	.24496
8006	.18890	.00186	.03719	.14986	.18029	.00303	.03192	.14534
8106	.28058	.01180	.00346	.26533	.26823	.00120	.00072	.26631
8206	.42298	.00953	.10390	.30955	.33727	.00462	.03652	.29613
8306	.28126	.02002	.08805	.17319	.21953	.00190	.05204	.16559
8406	.20820	.04548	.00136	.16135	.17843	.02277	.00178	.15388
8506	.21761	.01581	.01671	.18510	.17188	.00008	.00350	.16830
8606	.14107	.00203	.04136	.09768	.13330	.01012	.02878	.09441
8706	.09544	.00808	.00283	.08454	.07764	.00034	.00113	.07617
8806	.13363	.02162	.00379	.10822	.12863	.02127	.00140	.10597
8906	.21994	.04644	.02058	.15292	.17577	.01366	.01136	.15075
9006	.17963	.02020	.01877	.14066	.15531	.00922	.00905	.13703
9106	.12440	.01614	.01382	.09444	.10322	.00622	.00666	.09034

At first sight it seems unlikely that the prediction rule derived in the previous section can improve beta forecasts. But as Table 6 shows, the instrumental variables approach using accounting ratios produces better predictions than the naive forecast in 14 of the 16 periods. The reason for this is that the instrumental variables approach, in which historical betas (naive forecast) are corrected in respect of the error term of the regression, reduces the variance of the cross-sectional betas in the same way as the autoregressive adjustment procedures and thus the inefficiency component of the MSE. Since the same values of the

---

by autoregressive adjustment procedures is small. Note that, by definition, the random component of the Blume predictors and of the naive forecasts are equal.

variables as were used to estimate the prediction function are also used to compute (correct) the beta forecast, it is not important that some coefficients of the prediction rule suffer from instability, insignificance, theoretically inexplicable signs, or bias caused by the collinearity of the independent variables. Tests were made of several prediction rules based on different accounting ratios. Forecasts superior to naive predictions are gained when a size variable and the "plant and equipment to total capital ratio" are included in the function. The other variables can be selected independently without seriously reducing forecast ability. Bauer (1992, pp. 211-215) employed a prediction rule that also used a size variable and the "plant to total capital ratio" (together with financial leverage and dividend yield) and found an improvement in fundamental prediction.[28]

Table 6: Mean squared errors for historical and fundamental predictions

End of prediction period	Historical		Fundamental			
	Naive	Bayes	Instrumental variables approach			
	MSE[1)]	MSE[1)]	MSE	Bias	Inefficiency	Random
7606	.27354	.23239	.25687	.04899	.00138	.20650
7706	.16240	.14469	.16725	.00023	.00204	.16498
7806	.27033	.21672	.22609	.01392	.01363	.19854
7906	.32607	.26287	.24172	.00056	.00074	.24042
8006	.27027	.18029	.19972	.00424	.02488	.17060
8106	.28872	.26823	.27304	.00087	.00213	.27004
8206	.48169	.33727	.35726	.00653	.02078	.32995
8306	.37049	.21953	.19699	.00084	.01826	.17789
8406	.22517	.17843	.19657	.02771	.00002	.16884
8506	.23877	.17188	.16873	.00000	.00000	.16873
8606	.19773	.13330	.11627	.01270	.00377	.09980
8706	.10370	.07764	.08792	.00083	.00039	.08671
8806	.14364	.12863	.16147	.02160	.00015	.13972
8906	.19174	.17577	.18932	.01403	.00202	.17327
9006	.20498	.15531	.16191	.01073	.00080	.15038
9106	.13084	.10322	.12319	.00665	.00113	.11541

[1)] The MSE components of these forecasts are displayed in Tables 4 and 5.

[28] These two variables were not used by Müller (1992) who had no success with fundamental predictions.

Compared with the Bayesian adjustment, the instrumental variable approach generates a lower MSE only in four periods. The small differences in the MSEs preclude the inference that either the fundamental prediction, or the Bayes procedure is the superior approach. This is not surprising, since the corrective effect of both methods in reducing the variance of the prediction is similar. Another fundamental prediction method is inserting the predicted values of the fundamental variables, or the ratios computed from the subsequent annual report, in the prediction rule. The forecast ability would not be altered, if the variables were stable. This can be assumed for size and the "plant and equipment to total capital ratio". But this contradicts the idea of forecasting changes in systematic risk from changes in fundamental variables. If we apply the ratios of the following year as predicted accounting ratios to the prediction rule, the MSE for this forecast is clearly higher than for the instrumental variables approach. However, an improvement compared with naive prediction could not be observed in this case.

4. Summary and conclusions

The findings of our study indicate that the values of beta estimates depend pre-eminently on the procedure selected for estimation, and especially on the length of the return interval. There is a substantial intervalling effect in the case of German stock betas. The beta coefficients of infrequently traded stocks computed with short-term intervals are seriously biased by this effect. Correction procedures proposed in the literature do not adjust adequately for this bias. Using weekly returns instead of the corrective methods yields similar values for systematic risk.

The relationships between accounting numbers and systematic risk are weak for German shares. Low, unstable, and insignificant correlations, or inexplicable signs are observed. Of the fundamental variables, size variables have the greatest explanatory power. The positive sign for this relation contrasts with U.S. findings and theoretical considerations. It can be explained by the fact that size is correlated with trading liquidity and thus represents a proxy for liquidity variables which show the highest correlations with systematic risk. These results are independent of the estimation procedure, the time-lag between the beta estimation period and the balance sheet date, and of the length of the estimation period.

Beta coefficients computed with daily returns are more stable and show a lower regression tendency than betas estimated with longer return intervals. Autoregressive adjustment procedures improve beta forecasts compared with naive prediction. The Bayesian adjustment of Vasicek (1973) is superior to the method of Blume (1971). Accounting-based beta predictions employing the instrumental variables approach facilitate better beta forecasts than naive historical predictions. For German stocks, a size variable and the "plant and equipment to total capital ratio" are the most important variables in the prediction rule. The inclusion of additional accounting ratios does not have a substantial effect on the accuracy of forecasts. The predictive power of the instrumental variables approach is similar to that of the Bayesian adjustment. Both methods reduce the variance of the cross-section of beta coefficients and thus the inefficiency of the forecast. We are not able to demonstrate the superiority of either of these procedures in predicting the systematic risk of German stocks. While the results for the relations between systematic risk and accounting variables are similar to those of Bauer (1992), the conclusions concerning the predictive ability of fundamental beta forecasts are different. The results reported here indicate that an application of fundamental beta forecasts - or a combination of historical and fundamental prediction employed by Bauer (1992) - for German stocks is questionable for the following reasons. The relations between systematic risk and accounting variables are insignificant for many accounting ratios, especially for financial leverage, with which a clear positive interaction would be expected. There is no theoretical explanation for the signs of the relations for size and operating leverage variables which are the most important variables for the corrective effect of the instrumental variables approach. The improvement of beta forecasts from the instrumental variables approach results from a correction of historical betas, but it is not based on the idea of explaining changes in systematic risk with changes in accounting numbers representing determinants of risk. An equivalent or better improvement, in the case of our sample, can be achieved by a Bayesian adjustment which also has lower costs of implementation.

References

Bauer, C. (1992): Das Risiko von Aktienanlagen - Die fundamentale Analyse und Schätzung von Aktienrisiken. Cologne (Müller Botermann).

Beaver, W.H., Kettler, P. and Scholes, M. (1970): The Association Between Market Determined and Accounting Determined Risk Measures, in: Accounting Review 45, 654- 682.

Beaver, W.H. and Manegold J. (1975): The Association Between Market-Determined and Accounting-Determined Measures of Systematic Risk: Some Further Evidence, in: Journal of Financial and Quantative Analysis 10, 231-284.

Black, F. (1993): Beta and Return - "Announcements of the 'Death' of Beta Seem Premature", in: Journal of Portfolio Management 20 (1), 8-18.

Blume, M.E. (1971): On the Assessment of Risk, in: Journal of Finance 26, 1-10.

Bowman, R.G. (1979): The Theoretical Relationship Between Systematic Risk and Financial (Accounting) Variables, in: Journal of Finance 34, 617-630.

Bowman, R.G. (1981): The Theoretical Relationship Between Systematic Risk and Financial (Accounting) Variables - Reply, in: Journal of Finance 36, 749-750.

Callahan, C.M. and Mohr, R. M. (1989): The Determinants of Systematic Risk: A Synthesis, in: Financial Review 24, 157-181.

Chung, K.H. (1989): The Impact of Demand Volatility and Leverages on the Systematic Risk of Common Stocks, in: Journal of Business Finance and Accounting 16, 343-360.

Cohen, K.J.,Hawawini, G.A., Maier, S.F., Schwartz, R.A., and Whitcomb, D.K. (1983a): Estimating and Adjusting for the Intervalling-Effect Bias in Beta, in: Management Science 29, 135-148.

Cohen, K.J., Hawawini, G.A., Maier, S.F., Schwartz, R.A., and Whitcomb, D.K. (1983b): Friction in the Trading Process and the Estimation of Systematic Risk, in: Journal of Financial Economics 12, 263-278.

Conine, T.E. (1983): On the Theoretical Relationship Between Systematic Risk and Price Elasticity of Demand, in: Journal of Business Finance and Accounting 10, 173-183.

Corhay, A. (1992): The Intervalling Effect Bias in Beta: A Note, in: Journal of Banking and Finance 16, 61-73.

Dimson, E. (1979): Risk Measurement when Shares are subject to Infrequent Trading, in: Journal of Financial Economics 7, 197-226.

Elgers, P.T. (1980): Accounting-Based Risk Predictions: A Re-examination, in: Accounting Review 55, 389-408.

Eskew, R.K. (1979): The Forecasting Ability of Accounting Risk Measures: Some Additional Evidence, in: Accounting Review 54, 107-118.

Fama, E.F. and French, K.R. (1992): The Cross-section of Expected Stock Returns, in: Journal of Finance 47, 427-465.

Frantzmann, H.-J. (1990): Zur Messung des Marktrisikos deutscher Aktien, in: Zeitschrift für betriebswirtschaftliche Forschung 42, 67-83.

Hawawini, G.A. (1980): Intertemporal Cross-Dependence in Securitities Daily Returns and the Short-Run Intervalling Effect on Systematic Risk, in: Journal of Financial and Quantative Analysis 15, 139-149.

Klemkosky, R.C. and John D. M. (1975): The Adjustment of Beta Forecasts, in: Journal of Finance 30, 1123-1128.

Lee, Ch.-F., Newbold, P., Finnerty, J.E., and Chu, Ch.-Ch. (1986): On Accounting-Based, Market-Based, and Composit-Based Beta Predictions: Methods and Implications, in: Financial Review 21, 51-68.

Mandelker, G.N. and Rhee, S.G. (1984): The Impact of the Degrees of Operating and Financial Leverage on Systematic Risk of Common Stock, in: Journal of Financial and Quantative Analysis 19, 14-57.

Marsh, P. (1979): Equity Issues and the Efficiency of the UK Stock Market, in: Journal of Finance 34, 839-862.

Mincer, J. and V. Zarnowitz (1969): The Evaluation of Economic Forecasts, in: Mincer, J. (ed.): Economic Forecasts and Expectations. New York (National Bureau of Economic Research), 3-46.

Möller, H.P. (1986): Bilanzkennzahlen und Ertragsrisiken des Kapitalmarkts. Stuttgart (C.E. Poeschel).

Müller, W. (1992): Bilanzinformation und Aktienbewertung. Frankfurt/Main (Knapp).

Pfennig, M. (1993): Zur fundamentalen Erklärung der Beta-Faktoren am deutschen Aktienmarkt. Frankfurt (Institut für Kapitalmarktforschung, University of Frankfurt).

Reilly, F.K. and Wright, D.J. (1988): A Comparison of Published Betas, in: Journal of Portfolio Management 14, 64-69.

Rosenberg, B. and Guy, J. (1976): Prediction of Beta from Investment Fundamentals - Part I, in: Financial Analysts Journal 32, 60-72.

Rosenberg, B. and Guy, J. (1976): Prediction of Beta from Investment Fundamentals - Part II, in: Financial Analysts Journal 32, 62-70.

Rosenberg, B. and Vinay, M. (1975): The Prediction of Investment Risk: Systematic and Individual Risk, in: Proceedings of the Seminar on the Analysis of Security Prices, University of Chicago, November 1975, Reprint No. 21 of the Institute of Business and Economic Research of the University of California. Berkeley, 85-225.

Schlag, Ch. (1994): Neues zum Intervalling-Effekt am deutschen Aktienmarkt, in: Kredit und Kapital 27, 437-460.

Scholes, M. and Williams, J. (1977): Estimating Beta from Non-Synchronous Data, in: Journal of Financial Economics 5, 309-327.

Steiner, M. and Bauer, Ch. (1992): Die fundamentale Analyse und Prognose des Marktrisikos deutscher Aktien, in: Zeitschrift für betriebswirtschaftliche Forschung 44, 347-368.

Steiner, M., Beiker, H. and Bauer, Ch. (1993): Theoretische Erklärungen unterschiedlicher Aktienrisiken und empirische Überprüfungen, in: W. Bühler, H. Hax and R. Schmidt (eds.): Empirische Kapitalmarktforschung. Zeitschrift für betriebswirtschaftliche Forschung, special issue 31, 99-129.

Vasicek, O.A. (1973): A Note on Using Cross-sectional Information in Bayesian Estimation of Security Betas, in: Journal of Finance 28, 1233-1239.

Zimmermann, P. (1993): Intervaling-Effekt und Anpassungsverfahren bei der Schätzung von Betawerten am deutschen Aktienmarkt. Working Paper, Lehrstuhl für Kreditwirtschaft und Finanzierung, University of Frankfurt, February.

Zimmermann, P. (1994): Systematisches Aktienkursrisiko und fundamentale Unternehmensdaten. Working Paper, Seminar für Kapitalmarktforschung und Finanzierung, University of Munich, September.

Measuring Portfolio Performance and the Empirical Content of the APT

Manfred Steiner, Thomas Nowak and Carsten Wittrock
University of Augsburg

1. Basic problems in performance measurement

The investment performance of mutual fund managers has been extensively evaluated in the literature, especially in the USA. To determine whether a manager has generated superior returns it is necessary to adjust his portfolio performance for risk by comparing that performance with the returns of a passive portfolio in the same risk class. In the earlier studies of Treynor (1965), Jensen (1968, 1969) and Sharpe (1966) the Capital Asset Pricing Model (CAPM) provided the expected risk-return relationship.

Two main issues have to be resolved in measuring fund performance. The one is the choice of an appropriate benchmark and the other results from timing-related problems which can upwardly bias estimates of systematic risk in the case of market timing strategies.

Roll (1977, 1978), who argued that the Security Market Line criterion gives ambiguous signals for portfolio evaluation, drew attention to the first issue. The apparent inefficiency of market proxies coupled with concern over the testability of the CAPM has stimulated recent research on the APT, developed by Ross (1976, 1977), which constitutes another potential benchmark with which to measure normal performance.

The theoretical objections raised by Roll appear to have been resolved by Grinblatt/Titman (1989) who show that an unconditional mean-variance efficient portfolio consisting of assets, which are considered tradable by the evaluated investor, classifies informed investors as positive performers and therefore allows correct inferences about an investor's performance. Thus, in contrast to the use of the market portfolio in tests of the CAPM, which requires the observability of all assets, this benchmark consists of a relatively small set of assets which is relatively mean-variance efficient in respect to those assets.

The insights of Grinblatt/Titman rest on the assumption that means, variances and covariances of excess returns of assets are computed from the perspective of the uninformed investor. Such investors view excess returns as being drawn from an independent and identical distribution over time. Hence, the distribution of returns is stationary and thus the mean and variance of the relatively efficient portfolio are constant. A further assumption is that the transactions of informed investors do not affect market prices so that the unconditional distribution of the returns is not a function of the information generated by informed traders.[1]

These insights are important in at least two respects, namely, in indicating that links between performance measures and particular equilibrium models are not necessary conditions, and, that legal or statutory restrictions are easier to take into account when looking for an appropriate benchmark. However, the problem of determining ex ante benchmark efficiency is still formidable.

Another difficulty in performance measurement concerns the measurement of portfolio risk when managers acting on private information revise the composition of their portfolios and thereby alter the risk level of their funds. In anticipation of positive, or negative, general market price movements managers may gain additional returns from market timing activities by switching from less to more risky equities. Jensen (1972), Grant (1977), Admati/Ross (1985) and Dybvig/Ross (1985) show that the resulting nonstationarity of portfolio return distributions can introduce bias into performance measures using simple regressions, such as the Jensen measure. These measures are based on the assumption that managers possess no market-timing ability and that any abnormal performance is due to stock selection. Several models were developed that allow for such forms of nonstationarity of the portfolio risk level.

This study deals with the performance of 21 German stock and balanced funds during the period from January 1974 to December 1991. Different methods are applied which do not require the observation of portfolio holdings and which are considered to be advanced techniques for the detection of superior performers both theoretically and empirically.[2] An empirical analysis of the APT provides a potential alternative benchmark for portfolio performance evaluation. In contrast to other studies, the factors which might be the common sources of systematic risk affecting security returns are prespecified.

---

[1] These issues are discussed in more detail in Nowak/Wittrock (1994), Wittrock/Steiner (1995), and Wittrock (1995).

[2] In general the approaches which require portfolio weights can reduce benchmark and timing-related problems. However, such data on portfolio holdings are difficult to obtain and the use of interim reports (Rechenschafts- and Zwischenberichte) means a somewhat long interval for measuring the performance of the funds. Empirical examinations using portfolio weights, can be found in Wittrock (1995).

2. Measures of performance

The widely used Jensen alpha, which is the intercept of a least squares regression of the excess returns of the managed portfolio $\tilde{r}_{Pt}$ on the excess returns of a proxy for the market portfolio $\tilde{r}_{Et}$ is given by

$$\tilde{r}_{Pt} \quad = \quad J_P + b_P \, \tilde{r}_{Et} + \tilde{\delta}_{Pt} \,, \qquad (1)$$

where:

$$b_P \quad = \quad \text{estimated least squares slope coefficient}$$

$$\tilde{\delta}_{Pt} \quad = \quad \text{error term}$$

$$E(\tilde{\delta}_{Pt}) \quad = \quad \mathrm{Cov}(\tilde{\delta}_{Pt}, \tilde{r}_{Et}) = \mathrm{Cov}(\tilde{\delta}_{Pt}, \tilde{\delta}_{Pt-1}) = 0$$

However, if a manager has timing abilities, J_P can be negative. Measures that cope with the problems associated with the shifting composition and changing risk of managed portfolios can be categorized either as measures which correct for the bias in Jensen's alpha that is induced by the effect of timing abilities; or, as methodologies which ascribe total performance to selectivity and timing abilities. In the case of the former, a direct test of timing abilities is an explicit possibility whereas in the latter case only the combined performance can be measured without an identification of the components. The measures applied in this study are summarized in Figure 1.

Grinblatt/Titman (1992), Shukla/Trzcinka (1992), Ippolito (1993), Steiner/Wittrock (1995) and Wittrock (1995) give a detailed survey of these and other performance measures.

It is important to note that portfolios can only be ranked by selectivity performance because performance attributable to timing abilities is affected by risk aversion (Grinblatt/Titman 1989, p. 410).

Regression-based timing measures include the quadratic regression proposed by Treynor/Mazuy (1966).[3] This regression is identical to the one used to compute Jensen' s alpha, except that an additional term, the squared excess return of the benchmark, is included as specified in equation (2).

---

[3] A formal treatment of the test is found in Pfleiderer/Bhattacharya (1983) and Admati/Bhattacharya/Pfleiderer/Ross (1986). Detailed descriptions of all approaches are given by Nowak/Wittrock (1993), Steiner/Wittrock (1994), Wittrock/Steiner (1995) and Wittrock (1995).

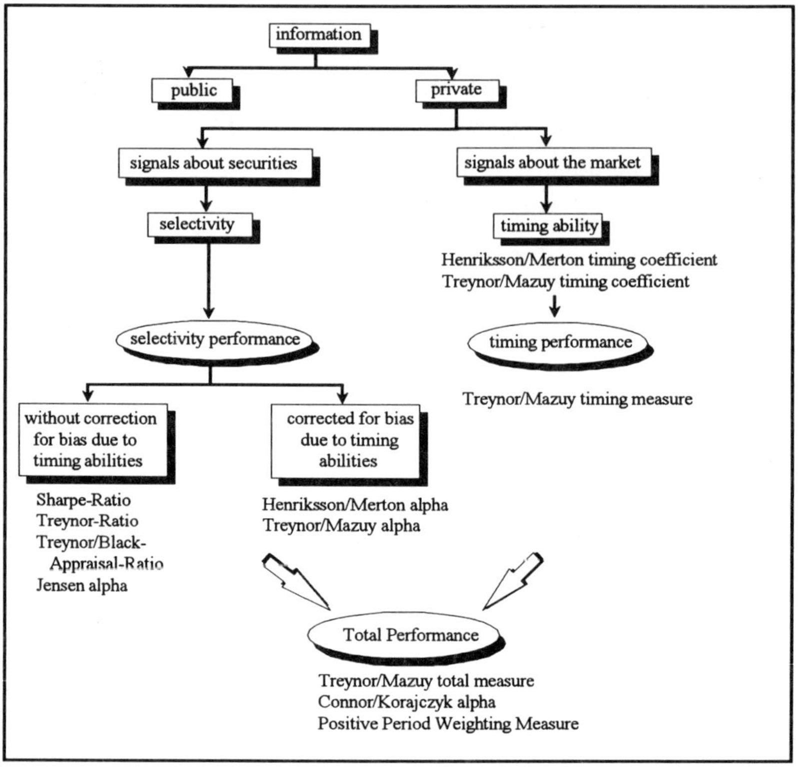

Figure 1: Measures for identifying private information

$$\tilde{r}_{Pt} = J_P^{T/M} + b_P \tilde{r}_{Et} + \gamma_P (\tilde{r}_{Et})^2 + \tilde{\delta}_{Pt}, \tag{2}$$

where $\tilde{r}_{Pt}$ = excess return of portfolio p

$\tilde{r}_{Et}$ = excess return of the relative mean-variance efficient portfolio

$J_P^{T/M}$ = Treynor/Mazuy alpha

Under certain conditions the coefficient on the quadratic term γ_P can be used to detect the precision of the manager' s timing forecasts. The timing component of performance is given by

$$\text{T/M-Tim.} = \gamma_P Var(\tilde{R}_E) \tag{3}$$

and the total performance can be calculated by adding $J_P^{T/M}$ and T/M-Tim.

A similar approach was developed by Merton (1981) and Henriksson/Merton (1981) in which the portfolio beta is assumed to switch between two betas conditioned on the forecast of the investor, namely, high beta corresponding to a positive excess return on the benchmark portfolio, and a beta of zero corresponding to a forecasted benchmark excess return which is positive as shown by equation (4).

$$\tilde{r}_{Pt} \quad = \quad J_P^{H/M} + \beta_{1P}\, \tilde{r}_{Et} + \beta_{2P} \max(0\,;\, -\tilde{r}_{Et}) + \tilde{\varepsilon}_{Pt}, \qquad (4)$$

The term max $(0; -\tilde{r}_{Et})$ in equation (4) can be regarded as an end-of-period value of a put option on the benchmark portfolio with a strike price equal to the risk-free return. As in the Treynor/Mazuy (1966) approach, a coefficient which is significantly positive indicates that the manager possesses, and utilizes, superior information on the returns on the market index.

The limitations of these methods lie in their restrictive behavioral assumptions and a misclassification of managers when stock returns are co-skewed with the benchmark returns or when co-skewness is generated by artifical timing.

Artificial timing is meant to be one of the reasons for the negative correlation, between the alpha and timing coefficient in the above mentioned approaches, which was identified by Chang/Lewellen (1984), Henriksson (1984), Lehmann/Modest (1987), Connor/Korajczyk (1991) among others.[4] The artifical timing components may be due to the dynamic trading strategies of managers who, without any superior information, replicate a put. Another explanation may be that, as pointed out by Jagannathan/Korajczyk (1986), there are nonlinearities in returns resulting from the leverage effects of the underlying asset return generating process. This would cause negative timing coefficients for funds investing in stocks having a lower leverage level than that of the benchmark portfolio. This is not unrealistic considering the fact that most funds invest in Blue Chips whereas broad indices also include smaller companies. On the other hand, funds which have specialized in investments in smaller companies should exhibit positive timing coefficients.

Connor/Korajczyk (1991) extend the Henriksson/Merton approach by allowing for costly market put options in the returns on the funds in order to capture artificial timing. This is effected by constructing a net put option as a variable in the regression

---

[4] However, it can be shown that the negative correlation is mainly due to a statistical error. A formal treatment is given by Wittrock (1995). Artificial timing should be at least one of the reasons for the preponderance of negative timing coefficients. Empirical evidence is given by Wittrock (1995).

$$\tilde{r}_{Pt} = J_P^{C/K} + \beta_{1P}\tilde{r}_{Et} + \beta_{2P}\Big[\underbrace{\max(0, R_{ft} - \tilde{R}_{Et}) - (1 + R_{ft})\, put_0}_{net\ put}\Big] + \tilde{\varepsilon}_{Pt}, \qquad (5)$$

where put_0 is the time-zero market value of the put. In contrast to the Henriksson/Merton (1981) regression, which implies that mutual funds own a costless option, the costs of the options due to artificial timing are reflected in the mean returns through the intercept in the Connor/Korajczyk (1986) model. The net put

$$put_{net} = put - (1 + R_f)\, put_0, \qquad (6)$$

where:

$$put = \max\,(R_{ft} - \tilde{R}_{Et}, 0)$$

$$put_0 = 2\,N\,(0{,}5\sigma\sqrt{t}\,) - 1,$$

equals a portfolio insurance contract and guarantees an investor, who holds it together with the market portfolio, the risk-free return minus the future value of the put price. Since the option is a European put option against a non-dividend-paying index, it can be priced with the formula developed by Black/Scholes (1973). The Connor/Korajczyk model allows for non-information based changes in mutual fund betas and simultaneously measures the sum of timing and selectivity performance.[5]

Another approach to the measurement of total performance is the positive period weighting measure developed by Grinblatt/Titman (1989).

The assumption that uninformed investors view excess returns as being drawn from an independent identical distribution implies (1) that the aforementioned unconditional mean-variance-efficient portfolio has constant portfolio weights and (2) that the beliefs of uninformed investors are independent of realised returns on individual assets and therefore also independent of realised returns on the relatively efficient portfolio. Hence their portfolio weights and portfolio beta will not change for different realised returns and the covariance between their portfolio weights and asset returns is zero. Contrastingly, an informed investor will change his portfolio weights in response to either selectivity or timing information thereby inducing a nonzero covariance between his portfolio weights and asset returns.

---

[5] Simulations of selectivity and timing abilities, for investigating the robustness of different performance measures, by Wittrock (1995) have shown favourable results applying the Connor/Korajczyk (1986) model in detecting private information compared with other measures including the aforementioned methods and the positive period weighting measure.

The Grinblatt/Titman measure, namely, the weighted sum of the period by period excess returns on the evaluated portfolio, is based on these insights. The sum of the weights w multiplied by the time series of excess returns of the relative mean-variance efficient benchmark portfolio must at the same time be zero. Grinblatt/Titman also show that, if these periodic weights are nonnegative, the weighted average of excess returns of an evaluated portfolio will be positive assuming it is managed by an investor whose forecasting ability enables him to time the market or select individual stocks. A formal description results in

$$\mathrm{PW} = \sum_{t=1}^{T} w_t \, r_{Pt} \tag{7}$$

where:

$$\mathrm{w_t} = w(r_{Et}, T)$$

$$\sum_{t=1}^{T} w_t \, r_{Et} \rightarrow 0 \ \ for \ \ T \rightarrow \infty,$$

$$\sum_{t=1}^{T} w_t = 1 \text{ and } \mathrm{w_t} > 0, \mathrm{t} = 1, \ldots, \mathrm{T}$$

where the large sample PW is zero for uninformed investors and positive for informed investors as long as the investor is a positive market timer.[6]

After choosing the appropiate benchmark portfolio the next concern is the choice of weights. Grinblatt/Titman (1994) and Cumby/Glen (1990) derive weights by assuming that uninformed investors have a power utility function

$$\mathrm{U}(\mathrm{W_t}) = \frac{1}{1-\theta} W_t^{1-\theta} \tag{8}$$

with:

$\mathrm{W_t}$ = wealth at the end of period t

θ = coefficient of relative risk aversion, where $\theta > 0$.

The choice of a power utility function has several advantages. In particular it does not exhibit satiation as does a quadratic utility function. Hence, the weights derived from a power utility function satisfy the nonnegativity constraint for the portfolio weights.

---

6 Another condition requires that either selectivity and timing information are independent; or, that the investor has constant absolute risk-aversion due to wealth effects, see Grinblatt/Titman (1989, p. 406). A more detailed description of this measure and its theoretical background can be found in Grinblatt/Titman (1994) and Wittrock/Steiner (1995).

Since the uninformed investor divides his wealth between the relative mean-variance efficient portfolio and the risk-free security, his wealth at the end of period t is

$$W_t = W_t(y) = 1 + y\tilde{R}_{Et} + (1-y)R_{ft} \qquad (9)$$

where: y = proportion of wealth invested in $\tilde{R}_{Et}$; and

$1 - y$ = proportion of wealth invested in R_{ft}.

The uninformed investor maximizes his expected utility by choosing y. To estimate the optimal choice of y, y*, an algorithm

$$E(U(W_t)) = (1-\theta)^{-1} \sum_{t=1}^{T} (1 + R_{ft} + y\tilde{r}_{Et})^{1-\theta} \qquad (10)$$

can be applied. Choosing the optimal y* computes the time series of gross returns on the optimal portfolio $(1 + R_{ft} + y^* \tilde{r}_{Et})$. Interpreting those gross returns as wealth levels, the marginal utility of wealth W at time t can be derived as the first order condition of the power function $(1 + R_{ft} + y^* \tilde{r}_{Et})^{-\theta} \tilde{r}_{Et}$. Therefore the weights are defined as $(1 + R_{ft} + y^* \tilde{r}_{Et})^{-\theta}$. Normalizing the weights to sum to unity implies that the PW can be interpreted as monthly abnormal returns in the same units as $\tilde{r}_{Et}$. Thus the weights are specified as

$$W_t = (1 + R_{ft} + y\,\tilde{r}_{Et})^{-\theta} / \sum_{t=1}^{T} (1 + R_{ft} + y\,\tilde{r}_{Et})^{-\theta} \qquad (11)$$

and are multiplied with the excess returns of the evaluated portfolio in computing the PW defined by equation (7).[7]

In this context the weights can be interpreted as the marginal utilities of an investor with a power utility function. If the active portfolio is managed without any special information, then adding it to the mean-variance efficient portfolio achieves no improvement, so the measure would take on a value of zero. It is interesting to note that the Jensen measure has implicit weights that satisfy all conditions of the PW except the nonnegative weight condition. Therefore the timing related problems of the Jensen-measure can be explained by interpreting

---

[7] A thorough description is given by Grinblatt/Titman (1994, p. 439). The test statistic is developed in detail by Cumby/Glen (1990, p. 500).

the weights of this measure as the marginal utilities of an investor with a quadratic utility function. The marginal utility becomes negative for large terminal wealth levels — an unrealistic situation in which the weights take on negative values for benchmark returns that are very high. Successful timers that have very high betas when market returns are high are thus penalized rather than rewarded by Jensen' s Alpha.[8]

All of the above mentioned approaches can be transferred to an APT framework. Connor/Korajczyk (1986) show that the intercept of a regression of portfolio returns on the values of the different factors may be interpreted in much the same way as the Jensen alpha. Grinblatt/Titman (1994) use a ten- and eight-portfolio benchmark to construct the relatively efficient portfolio. Lehmann/Modest (1987) employ the Treynor/Mazuy (1966)-approach in an APT context.

3. Empirical analysis

3.1. The arbitrage pricing theory as a benchmark

3.1.1 The basic empirical methodology

The APT formulated by Ross (1976, 1977) assumes that asset returns are affected by a small number of exogenous factors, i.e., individuals believe that returns on assets are generated by a k-factor model which can be expressed as

$$R_i = E(R_i) + b_{i1} f_1 + b_{i2} f_2 + ... + b_{ik} f_k + \varepsilon_i \qquad (12)$$

where: $E(R_i)$ = expected return of the ith asset, if all factors have a value of zero

f_k = $[F_k - E(F_k)]$

= value of the random, **unanticipated** systematic kth (risk)-factor

b_{ik} = sensitivity of the return on asset i (factor beta) to the fluctuations in factor k

---

8 However, it can be shown that a negative bias in Jensen' s alpha only occurs under certain circumstances (Shukla/Trzcinka 1992, p. 14, Wittrock 1995, p. 88).

ε_i = unsystematic risk component, idiosyncratic to the ith asset.

Different assets have different levels of sensitivities (b_{ik}) to these unknown factors and such sensitivities are interpreted as measures of systematic risk. Every asset's value changes when one of these variables undergoes an unanticipated change. Adducing arbitrage arguments it can be shown that expected asset returns are approximately, or strictly, linear in the sensitivities of the assets to the exogenous factors

$$E(R_i) = \lambda_0 + \lambda_1 b_{i1} + \lambda_2 b_{i2} + ... + \lambda_k b_{ik} \qquad (13)$$

Equation (13) is the core of the APT and implies that the expected return on any asset i can be written as the product of a linear combination of the factor betas and the risk premia (λ_K) associated with the k factors.

Although the model has gained theoretic importance, practical applications of (13), its pricing equation, have been hampered by difficulties in estimating the unkown factors. The APT assumes a factor model of returns a priori, namely, equation (12), and does not generate the returns process endogenously in giving effect to economic influences on asset prices. As a consequence there is a large amount of ambiguity in the empirical predictions of the APT, particulary when compared with the CAPM.[9]

Following this interpretation of the APT as a statistical model with unobservable factors, factor analytical procedures developed by Roll and Ross (1980) can be used to estimate the unknown factors, f_k, and factor betas, b_{ik}, simultaneously.[10] However, here we conform to the current trend by prespecifying factors[11] and use innovations in German macroeconomic variables as proxies for the underlying risk factors driving security returns, as in the seminal study by Chen/Roll/Ross (1986).

Apparently, the first, and crucial, task in this process of implementing APT for performance measurement lies in the prespecification of the factors which are hypothesized to impact average returns. Unfortunately there is no complete theory to justify replacing the unobserved factors with any set of observed

[9] A comparison of factor models and models from capital market theory can be found in Steiner/Nowak (1995).

[10] A brief description of this procedure and first results for the German stock market is given by Adelberger/Lockert (1995).

[11] The reason for choosing this kind of empirical implementation lies in the fact that performance measurement only makes sense with a fully identified benchmark. More detailed discussion of this subject can be found in Nowak/Wittrock (1993).

variables. Nor is there a correct set of factors and every selection reflects a substantial degree of subjectivity. The following selection of macroeconomic variables therefore gives effect to our economic intuition.[12]

Factor-selection is followed by the construction of the variables and, in particular, the isolation of their unanticipated component. This is necessary since efficient market theory implies that only innovations in the factors, i.e., economic news, have a pervasive influence on returns. Following Löflund (1992), our goal is to approximate the information set available to investors and then to extract the expected portion from the realised values of the macroeconomic variables. We assume that investors have a very reduced information set, use naive or simple forecasts and adopt an ARIMA-model. As a third technique and methodological innovation in this context, we employ a neural network.[13]

Table 1: Macroeconomic variables in the tests

Variable	Symbol	Definition
Exchange rate	**EX**	trade-weighted exchange rate of the German mark; 1972 = 100
Business climate	**BUC**	Index; seasonally adjusted
Money supply	**MON**	M1; seasonally adjusted
Order receipts	**ORD**	values; 1985 = 100; seasonally adjusted
Energy-price-index	**OIL**	in DM; 1985 = 100; HWWA-Index
Interest rate	**RATE**	yield of German medium-term Government bonds (4 years)
Terms of trade	**TOT**	price-index;1985 = 100; seasonally adjusted
Term structure	**TERM**	yield-difference: German long-term Government bonds (10 years) ./. German short-term Government bonds (1 year)

In a third, and last, step it is necessary to examine econometric issues related to the testing of the APT (Nowak 1994). The task of testing a prespecified APT model is conceptually related to the original proofs of the CAPM. The most commonly used test is the two-step procedure developed by Black/Jensen/Scholes (1972) and Fama/MacBeth (1973), in which the factor betas are first estimated in a time-series regression and thereafter, used as data for a cross-sectional regression to yield estimates of risk premia. However, the most recent proofs of the APT are based on rather advanced econometric techniques because the two-step approach has long been recognized to be subject to an errors-in-the-variables

[12] These variables emerged from a thorough discussion in Steiner/Nowak (1994).
[13] The General Regression Neural Network employed is described by Wittkemper (1994).

defect. McElroy/Burmeister (1988) employ a regression method which not only circumvents those econometric pitfalls but also recognises that the return generating process (12) and the asset pricing relationship (13) are related via $E(R_i)$. Substituting (13) into (12) yields a multivariate nonlinear regression with which factor betas and their associated 'prices' using Gallant's (1975,1987) iterated non-linear seemingly unrelated regression technique (INSUR) can be jointly estimated.[14]

3.1.2 Macroeconomic variables and asset pricing: the basic results

The tests were conducted with monthly stock returns from 1968 - 1991 and the macro-economic variables are monthly time-series for the same period. For the Fama/MacBeth (1973) tests the total time period is divided into 20 four-year estimation periods (time-series regressions) and corresponding 20 one-year testing periods (cross-sectional regressions). The cross-sectional regression is run for each of the 12 months in the testing period and creates monthly estimates of risk premia from which the time-series means are computed for four five-year periods. Table 2 summarizes the main findings from the APT tests using individual securities and different innovation specifications.[15]

Table 2 demonstrates weak relationships between average stock returns and factor risk measures.[16] Furthermore, the results are not robust to different modellings of the unanticipated component. Here the neural network gives the best performance. Since such disturbing results might be attributable to estimation errors, that are inherent in the Fama/MacBeth (1973) approach, we now try to pool all the data into one multivariate analysis.

These tests necessitate a recognition that the computer intensiveness of the estimation procedure (nonlinear and simultaneous) rules out the usage of the complete data and factor set. One way to reduce the number of cross-sectional units is to group assets into portfolios. Since it was desired to preclude such a bias from the test, only subsets of the German stock market were analyzed, namely, by classifying individual assets according to the market segment they belong to and analyzing each segment separately.[17] Additionally the model was restricted to four factors only.

---

[14] The basic econometric principles are presented in Judge et. al. (1988) and Srivastava/Giles (1987).

[15] The results can only be presented at a high level of aggregation and for individual stocks. For the comprehensive results of our additional tests with different portfolio sorting criteria see Nowak (1994).

[16] The results using different portfolio principles were much better but still too weak.

[17] Apart from the econometric necessities there is also an economic justification for this procedure. Levy (1978) introduced a GCAPM which incorporated individual securities

Table 2: Summary of Fama-MacBeth cross-sectional regressions of stock returns on factor betas over five subperiods: individual securities and different innovation specifications

SIMPLE								
Period	**EX**	**BUC**	**MON**	**OIL**	**ORD**	**RATE**	**TERM**	**TOT**
72-76								
77-81					+		+	
82-86	+					⊖		
87-91								
ARIMA								
Period	**EX**	**BUC**	**MON**	**OIL**	**ORD**	**RATE**	**TERM**	**TOT**
72-76								
77-81								
82-86		⊕						
87-91						⊕		⊖
NETWORK								
Period	**EX**	**BUC**	**MON**	**OIL**	**ORD**	**RATE**	**TERM**	**TOT**
72-76							+	
77-81		-		-	+			
82-86		⊕						
87-91						⊕		-

EX = trade-weighted exchange rate; BUC = Business climate; MON = Money supply; OIL = Energy price-index; ORD = Order receipts; RATE = Interest rate; TERM = Term structure; TOT = Terms of Trade; ⊕/⊖ = significant on the 5%-level and sign is pos./neg.;

+ / - = significant on the 10%-level and sign is pos./neg.

It is obvious from the results in Table 3 that the number of priced risk factors is again disappointing. While the results for the first two segments are quite encouraging, there are virtually no significant risk premia in the lowest market segments.[18] Hence, the extremely weak risk-return relationship of this APT model clearly demonstrates that our APT specification is not a viable tool for risk-adjustments in performance measurement.

market lines for different market segments. Beiker (1993) shows that the market segment influences the securities specific risks.

[18] It must be remembered however that this regression-technique is highly sensitive to variations in the starting values and the factor set in the optimization algorithm.

Table 3: Summary of INSUR-techniques over five subperiods: individual securities, different innovation specifications and different subsamples

Factor	BUC			MON			OIL			RATE		
	SIMPLE	ARIMA	NETWORK	SIMPLE	ARIMA	NETWORK	SIMPLE	ARIMA	NETWORK	SIMPLE	ARIMA	NETWORK
Period						DAX						
72-76		⊖	-		⊖	-					⊕	⊕
77-81												
82-86												
87-91	+			⊖		⊖	⊕		⊕	-		-
Period						VAR						
72-76	⊕	⊕							⊕	⊕	⊕	
77-81												
82-86												
87-91		⊖									⊖	
Period						KASSA						
72-76												
77-81												
82-86												
87-91			+									
Period						FREI						
72-76												
77-81												
82-86												
87-91												

RATE = Interest rate; TERM = Term structure; TOT = Terms of Trade; DAX = Stocks of Deutscher Aktienindex ; VAR = Stocks with variable trading.; KASSA = Stocks without variable trading; FREI = Stocks in the Freiverkehr; ⊕/⊖ = significant on the 5%-level and sign is pos./neg.

+ / - = significant on the 10%-level and sign is pos./neg..

3.2 The performance of German Mutual Funds

3.2.1 Benchmark efficiency

Hsia (1986), Gibbons/Ross/Shanken (1989) and Cumby/Glen (1990), among others, all propose procedures for testing the mean-variance efficiency of a candidate benchmark portfolio. As already mentioned, Grinblatt/Titman (1989) have pointed out that such a portfolio may consist of a relatively small set of assets that are considered tradable by the evaluated investor. Thus, since we lack returns data on the full set of equities available to fund managers we adopt commonly used indices as candidate benchmarks. Of these, the DAFOX, a broadly diversified value-weighted performance index qualifies as a benchmark portfolio in that it covers the most important market for fund investments which mainly comprises assets that can be considered as tradable by the managers. Göppl/Schütz (1992) could not reject its efficiency using a Hotelling-T^2 statistic as in Shanken (1985).[19]

Grinblatt/Titman (1994) construct an eight portfolio benchmark modelling the known anomalies in the benchmark. However, modelling anomalies in the benchmark is subject to criticism as noted by Wittrock (1995) and Grinold (1993).[20]

3.2.2 Evidence on mutual fund performance

Mutual fund data were obtained from the BVI Bundesverband Deutscher Investment-Gesellschaften e.V.[21] The sample period is for 5/1974 to 12/1991 and is divided in three sub periods, namely, from 5/1974 to 12/1979, 1/1980 to 12/1985 and from 4/1986 to 12/1991, thus comprising periods with stable, rising and volatile periods. The German-based funds consists of 21 funds which mainly invest in German stocks and include 3 balanced funds. 21 funds existed from 4/1986 to 12/1991 and only 16 in the complete period from 5/1974 to 12/1991.

---

[19] Tests proposed by Cumby/Glen (1990) were carried out using all of the available indices. These tests included an equally weighted index constructed by Wittrock (1995). Using that index, the efficiency of DAFOX was rejected at the 5 % significance level. However, it has been noted by Lehmann/Modest (1987, p. 260) and Hendricks/Patel/ Zeckhauser (1993, p. 123) that equally weighted indices are not suitable for measuring the performance of mutual funds.

[20] This includes the questionable procedures for identifying anomalies, their instability over time and the justification not to credit a manager for identifying anomalies. These aspects are discussed in more detail in Grinold (1993), Krämer/Runde (1991, 1993), Wittrock (1995) and Elton/Gruber/Das/Hlavka (1993, p.12, footnote 13).

[21] Descriptive statistics of the funds can be found in Steiner/Wittrock (1994).

As shown in Steiner/Wittrock (1994) and Nowak/Wittrock (1994), the effect of survivorship, bias, if any, is negligable. The monthly returns were adjusted for cash-distributions. The risk-free interest rate is proxied with the 30-day money market rate in the Frankfurt interbank market.

Table 4 repeats the results of applying all measures obtained with the DAFOX as the benchmark. The reported number of significant coefficients is based on a 5 % significance level whereby the t-statistics are computed with the covariance matrix estimator proposed by White (1980).[22]

The Jensen measures are mostly negative and in no case is there evidence of statistically significant superior performance. As expected, especially funds with high capitalizations have high R^2s due to their broad diversification. The values of Jensen's alpha are **very sensitive** to the index used as a proxy which also influences the t-values. Using the DAX as a proxy in period 80/85 for example, all alphas were found to be positive, with two of them significantly different from zero. Introducing the DAFOX as a proxy there are 14 negative alphas, of which two are significant at the 10 % level. In contrast, the ranking is not affected by varying the indices. The Sharpe ratio, which does not need an index for estimating a beta, gives approximately the same rankings.

Applying the models of Treynor/Mazuy (1966) and Henriksson/Merton (1981) most of the timing coefficients were found to be negative and only a small proportion were significant. These findings are consistent with other investigations. As reported in earlier studies the estimated timing coefficients are negatively correlated with the estimated alphas, that a fact which indicates selectivity in almost all cases as shown in Table 5.

---

[22] It can be shown that the residuals of the proposed regressions may not be homoskedastic when the composition of an actively managed portfolio is changing due to private information. Breen/Jagannathan/Ofer (1986), who test other procedures for correcting the bias due to heteroskedasticity including weighted least squares regression, recommend the use of White's procedure. Using Monte Carlo simulation Cumby/Modest (1987) find that appropriate results with this method can be expected with sample sizes of 60 to 100. Tests for autocorrelation and the distribution of residuals are not reported here. There are no signs of autocorrelation in the residuals using the Durbin-Watson test and the hyphothesis of normally distributed residuals could not be rejected using Kolmogorov-Smirnov and Shapiro/Wilk-statistics.

Table 4: Tests of mutual fund performance with the DAFOX as the benchmark in the subperiods

	Average alphas = alpha*10^3			Number of positive (+) and negative (-) values in brackets number of values significantly different from zero using White (1980) heteroscedastic standard errors						Minimal values			Maximal values		
Period	74-79	80-85	86-91	74-79		80-85		86-91		74-79	80-85	86-91	74-79	80-85	86-91
Jensens' s alpha - equation (1)															
J_P	-0,391	-0,910	-0,102	5+/11-	(0)/(0)	4+/14-	(0)/(2)	9+/12-	(0)/(0)	-2,592	-2,397	-2,385	0,634	3,821	4,533
β_P	0,815	0,757	0,812							0,58	0,34	0,45	0,99	0,95	0,98
R^2	0,883	0,850	0,925							0,56	0,41	0,71	0,97	0,96	0,98
Jensens' s alpha - 3-index model equation (1)															
$J/3_P$	-0,62	-0,62	-0,13	7+/9-	(0)/(1)	4+/14-	(0)/(0)	10+/11-	(0)/(0)	-2,43	-2,0	-3,13	0,86	2,59	4,68
R^2	0,899	0,877	0,934							0,61	0,48	0,72	0,98	0,97	0,99
Treynor/Mazuy model - equation (2)															
J^{T/M_a}	0,06	-0,49	1,11	9+/7-	(0)/(0)	4+/14-	(1)/(2)	15+/6-	(1)/(0)	-1,99	-3,90	-1,27	2,75	6,33	4,75
β_P	0,82	0,77	0,79							0,603	0,37	0,43	0,99	0,97	0,97
γ_P	-0,426	-0,298	-0,301	5+/11-	(1)/(1)	6+/12-	(1)/(1)	4+/17-	(0)/(7)	-2,687	-1,762	-1,416	0,901	1,369	0,659
R^2	0,89	0,86	0,93							0,59	0,41	0,83	0,97	0,97	0,98
Henriksson/Merton model - equation (4)															
$J^{H/M}$	0,06	-0,16	1,17	7+/9-	(0)/(0)	6+/12-	(1)/(1)	16+/5-	(0)/(0)	-2,92	-6,10	-0,98	4,27	8,37	6,00
β_{1P}	0,80	0,74	0,76							0,63	0,31	0,40	1,04	0,97	0,99
β_{2P}	-0,037	-0,050	-0,080	5+/11-	(1)/(0)	6+/12-	(1)/(1)	3+/18-	(1)/(1)	-0,375	-0,303	-0,294	0,251	0,276	0,113
R^2	0,89	0,85	0,93							0,58	0,40	0,72	0,97	0,96	0,98
Connor/Korajczyk model - equation (5)															
$J^{C/K}$	-0,45	-0,96	-0,41	7+/9-	(0)/(0)	4+/14-	(1)/(4)	12+/9-	(1)/(1)	-2,85	-2,41	-4,42	0,67	3,50	4,97
β_{1P}	0,80	0,74	0,76							0,63	0,31	0,40	1,04	0,97	0,99
β_{2P}	-0,037	-0,496	-0,080	5+/11-	(1)/(0)	6+/12-	(1)/(1)	3+/18-	(0)/(1)	-0,375	-0,302	-0,294	0,215	0,276	0,113
R^2	0,89	0,85	0,93							0,58	0,40	0,72	0,97	0,96	0,98
Positive period weighting measure - (7)															
PW	-0,37	-0,94	-0,15	5+/11-	(0)/(0)	4+/14-	(0)/(2)	9+/12-	(0)/(0)	-2,58	-2,37	-3,92	0,65	3,44	4,54
Treynor/Mazuy total measure - equation (4) + $J^{T/M}$															
Tot	-0,4	-0,98	-0,19	5+/11-	(1)/(0)	4+/12-	(0)/(2)	9+/12-	(0)/(0)	-2,63	-2,47	-4,07	0,64	3,43	4,73

Table 5: Pearson correlation coefficients between estimated timing coefficients and estimated alphas with the DAFOX as the benchmark

Period	74-79	80-85	86-91	74-91
Correlation between $J^{T/M}$ and γ_P	*-0,7183	*-0,7765	-0,3410	*-0,6083
Correlation between $J^{H/M}$ and β_{2P}	*-0,8718	*-0,8387	*-0,5888	*-0,5893
Correlation between $J^{C/K}$ and β_{2P}	**0,3325**	**-0,2637**	*0,6860	*0,6796

Where significant negative timing coefficients were found, the alphas indicating selectivity were significantly positive. This behavior is difficult to explain economically and caused doubts about the appropriateness of these models. One explanation could be artifical timing which can be taken into account by applying the Connor/Korajczyk (1986) model.[23] The negative correlation was in fact eliminated as indicated in Table 2. The average alpha was negative, indicating that the funds did not exhibit superior performance. However, since this method only compositely measures the sum of timing and selectivity, inferences about the determinants of performance cannot be drawn.

The results of applying the PW measure are almost identical to the other total performance measures, i. e. to the Connor/Korajczyk alpha and the Treynor/Mazuy-total measure. Overall the measure took on a negative value, indicating a negative total performance, which was statistically insignificant in most cases.[24] The results obtained with these measures are, for the majority of the funds, almost identical to the results derived with the Jensen measure. Since Jensen's alpha only indicates performance due to selectivity it seems that on average timing ability was absent. It may however be noted that when certain conditions are met, Jensen's alpha is negatively biased in respect to timing abilities only. Otherwise, as has been shown both theoretically and empirically by Wittrock (1995), Jensen’s measure also captures timing performance. In the periods chosen, the chances that Jensen’s measure would negatively bias the empirical results are quite small. Nevertheless it seems unlikely that successful

---

[23] An estimate of the variance is necessary to price the put-option by using the Black/Scholes formula. The estimated variance of the returns on the market index in the period considered was used.

[24] The coefficient of relative risk aversion was assumed to be 0,05. The results did not appear to be sensitive to the choice of that parameter value. We also used a value of 2, which was identified in an empirical examination of Friend/Blume (1975), and 8 which was used by Grinblatt/Titman (1994). The results were virtually identical although the division between the risk-free asset and market index was quite different (see equation 9).

market timing has contributed to performance after allowing for transaction costs, as the negative timing coefficients of the Treynor/Mazuy (1966) and Henriksson/Merton (1981) models show.[25]

The extent to which different benchmarks matter can be determined by analyzing the correlations between the performance scores generated with different indices. Table 6 reports the correlations for the three total performance measures using the DAFOX, DAFOX Blue Chip and the DAX.

Table 6: Pearson correlations between abnormal returns using positive period weighting with different benchmarks

lower left triangle: period 74/79
1upper right triangle: period 80/85

Indices	DAFOX	DAFOX	DAX
DAFOX	1	0,994	0,909
BC	0,9999	1	0,949
DAX	0,917	0,912	1

lower left triangle: period 86/9
upper right triangle: period 74/91

Indices	DAFOX	DAFOX	DAX
DAFOX	1	0,999	0,970
BC	0,999	1	0,973
DAX	0,999	0,999	1

The results suggest that the ranking of portfolios is unlikely to be sensitive to the choice of benchmark index. However, the absolute performance of each fund differed in respect of each individual index. The results were almost identical for the other measures. The correlations between all of the performance measures that were investigated were computed in testing whether the particular choice of measure is crucial. Table 7 illustrates the results for 74/79 and 80/85.

The results show very similar rankings irrespective of the measures used except for the selectivity measures which correct for the bias in case of timing abilities. However, Wittrock (1995) has shown that selectivity measures are biased because of their statistical relationship with the timing coefficient.

Elton/Gruber/Das/Hlavka (1991) found that the superior performance identified by Ippolito (1989) is eliminated when using a three index model with a small cap and bond index in addition to a blue chip index (S&P 500). Assuming no timing abilities an attempt was also made to determine whether there are significant differences in the case of funds which invest in both stocks and bonds. This seems to be important, especially for balanced funds. The different asset allocation policies of the funds were investigated at the same time by resorting to a three index model including the DAFOX Blue Chip, the DAFOX Small Cap

[25] It has also been demonstrated empirically that the timing coefficients prove to be almost indentically the same as those of purely random portfolios. See Wittrock (1995) for further details.

and the REX-Performance-Index. The alphas (J/3) reported in Table 4 did not change much, indicating that the influence of the capital invested in bonds is small. However, the significance of the results was reduced somewhat. This is supported by the high correlation in Table 4 between J/3 and the other measures.

Table 7: Pearson correlations between abnormal performance using different performance measures in period 74/79 (lower left triangle) and in period 80/85 (upper right triangle); benchmark: DAFOX

Performance timing	Selectivity performance							Total performance		
	without correcting for bias due to timing abilities					corrected for bias due to timing abilities		selectivity- and timing		
class of measure	ranking			absolute		absolute		absolute		
Measures	S	T	T/B	J	J/3	T/M-Alpha	H/M-Alpha	T/M-Tot.	C/K-Alpha	PW
Sharpe	1	0,89	0,85	0,94	0,90	0,86	0,72	0,94	0,94	0,95
Treynor	1,00	1	0,89	0,94	0,94	0,87	0,71	0,94	0,94	0,94
Trey./ Black	0,92	0,92	1	0,96	0,91	0,87	0,72	0,96	0,97	0,96
Jensen	0,99	1,00	0,95	1	0,95	0,93	0,80	1,00	1,00	1,00
Jensen/3	0,92	0,91	0,86	0,91	1	0,86	0,71	0,95	0,95	0,95
T/M-Alpha	0,56	0,59	0,68	0,62	0,59	1	0,95	0,89	0,90	0,90
H/M-Alpha	0,33	0,36	0,47	0,39	0,40	0,95	1	0,74	0,75	0,75
T/M-Tot.	0,99	1,00	0,95	1,00	0,91	0,60	0,37	1	1,00	1,00
C/K-Alpha	0,98	0,98	0,90	0,97	0,87	0,43	0,17	0,98	1	1,00
PW	0,99	1,00	0,95	1,00	0,91	0,61	0,39	1,00	0,97	1

numbers shaded gray are not significant at the 5 % significance level

We found no evidence that, on average, funds provide investors with a performance that is superior to that of a broadly-based equity index over the sample periods.[26] This result is independent of the performance measure used and the period considered. Our conclusions are based on a limited number of German funds. However, in that they are consistent with other empirical findings reported elsewhere, they might have a more general validity than that which can be inferred from our relatively small set of data.

[26] Our findings were supported by stochastic dominance criteria which utilize the entire probability density function of returns rather than a finite number of moments such as mean and variance (see Wittrock/Steiner 1995).

The APT is not a valid performance benchmark in the present state of knowledge if its constituent factors are prespecified. However, prespecification seems to be a necessary condition for a tool which can combine performance measurement and performance attribution. We leave this issue for further research.

References

Adelberger, O.L. and Lockert, G.(1993): Empirische Ergebnisse zur Anzahl und Bewertung der APT-Risikofaktoren am deutschen Aktienmarkt, Working Paper, University-GH of Essen.

Admati, A.R., Bhattacharya, S., Pfleiderer, P. and Ross, S.A. (1986): On Timing and Selectivity, in: Journal of Finance 41, 715 - 732.

Admati, A.R. and Ross, S.A. (1985): Measuring Investment Performance in a Rational Expectations Equilibrium Model, in: Journal of Business 58, 1 -26.

Beiker, H. (1993): Überrenditen und Risiken kleiner Aktiengesellschaften - Eine theoretische und empirische Analyse des deutschen Kapitalmarktes von 1966 bis 1989, Cologne (Botermann).

Black, F., Jensen, M. and Scholes, M. (1972): The Capital Asset Pricing Model: Some Empirical Tests, in: Jensen, M. (ed.): Studies in the Theory of Capital Markets. New York (Praeger), 79-121.

Black, F. and Scholes, M. (1973): The Pricing of Options and Corporate Liabilities, in: Journal of Political Economy 81, 637 - 659.

Breen, W., Jagannathan, R. and Ofer, A.R. (1986): Correcting for Heteroscedasticity in Tests for Market Timing Ability, in: Journal of Business, 59, 585 - 598.

Chang, E.C. and Lewellen, W.G. (1984): Market Timing and Mutual Fund Investment Performance, in: Journal of Business 57, 57 - 72.

Chen, N.-F., Roll, R. and Ross, S.A. (1986): Economic Forces and the Stock Market, in: Journal of Business 59, 383-403.

Connor, G. and Korajczyk, R.A. (1986): Performance Measurement with the Arbitrage Pricing Theory, in: Journal of Financial Economics 15, 373 - 394.

Connor, G. and Korajczyk, R.A. (1991): The Attributes, Behavior, and Performance of U.S. Mutual Funds, in: Review of Quantitative Financial Analysis 1, 5 - 26.

Cumby, R.E. and Glen, J.D. (1990): Evaluating the Performance of International Mutual Funds, in: Journal of Finance 45, 497 - 521.

Cumby, R.E. and Modest, D.M. (1987): Testing for Market Timing Ability, in: Journal of Financial Economics 19, 169 - 189.

Dybvig, P.H. and Ross, S.A. (1985): Differential Information and Performance Measurement Using a Security Market Line, in: Journal of Finance 40, 383 - 399.

Elton, E.J., Gruber, M.J., Das, S. and Hlavka, M. (1993): Efficiency with Costly Information: A Reinterpretation of Evidence from Managed Portfolios, in: Review of Financial Studies 6, 1 - 22.

Fama, E.F. and MacBeth, J.D. (1973): Risk, Return and Equilibrium: Empirical Tests, in: Journal of Political Economy 38, 607-636 .

Friend, I. and Blume, M.E. (1975): The Demand for Risky Assets, in: American Economic Review 65, 900 - 922.

Gallant, A.R. (1975): Seemingly Unrelated Nonlinear Regressions, in: Journal of Econometrics 3, 35-50.

Gallant, A.R. (1987): Nonlinear Statistical Models. New York et al. (John Wiley).

Gibbons, M.R., Ross, S. A. and Shanken, J. (1989): A Test of Efficiency of a Given Portfolio, in: Econometrica 57, 1121 - 1152.

Göppl, H. and Schütz, H.(1992): Die Konzeption eines Deutschen Aktienindex für Forschungszwecke (DAFOX), Discussion Paper No. 162, Department of Decision, Theory and Operations Research, University of Karlsruhe.

Grant, D. (1977): Portfolio Performance and the Cost of Timing Decisions, in: Journal of Finance 32, 837 - 846.

Grinblatt, M. and Titman, S. (1989): Portfolio Performance Evaluation: Old Issues and New Insights, in: Review of Financial Studies 2, 393 - 421.

Grinblatt, M. and Titman, S.(1992): Performance Evaluation, Working Paper No. 3-92, John E. Anderson, Graduate School of Management, University of California, Los Angeles.

Grinblatt, M. and Titman, S. (1994): A Study of Monthly Mutual Fund Returns and Performance Evaluation Techniques, in: Journal of Financial and Quantitative Analysis 29, 419 - 444.

Grinold, R.C. (1993): Is Beta Dead Again?, in: Financial Analysts Journal 49, 28 - 34.

Hendricks, D., Patel, J. and Zeckhauser, R. (1993): Hot Hands in Mutual Funds: Short-Run Persistence of Relative Performance, 1974-1988, in: Journal of Finance 48, 93 - 130.

Henriksson, R.D. (1984): Market Timing and Mutual Fund Performance: An Empirical Investigation, in: Journal of Business 57, 73 - 96.

Henriksson, R.D. and Merton, R.C. (1981): On Market Timing and Investment Performance II. Statistical Procedures for Evaluating Forecasting Skills, in: Journal of Business 54, 513 - 533.

Ippolito, R.A. (1989): Efficiency with Costly Information: A Study of Mutual Fund Performance, 1965-1984, in: Quarterly Journal of Economics 104, 1 - 23.

Ippolito, R.A. (1993): On Studies of Mutual Fund Performance, 1962-1991, in: Financial Analysts Journal 49, 1993, S. 42 - 50.

Jagannathan, R. and Korajczyk, R.A. (1986): Assessing the Market Timing Performance of Managed Portfolios, in: Journal of Business 59, 217 - 235.

Jensen, M.C. (1968): The Performance of Mutual Funds in the Period 1945-1964, in: Journal of Finance 23, 389 - 416.

Jensen, M.C. (1969): Risk, the Pricing of Capital Assets, and the Evaluation of Investment Portfolios, in: Journal of Business 42, 167 - 247.

Jensen, M.C. (1972): Optimal Utilization of Market Forecasts and the Evaluation of Investment Performance, in: Szegö, G. and K. Shell (eds.): Mathematical Methods in Investment and Finance. New York (North-Holland), 310 - 335.

Judge, G., Griffiths, W.E., Hill, R.C., Lütkepohl, H. and T.C. Lee (1988): Introduction to the Theory and Practice of Econometrics. 2nd ed. New York et al.

Krämer, W. and Runde, R. (1991): Wochentagseffekte am deutschen Kapitalmarkt, Research Paper No. 91/5, Department of Statistics, University of Dortmund.

Krämer, W. and Runde, R. (1993): Kalendereffekte auf Kapitalmärkten, in: Bühler, W., Hax, H. and R. Schmidt (eds.): Empirische Kapitalmarktforschung. Zeitschrift für betriebswirtschaftliche Forschung, special issue 31, 87 - 98.

Lehmann, B.N. and Modest, D.M. (1987): Mutual Fund Performance Evaluation: A Comparison of Benchmarks and Benchmark Comparisons, in: Journal of Finance 42, 233 - 265.

Levy, H. (1978): Equilibrium in an Imperfect Market: A Constraint on the Number of Securities in the Portfolio, in: American Economic Review 68, 643-658.

Löflund, A. (1992): Arbitrage Pricing Theory in a Small Open Economy - Empirical Evidence from the Swedish Stock Market, Swedish School of Economics and Business Administration Research Reports 26, Helsingfors.

McElroy, M.B. and Burmeister, E. (1988): Arbitrage Pricing Theory as a Restricted Nonlinear Multivariate Regression Model, in: Journal of Business Economics and Statistics 6, 29-42.

Merton, R.C. (1981): On Market Timing and Investment Performance I. An Equilibrium Theory of Value for Market Forecasts, in: Journal of Business 54, 363 - 406.

Nowak, Th. (1994): Faktormodelle in der Kapitalmarkttheorie. Cologne (Botermann).

Nowak, Th. and Wittrock, C. (1993): Kapitalmarkttheoretische Ansätze zur Performance-Messung, Working Paper, Department of Finance, University of Münster.

Nowak, Th. and Wittrock, C. (1994): Empirische Ergebnisse zur Messung der risikobereinigten Performance von Investmentfonds, Working Paper, Department of Finance, University of Münster.

Pfleiderer, P. and Bhattacharya, S. (1983): A Note on Performance Evaluation, Technical Report 714, Graduate School of Business, Stanford University.

Roll, R. (1977): A Critique of the Asset Pricing Theory' s Tests - Part I: On Past and Potential Testability of the Theory, in: Journal of Financial Economics 4, 129 - 176.

Roll, R. (1978): Ambiguity When Performance is Measured by the Securities Market Line, in: Journal of Finance 33, 1051 - 1070.

Roll, R. and Ross, S.A. (1980): An Empirical Investigation of the Arbitrage Pricing Theory, in: Journal of Finance 35, 1073 - 1103.

Ross, S.A. (1976): The Arbitrage Theory of Capital Asset Pricing, in: Journal of Economic Theory 13, 341 - 360.

Ross, S.A. (1977): Return, Risk and Arbitrage, in: Friend, I. and J.L. Bicksler (eds.): Risk and Return in Finance. Cambridge/Massachusetts (Ballinger).

Shanken, J. (1985): Multivariate Tests of the Zero-Beta CAPM, in: Journal of Financial Economics 14, 327 - 348.

Sharpe, W.F. (1966): Mutual Fund Performance, in: Journal of Business 39, 119 - 138.

Shukla, R. and Trzcinka, C. (1992): Performance Measurement of Managed Portfolios, Financial Markets, Institutions & Instruments, New York University Salomon Center 1, No. 4. New York.

Srivastava, V.K. and D.A.E. Giles (1987): Seemingly Unrelated Regression Equation Models: Estimation and Inference. New York/Basel (Dekker).

Steiner, M. and Nowak, Th. (1994): Zur Bestimmung von Risikofaktoren auf Basis der Arbitrage Pricing Theory, in: Die Betriebswirtschaft 54, 347 - 362.

Steiner, M. and Nowak, Th. (1995): Mehrfaktorenmodelle, in: Gerke, W. and M. Steiner, (eds.): Handwörterbuch des Finanz- und Bankwesens. 2. ed., Stuttgart (Schäffer-Poeschel), 1433 - 1443.

Steiner, M. and Wittrock, C. (1994): Timing-Aktivitäten von Aktieninvestmentfonds und ihre Identifikation im Rahmen der externen Performance-Messung - Eine theoretische und empirische Untersuchung der Leistungen von Investmentfonds, in: Zeitschrift für Betriebswirtschaft 64, 593 - 618.

Steiner, M. and Wittrock, C. (1995): Performance-Messung von Wertpapierportfolios, in: Gerke, W. and M. Steiner (eds.): Handwörterbuch des Finanz- und Bankwesens. 2. ed., Stuttgart (Schäffer-Poeschel), 1514 - 1526.

Treynor, J.L. (1965): How to Rate Management of Investment Funds, in: Harvard Business Review 43, 63 - 75.

Treynor, J.L. and Black, F. (1973): How to Use Security Analysis to Improve Portfolio Selection, in: Journal of Business 46, 66 - 86.

Treynor, J.L. and Mazuy, K.K. (1966): Can Mutual Funds Outguess the Market?, in: Harvard Business Review 44, 131 - 136.

White, H. (1980): A Heteroscedasticity-Consistent Covariance Matrix Estimator and a Direct Test for Heteroscedasticity, in: Econometrica 48, 817 - 838.

Wittkemper, H.-G. (1994): Neuronale Netze als Hilfsmittel zur Rendite- und Risikoschätzung von Aktien. Cologne (Botermann).

Wittrock, C. (1995): Messung und Analyse der Performance von Wertpapierportfolios - Eine theoretische und empirische Untersuchung. Bad Soden/Ts. (Uhlenbruch).

Wittrock, C. and Steiner, M. (1995): Performance-Messung ohne Rückgriff auf kapitalmarkttheoretische Renditeerwartungsmodelle - Eine Analyse des Anlageerfolges deutscher Aktieninvestmentfonds, in: Kredit und Kapital 28, 1 - 45.

D Futures and Options

Analysis of the Call Policy of Bund, Bahn, and Post in the German Bond Market

Wolfgang Bühler and Michael Schulze
University of Mannheim

1. Introduction

It is well understood that the call feature of a callable bond can be regarded as the issuer's option to redeem the bond prematurely. Typically, this call option can be exercised at a finite number of points of time with possibly varying call premia.

An issuer's main reason for endowing a bond with a call option is to redistribute future interest rate risk between himself and the bond holders[1]. Whether the issuer of the bond exercises his option optimally is an interesting question which can be elucidated with either of two approaches. The first uses the market prices of the callable bond and basically determines whether, at call dates, these prices are above, or below, the call value or, in case of a callable and convertible bond, above or below its conversion value. The second approach is based on a valuation model of the call feature. In this case the bond should be called whenever the call option is worth more dead, i.e., exercised, than alive.

Most empirical studies use market prices to analyze call policy. Ingersoll (1977) finds that, in a sample of 179 callable and convertible bonds, they were, with only 9 exceptions, called too late. Asquith/Mullins (1991) and Campbell/Ederington/Vankudre (1991) offer reasons why firms do not call convertible bonds when their conversion prices exceed their call prices. Contrastingly Vu (1986) reports that in a sample of nonconvertible corporate bonds, the majority were called when their market prices were quoted below their call prices. Finally, Longstaff (1992) analyzes the call policy of the US-Treasury. He finds that in 25 out of 42 cases the Treasury followed an optimal call policy.

---

[1] Other reasons could be „asymmetric information on future interest rates", „asymmetric taxation of call premia for the corporation and the private investor" and „reduction of agency costs" (see e.g. Robbins/Schatzberg 1986, p. 935).

As far as we are aware, only one study uses the second approach. Using a two-factor model, Brennan/Schwartz (1979) analyze the exercise policy of the owners of Canadian saving bonds. These bonds can be redeemed at the discretion of the bondholders. The results are ambiguous in that the aggregated redemption data show that a substantial proportion of bondholders do not follow an optimal strategy, whilst, on the other hand, observed behaviour to some extent conforms to an optimal redemption strategy.

The present paper is concerned with the call policy of the German Government (Bund), the German National Railways (Bahn) and the German National Post Office. This study differs in a number of important respects from the studies mentioned above, in that:

(i) Market prices and a valuation model are used to assess the observed call strategy.

(ii) Bonds issued by Bund, Bahn and Post constitute a homogenous market segment with respect to (non-existent) bankruptcy risk, taxation, characteristics of the call feature, liquidity and market frictions.

(iii) The callable and noncallable bonds of these issuers are quoted simultaneously. This is important as the valuation model is based on the dynamics of the term structure of interest rates.

(iv) The call features for different bonds are identical.

(v) The notice period in calling bonds introduces an exercise risk into the call feature.

(vi) The bonds have no specific collaterals and are not convertible. The debt management of the issuers does not depend on their investment policy. From the „clean" nature of the bonds it follows that the only reason for calling a bond is decreasing interest rates.

It can be expected, that this „clean" sample of bonds, together with a valuation model which was specifically designed to fit the available data, considerably reduce the impact of other motives to call bonds as well as the noise in the data.

The paper is organized as follows. The characteristics of the identical call feature of Bund, Bahn, Post bonds are described in the following section as are the analysis of call policy and the valuation model approach. Section 3 contains the main body of the study. It deals with the data base, the dynamics of the term structure of interest rates, and an evaluation results of the call policy. Section 4 concludes the paper.

2. Methods of examining call politics

2.1 Characteristics of call features

Call features embedded in the callable bonds of Bund, Bahn and Post possess the following standardized characteristics:

(i) They permit call announcements only for a coupon date.

(ii) Their redemption date is always the first or last day of a month.

(iii) Their announcement period covers at least three months.

(iv) Their call price is equal to their face value.

(v) On the refunding of a called bond, the issuer incurs transaction costs of about 1% of its face value[2].

Furthermore, all bonds have an initial a call free period of several years. The mixed European-American characteristic of the call option is a consequence of the first of these features.

The intrinsic value of a call option is defined as the net present value of future interest cost savings that can be achieved by calling the bond and refunding it with a par bond with a maturity equal to the residual maturity of the callable bond. Because of (ii) above, this intrinsic value is uncertain because during the announcement period the term structure of interest rates, and therefore the coupon of the newly issued par bond, may change.

Calling a bond is financially expedient only if the transaction costs involved are covered by interest cost savings. Therefore, transaction costs may delay an optimal call and reduce the value of the call option. The first consequence has to be considered in both approaches in assessing observed call policy, whereas the second is a relevant consideration only if an option pricing model is used.

---

[2] The issuing costs comprise 0.875 % of the face value as fee for the underwriting syndicate, 100,000 DM fee for listing the new bond at 8 German exchanges (12,500 DM each), and the costs of announcing the issue.

2.2 Examination of call policy using market prices

The owner of a callable bond can interpret this instrument as a portfolio comprising an identical noncallable bond and a short position in a call option on this bond. Hereafter the noncallable bond is described as the underlying bond. Ignoring the announcement period and transaction costs, and assuming that call dates are coupon payment dates, the intrinsic value Φ_s of a call feature at a call date t_C is:

$$\Phi_s = \max\{0; B - E\} \tag{1}$$

Whereby B denotes the price of the underlying bond and E the call price of the callable bond. Under the simplifying assumptions made here, Φ_s is certain and equals the present value of interest cost savings which result from calling the bond and refinancing it with the underlying bond at current market rates (see Bühler/Köndgen/Schmidt 1990, p. 59.).

Transaction costs of amount TC increase the exercise price from E to E + TC. The risk caused by an announcement period of length AP can be hedged with an ideal forward contract on the underlying bonds. This is equivalent to a forward issue of the underlying bond at the redemption date t_R with an issue price equal to the forward price F_B. On the usual cost of carry argument this forward price at the call date $t_C = t_R$ - AP equals

$$F_B = [B + c(1 - AP)] \cdot (1 + r)^{AP} - c, \tag{2}$$

where c denotes the coupon of the underlying bond and r the relevant short-term interest rate for the period AP. The hedged intrinsic value of a call option at t_R is obtained from (1) by substituting E with E + TC and B with F_B. Discounting this value back to the call date yields the hedged intrinsic value Φ at t_C:

$$\Phi = \max\left\{0; B + c(1 - AP) - [E + c + TC] \cdot (1 + r)^{-AP}\right\} \tag{3}$$

Equation (3) can be motivated by a strategy in which the underlying bond is issued at t_C at the current price including accrued interest $B + c(1 - AP)$. Transaction costs are deferred until t_R and are payed together with the call price E and the full coupon. These payments are made comparable with the issue proceeds by discounting.

Recalling that a callable bond can be stripped into the underlying bond and a written call, its price CB equals

$$CB = B - C, \tag{4}$$

where C denotes the call price. At a call date t_C the call value C is not smaller than the hedged intrinsic value Φ. This implies the inequality

$$CB \leq B - \Phi =: CB_{crit}. \tag{5}$$

Whenever $\Phi > 0$ and inequality (5) is violated, the call is priced implicitly below its hedged intrinsic value and (5) signals a theoretical arbitrage opportunity. This signal is based only on the observable market price CB, the interest rate r and on known contract specifications E, c, AP, TC. The unobservable price B of the underlying bond cancels out. In section 3.4 the call policy of Bund, Bahn and Post is evaluated by examining the no arbitrage condition (5).

2.3 Examination of the call policy using a bond option pricing model

The second approach to assessing call policy is, like the first, based on inequality (5). However, theoretical values of the callable bond are used instead of market prices. Whenever Φ is positive at a call date, CB_{crit} is equal to the value of the callable bond if called. This critical value has to be compared with the theoretical value of the callable bond if it is not called and an optimal call policy is pursued in the future. This procedure is equivalent to examining whether the theoretical value of the call option when not exercised is below, or above, its hedged intrinsic value Φ. The second approach, therefore, depends basically on a valuation model for interest rate options.

2.3.1 A trinomial model for pricing bond options

The valuation model developed here represents a trinomial generalization of the well known binomial model of Ho/Lee (1986). A third state was added in order to adapt the model to the time-series of monthly bond data. An analysis of these data showed that, besides upward and downward shifts in the term structure of interest rates, a third possibility should be considered which can be identified as "no change"[3].

---

[3] It schould be noted that the trinomial model differs from a Ho/Lee-model with a period length of one half month. The two models result in different representations of future term structure of interest rates.

The basic assumptions of the trinomial model are identical to those of the discrete Ho/Lee-model[4]. There are M zero bonds with maturities T = 1, ..., M periods (months) which are traded in a frictionless market at points of time t = 0, ..., N. At point of time t there are $I_t + 1$ possible states i. In every state i the zero bond prices

$$P_t^i(T) \qquad (T = 1, ..., M) \tag{6}$$

characterize the term structure of interest rates ($i = 0, ..., I_t$; t = 0, ...,N). At t = 0 there is only one state ($I_0 = 0$), and the corresponding term structure of interest rates is given exogenously.

The transition from discount function $P_t^i(T)$ to one of three possible discount functions, $P_{t+1}^i(T)$, $P_{t+1}^{i+1}(T)$ or $P_{t+1}^{i+2}(T)$, in the next period, is modelled relative to the implied forward discount function $F_t^i(T) = P_t^i(T+1)/P_t^i(1)$ through three time and state independent perturbation functions $h^u(T)$, $h^n(T)$ and $h^d(T)$ in the following way:

$$P_t^i(T) \rightarrow \begin{cases} P_{t+1}^{i+2}(T) = F_t^i(T) \cdot h^u(T) & \text{"UPSTATE"(U)} \\ P_{t+1}^{i+1}(T) = F_t^i(T) \cdot h^n(T) & \text{"NO CHANGE"(N)} \\ P_{t+1}^{i}(T) = F_t^i(T) \cdot h^d(T) & \text{"DOWNSTATE"(D)} \end{cases} \tag{7}$$

Adding three path independence conditions, e.g. the sequence (U,N) should result in the same discount function as the sequence (N,U), and a standard no arbitrage condition, the three perturbation functions can be characterized by a system of nonlinear difference equations. It can be shown that this system is solved by reference to the following functions:

$$h^u(T) = \frac{1}{\pi^2 + 2\pi(1-\pi)\delta^T + (1-\pi)^2\delta^{2T}}, \; h^n(T) = \delta^T h^u(T), \; h^d(T) = \delta^{2T} h^u(T), \tag{8}$$
$$0 < \pi, \; \delta < 1$$

A recursive application of (7) and (8) shows that in any state (t,i) the discount function $P_t^i(T)$ depends only on the exogenous initial discount function $P_0^0(T)$ and the two parameters π and δ.

---

[4] For a detailed description of the model see Bühler/Schulze (1991) or Bühler/Schulze (1993).

2.3.2 Optimal call policy

The optimal call policy is determined by a recursive procedure which is standard practice in option pricing theory. At the last call date N_C the value of the call option in state i equals

$$C(N_C,i) = \max\left\{0; B(N_C,i) + c(1-AP) - E^*[1+r(N_C,i)]^{-AP}\right\}$$

where $B(N_C,i)$ and $r(N_C,i)$ are the price of the underlying bond and the short-period interest rate in state (N_C,i). E^* denotes the sum E + c +TC.

In an arbitrary noncall state (t,i), t < N_C, the value of the call option, C(t,i), is equal to

$$C(t,i) = \left[\pi^2 C(t+1,i+2) + 2\pi(1-\pi)\cdot C(t+1,i+1) + (1-\pi)^2 C^2(t+1,i)\right]\cdot P_t^i(1) \tag{9}$$

If (t,i) coincides with a call date, the hedged intrinsic value

$$\Phi(t,i) = \max\left\{0; B(t,i) + c(1-AP) - E^*[1+r(t,i)]^{-AP}\right\} \tag{10}$$

is compared with the call value $C^*(t,i)$ computed according to (9) under the assumption that the call is not exercised. The maximum of $C^*(t,i)$ and Φ(t,i) equals the call value C(t,i) on a call date. The optimal decision in state (t,i) is simultaneously determined.

The theoretical price of a callable bond is equal to the difference between the underlying bond price and the call value. Especially, at t = 0:

$$CB(0,0) = B(0,0) - C(0,0) \tag{11}$$

This result is used in section 3.5 where the call policy is assessed using theoretical values.

3. Empirical results

3.1 Data basis and empirical design

Table 1 shows the numbers of outstanding callable and noncallable bonds issued by Bund, Bahn or Post in the years 1960-1988. The numbers in parentheses indicate the new issues in the individual years in question.

The second approach necessitates an estimate of the term structure of interest rates. In this study a cubic spline regression is used as the discount function. The empirical results show that for an estimation of acceptable quality at least 20 market prices of noncallable bonds are necessary. 1968 is the first year which satisfies this condition. Therefore, January 1968 defines the first month of the research period. The last month in which an outstanding bond can be called is February 1987.

Table 1: Callable and noncallable bonds 1960 - 1988

Year	Noncallable bonds		Callable bonds		Total number	
1960	0	(0)	8	(2)	8	(2)
1962	0	(2)	9	(7)	9	(9)
1964	7	(4)	24	(5)	31	(9)
1966	15	(1)	28	(0)	43	(1)
1968	22	(6)	28	(1)	50	(7)
1970	32	(9)	28	(0)	60	(9)
1972	49	(7)	28	(1)	77	(8)
1974	62	(12)	31	(0)	93	(12)
1976	74	(12)	30	(0)	104	(12)
1978	91	(14)	25	(0)	116	(14)
1980	106	(9)	14	(0)	120	(9)
1982	89	(15)	12	(0)	101	(15)
1984	92	(12)	2	(0)	94	(12)
1986	100	(15)	2	(0)	102	(15)
1988	120	(11)	1	(0)	121	(11)

Established at the end January of each year;
in the parentheses: number of issues during that year.

This period was divided into monthly subperiods for a number of reasons. First, the call dates differ by a multiple of months. Therefore the length of the subperiod should not exceed one month. Second, using monthly data provides an adequate number of observations. Third, in quiet periods of the bond market, the noise in bond prices with a time distance of less than one month is relatively too strong. Fourth, the accuracy of a discrete valuation model is adequate.

The computation of the theoretically optimal call strategy consisted of three steps. First, the term structure of interest rates was estimated for the last trading day in each of the 230 months from January 1968 to February 1987. Second, the stochastics of the term structures of interest rates, defined by the two parameters π and δ, were estimated on the basis of the last 12 observations. This resulted in 218 estimates for π and δ from January 1969 to February 1987. For these months, as a third step, the call option was evaluated and it was ascertained whether a call, if possible, was optimal.

During these 218 months 31 different callable bonds were outstanding. They offered a total of 390 call possibilities. Since the market price of the callable bond is needed for this first approach, those cases were excluded, for which no transaction price was quoted in the daily auction. This left 359 usuable observations, the call policies of which were evaluated by reference to the two alternative approaches.

3.2 Estimation of the term structure of interest rates

As in the studies of Mc Culloch (1971), Carleton/Cooper (1976), Schaefer (1981), Chambers/Carleton/Waldman (1984), Shea (1984), Litzenberger/Rolfo (1984) and others, an estimate of the discount function was transformed into the term structure of interest rates. The discount function was approximated by a cubic spline function using fixed knots and basic functions as recommended by Seber/Wild (1989, pp. 481-484).

For the estimation of discount functions, a data set of 17,211 market prices from 227 different noncallable bonds was available. 126 of these bonds were issued by Bund, 58 by Bahn, and 43 by Post. The coupons ranged from 5 % to 10.75 % and the time to maturity at issuance varied from 5 to 30 years. For each of the 230 months the term structure of interest rates was estimated up to a maturity date of 10 years. The number of available bonds varied from a minimum of 22 bonds in January 1968 to a maximum of 111 bonds in February 1987.

The quality of the estimation procedure is measured in the sample by the absolute deviation between the market prices (including accrued interest) of coupon bonds and their theoretical values.The latter computed by discounting the future cash flows of a bond using the estimated discount function.

An overall MAD of 0.34, signifies an estimation procedure, acceptable of quality. A residual analysis, whose results are not reported here, shows that the results are unbiased with respect to the coupon level, the residual time to maturity and the bond price.

Summary statistics of the mean absolute deviations (MAD) of the 230 estimations are presented in Table 2.

Table 2: Summary statistics of the differences between observed and theoretical prices

Estimation period	Jan.1968 - Feb. 1987
Number of estimations	230
Total number of bond prices	17211
Min. number of bond prices	22 (Jan. 1968)
Max. number of bond prices	111 (Feb. 1987)
Mean absolute deviation (MAD)	*Number of estimations*
$0 \leq$ MAD ≤ 0.20	*28*
$0.20 <$ MAD ≤ 0.40	*132*
$0.40 <$ MAD ≤ 0.60	*65*
$0.60 <$ MAD ≤ 0.80	*5*
$0.80 <$ MAD	*0*
Minimum MAD	0.14 (November 1981)
Maximum MAD	0.76 (January 1970)
Overall MAD	0.34

3.3 Estimation of the transaction behavior of the term structures of interest rates

Equations (7) and (8) indicate that for an estimation of the parameters π and δ, which define the stochastics of the discount functions, consecutive movements of these functions should be classified as UPSTATE, NO CHANGE or DOWNSTATE. To this end the estimated discount functions were considered at the discrete maturities of 1, 2, 3, ..., 119 months and the following somewhat arbitrary classification procedure was used. Whenever more than 100 out of 119 discount factors are larger (smaller) than the corresponding implied forward factors, the transition is classified as UPSTATE (DOWNSTATE). If a comparison results neither in an UPSTATE nor in a DOWNSTATE classification, the transition is defined as NO CHANGE. According to this procedure, 101 transitions out of 229 are classified as UPSTATE, 70 as NO CHANGE, and 58 as DOWNSTATE.

In the regression model (12), formulated below, the type of transition is characterized by 0-1 indicator variables $\alpha_i(t)$, t = 1,2,3. $\alpha_1(t)$ equals 1 if the transition from t to t + 1 is classified as an UPSTATE. $\alpha_2(t)$ refers to NO CHANGE and $\alpha_3(t)$ to a DOWNSTATE transition. If bond maturity is measured in years, one month corresponds 1/12 of a year and equations (7) and (8) can be transformed to the following nonlinear regression model with the error term u_i:

$$P_{t+1}(T_i) = F_t(T_i) \times \frac{\alpha_1(n) + \alpha_2(n)\delta^{T_i} + \alpha_3(n)\delta^{2T_i}}{\pi^2 + 2\pi(1-\pi)\delta^{T_i} + (1-\pi)^2\delta^{2T_i}} + u_i \ , \tag{12}$$

$$T_i = i/12 \text{ years}, i = 1, 2, \ldots, 119.$$

In principle, at every point in time t estimates of π and δ can be obtained by minimizing the sum of squared errors of the 119 cases of equation (12). However, these estimates would depend only on one transition and its classification. They would also ignore the fact that π and δ have to explain the whole (stationary) transition process, including the other two transition possibilities. An analysis of the 229 classifications showed that each series of 13 consecutive discount functions contained at least two different types of transition. For this reason the nonlinear regression (12) was extended to explain simultaneously the 12 last transitions of the discount functions P_{t-11}, $P_{t-10}, \ldots, P_t$, P_{t+1}. This increases the number of cases of equation (12) from 119 to 1,428.

The parameters π and δ were estimated for each of the 218 months from January 1969 to February 1987. In each case, the sum of squared errors of the extended nonlinear regression (12) was minimized using the Newton-Raphson algorithm. The results are summarized in Table 3.

Table 3: Summary statistics of parameter estimation

	π	δ
Number of estimations	218	218
Arithmetic mean	0.5547	0.9977
Standard deviation	0.1203	$8.117 \cdot 10^{-4}$
Minimum	0.1775	0.9957
Maximum	0.9975	0.9994
Median	0.5500	0.9978
Upper quartile	0.6010	0.9982
Lower quartile	0.4914	0.9972

An analysis of the time series of π and δ showed that π fluctuates considerably more than δ. This is important as δ is closely related to the volatility of bond prices, the fundamental factor for the value of a call feature and the call policy. A more detailed analysis of π and δ is given in Bühler/Schulze (1991, pp. 293 - 295).

3.4 Examination of the call policy using market prices

According to inequality (5) there exists a theoretical arbitrage opportunity whenever, at a call date, the market price CB of a callable bond is larger than the critical value CB_{crit}. This critical value depends only on the observable variables E, c, TC, AP and r.

As stated in section 3.1, there were 359 possible occasions on which one of 31 callable bonds could have been called. In 329 cases inequality (5) was not violated. As none of the call options was exercised in these situations, the issuers' behaviour was optimal. In the remaining 30 cases it would have been optimal to call, but no call was observed. The characteristics of the callable bonds and the missed interest savings are presented in Table 4. The italicised cases are discussed in section 3.5.2.

The first column in Table 4 shows the bonds for which a call opportunity was missed. The initial time to maturity T_I (column T_I) varied between 15 and 20 years. Since, for most bonds, a call opportunity was missed more than once, the 30 observations are distributed only among 17 different bonds. As expected, the missed calls are concentrated in the respective periods 1977 to the first quarter of 1979 and May 1983 to May 1985. In the first period the average yield to maturity dropped to its post war minimum of 5.2 %, whilst in the second period the minimum was 5.5 %. The unweighted mean of interest savings $CB\text{-}CB_{crit}$ per 100 DM face value amounts to 0.78 DM with a minimum of 0.04 DM. Ten of these differences are larger than 1 DM (or 1 %), but only one exceeds 2 DM.

The absolute level of missed theoretical arbitrage profits is of more interest than the relative values $CB\text{-}CB_{crit}$, because all bonds in Table 4 - with exeption of the 8 % Post 1972 bond - are lottery bonds. These issues are repayed on a regular basis in constant amounts.

A comparison of the time of maturity at the missed call dates T_C with the original time to maturity T_I shows that the missed calls are concentrated in the last quarter of the bonds' maturities. An analogous conclusion can be drawn from column #c. This column represents the position of the missed call dates within the series of call possibilities. The numbers in parenthesis are the total numbers of call dates.

Table 4: Characteristics and consequences of missed bond calls (observed prices)

Bond	t_C	CB-$CB_{crit.}$	T_I	T_C	#c	E_I	E_C	Loss
7% *Bahn 1958*	30.01.1969	1.50	20	9.25	9 (26)	250	188	2,820,000
7% Bahn 1958	30.07.1969	0.11	20	8.75	10 (26)	250	188	206,800
7% *Bund 1965*	30.03.1977	0.22	15	3.25	6 (8)	350	140	308,000
6% Bahn 1964	29.04.1977	0.08	15	2.26	4 (5)	250	50	40,000
7% *Bahn 1958*	29.07.1977	0.24	20	0.76	26 (26)	250	25	60,000
6% *Bund 1962*	30.09.1977	0.39	20	4.75	12 (20)	400	133	518,700
6% *Bahn 1962*	30.10.1977	0.71	20	4.25	13 (20)	210	56	397,600
6% *Post 1962*	30.10.1977	0.71	20	4.75	12 (20)	210	70	497,000
6% *Bahn 1962 II*	30.11.1977	0.63	20	4.75	12 (20)	250	83	522,900
6% *Bund 1963 II*	29.12.1977	0.44	20	5.26	6 (10)	500	300	1,320,000
6% *Bahn 1963 II*	28.02.1978	0.63	19	4.26	6 (9)	265	106	667,800
6% *Bund 1964 II*	28.02.1978	0.53	15	1.26	5 (5)	300	60	408,000
6% Post 1964	28.02.1978	0.68	15	1.26	9 (10)	320	64	339,200
6% *Bund 1962*	30.03.1978	1.31	20	4.25	13 (20)	400	107	1,401,700
6% *Bund 1963 III*	30.03.1978	1.81	19	4.25	6 (9)	400	160	2,496,000
6% *Post 1963 II*	30.03.1978	1.56	20	5.25	6 (10)	210	126	2,280,600
7% *Bund 1965*	30.03.1978	2.41	15	2.25	7 (8)	350	70	1,687,000
6% *Bahn 1962*	28.04.1978	0.76	20	3.76	14 (20)	210	56	425,600
6% *Post 1962*	28.04.1978	1.26	20	4.26	13 (20)	210	56	705,600
6% *Bahn 1964*	28.04.1978	0.91	15	1.26	5 (5)	250	50	455,000
6% Bahn 1962 II	30.05.1978	0.51	20	4.25	13 (20)	250	67	341,700
6% *Post 1964 II*	30.05.1978	1.01	15	1.25	5 (5)	210	42	424,200
6% Post 1964	30.08.1978	0.04	15	0.75	10 (10)	320	64	25,600
6% Bund 1964	29.09.1978	0.15	20	5.26	6 (10)	400	240	360,000
6% Post 1962	30.10.1978	0.28	20	3.75	14 (20)	210	56	156,800
7% *Bund 1965*	30.03.1979	0.64	15	1.25	8 (8)	350	70	448,000
8% Post 1972	30.05.1983	0.32	15	4.25	2 (5)	400	400	1,280,000
8% *Post 1972*	30.05.1985	1.21	15	2.25	4 (5)	400	400	4,840,000
6.5% *Post 1968*	28.02.1986	1.31	20	2.26	8 (9)	210	42	550,200
8% *Post 1972*	30.05.1986	1.96	15	1.25	5 (5)	400	400	7,840,000

t_C: Date of missed call
CB-$CB_{crit.}$: Missed interest savings per DM 100 face value
T_I: Initial maximum time to maturity [years]
T_C: Maximum time to maturity at t_C [years]
#c: Position of t_C in the series of possible call dates
E_I: Nominal amount at date of issue [Mio. DM]
E_C: Outstanding amount at t_C [Mio. DM]
Loss: Missed interest savings [DM]

From columns E_I and E_C it can be concluded that on average only 43 % of the bonds initial nominal amount is still outstanding at the missed call dates. Multiplying E_C with CB-CB_{crit} results in the absolute missed arbitrage profit which is reported in the last column. This loss varies between 25,600 DM and

7,840,000 DM. The average loss amounts to 1,127,447 DM. The two largest losses are related to the only conventional bond in the sample, namely the 8 % Post 1972 bond, which has the maximum outstanding value of 400 million DM. The loss of 4.84 million DM represents 15.1 % of the annual interest payments, but the larger loss of 7.84 million DM constitutes 24.5 % thereof. That Post refrained from taking these large arbitrage profits was possibly a consequence of an intense public criticism of two calls of Bund bonds some years ago. In these two cases the Bund were accused of acting against the interest of the "small" saver (widows and orphans).

If the straight Post bond is deleted from the sample, the average loss is reduced to 735,682 DM. This loss corresponds approximately to interest payments for a period of 1.5 months. It can be argued that the loss of reputation that is suffered when a public issuer calls a bond outweigh this financial disadvantage.

3.5 Examination of the call policy using the valuation model

3.5.1 General results

The analysis in this section is also based on the 359 possible occasions on which one of 31 callable bonds could have been called. In 332 of these 359 cases the issuers' behavior was consistent with the model's recommendation. In 330 situations the value of the call option was lower when exercised than when not exercised and the issuers did not call the bond. In the two cases in which the intrinsic value of the call exceeded the non-exercised call value, calls were observed. The 27 cases in which a call was missed are reported in Table 5, which can be directly compared with Table 4. These tables differ only in respect of the definitions of their third and last columns. In Table 5, V_E - V_N denotes the difference between the intrinsic value of the call ($V_E > 0$) and its theoretical value if not exercised (V_N). The last column is the product of the difference V_E - V_N and the amount E_C outstanding at the call date t_C.

The 27 missed calls are distributed among 16 different bonds. The average loss V_E-V_N in not calling the bond amounts to 0.67 DM or 0.67%. This difference represents the forgone interest savings per 100 DM nominal face value up to the next call date or until the maturity of the bond. Calling these 16 bonds optimally during the period from January 1969 to February 1987 would have reduced the average maximum time to maturity by only 20.5 %. The average face value outstanding at the call dates amounts to 42 % of the nominal values at the date of issue.

Table 5: Characteristics an consequences of missed bonds (theoretical values)

Bond	t_C	V_E-V_N	T_I	T_C	#c	E_I	E_C	Loss
7% *Bahn 1958*	30.01.1969	1.04	20	9.25	9 (26)	250	188	1,955,000
7% *Bund 1965*	30.03.1977	0.45	15	3.25	6 (8)	350	140	630,000
7% *Bahn 1958*	29.07.1977	0.19	20	0.76	26 (26)	250	25	47,500
6% Post 1964	30.08.1977	0.32	15	1.75	8 (10)	320	128	409,600
6% *Bund 1962*	30.09.1977	0.66	20	4.75	12 (20)	400	133	877,800
6% *Bahn 1962*	30.10.1977	0.27	20	4.25	13 (20)	210	56	151,200
6% *Post 1962*	30.10.1977	0.60	20	4.75	12 (20)	210	70	420,000
6% *Bahn 1962 II*	30.11.1977	0.61	20	4.75	12 (20)	250	83	506,300
6% *Bund 1963 II*	29.12.1977	0.73	20	5.26	6 (10)	500	300	2,190,000
6% *Bahn 1963 II*	28.02.1978	0.57	19	4.26	6 (9)	265	106	604,200
6% *Bund 1964 II*	28.02.1978	0.71	15	1.26	5 (5)	300	60	426,000
6% *Bund 1962*	30.03.1978	0.49	20	4.25	13 (20)	400	107	524,300
6% *Post 1963 II*	30.03.1978	0.66	20	5.25	6 (10)	210	126	1,953,000
6%*Bund1963 III*	30.03.1978	1.55	19	4.25	6 (9)	400	160	1,056,000
7% *Bund 1965*	30.03.1978	0.35	15	2.25	7 (8)	350	70	245,000
6% *Bahn 1962*	28.04.1978	1.07	20	3.76	14 (20)	210	56	599,200
6% *Post 1962*	28.04.1978	0.51	20	4.26	13 (20)	210	56	285.600
6% *Bahn 1964*	28.04.1978	0.73	15	1.26	5 (5)	250	50	365.000
6% *Bahn 1962 II*	30.05.1978	0.48	20	4.25	13 (20)	250	67	321.600
6% *Post 1964 II*	30.05.1978	1.04	15	1.25	5 (5)	210	42	436.800
6% Bund 1962	29.09.1978	0.09	20	3.76	14 (20)	400	107	96,300
7% *Bund 1965*	30.03.1979	0.40	15	1.25	8 (8)	350	70	280,000
8% Post 1972	30.05.1984	0.01	15	3.25	3 (5)	400	400	40,000
8% *Post 1972*	30.05.1985	1.70	15	2.25	4 (5)	400	400	6,800,000
6.5% *Post 1968*	28.02.1986	0.56	20	2.26	8 (9)	210	42	235,200
8% *Post 1972*	30.05.1986	2.27	15	1.25	5 (5)	400	400	9,080,000
6.5% Post 1968	27.02.1987	0.03	20	1.26	9 (9)	210	21	6,300

V_E-V_N: Missed interest savings per DM 100 face value
t_C ,T_I ,T_C ,#c, E_I ,E_C defined as in table 4
Loss: Theoretical missed interest savings [DM]

The issuers missed interest savings ranging from 6,300 DM to 9,080,000 DM (mean value 1,131,189 DM). The two highest losses are again related to the straight 8 % Post 1972 bond. If this bond is deleted from the sample, the average loss reduces by 50 % to 586,484 DM. This corresponds to an average interest payment for 1.2 months which could have been avoided. Compared with the loss of reputation if Bund, Bahn or Post call one of their issues, this average saving is rather small.

3.5.2 A comparison of the market based and the model based results

The two methods used to examine the call policy differ substantially. Whereas the first examines whether the unobservable market prices of call options are below their intrinsic values, the second utilises the theoretical values of unexercised call options. Therefore, the optimal issuer behaviours specified by these two methods do not necessarily coincide.

A comparison of Tables 4 and 5 shows however, that, in 23 cases, missed calls were uncovered by both approaches. These cases are indicated with italicised letters in the first column. They characterize situations in which simultaneously the call feature was priced in the market below its intrinsic value and in which the call was worth more if exercised than if not. 23 out of 30 observations in Table 4 were also identified by the model. Conversely 23 out of 27 or 85 % of the missed calls reported in Table 5 were also observable in the market.

Seven arbitrage opportunities reported in Table 4 were not uncovered by the model. The average relative loss in these 7 cases amounts to 0.24 %, whilst the average absolute loss is 343,940 DM. Both numbers are considerably smaller than the corresponding losses in the complete sample. The four missed optimal calls in Table 5 which were not "discovered" by the issuers result in a theoretical average loss of 0.11 % or 138,050 DM. Both numbers are extremely small. These results can be interpreted as a positive qualitative test of the valuation model. The "test statistic" is not the customary difference between observed and theoretical option values, it is the difference between observed and theoretical call policies.

3.5.3 Detailed analysis of observed calls

Only two of the 31 callable bonds, the 10 % Bund 1973 and the 10 % Bund 1973 III, were called within the period investigated. These bonds were first quoted on the Frankfurt exchange on July 23, 1973, and September 12, 1973, respectively. After a 5 year call protection period they were callable with a three month minimum announcement period in the years 1978, 1979, and 1980 with repayment dates on August 1 and October 1, respectively.

Both bonds were called on March 8, 1978. Calling a bond earlier than three months before repayment is permissible although such a decision, if unhedged, is not optimal. If hedged, a premature call does not add to the value of the call option.

In March 1978 interest rates in the German bond market dropped to their lowest level within the period investigated. It was possible to refund the two bonds at a rate of about 5 %. Both issues are straight bonds with a 500 million

DM nominal value. Calling these bonds and refunding them with two 5 % par bonds results in interest savings of 50 million DM a year.

The theoretical values of the call options if exercised or not are presented in Table 6. In the case of the first bond, the difference V_E-V_N = 5.56 represents interest savings of 27.8 millions had the bond been called, compared with the adopting of the optimal call strategy in April 1979. For the second bond, the interest savings amount to 5.28 % or 26.4 million DM. These interest savings differ considerably from those reported in Table 5.

Table 6: Characteristics and consequences of the two called bonds

Bond	t_C	V_E-V_N	T_I	T_C	#c	E_I	E_C	Savings
10 % Bund 1973	30.04.1978	5.56	8	3.25	1 (3)	500	500	27.8
10 % Bund 1973 III	30.06.1978	5.28	8	3.25	1 (3)	500	500	26.4
For definition of variables see table 5.								

In addition to the analysis of the call policy it is interesting to question whether these calls were anticipated by the market. The answer may lie in a comparison of the prices of two 10% Bund bonds with the prices of noncallable bonds maturing on the first payment dates. Because no bonds with these terms were quoted in the market, theoretical prices were computed using the estimated term structure of interest rates. The observed prices of the 10 % Bund bond 1973 and the theoretical prices are depicted in Figure 1 for a time period of about three years. The analogous figure for the 10 % Bund 1973 III gives no additional insights.

The letter "A" represents the announcement date of the call. After this date the future cash flows of the callable bond are certain and the market prices are close to the theoretical prices of the straight bond. During a period of more than 2.5 years, prior to the announcement date A, the callable bond's prices considerably and systematically exceed the theoretical prices. This is surprising as a callable bond should be quoted below the price of every non-callable bond with a maturity date coinciding with one of the redemption dates. Figure 1 suggests that the market paid a positive premium for the chance that the 10 % Bund would be not called on the first call date, instead of subtracting a risk premium from the price of the straight bond maturing in August 1978. Another interpretation could be that, despite the fact that the average yield to maturity was more than two percentage points below the 10 % coupon during the period underlying Figure 1, the market did not expect the bond to be called as the Bund had never previously called a bond.

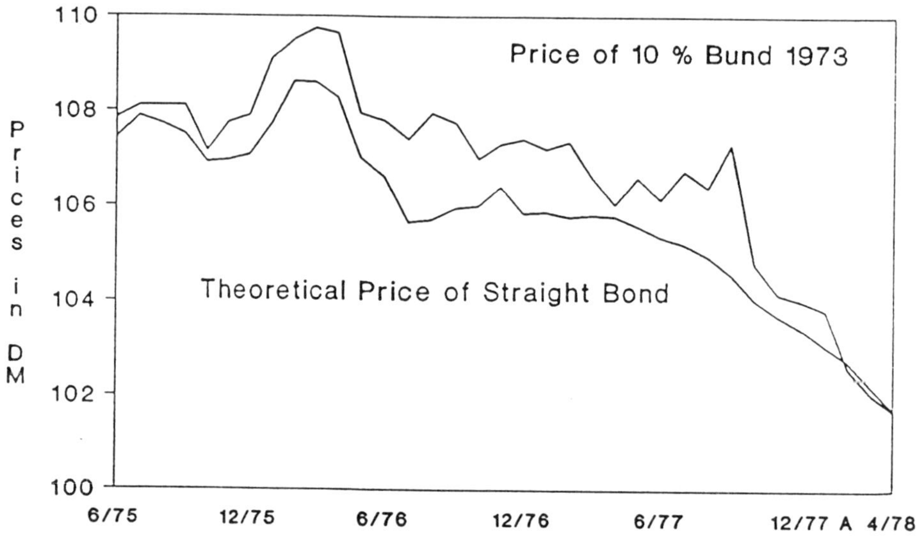

Figure 1: Prices of 10 % Bund 1973 (repayed August 1978) and theoretical prices of a 10 % straight bond with maturity date August 1978

A second interesting comparison is that of a straight bond which was redeemable simultaneously in 1981 with one of the two called bonds. Fortunately, the noncallable 10 % Post 1973 bond matured only one month later than the 10 % Bund 1973 III. The market prices of these two bonds are presented in Figure 2.

Beginning with the initial quotation of the 10 % Post bond in October 1973, the market prices of the two bonds were closely approximated until June 1976. As from the latter date, the two bond prices begin to differ considerably. The market became aware of the call risk and priced the callable bond at a discount to the straight bond. Figure 1 shows that the call option was in the money after December 1974, compared with both the standard definition of the intrinsic value and the hedged intrinsic value. Therefore, the call option was heavily underpriced until May 1975.

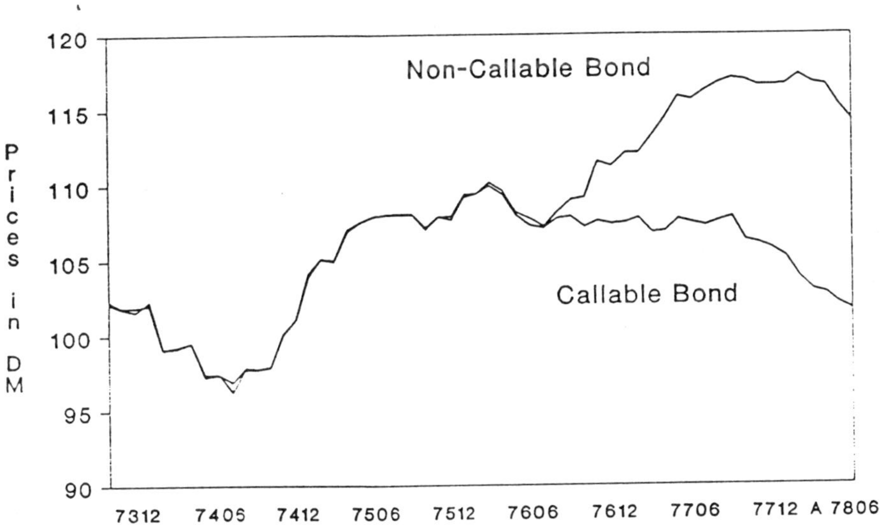

Figure 2: Prices of the callable 10 % Bund 1973 III and the noncallable 10 % Post 1973

4. Summary and conclusion

This study contains an analysis of the call policy of the German Government (Bund), the German National Railways (Bahn) and Post Office in respect of their bond market issues. Two different analytical methods were applied. The first is based on directly observable data only and attempts to elicit arbitrage opportunities in the bond market. The second procedure uses a bond option pricing model and determines an optimal call policy in accordance with this model.

The issuers followed an optimal call policy in that they never called a bond when it was optimal not to call. Furthermore, in both cases when a bond was called this was the optimal decision. However, there were a number of missed calls.

Indged by reference to market prices in 30 out of 359 possibilities an optimal call was not exercised. In most cases the resultant financial loss was small. However, a call of the 8 % Post bond in May 1985, or May 1986, would have saved interest payments for three periods until August 1987 of 4,840,000 DM and 7,840,000 DM, respectively.

Similar results were found using an option pricing model. In 27 situations an optimal call was missed. With the exception of two cases the financial loss was small. Again the two cases with notable losses refer to the May 1985 and May 1986 call dates of the 8% Post 1972 bond.

The model correctly forecasts the two calls of the 10 % Bund bonds in 1978. Taken together these two cases enabled the issuer to save interest payments of about 150 million DM in the remaining three years until maturity of the two bonds.

References

Asquith, P. and Mullins, D.W. (1991): Convertible Debt: Corporate Call Policy and Voluntary Conversion, in: Journal of Finance 46, 1273-1289.

Brennan, M.J. and Schwartz E.S. (1979): Savings Bonds: Theory and Empirical Evidence, in: Monograph Series in Finance and Economics, Monograph 1979-4, New York University. New York.

Bühler, W., Köndgen, J. and Schmidt, H. (1990): Schutz und Diskriminierung nach Paragraph 609a BGB, in: Zeitschrift für Bankrecht und Bankwirtschaft 2, 49-75.

Bühler, W. and Schulze, M. (1991): Estimation of the Transition Behaviour of Term Structures of Interest Rates, in: Statistical Papers 32, 281-297.

Bühler, W. and Schulze, M. (1993): Zur Bewertung kündbarer Anleihen - Eine empirische Studie am deutschen Rentenmarkt, in: Bühler, W., H. Hax and R. Schmidt (eds.): Empirische Kapitalmarktforschung. Zeitschrift für betriebswirtschaftliche Forschung, special issue 31, 61-85.

Bühler, W., H. Hax and R. Schmidt (eds.) (1993): Empirische Kapitalmarktforschung, Zeitschrift für betriebswirtschaftliche Forschung, special issue 31.

Carleton, W.T. and Cooper, I.A. (1976): Estimation and Uses of the Term Structure of Interest Rates, in: Journal of Finance 31, 1067-1084.

Chambers, D.R., Carleton, W.T. and Waldman, D.W. (1984): A New Approach to Estimation of the Term Structure of Interest Rates, in: Journal of Financial and Quantitative Analysis 19, 233-255.

Campbell, C.I., Ederington, L.H. and Vankudre, P. (1991): Tax Shields, Sample-Selection Bias, and the Information Content of Conversion-Forcing Bond Calls, in: Journal of Finance 46, 1291-1324.

Ho, T. and Lee, S.B. (1986): Term Structure Movements and Pricing Interest Rate Contingent Claims, in: Journal of Finance 41, 1011-1029.

Ingersoll, J. (1977): An Examination of Corporate Policies on Convertible Securities, in: Journal of Finance 32, 463-478.

Litzenberger, R. and Rolfo, J. (1984): An International Study of Tax Effects on Government Bonds, in: Journal of Finance 39, 1-22.

Longstaff, F.A. (1992): Are Negative Option Prices Possible? The Callable U.S. Treasury-Bond Puzzle, in: Journal of Business 65, 571-592.

Mc Culloch, J.H. (1971): Measuring the Term Structure of Interest Rates, in: Journal of Business 44, 19-31.

Robbins, E.H. and Schatzberg, I.D. (1986): Callable Bonds: A Risk-Reducing Signalling Mechanism, in: Journal of Finance 41, 935-949.

Schaefer, S.M. (1981): Measuring a Tax-Specific Term Structure of Interest Rates in the Market for British Government Securities, in: The Economic Journal 91, 415-438.

Seber, G. and Wild, C. (1989): Nonlinear Regression. New York 1989.

Shea, G. (1984): Pitfalls from Smoothing Interest Rate Term Structure Data: Equilibrium Models and Spline Approximations, in: Journal of Financial and Quantitative Analysis 19, 253-269.

Vu, Y.D. (1986): An Empirical Investigation of Calls of Non-Convertible Bonds, in: Journal of Financial Economics 16, 235-265.

Time-lags between Price Changes of Stocks and Stock Options

Martina Gais, Renate Hecker and Ekkehard Wenger
University of Würzburg

1. Introduction

According to basic welfare economics, two fundamental reasons explain the existence of option markets. On the one hand, introducing additional securities like options into an incomplete stock market will create more opportunities for spreading risks among market participants, and therefore may lead to an improved risk allocation[1]. On the other hand, the option market increases the informational efficiency of the capital market, if option trading causes prices to adjust more rapidly to new information[2]. This study is restricted to the latter possibility. Thus, the welfare consequences of the option market is to be judged by its impact on stock prices.

Interdependencies between option and stock prices have attracted the attention of empiricists for at least two decades. To clarify the relationship of this study to previous work, two criteria facilitating the classification of different lines of pertinent research may be helpful. The first criterion refers to the question of whether the flow of information between the option and stock markets takes a well-defined direction. Relevant American studies like the papers of Panton (1976), Manaster/Rendleman (1982, hereafter M/R), and Bhattacharya (1987) assume that the option market adjusts more rapidly to new information than does the stock market. Only few studies, for example, Stephan/Whaley (1990), do not start from the hypothesis that information spreads from the option market to the stock market. In accordance with the second criterion, studies can be classified either by reference to a data base comprising no more than a series of consecutive price quotations; or, to a data base which is restricted to certain time intervals covering pre-specified events. Most of the studies just mentioned are not

[1] Better risk allocation, however, requires only certain kinds of options, if any (Ross 1976, Cass/Stiglitz 1970, and Hakansson 1982, p. 1001).

[2] A third possible reason is that trading options instead of the underlying stock may save transactions costs. But in the absence of the two reasons mentioned above it is difficult to imagine how market participants can save transactions costs if they establish an option market in addition to the market for the underlying securities.

restricted in this sense[3], whereas others have focused on events like expiration dates of options (Klemkosky 1978, Officer/Trennepohl 1981, and Lion 1989), the introduction of new options (Trennepohl/Dukes 1979, Klemkosky/Mannes 1980, Whiteside/Dukes/Dunne 1983, Gemmill 1989, Skinner 1989, and Conrad 1989), or the disclosure of new information by the company which issued the underlying stock[4].

The results of the American studies are mixed. According to Panton (1976, pp. 111 f.), there is no reliable evidence that option prices can predict stock prices: With few exceptions, future stock price performance showed no significantly positive correlation with observed differences between actual call prices and theoretical call values based on the concurrent stock price. On the other hand, M/R (1982) report evidence that option prices reflect new information earlier than the stock market. However, trading strategies designed to exploit information from the option market in the lagging stock market failed to earn significant excess profits (M/R 1982, p. 1055). Bhattacharya also concludes that, whilst option prices contain some information that is not contained in contemporaneous stock prices, such information does not allow to earn excess profits in the stock market (Bhattacharya 1987, p. 14). These findings are at odds with those of Stephan/Whaley who present evidence of a fifteen to twenty minute lead of stock prices over the option market[5].

This study is based on time series of option and stock prices from the Frankfurt Stock Exchange and investigates whether there are systematic interdependencies between option and stock prices. The empirical analysis that follows is divided into two main parts. The first part is presented in section 2. It is free of restrictions on certain events in the stock or option market, and is not based on the assumption that the flow of information between the two markets takes a well-defined direction. The purpose of section 2 is to examine whether option prices anticipate stock price movements or *vice versa*.

Theoretical reasons can be advanced for both time patterns and it is impossible to decide *a priori*, which is the more dominant in practice. If investors use options to hedge a previous investment in the stock market, a lagging option market may be the consequence. On the other hand, traders with privileged access to information not yet publicly available will invest in options, because the

---

[3] The papers of Panton (1976), M/R (1982), and Stephan/Whaley (1990) fall into this category whereas Bhattacharya (1987) proposes an "all days" and a "pre-event days" version of his tests.

[4] Dividend and earnings announcements are the focus of Bhattacharyas "pre-event days" test version; see footnote 3.

[5] With respect to trading activity, the lead of the stock market over the option market seems to be larger (Stephan/Whaley 1990, p. 214).

profit on a given investment in options rather than in stocks will be much higher (Black 1975, p. 61).

Privileged traders, however, are not likely to have informational advantages which remain constant over time. Consequently, they can be expected to adjust their trading activity in the option market. If so, the predictive power of option prices will increase in advance of strong abnormal performance of stock prices. This hypothesis is examined in section 3 which contains the second part of the empirical findings. Here, the analysis is guided by the question of whether option prices predict abnormal performance of the underlying stock.

2. Chronological order of option and stock price changes

Observed and implied stock prices are compared to investigate the relationship between the prices of options and stocks. Implied stock prices are derived from observed option prices by resorting to conventional option pricing models. Implied prices serve as a proxy for option price movements and can be directly compared with the corresponding time series for the stock market. Section 2.1 shows in detail how implied stock prices are computed. In section 2.2 the correlation between implied and observed stock returns is examined for different lead/lag periods. Section 2.3 is concerned with trading strategies designed to exploit potential lead/lag structures.

This part of the study is based on a sample of 14 firms[6] with actively traded options listed on the Frankfurt Stock Exchange. The sample covers all trading days from April 1, 1983 to December 31, 1989[7]. This time frame was chosen because rules of option trading in Germany were subject to considerable changes on both its opening and closing dates. The analysis hereafter refers to call options unless put options are explicitly mentioned.

2.1 Calculation of implied stock prices

The prices of all option series[8] with the same underlying stock have been used to calculate the implied price of the stock in question. The implied stock price can

---

[6] BASF AG, Bayer AG, Hoechst AG, BMW AG, Daimler-Benz AG, VW AG, Commerzbank AG, Deutsche Bank AG, Dresdner Bank AG, Mannesmann AG, RWE AG, Siemens AG, Thyssen AG and Veba AG.

[7] Stock and option market transaction data were provided by Deutsche Finanzdatenbank (DFDB) Karlsruhe.

[8] During the relevant period of 1684 trading days in this study, there is usually not more than one price per day for each option series (defined by exercise price, expiration date

be interpreted as the "translation" of all price signals of the option market into a single stock price.

The implied stock price S^* is calculated simultaneously with the implied volatility[9] σ^* for each stock i and each day t using the option market data mentioned above. The idea underlying the determination of S^* and σ^* is the minimization of the sum of the squared differences between observed option prices and theoretical option values derived from a suitable pricing model. Consequently, if S^* and σ^* are used as input data of the pricing model, they must solve the following minimization problem:

$$\underset{S_{it},\sigma_{it}}{Min} \quad Q = \sum_{j=1}^{n_{it}} \left(M_{ijt} - C_{ijt}\left(S_{it}, \sigma_{it}\right)\right)^2 \tag{1}$$

For underlying security i, M_{ijt} is the observed price of option series j on day t; C_{ijt} (S_{it}, σ_{it}) is a function of the stock price and its volatility determining the theoretical option value in accordance with the chosen pricing model; n_{it} indicates how many option series for underlying stock i have been traded on day t[10]. Solving the minimization problem with respect to S_{it} and σ_{it} yields the implied stock price and its implied volatility for security i on day t.

The choice of an appropriate pricing model has to take into account that options which expired before the end of 1987 were essentially dividend protected whereas, thereafter, the dividend protection was eliminated. In the case of the earlier maturities, the exercise price was reduced by the dividend as soon as the dividend had been paid out[11]. Although all options in the sample could have been exercised at any time before maturity, the dividend protection for options expiring before the end of 1987 rendered the exercise of calls before maturity unattractive to the holder[12]. Consequently, the theoretical values of the respective options were derived from the Black/Scholes (BS) model (Black/Scholes 1973)[13].

---

and underlying stock). The annual average for the number of option series traded per day for each of the 14 firms lies between 5 and 12.

[9] Values of σ based on historical stock return data may not be satisfactory for the purpose pursued here. For the conception of implied volatility (Cox/Rubinstein 1985, pp. 278 f.).

[10] Only prices of effective trades have been included; bid and ask prices without trades have not been considered.

[11] Of course, the mere reduction of the exercise price is only an incomplete protection against payouts. If an option has an exercise price K prior to the payout of a dividend D leading to an ex dividend stock price S^{ex}, perfect dividend protection requires that the original option has to be exchanged for (1+D/Sex) options with exercise price [K/(1+D/Sex)] (Merton 1973).

[12] The conditions, under which early exercise will never occur, if options are dividend protected as described above, are given by Geske/Roll/Shastri (1983, pp. 1272 f.).

[13] If a dividend is paid during the life of an option, the logic of the BS-model requires that the reduction in the exercise price is taken account of even before the dividend is paid.

For calls expiring after the end of 1987, a suitable valuation model has to take account of potential exercise before dividend dates. In the relevant cases, the Roll/Geske/Whaley (RGW) model (Whaley 1981) was chosen[14]. It applies to options on stocks paying a single dividend before the option expires. Cases with more than one dividend during the life of an option did not occur. The corporations in the sample pay dividends only once a year, whereas the life of the options has an upper bound of nine months and 15 days (Hecker 1993, p. 86).

The valuation models applied have the following parameters: the stock price and its volatility, the exercise price of the option, the remaining time until the option expires, the risk free interest rate, the amount of a potential dividend and its payment date. For two of these parameters, the empirical specification ist not self-evident[15]. The risk free interest rate is adjusted monthly to the average three month interbank rate in Frankfurt as published in "Monatsberichte der Deutschen Bundesbank". The dividend on the stock is the amount declared by the company net of corporate taxes but before the usual 25 percent withholding tax[16].

The minimization problem underlying the concept of the implicit stock price has no analytical solution[17] and the iterative computational procedure, which is used to find numerical values for implicit stock prices, is explained in detail in Wenger/Hecker/Gais (1993, pp. 138 f.).

The necessary adjustments, however, are not made because their effects are too small to justify the effort.

[14] This approach duplicates the relevant cash flows of the American call option with a portfolio of a European option and an option on this option.

[15] The empirical specification of the stock price and its volatility are also usually not self-evident. As long as their implied values are needed, however, the problem is meaningless.

[16] The 25 percent withholding tax is treated as tax prepayment of the stockholder himself whereas corporate taxes on distributed profits are imputed to the domestic stockholder as a tax prepayment on the "gross" dividend before the imputed corporate tax. Depending on the individual tax rate of the stockholder, the "effective" dividend he receives net of all taxes may be higher or lower than the amount declared by the company. Because the corporate tax on distributed profits was levied at a rate of 36 percent during the entire period in question, the specification of the dividend parameter implies that the tax rate of the representative investor is 36 percent.

[17] M/R (1982, p. 1047) solve the minimization problem numerically using a Newtonian search in which partial derivatives with respect to S and σ are simultaneously set close to zero. Their technique can be applied if these derivatives can be determined analytically. This can be done as long as only the BS-model is used for calculating the theoretical option prices. The simple BS-model, however, does not take account of potential exercise before dividends. M/R avoid the problem by excluding the options in question. In a study of the German market, this is not a viable strategy because the ensuing loss of data can only be afforded in a sufficiently broad market like that of the US.

2.2 Serial correlation of implied and observed stock returns

If the option market leads the stock market or *vice versa*, this may be detected by analyzing the serial correlation between implied and observed stock returns[18]. For that reason, correlation coefficients of implied and observed stock returns[19] are calculated for lead and lag periods of up to 10 days. Thus the lag of the implied returns behind the observed returns which is fed into the correlation analysis can be expressed by an integer k ranging from -10 to +10. If it turns out that, for the highest correlation coefficient, the sign of k is negative, this would suggest a lead of the option market over the stock market. The reverse conclusion may be drawn if the correlation coefficient reaches its maximum for a positive value of k.

The correlation analysis was carried out for 91 different combinations of firm and year[20]. Consequently, there are 91 correlation coefficients for each value of k. Table 1 gives the number of positive and significantly positive correlation coefficients as well as the average correlation coefficient as a function of k:

Only for k=0 and k=1 does a clear majority of the total of 91 correlation coefficients turns out to be positive. For contemporaneous price changes 86 coefficients were positive; 68 of them were significantly larger than zero at the 0.01 level. For a stock market lead of one day, 76 coefficients were positive and 37 of them were significant. For all other values of k, the average correlation coefficient was very close to zero and the number of significantly positive correlation coefficients did not exceed five. Evidently there are no indications that the option market leads the stock market[21].

---

[18] Observed stock returns are calculated by using odd lot prices ("Kassakurse"). In Germany, odd lot prices are the most widely used stock price quotations. Deutsche Finanzdatenbank could not provide other quotations.

[19] To compute daily returns, stock prices must be adjusted by dividends and preemptive subscription rights. Implied stock prices are not available for days without trades in an adequate number of option series. In the time series for the respective security such days are excluded. If day t is excluded, the observed stock return R and the implied stock return R^* on day t+1 are calculated as follows:

$$R_{t+1} = \frac{S_{t+1}}{S_{t-1}} - 1 \quad \text{and} \quad R^*_{t+1} = \frac{S^*_{t+1}}{S^*_{t-1}} - 1$$

For each stock and calendar year not more than 40 percent exclusions are allowed. Otherwise stock returns for the respective calendar year were omitted from the analysis.

[20] The upper bound for the number of coefficients is 14x7=98. In fact, only 91 coefficients have been computed. 7 cases have not been analyzed because the option market was too thin; see the preceding footnote.

[21] This conclusion is corroborated by the results which follow from ordering the 21 correlation coefficients for each of the 91 firm-year-combinations by their size. The correlation coefficient for k=0 was the highest one in 60 of 91 cases and ranked second in

Table 1: Results of the correlation analysis

Time-lag k in days	Number of **positive** correlation coefficients	Number of **significant**[22] positive corr. coeff.	Average correlation coefficient
-10	50	2	0.0094
-9	49	2	0.0022
-8	47	2	0.0015
-7	50	4	0.0142
-6	41	1	-0.0164
-5	49	3	0.0005
-4	51	3	0.0080
-3	51	1	0.0097
-2	39	1	-0.0174
-1	39	0	-0.0123
0	86	68	0.3060
1	76	37	0.1242
2	38	5	-0.0141
3	47	1	0.0034
4	39	2	-0.0109
5	52	4	0.0071
6	43	1	-0.0039
7	55	0	0.0143
8	39	3	0.0004
9	42	3	0.0015
10	50	3	0.0046

If there is any lead at all, the stock market leads the option market, at least on an average. But the average lead is too small to make for a stronger correlation between observed stock returns and implied stock returns one day later than between the corresponding returns on the same day. Taking account of the fact that time lags of less than one day are meaningless if implied stock prices can be calculated only once a day, these results come remarkably close to those of Stephan/Whaley, whose 5-minute-data for the American market give evidence of a stock market lead of less than half an hour.

Considering the results of the American studies it is not surprising that contemporaneous price changes show the strongest correlation. But the average correlation coefficient of 0.306 for k=0 corresponds to a coefficient of determination of only 0.09 in a univariate regression of one time series on the other. The conclusion is that the intensity and direction of stock price movements

11 cases; the value for k=1 ranked first in 11 and second in 31 cases. For k=-1, however, the correlation coefficient was ranked first only once and second only once.

[22] Significant at the 0.01 level.

are not very well reflected in the option market because the two markets are exposed to substantially different influences. This result also confirms similar findings of Stephan/Whaley (1990, p. 206)[23].

2.3 Tests of trading rules

If option prices contain information other than stock prices, arbitrage opportunities may exist which can be exploited by traders. Assuming that option prices contain more information than stock prices, the observed stock price can be expected to adjust to the implied stock price if there is a difference between them. If there is more information in stock prices, the implied stock price should move towards the observed stock price and option prices should adjust accordingly.

Two simple trading rules are designed to exploit the potential price adjustments. The difference between the implied and the observed stock price is computed for each day t and each firm i. Two portfolios are formed daily. The first contains all stocks for which the observed stock price is higher than the implied stock price whereas, in the second portfolio, implied stock prices are higher. Equal sums are invested in each stock[24]. According to trading rule I, price information of day t is used to form portfolios bought on day t and sold on day t+1. This trading rule is clearly of an *ex post* nature because the information needed for trading is not available when the portfolios are bought. As it cannot be applied in practice, an *ex ante* trading rule is tested which is based on information already available before trades are made. According to trading rule II, therefore, price information of day t is used to buy stocks on day t+1 which are sold one day later.

If no information is contained in option prices that is not contained in stock prices, there will be no difference between the returns of the two portfolios, and the following null hypothesis can therefore be defined:

$$H_0 : W(R_t(P_1) < R_t(P_2)) = W(R_t(P_1) \geq R_t(P_2)) = 0.5 \qquad \text{for } t = 1 \ldots n$$

where P_i = portfolio i, i = 1, 2
R_t = return between day t-1 and day t

[23] Even for a multiple time series regression with implied stock returns regressed on contemporaneous, leading, or lagging stock price changes they report a coefficient of determination of only 0.07. In accordance with their study, we found implied stock prices to be more volatile than observed stock prices.

[24] Problems of indivisibility are ignored.

W ( ) = probability of the event in the brackets

According to the null hypothesis, the probability that the first portfolio will have a higher return than the second is equal to the probability of the opposite case. This hypothesis is subjected to a two-sided sign test (Kendall/Stuart 1979, pp. 542 f.). The following table shows the number of days on which the first portfolio had a higher return than the second and *vice versa*. The average daily returns for each year are reported in columns 5 and 6. The last column contains the probability that the null hypothesis is rejected even when it is true[25].

Table 2: Test of *ex post* and *ex ante* trading rule

Year	Number of trading days	Number of days where $R_t(P_1)<R_t(P_2)$	$R_t(P_1)\geq R_t(P_2)$	Average daily return Portfolio 1	Portfolio 2	Error probability of the Two-sided sign test
Trading rule I (*ex post*)						
1983	173	78	95	0.0010278	0.0005919	0.2238
1984	235	109	126	0.0004502	-0.0000930	0.2966
1985	242	124	118	0.0026332	0.0026019	0.7479
1986	241	134	107	0.0005589	0.0002106	0.0940
1987	248	111	137	-0.0007108	-0.0014633	0.1124
1988	247	115	132	0.0016249	0.0015262	0.3389
1989	246	124	122	0.0013005	0.0012834	0.9492
Trading rule II (*ex ante*)						
1983	173	78	95	0.0015441	0.0005674	0.2238
1984	235	125	110	-0.0000727	0.0003371	0.3268
1985	242	121	121	0.0026324	0.0021784	1.0000
1986	241	134	107	-0.0002379	-0.0000832	0.0940
1987	248	108	140	-0.0004189	-0.0016625	0.0490
1988	247	108	139	0.0012903	0.0013020	0.0645
1989	246	116	130	0.0014208	0.0009573	0.4433

25 The error probability is calculated by summing the probabilities of a binomial distribution for the "extreme cases" below the minimum and above the maximum of n and n-m:

$$\alpha = \sum_{k=0}^{\min(m,n-m)} 0.5^n \binom{n}{k} + \sum_{k=\max(m,n-m)}^{n} 0.5^n \binom{n}{k} = 2 \cdot 0.5^n \cdot \sum_{k=0}^{\min(m,n-m)} \binom{n}{k}$$

n is the number of trading days and m the number of days with Rt (P1) < Rt(P2). The second equation is due to the symmetry of the distribution.

The null hypothesis cannot be rejected at the 0.01 significance level in any year. Nor is rejection admissible on the basis of one significant result at the 0.05 level since fourteen tests have been carried out. Consistent with the results reported in section 2.2, there is no evidence that the option market anticipates stock price movements. On the contrary, the mean return of portfolio 1 is higher than the mean return of portfolio 2 in most cases.

3. Informational content of option prices regarding future abnormal stock price activity[26]

According to section 2, there is no evidence that option prices reflect new information earlier than do contemporaneous stock prices. This conclusion, however, is based on an analysis which has not been restricted to certain pre-specified events. Hence it may still be questioned whether option prices predict stock prices during specific time periods when information is available to corporate insiders but not yet available to the capital market. Investors with an important piece of non-public information may prefer to deal in options because some characteristics of options are likely to appeal to informed traders. In particular, options require lower cash outlays than a leveraged position in the underlying stock, but have a similar capacity for exploiting superior information (Manne 1966, p. 90, Black 1975, p. 61). The implication is that call option prices may predict abnormal performance of the underlying stock if privileged traders use the option market to exploit information which is not yet publicly available. The empirical content of this implication is examined in the remaining part of this study. For this purpose, a statistical test is used to ascertain whether call options are significantly more likely to be substantially overpriced (underpriced) relative to their theoretical values if, subsequently, the underlying stock outperforms (underperforms) the market. Whether the mispricing of an option is classified as "substantial" depends on how it is ranked by amount among all observed mispricings within the respective test period. The test is clearly of an *ex post* nature, as it is based on information which is not available before the conclusion of the test period. Not investigated is the question of whether the potential informational content of call prices could have been exploited to earn excess returns by a trader who lacked direct access to the information which subsequently led to the abnormal performance of the underlying stock. The tests involve a sample of six firms[27] listed on the Frankfurt Stock Exchange; the price data are taken from a time interval running from April 1, 1983 to December 31, 1987.

---

[26] A more complete discussion of this topic is given by Hecker (1993).

[27] BASF AG, Bayer AG, Hoechst AG, BMW AG, Daimler-Benz AG, and VW AG.

If the tests confirm that call prices predict abnormal performance of the underlying stock they constitute an important argument against allegations that the existence of an option market reduces the efficiency of the market for the underlying stock[28]. Moreover, the test results may be helpful in deciding whether additional research should be undertaken to explore how information spreads from the option market to the stock market and *vice versa*.

The intensity of potential insider trading in the option market is presumably influenced by various factors (Hecker 1994a, pp. 410-418). As the further analysis is restricted to the call market, pertinent insider activity might be expected to be much lower for negative than for positive inside information. An insider with negative non-public information is more likely to buy puts instead of selling calls. Selling calls would limit potential profits to the price of the option and would trigger considerable margin requirements.

Furthermore, insiders are likely to prefer those segments of the option market which are characterized by sufficient liquidity and high elasticity of the option price with respect to the stock price; on the other hand, they must choose expiration dates according to the time the market will presumably need to bring prices into line with the information in question. Finally it has to be kept in mind that the extent of insider trading in the option market might also be influenced by a long-lasting bull or bear market.

The remainder of the paper is organized as follows: section 3.1 starts with the market model that is used to determine the daily abnormal performance in the stock market. This is followed by an explanation of the procedure for selecting days with "conspicuous" residual stock price movements. Section 3.2 is concerned with the selection of "potential insider trading days" which precede intervals with conspicuous residuals as already defined in the previous section. Section 3.3 introduces the concept of "option mispricing" that is adopted in this study. Thereafter, criteria are proposed for separating irrelevant and "substantial" mispricings. In the first part of section 3.4, a statistical test is developed which detects whether the substantial mispricing of options is significantly more frequent on potential insider trading days. The second part of section 3.4 deals with the implications of various test runs; in the last part, the test results are presented.

---

[28] A discussion of this hypothesis is given by Gemmill (1989, p. 15) or Klemkosky (1978, pp. 508 f.).

3.1 Identification of abnormal performance in the stock market

3.1.1 The single index model and the estimation of the model parameters

The return on an individual stock is adjusted for general market conditions by resorting to the following logarithmic form of the single index model (See Fama/Fisher/Jensen/Roll, 1969, p. 4):

$$\ln(1 + r_{it}) = \alpha_i + \beta_i \cdot \ln(1 + r_{mt}) + \varepsilon_{it} \qquad (2)$$

where r_{it} = effective rate of return on security i for the period from t-1 to t

r_{mt} = effective rate of return on the market index for the period from t-1 to t[29]

$$\beta_i = \frac{\text{cov}\left[\ln(1 + r_{it}), \ln(1 + r_{mt})\right]}{\text{var}\left[\ln(1 + r_{mt})\right]}$$

$$\alpha_i = E\left[\ln(1 + r_{it})\right] - \beta_i \cdot E\left[\ln(1 + r_{mt})\right]$$

ε_{it} = normally distributed random disturbance term of security i for the period from t-1 to t. It is assumed that ε_{it} satisfies the usual assumptions of the linear regression model. That is, ε_{it} has zero expectation and constant variance independent of t; the ε_{it} are serially independent and the distribution of ε_{it} is independent of $\ln(1+r_{mt})$.

Least squares estimates based on daily returns[30] are used to determine α_i and β_i for each of the six securities in the sample and for each year in the data base. The corresponding estimates of disturbance terms are identical with daily residuals measuring abnormal stock price performance.

---

[29] The "general market conditions" are represented by the "Deutsche Aktienindex (DAX)" for the year 1988 and by the "Index der Börsen-Zeitung (BZ-Index)" (transformed to the new base of the DAX) for the test period from 1983 through 1987.

[30] Evaluating the efficiency of the estimation procedure uncovered several cases of significant auto-correlation and heteroscedasticity of the disturbance terms. For that reason, alternative methods of estimating the abnormal performance have been considered. As the estimation procedure has essentially had no influence on the outcome of the selection procedure described in subsection 3.1.2, only ordinary least squares estimates were used in the following tests.

3.1.2 Selection of days with conspicuous residuals

The test design requires a selection procedure for "critical days" which are characterized by "conspicuous" abnormal performance in the stock market. The selection procedure consists of two steps:

First step: For each year of the total sample period, select
- 10 days ranking highest according to the absolute value of the daily residual
- 10 two-day intervals ranking highest according to the absolute value of the sum of their residuals
- ...
- 10 ten-day intervals ranking highest according to the absolute value of the sum of their residuals[31].

There is a sound reason why, in the first step, not only single days are selected, namely, that it is highly unlikely that every piece of new information is always fully reflected in the stock return of a single day.

Second step: The intervals selected in the first step are curtailed whenever the absolute value of the sum of the residuals of the curtailed interval is larger than the absolute value of the sum of the residuals of the original interval. This ensures that intervals remaining in the selection do not begin, or end, with abnormal stock price movements running counter to the direction of the abnormal performance due to which the respective interval has been selected.

The days remaining after the second step are considered as "critical days" with conspicuous residual stock price performance. In so far as the second step leads to time intervals which are overlapping, or bordering, on each other, they are merged into one interval whenever the sums of their residuals have the same sign. This implies that every interval is eliminated, if it is fully covered by a longer one that is still in the selection after step two.

3.2 Selection of potential insider trading days

Potential insider trading days in the option market are assumed to be trading days prior to the "critical intervals" selected according to the previous section. The former may be followed by the latter without a single day in between or with a pre-specified time lag. The length of this lag, as well as the total number of

---

[31] For 1983, the number of days or intervals selected in each group has been reduced from 10 to 7 because the test period includes only the last nine months of the year.

consecutive days classified as potential insider trading days, is varied according to 25 different combinations examined in the test runs.

3.3 Selection of days with substantial relative mispricing of options

The mispricing of an option is defined as the relative deviation of the option's price from its corresponding theoretical value. In accordance with section 2.1, the theoretical value of all options expiring before the end of 1987 is derived from the BS-model. For options with later maturities, the same model is applied unless the underlying stock pays dividends before the option expires. Should such payouts occur, the respective theoretical values are determined according to a numerical integration technique which takes account of potential exercise before dividend dates[32].

The parameters entering the valuation models are specified as follows. The relevant stock price is recorded daily and is measured by the first transaction price of the underlying stock on the day in question[33]. The future stock price volatility is determined by an estimate based on historical stock price data for an annual period ending on the day before the valuation date. The risk free interest rate and the amount of a potential dividend are chosen in accordance with section 2.1.

For option series[34] with the same underlying stock, which are traded on the same day[35], a weighted average mispricing per day is calculated; the weights fed

---

[32] The numerical integration approach rests on the same assumptions as the Roll/Geske/Whaley-model with one exception. As long as dividends have not been paid out, the Brown-Wiener-process underlying the valuation model applies to the cum dividend stock price and not to the stock price diminished by the discounted future dividend.

[33] For the smaller sample used in the second part of this study, prices of first daily stock transactions, which could not be provided by the Deutsche Finanzdatenbank, were collected by the authors themselves. First daily transactions in the relevant stocks are usually effected in closer proximity to the time of the option price quotation than the quotation of the daily odd lot price used in the larger sample of the first part of this study; see footnote 18.

[34] If there is more than one transaction price for the same option series on the same day, every transaction price is treated as the price of a separate option series. Such cases, however, occurred very rarely.

[35] The average mispricing per day does not take account of those option series which have a remaining life of less than 15 days because complete data for these options are not available. As in the first part of this study, quotations of bid and ask prices without trades have also been ignored.

into the average MP_{it} correspond to the theoretical values of the respective option series:

Table 3: Selection alternatives for potential insider trading days (see also p. 270)

Number of potential insider trading days preceding the days with large residuals Large residuals in the stock market 60 50 40 30 20 15 10 5 ———— — —— ——— ———— ————— —————— ——————— ————————	The 5, 10, ..., 60 days immediately preceding the days with conspicuous residuals in the stock market are considered as potential insider trading days. (= 8 test runs)
Number of potential insider trading days preceding the days with large residuals Large residuals in the stock market 20 15 10 5 ———— — —— ——— ————	There is a lag of 5 trading days between the potential insider trading days and the selected interval with conspicuous residuals. (= 4 test runs)
Number of potential insider trading days preceding the days with large residuals Large residuals in the stock market 20 15 10 5 ———— — —— ——— ————	There is a lag of 10 trading days between the potential insider trading days and the selected interval with conspicuous residuals. (= 4 test runs)

Number of potential insider trading days preceding the days with large residuals 60 50 40 30 20 15 10 5 Large residuals in the stock market	In addition to the days preceding the interval with conspicuous residuals the first half of the interval is also considered as a potential insider trading period. (= 8 test runs)
Large residuals in the stock market Potential insider trading days	All selected days with conspicuous residuals are considered as potential insider trading days[36]. (= 1 test run)
	= 25 test runs

$$MP_{it} = \sum_{j=1}^{n_{it}} \frac{C_{ijt} - M_{ijt}}{C_{ijt}} \cdot \frac{C_{ijt}}{\sum_{j=1}^{n_{it}} C_{ijt}} \Leftrightarrow MP_{it} = \sum_{j=1}^{n_{it}} \frac{C_{ijt} - M_{ijt}}{\sum_{j=1}^{n_{it}} C_{ijt}} \qquad (3)$$

The symbols are defined as in section 2.1.

An average mispricing based on weights reflecting the theoretical values of the individual options has the advantage that the resulting daily mispricing signal is not influenced over-proportionally by high percentage mispricings of option series with small absolute values. Markets for the latter are often very thin and even relatively small orders are sufficient to cause huge price swings in percentage terms. Moreover, the respective option prices may be distorted by high

[36] This test run only serves for control purposes. It may answer the question of whether the test results indeed show that option prices lead stock prices.

transactions costs and discrete price steps of 0.05 DM to which price quotations are restricted [37].

Average option mispricings are not only calculated per company and per day but also per company, day and expiration date. As maturity dates are quarterly, and the life of an option has an upper bound of 9 months and 15 days, three maturity dates are available[38] for calculating "specific" mispricing signals. The "overall" mispricing including all relevant option series is, as explained above, a weighted average of the three maturity-specific mispricing signals. The reason for tests based on maturity-specific mispricing signals follows from the assumption that the remaining life of an option is an important factor in the calculus of an insider[39]. If insider activity is concentrated on a single maturity, it may go undetected without analyzing data specific to that maturity. The overall mispricing will not reflect insider trading in a single maturity, if the weight of the mispricings of the respective option series is too low compared to option series with other expiration dates.

As differences between observed option prices and theoretical option values will always occur, mispricings are meaningless for the purpose of this study, unless they are "substantial". Consequently, a selection procedure for days with "substantial" mispricings has to be designed. For the purpose of this study it does not make much sense to determine these days by comparing the daily mispricing with an upper, or lower bound which is constant and equal for all companies, test periods and test variants. Due to the fact that mispricings within a certain test period do not necessarily average zero, the mispricings are classified relative to the special circumstances of the respective test period. The values of MP_{it} are ranked according to size separately for each company and each test variant within the respective test period. Then all mispricings belonging to a certain quantile at the upper or lower end of the ranking are considered as substantial relative under- or overpricings, respectively. The quantiles being used for the alternative test runs vary in 5 percent-steps from 5 percent to 50 percent of the total number of trading days in the respective test period.

Running test variants with different quantiles has important advantages. Restricting the selection of days with substantial relative mispricings to a small

---

37 Using the BS-model there is also a problem of systematic mispricings especially with deep-out-of-the-money options; see for example Merton (1976, p. 345) and Galai (1983, p. 59). Calculating weighted averages renders this problem less severe.

38 During the last 15 days before expiration dates, four maturities are traded. Complete data are available for only three of them; see footnote 36.

39 The remaining life of the option exercises an important influence on how strongly the option value reacts to stock price changes (Hecker 1994a, pp. 414-416). How the option delta and the elasticity of an option depend on the remaining life of the option is explained in detail in Cox/Rubinstein (1985, pp. 222 f. and pp. 228 f.).

quantile like 5 percent would introduce a high risk of the test results being biased by a single outlier. Moreover, there is no reason to assume that the potential buying and selling of insiders at a certain day will always have the same effect on option prices. If the pressure on option prices varies from case to case, it makes sense to run the tests with quantiles of varying sizes.

3.4 The statistical test and the interpretation of the test results

3.4.1 The statistical test

If mispricings in the option market occur by chance, and not due to trading by insiders anticipating excess returns in the stock market, the likelihood of substantial relative mispricings should not increase during periods of potential insider trading days. Consequently, the value of p_1, denoting the probability of substantial relative mispricings on potential insider trading days, should coincide with p_2, the respective mispricing probability on other days. But if, as assumed in this study, insiders initially try to exploit their informational advantage in the option market, the probability p_1 should be higher than p_2. Prior to the conspicuous overperformance (underperformance) of the underlying stock, there should be a higher probability of substantial relative overpricing (underpricing) of call options[40].

A significant difference between p_1 and p_2 can be detected by the one-sided exact Fisher test (Kendall/Stuart 1979, pp. 580-583). For each of the investigated companies the null hypothesis H_0: $p_1 = p_2 = p$ is tested against the alternative hypothesis H_1: $p_1 > p_2$. As conspicuous residual stock price performance is always examined separately for positive and negative values, p_k is the probability of substantial relative overpricing in the call option market in cases of subsequent overperformance of the underlying stock. In cases of subsequent underperformance, p_k is the probability of substantial relative underpricing in the call option market.

The relevant data of the sample can be arranged in the following 2 x 2 table:

[40] This specification of the "insider hypothesis" rests on the assumption that insiders have a noticeable influence on option prices. This implies that insiders generate a sufficiently high percentage of the trading-volume in the respective call option market segment.

Table 4: Classification of the data

	E_1: substantial relative daily mispricing	E_2: no substantial relative daily mispricing	
D_1: potential insider trading day	n_{11}	n_{12}	$n_{1.}$
D_2: no potential insider trading day	n_{21}	n_{22}	$n_{2.}$
	$n_{.1}$	$n_{.2}$	$n_{..}$

where n_{rs} = number of trading days of class D_r with a mispricing of category E_s.

$n_{.s}$ = number of all trading days with a mispricing of category E_s.

$n_{r.}$ = number of all trading days of class D_r.

$n_{..}$ = number of all trading days.

Observing $x_{11} = n_{11}$ substantial relative mispricings at potential insider trading days, the null hypothesis $p_1 = p_2$ may be rejected at the level of significance α given by:

$$\alpha = p\left(x_{11} \geq n_{11} \middle| H_0\right) = \sum_{x_{11}=n_{11}}^{\min(n_{1.},n_{.1})} \frac{\binom{n_{.1}}{x_{11}} \cdot \binom{n_{..} - n_{.1}}{n_{1.} - x_{11}}}{\binom{n_{..}}{n_{1.}}} \tag{4}$$

3.4.2 Description of the test runs and methodological remarks

The sample period is divided in five separate test periods of one year[41]. In each test period the test is carried out for each company in four different variants. The first variant includes all traded call options on the stock of the respective company in the respective test period. Each of the other three variants is based exclusively on calls with the same standardized expiration date[42].

The null hypothesis is divided into two partial hypotheses, as described above, whereby one applies to positive and the other to negative abnormal stock price performance. Instead of only one test run per partial hypothesis, company,

---

41 The only exception is the first test period. As the sample period starts on April 1, 1983, the first test period consists only of nine months from April 1, 1983, through December 31, 1983.

42 This is valid except for BMW and Daimler-Benz. As regards these two companies, the test variant based exclusively on call options with the longest time to expiration has not been carried out for the test period 1984. For both companies the respective options were traded on less than 20 percent of all trading days in 1984.

calendar year, and class of maturity, 250 test runs were carried out for each combination of the four criteria just mentioned[43]. The 250 cases include all possible combinations of 25 selection alternatives for potential insider trading days preceding abnormal stock price movements[44] and of 10 different quantiles used to determine the days with substantial relative mispricings[45]. The variety of test runs is necessary because it cannot be decided *a priori*, when insiders trade and how strongly they influence option prices. This has to be taken into account by alternative specifications of the test hypothesis. Otherwise, the most striking results may go undetected.

If there are 250 test runs for each combination of the four criteria mentioned above, the null hypothesis cannot be rejected at a pre-specified level of significance simply because one single test run suggests rejection at the significance level in question. If it is intended to make rejection dependent on the most significant result of a single test run, critical values for that result have to be determined. These critical values depend on the statistical relationship between the results of the 250 different test runs and on the pre-specified significance level required for the rejection of the null hypothesis. Although it is certainly wrong to assume statistical independence for the results of the 250 test runs per combination of the four criteria mentioned above, critical values for the result of the most significant test run are calculated on the assumption of statistical independence. Obviously, this is a very conservative approach implying more rigorous standards for the rejection of the null hypothesis than the pre-specified level of significance implies.

If 0.01 is the significance level required for the rejection of the null hypothesis, and if results of test runs are treated as though they are statistically independent, the critical value of the significance level of the most significant test run is $\alpha = 0.00004$[46]. Con-sequently, the null hypothesis is rejected with respect to a single combination of the four criteria mentioned above, if there is at least one test run with $\alpha \leq 0.00004$. This ensures that the probability of erroneously rejecting the null hypothesis is not higher than 0.01[47].

---

43 In a few cases, the number of test runs was less than 250, because days without trades in the relevant option series were more frequent than days with trades (Hecker 1994b, footnote 118).

44 See section 3.2.

45 See section 3.3.

46 For $\alpha = 0.00004$ the level of significance is $(1 - (1-\alpha)^{250}) = (1-0.99996)^{250} = 0.00995 \approx 0.01$.

47 At least for the cases with positive abnormal performance in the stock market, it is of little practical importance that the upper limit of α which still ensures a level of significance of 0.01 cannot be determined precisely as long as the statistical relationship between the results of the 250 test runs is unknown. In overperformance cases the calculated alphas of the test variants based on "overall" mispricing signals are either

3.4.3 The test results

According to the tests[48], the partial hypothesis concerned with positive residual stock price performance is rejected for each company at least in the majority of the five test periods. For Daimler-Benz, the test variant based on overall overpricing permits the rejection of the null hypothesis every year. As regards the maturity-specific test variants, there are only few exceptions. The results for VW are similar; but in 1984 and 1986, alphas below 0.00004 were only found in maturity-specific test variants[49]. As far as Bayer and BMW are concerned, for every test period but the first, at least one test variant permits the rejection of the null hypothesis[50]. In the case of BASF, the null hypothesis is not rejected in 1985 for any test variant; the same is true for Hoechst in 1983 and 1985[51].

In the case of each company, the majority of the test periods supports the conclusion that the probability of substantial relative overpricing of call options is significantly higher before positive residual stock price movements. These findings, however, are not borne out for each class of maturity in the same way. The same is true with respect to alternative classifications of mispricings and alternative selection rules for potential insider trading days. Moreover, the test results frequently turn out to be significant when the potential insider trading period selected for running the test is extended into the first half of the interval with conspicuous abnormal stock price performance instead of being restricted to days preceding the interval in question. At any rate, call option prices do lead, because the findings support the conclusion that option prices reflect the positive residuals of the underlying stock in advance. This conclusion is corroborated by test runs which are carried out for control purposes and rest on the assumption that potential insider trading days are coincident with periods of conspicuous stock price overperformance. Even if the results of such test runs turn out to be significant, almost without exception other tests for the same combination of

---

smaller than 0.00004 or they do not even fall below the thresholds of 0.01 or 0.05. This is true except for VW during the years 1984 and 1986.

[48] A summary of the test results in tables can be found in Hecker (1994b, pp. 541 f. and pp. 554-565). A comprehensive presentation and interpretation of the test results is given by Hecker (1993, pp. 241-308).

[49] For long-maturity options in 1984 and for short- as well as long-maturity options in 1986. Short-maturity options have a remaining life of about 10 to 70 trading days, long-maturity options of about 130 to 190 trading days. Middle-maturity options lie in between.

[50] For BMW there is not a single α below 0.01 in 1983. As regards Bayer, in 1983 only one α below 0.01 was detected for one of the test runs based on long-maturity options. The test result in question is $\alpha = 0.00172291$; this is far above the critical value 0.00004, which is required for rejection of the null hypothesis.

[51] As regards the results for Hoechst in 1983, some alphas lie between 0.002 and 0.008; this is due to the test variant based on short-maturity options. Apart from this exception, there are no test runs with alphas below 0.01 for Hoechst in 1983. In 1985 this is true without exception as far as Hoechst and BASF are concerned.

relevant criteria can be found which are free from any such coincidence and lead to a higher, or at least the same, level of significance. This is true without exception for the test variant based on overall overpricing.

As far as negative residual stock price movements are concerned, the relationship between leading option mispricings and subsequent stock performance seems to be clearly less pronounced than in the case of positive abnormal performance. This is particularly obvious for the test variant based on overall mispricing. Here the relevant null hypothesis for the case of negative abnormal performance is not rejected for 15 out of a total of 30 combinations of companies and test periods[52]. In 1983 this is the case for BASF, Hoechst and VW, in 1984 for Daimler-Benz, in 1985 for BASF and Daimler-Benz, in 1986 for Hoechst, Daimler-Benz and VW and in 1987 for all six companies[53]. These findings are substantially different from those for positive abnormal stock price performance. If maturity-specific test variants are considered, too, the evidence of a lead of option prices over the negative residuals of the underlying stock remains weak: for 9 of 15 combinations listed above, the maturity-specific test variants do not permit the rejection of the null hypothesis either[54].

But even when the null hypothesis is rejected at the 0.01 level, the actual values of error probabilities are not as small as in the overperformance cases. Moreover, there is not even a single company for which the null hypothesis can be rejected in all five test periods, if the tests are based on negative abnormal performance. On the contrary, it is only rejected in a single test period, as far as BASF and Daimler-Benz are concerned. Even if the results of the maturity-specific test variants are taken into account, this finding remains unchanged for both firms.

The results can be summarized as follows: in an overwhelming majority of cases there is significant evidence that call option prices anticipate conspicuous

---

[52] For 6 of the remaining 15 combinations of companies, and test periods, the results are inconclusive. While alphas fall frequently and markedly below one percent for these combinations, they do not fall below the critical value of 0.00004. Keeping in mind that the latter has been calculated under the conservative assumption that different test runs are statistically independent, it remains unclear whether the null hypothesis can be rejected at the 0.01 level.

[53] For 14 of these 15 combinations of companies, and test periods, there is not even a single α below 0.01 for the test variant based on overall underpricing. This is true except for VW in 1986; in this case α falls below 0.01 in a single test run. The test result in question is $\alpha = 0.00675315$. As this is still close to 0.01, there is no reliable basis for rejecting the null hypothesis at the one percent level. Moreover, there are no alphas below one percent for maturity-specific test variants.

[54] For 5 of the remaining 6 combinations of companies, and test periods, there are alphas below one percent in some market segments; however the alphas are higher than the critical value of 0.00004.

overperformance of the underlying stock. The evidence is rather weak, however, as far as conspicuous underperformance is concerned. Trading in options, which are comparatively overpriced with respect to their theoretical values, is significantly more frequent on days preceding abnormal upward stock price movements than on other trading days. In most cases, the relevant null hypothesis that the probability of comparatively overpriced options is independent of the following stock price movement is rejected at a significance level of less than one percent. In many cases, however, the analogous null hypothesis, that trades of comparatively underpriced options are as likely on days preceding abnormal downward stock price movements as on other days, cannot be rejected.

The statistically significant concentration of comparatively overpriced options prior to abnormal stock price increases might be interpreted as an indication that insiders exploit positive non-public information preferably, or at least initially, in the call option market and not in the stock market. According to the test results, however, the exact size of the time-lag between the first insider activity in the call option market and the subsequent stock price adjustment, as well as the intensity of the price reaction in the option market, seem to vary considerably.

The test results of the second part of this study may have more explanations than insider trading; but the findings have many peculiarities which are consistent with specific expectations derived from the assumption that insider trading is indeed a dominant factor[55]. For instance, in most cases a consistent explanation can be found even for those test results which come from the few combinations of firm and year with no significant relationship between option mispricing and subsequent overperformance of the underlying stock.

Particularly in line with expectations are the weak findings on the question of whether the relative underpricing of call options anticipates abnormal stock price decreases. Unlike buying calls in advance of expected upward movements of the underlying security, selling calls in advance of expected stock price decreases does not seem to be a very effective strategy for exploiting inside information. Instead of trading calls, insiders with negative non-public information will prefer to buy puts if they expect a marked decrease in the price of the underlying stock. Consequently, a theory based on rational insider behaviour suggests that the overpricing of put options will be much more important than the underpricing of calls, if option traders with superior information expect the price of the underlying stock to fall. Further research on this hypothesis will have to include the put option market which has not been investigated here.

---

[55] Some of these peculiarities are not very pronounced; in such cases it is not clear whether they are of any importance for the interpretation of the findings. Among these are various findings for negative abnormal performance which are not completely in line with expectations derived from the "insider hypothesis". A comprehensive presentation and analysis is given by Hecker (1993, pp. 241-308).

Admittedly, there is still a lack of conclusive evidence on the question of whether option trading has a beneficial, or destabilizing impact on the stock market and its ability to produce "fundamentally correct" prices. But if the results of the second part of this study are interpreted according to the "insider hypothesis", they support the conclusion that trading activities in the option market might accelerate the adjustment of stock prices to new information.

References

Bhattacharya, M. (1987): Price Changes of Related Securities: The Case of Call Options and Stocks, in: Journal of Financial and Quantitative Analysis 22, 1-15.

Black, F. (1975): Fact and Fantasy in the Use of Options, in: Financial Analysts Journal 31, 36-72.

Black, F. and Scholes, M. (1973): The Pricing of Options and Corporate Liabilities, in: Journal of Political Economy 81, 637-654.

Cass, D. and Stiglitz, J. E. (1970): The Structure of Investor Preferences and Asset Returns, and Separability in Portfolio Allocation: A Contribution to the Pure Theory of Mutual Funds, in: Journal of Economic Theory 2, 122-160.

Conrad, J. (1989): The Price Effect of Option Introduction, in: Journal of Finance 44, 487-498.

Cox, J. C. and Rubinstein, M. (1985): Options Markets. Englewood Cliffs (Prentice-Hall).

Fama, E. F., Fisher, L., Jensen, M. C. and Roll, R. (1969): The adjustment of stock prices to new information, in: International Economic Review 10, 1-21.

Galai, D. (1983): A Survey of Empirical Tests of Option Pricing Models, in: Brenner, M. (ed.): Option Pricing: Theory and Applications. Lexington (Lexington Books), 45-80.

Gemmill, G. (1989): Stock Options and Volatility of the Underlying Shares, in: Journal of International Securities Markets 3, 15-22.

Geske, R., Roll, R. and Shastri, K. (1983): Over-the-Counter Option Market Dividend Protection and "Biases" in the Black-Scholes Model: A Note, in: Journal of Finance 38, 1271-1277.

Hakansson, N. H. (1982): Changes in the Financial Market: Welfare and Price Effects and the Basic Theorems of Value Conservation, in: Journal of Finance 37, 977-1004.

Hecker, R. (1993): Informationsgehalt von Optionspreisen - Eine empirische Untersuchung der Preisbildung am Markt für Kaufoptionen im Vorfeld abnormaler Kursbewegungen am Aktienmarkt. Heidelberg (Physica).

Hecker, R. (1994a): Insiderhandel am Markt für Kaufoptionen (Teil I) - Eine empirische Studie, in: Kredit und Kapital 27, 396-436.

Hecker, R. (1994b): Insiderhandel am Markt für Kaufoptionen (Teil II) - Eine empirische Studie, in: Kredit und Kapital 27, 536-570.

Kendall, M. and Stuart, A. (1979): The Advanced Theory of Statistics, Vol. 2: Inference and Relationship, 4th ed., London (Griffin & Company).

Klemkosky, R. (1978): The Impact of Option Expirations on Stock Prices, in: Journal of Financial and Quantitative Analysis 13, 507-518.

Klemkosky, R. and Maness, T. (1980): The Impact of Options on the Underlying Securities, in: Journal of Portfolio Management 9, 12-18.

Lion, J. (1989): Marktrationalität und Markteffizienz. Frankfurt/Main/Berlin/Bern/New York/Paris/Wien (Peter Lang).

Manaster, S. and Rendleman, R. J. (1982): Option Prices as Predictors of Equilibrium Stock Prices, in: Journal of Finance 37, 1043-1057.

Manne, H. G. (1966): Insider Trading and the Stock Market. New York (The Free Press).

Merton, R. C. (1973): Theory of Rational Option Pricing, in: The Bell Journal of Economics & Management Science 4, 141-183.

Merton, R. C. (1976): The Impact on Option Pricing of Specification Error in the Underlying Stock Price Returns, in: Journal of Finance 31, 333-350.

Officer, D. T. and Trennepohl, G. L. (1981): Price Behavior of Corporate Equities Near Option Expiration Dates, in: Financial Management 10, 75-80.

Panton, D. (1976): Chicago Board Call Options as Predictors of Common Stock Price Changes, in: Journal of Econometrics 4, 101-113.

Ross, S. A. (1976): Options and Efficiency, in: Quarterly Journal of Economics 90, 75-89.

Skinner, D. J. (1989): Option Markets and Stock Return Volatility, in: Journal of Financial Economics 23, 61-78.

Stephan, J. A. and Whaley, R. E. (1990): Intraday Price Changes and Trading Volume Relations in the Stock and Stock Option Markets, in: Journal of Finance 45, 191-220.

Trennepohl, G. L. and Dukes, W. P. (1979): CBOE Options and Stock Volatility, in: Review of Business and Economic Research 14, 49-60.

Wenger, E., Hecker, R. and Gais, M. (1993): Interdependenzen zwischen der Preisbildung am Aktien- und am Optionsmarkt, in: Bühler, W., H. Hax and R. Schmidt (eds.): Empirische Kapitalmarktforschung. Zeitschrift für betriebswirtschaftliche Forschung, special issue 31, 131-167.

Whaley, R. E. (1981): On the Valuation of American Call Options on Stocks with Known Dividends, in: Journal of Financial Economics 9, 207-211.

Whiteside, M., Dukes, W. P. and Dunne, P. M. (1983): Short Term Impact of Option Trading on Underlying Secutities, in: Journal of Financial Research 6, 313-321.

The DAX Futures Market and Dividends

Klaus Röder and Günter Bamberg
University of Augsburg

1. Introduction

The German futures market "Deutsche Terminbörse" started trading in DAX futures contracts on November 23, 1990. The foundation of these futures contracts, the DAX[1], is based on the prices of 30 German Blue Chips. The standardised delivery months are March, June, September, December. The German Options and Futures Exchange simultaneously lists three subsequent delivery dates. The final cash settlement takes place on the third Friday of the delivery month.

The purpose of this paper is to introduce the international reader to the computational formula of the DAX performance index and its impact on the corresponding index futures' fair value. The unique features of the DAX are its treatment of dividends, capital changes, stock splits etc. in the capital-weighted DAX calculation formula. This formula ignores taxes on capital gains, but allows for a 36% tax rate on dividend income[2]. Since in Germany dividends are paid once a year, dividend yield per payment is relatively high. In the year to September 1992, the annual German dividend yield based on the pre-tax dividend payments of the 30 constituent DAX companies was about 4.3%. One aim of this paper is to illustrate the effect of seasonality in German dividend payments on the arbitrage returns for private and institutional investors.

The specification of our fair valuation estimating model takes account of income and corporate taxes, taxation of dividends and short sales restrictions.

Trading in Germany differs from trading in other countries. Trading in the spot and futures markets takes place without the use of market makers. At the stock market three different stock prices are listed per trading day. The opening price containing all overnight round-lot (50 Stocks) orders is calculated in order

---

[1] DAX = "**D**eutscher **A**ktieninde**x**" (German stock index).

[2] German tax rates changed after 1992. See footnote no. 9.

to guarantee a maximum opening trading volume. All overnight at the market orders are settled at this price. The corresponding price for odd-lot orders (Kassakurs) is calculated at about 12 noon. During the rest of the trading day round-lot order transactions result from direct trading. The trading procedure at the futures market is analogous except for the odd-lot orders' price[3].

Direct short selling is not possible on the Frankfurt Stock Exchange. But institutional investors can borrow stocks from other investors or from the "Deutscher Kassenverein AG", a German clearing corporation[4]. Hence, private German investors are usually not able to shortsell stocks. We include additional lending costs and point out stock lending problems resulting from seasonality in German dividend payments.

In Germany private investors and corporations are taxed differently. Private investors pay progressive personal tax at rates from 0% to 53% while the corporate tax rate is 50%. German corporations pay additional taxes (trade taxation) which we ignore here.

Arbitrageurs facing the best conditions with respect to transaction costs and reaction possibilities fix the fair arbitrage price of futures contracts. The possibility of deducting transaction costs and other costs as security lending fees from pre-tax earnings has been neglected in recent research. Therefore, we derive a valuation model for the DAX futures contract assuming institutional investors. An institutional investor (as opposed to private investors) has to pay 50% corporate tax on dividend and interest income and on capital gains. We compare the empirical results for institutions with those for private investors. Private investors in Germany are not subject to taxes on long-term capital gains or on profits from futures cash settlement.

Previous research has documented existing reverse cash and carry index arbitrage profits in the German markets (see Bühler/Kempf 1993, Bamberg/Röder 1993, 1994a, b, Grünbichler/Calahan 1993). In this paper we show that most of these arbitrage profits result from dividend payments. Neglecting additional costs caused by dividend-induced portfolio reconstruction overestimates German arbitrage profits.

---

[3] Odd-lot orders do not exist at the futures market. A minimum volume of one contract can also be settled at the opening price.

[4] Since in Germany delivery of stocks must take place two trading days after selling, institutional investors can short stocks for short periods. Pope/Yadav (1994) exploit the impact of short-sales constraints on arbitrage possibilities in the U.K.. Investors who already own the index portfolio and want to hold it until maturity of the futures contract have the possibility to create short selling.

2. Construction and replication of the DAX

2.1 Construction of the DAX

The construction of the "Deutscher Aktienindex DAX" differs from that of such other indexes, as e. g. S&P 500, Dow Jones, Major Market or Value Line Index[5]. The underlying of the German futures contract is a performance index which is adjusted in respect of dividends and capital changes. The DAX is calculated every minute during trading hours using the prices of 30 Blue Chips listed on the Frankfurt Stock Exchange. The general formula for computing the DAX index S_t is given by:

$$S_t = DAX_t = K_{T_1} \cdot \frac{\sum_{i=1}^{30} p_{i,t} \cdot q_{i,T_1}}{\sum_{i=1}^{30} p_{i,t_0} \cdot q_{i,t_0}} \cdot 1000\,, \tag{1}$$

where:

t_0 = 12/30/1987 as basis date.

t = calculation dates expressed in minutes.

T_1 = closing date for adjusting the subscribed capital of constituent companies.

T_2 = last day of dividend payment (T_2 depends on i).

$p_{i,t}$ = stock price of company i at time t.

q_{i,T_1} = subscribed capital of company i at T_1.

p_{i,t_0} = closing stock price of company i at 12/30/1987.

q_{i,t_0} = subscribed capital of company i at 12/30/1987.

$c_{i,t}$ = dividend and rights issue corrective for company i at time t, where: $c_{i,t} = \begin{cases} 1 & for \quad t < T_2 \\ c_{i,T_2} & for \quad t \geq T_2 \end{cases}$.

K_{T_1} = constant linking factor. Once a year, at T_1, all correction factors c_{i,T_2} are set equal to 1 and the capital weights are actualised. The linking factor prevents the index from jumping.

---

[5] Great parts of this chapter are taken from Bamberg/Röder (1994b). We think that interested readers need this part of the paper to understand the valuation model of the DAX futures contract. Therefore, we accept some redundancy.

In this paper we take only dividends into consideration[6]. After the dividend distribution at the ex-dividend day T_2, the correction factor $c_{i,t}$ is adjusted from 1 to:

$$c_{i,T_2} = \frac{stock\ price_{i,cum}}{stock\ price_{i,cum} - cash\ div_i}, \tag{2}$$

where:

$stock\ price_{i,cum}$ = cum-dividend closing stock price of company i.

$cash\ div_i$ = dividend per share after deduction of 36 % corporate tax per share (cash dividend).

This correction of the DAX implies the reinvestment of the cash dividend in the shares of the distributing company. Since the marginal tax rate of most investors is not 36 %, they need to adjust their investment in the index portfolio in order to duplicate the DAX.

2.2 Replication of the DAX

Equation (2) assumes the reinvestment of dividends at a stock price equal closing price before dividend distribution minus the cash dividend. In fact, the earliest possible effective reinvestment is at the opening price on the next trading day. Due to new information and the differing marginal tax rates of market participants, the next day's opening price does not usually equal the cum-dividend closing price minus cash dividend. Consequently a riskless rebuilding of the index portfolio is not possible. In the empirical analysis which follows the difference between the closing price before distributing dividends minus cash dividend and the next day's opening price is ignored[7].

Arbitrageurs are interested in the value of the index portfolio, or the value of the index replicating portfolio, in comparison with the DAX index. This value depends on the investor's personal tax rate s. Thus,

$$FW_T\left(S_t^{Pf}\right) = S_T + FW_T\left(\sum_{i=1}^{30} DIV_i^{\Delta}\right) = S_T + \Delta DIV_T, \tag{3}$$

[6] The DAX-index is also corrected for capital increases or decreases, stock splits etc..

[7] We ignore divisibility restrictions on the stock market. In fact, dividend payments induce arbitrageurs to buy small numbers of stocks. These orders are settled at a special price around 12 a.m.. We also ignore additional transaction costs for this adjustment of the arbitrage portfolio.

where:

$FW_T(.)$ = final value at time T.

S_t^{Pf} = market value of the index replicating portfolio at time t.

DIV_i^{Δ} = $(0.36 - s) \cdot DIV_i^{gr}$

The investor has to reinvest 64 % of the gross dividends in the dividend-distributing company's stocks. The after-tax dividend equals this investment only when the investor's marginal tax rate is 36%. In order to maintain a risk-free arbitrage position, the arbitrageur has to invest, or disinvest, the difference in risk-free bonds. The final value of the index portfolio contains two parts: the index portfolio and the dividend difference account. The value of this latter account dearly depends on the investors' marginal tax rate. The final value ΔDIV_T at time T of all dividend difference cash flows between t and T is given by:

$$\Delta DIV_T = FW_T\left(\sum_{i=1}^{30} DIV_i^{\Delta}\right) = \sum_{i=1}^{30}\left(DIV_i^{\Delta} \cdot e^{r(1-s)(T-t_i)}\right) \tag{4}$$

where:

t_i = ex dividend day (T_2) of company i.

3. Pricing of the DAX Futures

3.1 Private investors

Stock index futures can be priced by arbitrage arguments. The fundamental equation for stock index futures was published by Cornell/French (1983) and Modest/Sundaresan (1983). Assuming that dividends and interest rates are nonstochastic, that markets are perfect and the absence of taxes, the fair value of a stock index futures contract is:

$$F_t^* = S_t \cdot e^{r(T-t)} - FW_t^T(D), \tag{5}$$

where:

F_t^* = futures (fair) value at time t.

S_t = stock index at time t.

r = risk-free continuously compounded interest rate.

T = maturity day of the futures contract.

$FW_t^T(D)$ = time T value of dividends paid on the component stocks in the index portfolio between t and T.

In the previous section we showed that taxes are an important feature of the DAX index structure.

The difference between the S&P 500 and other futures and the DAX futures contract is demonstrated elsewhere (see Bamberg/Röder 1993, 1994b, Bühler/Kempf 1992, Prigge/Schlag 1992 or Grünbichler/Callahan 1993). Neglecting taxes on dividends results in the following valuation formula of the DAX futures contract:

$$F_t^* = S_t \cdot e^{r(T-t)} \tag{6}$$

Formula (6) also ignores the taxes on dividends that are repayable to tax-exempt investors. In this paper we show the effect of dividends on the futures' fair value.

The German taxation system taxes all income cash flows at the same rate. Let s denote the marginal tax rate of a private arbitrageur. Assume also that private investors pay taxes only on dividends and interest received[8]. Suppose the futures price at time t is higher than the fair value. The arbitrageur acts as follows:

- he borrows S_t at the risk-free rate and buys the index portfolio.
- he short sells a futures contract.

The net cash flow of these transactions is zero. The arbitrageur closes his position on the maturity date of the futures contract and receives the following cash flow:

- $-S_t \cdot e^{r(1-s)(T-t)}$ redemption of debt and after tax interest on the risk-free debt.
- S_T from stock.
- $F_t - S_T$ from cash settlement of the short futures position.
- ΔDIV_T value of the risk-free investment of the difference dividend at time T. ($\Delta DIV_T < 0$ when $s > 0.36$).

[8] As already mentioned, the earnings of the cash settlement or early unwinding (daily settlement) of the DAX futures contract are not taxed in the case of private investors in Germany (see Hoffmann/Ramke 1990 p.80, Bröker 1991 or Jung/Redanz 1993). We further assume that capital gains on stocks are tax exempt. In Germany, private investors suffer taxes on capital gains for holding periods not exceeding 6 months.

In an arbitrage-free economy the net cash flow of this closing out must equal zero (or, in this case, it must be greater than zero in order to yield an arbitrage gain.):

$$F_t - S_t \cdot e^{r(1-s)(T-t)} + \Delta DIV_T = 0 .$$

Hence the fair value of the DAX futures contract F_t^* is:

$$F_t^* = S_t \cdot e^{r(1-s)(T-t)} - \Delta DIV_T \tag{7}$$

If the futures price falls below the value given by equation (7) the arbitrageur has to undertake the reverse transactions. This reverse cash and carry strategy implies the shorting of the DAX index portfolio. Since in Germany private investors cannot short stocks, this strategy is only practicable if investors already own this portfolio and desire to hold it until day T.

For some selected investor's tax brackets we get:

$$\begin{aligned} s = 0\% \quad &\Leftrightarrow \quad F_t^* = S_t \cdot e^{r(T-t)} - 0.36\sum_{i=1}^{30}\left(DIV_i^{gr} \cdot e^{r(T-t_i)}\right) \\ s = 36\% \quad &\Leftrightarrow \quad F_t^* = S_t \cdot e^{r \cdot 0.64 \cdot (T-t)} \\ s = 50\% \quad &\Leftrightarrow \quad F_t^* = S_t \cdot e^{r \cdot 0.5 \cdot (T-t)} + 0.14\sum_{i=1}^{30}\left(DIV_i^{gr} \cdot e^{r \cdot 0.5 \cdot (T-t_i)}\right) \end{aligned} \tag{8}$$

In the case of tax-exempt investors, dividend payments lower the fair price of the DAX futures contract. Ceteris paribus dividend payments ceteris paribus increase cash and carry arbitrage gains and decrease reverse cash and carry arbitrage profits for tax-exempt investors.

3.2 Institutional investors and the impact of corporate taxes

In Germany institutional investors and private investors are taxed differently. Institutional investors have to pay taxes on realised capital gains and on earnings stemming from futures contracts. In this section we consider a tax rate k of 50% on all gains from index arbitrage[9]. An arbitrageur undertaking the cash and carry

[9] Prior to 1993 the German corporate tax rate was 50%. After the 1993 corporate tax reform (beginning September 1993, but depending on a company's financial year) the tax

arbitrage transactions referred to in the previous section is confronted with the following after tax cash flows at time T:

- $-S_t \cdot e^{r(1-k)(T-t)}$ — redemption of debt and after tax interest on the risk-free debt.
- S_T — from stock.
- $-\left(S_T - S_t - \sum_{i=1}^{30} DIV_i^{cash}\right) \cdot k$ — tax payment, or tax shield, caused by realised capital gains or losses. The amount to be invested is the initial investment plus reinvestment of 64% of gross dividends. Therefore, $\sum_{i=1}^{30} DIV_i^{cash} = 0.64 \cdot \sum_{i=1}^{30} DIV_i^{gr}$
- $F_t - S_T$ — from cash settlement of the short futures position.
- $-(F_t - S_T) \cdot k$ — tax payment, or tax shield, caused by cash settlement of the short futures position.
- ΔDIV_T — value of the risk-free investment of the dividend difference at time T. ($\Delta DIV_T < 0$ when $k = 0.5$).

In order to prevent index arbitrage, this cash flow has to be equal to zero. As a fair value of the DAX futures contract for institutional investors we obtain:

$$F_t^* = \frac{S_t \cdot \left(e^{r(1-k)(T-t)} - k\right) - \Delta DIV_T - k \cdot \sum_{i=1}^{30} DIV_i^{cash}}{(1-k)} \tag{9}$$

or

$$F_t^* = \frac{S_t \cdot \left(e^{r(0.5)(T-t)} - 0.5\right) + \sum_{i=1}^{30}\left(0.14 \cdot DIV_i^{gr} \cdot e^{r(0.5)(T-t_i)}\right) - 0.5 \cdot \sum_{i=1}^{30} DIV_i^{cash}}{0.5} \tag{10}$$

Ignoring interest payments on dividends differences DIV_i^{Δ} in formula (4) we can estimate the expected impact of dividend payments on the fair value of the futures contract, i. e.,

---

rate was set at 45% and the corporate tax rate on dividend payments fell from 36% to 30%. Since 1/1/1995 the German reunification tax has increased the corporate tax rate to $0.45 \cdot 1.075 = 48.375\%$. German private investors pay personal taxes on all income and, under the imputation tax system, receive a dividend tax credit in respect of a proportion of assessed corporate taxes. We ignore the additional taxes to which institutional investors in Germany are liable, e.g. trade tax on earnings and trade tax on capital.

$$\Delta DIV_T = FW_T\left(\sum_{i=1}^{30} DIV_i^{\Delta}\right) = \sum_{i=1}^{30} DIV_i^{\Delta} = \sum_{i=1}^{30}(0.36-k)\cdot DIV_i^{gr}\ .$$

Therefore we get:

$$F_t^* = \frac{S_t \cdot \left(e^{r(0,5)(T-t)} - 0.5\right)}{0.5} - 0.36 \cdot \sum_{i=1}^{30} DIV_i^{gr}\ . \tag{11}$$

3.3 Institutional investors: reverse cash and carry arbitrage and stock short sales

If the costs of purchasing the stock and delivering it at time T exceed the futures price F_t, the arbitrageur reverses his arbitrage position, i. e.,

- he shorts the index portfolio S_t and invests the proceeds S_t at the risk-free rate.
- he buys a futures contract.

As previously mentioned, in Germany short sales are not possible. However it is possible to borrow stocks from t to T, to sell them at t and to repurchase them at time T. For example, the "Deutscher Kassenverein" offers a clearing service for stock borrowing (see Deutscher Kassenverein AG 1992, Hohmann 1991, Bühler/Kempf 1992 p.22)[10]. The borrowing costs are paid at the end of the borrowing period $[t,T]$. Let SL_T denote the total lending costs at T:

$$SL_T \cdot (1-k) = S_t \cdot l \cdot (1-k) \cdot (T-t)\ , \tag{12}$$

where:

SL_T = total pre-tax borrowing costs at time T.

l = annual lending rate.

We assume that institutional investors have unrestricted access to this service and can realise the full proceeds of the borrowed stocks[11]. Analogously to formula (9) in the previous section the fair value F_t^* is given by:

---

[10] The borrowing costs (in 1991) are about 2.5% of the market value.

[11] This emphasises a critical aspect of the German stock borrowing system. For technical reasons it is in practice not possible to borrow the stocks of the Allianz AG, a stock with one of the highest weights in the DAX.

$$F_t^* = \frac{S_t \cdot \left(e^{r(1-k)(T-t)} - k\right) - \Delta DIV_T - k \cdot \sum_{i=1}^{30} DIV_i^{cash}}{(1-k)} - SL_T \tag{13}$$

Inserting $k = 0.5$ we get:

$$F_t^* = \frac{S_t \cdot \left(e^{r(0.5)(T-t)} - 0.5\right) + 0.14 \cdot \sum_{i=1}^{30}\left(DIV_i^{gr} \cdot e^{r(0.5)(T-t_i)}\right) - 0.5 \cdot \sum_{i=1}^{30} DIV_i^{cash}}{0.5} - SL_T \tag{14}$$

The institutional arbitrageur receives a reverse cash and carry arbitrage signal if the actual futures price F_t is less than the theoretical futures price F_t^*, i. e., $F_t < F_t^*$.

3.4 Comparison of the fair values

To facilitate a comparison of the fair value assuming income taxes with that assuming corporate taxes, we exclude dividend payments according to formula (10). Thus,

$$F_t^* = \frac{S_t \cdot \left(e^{r(05)(T-t)} - 0.5\right)}{0.5}. \tag{15}$$

The tax rate s of the private investor leads to exactly the same fair value if:

$$\frac{S_t \cdot \left(e^{r(0.5)(T-t)} - 0.5\right)}{0.5} = S_t \cdot e^{r(1-s)(T-t)}$$

This means:

$$s = 1 - \frac{\ln\left(\frac{\left(e^{r(0,5)(T-t)} - 0.5\right)}{0.5}\right)}{r \cdot (T-t)}$$

Assuming realistic numbers for the time to maturity (T-t < 277 days) and the interest rate (r = 8%) the marginal income tax rate s takes on a (negligible) value within the range 0.005 and 0.015.

Under linear interest and the exclusion of dividend payments, taxes have no effect on the fair futures value F_t^*:

$$F_t^* = \frac{S_t \cdot [1 + r \cdot (1-s)(T-t) - s]}{(1-s)} = \frac{(1-s) \cdot S_t \cdot [1 + r \cdot (T-t)]}{(1-s)} = S_t \cdot [1 + r \cdot (T-t)]. \quad (16)$$

In the case of institutional investors it thus follows that if dividends are ignored, taxes may also be omitted. Assuming no dividend payments and continuously-compounded interest, the fair value of the DAX futures contract for a tax-exempt investor approximates that of an institutional investor who pays corporate taxes.

Additionally assuming no interest payments on the dividend difference account as in formula (11), the fair value for institutional investors equals the futures' fair value assuming tax-exempt investors in formula (8):

$$\begin{aligned} F_t^* &= \frac{S_t \cdot [1 + r \cdot (1-s)(T-t) - s]}{(1-s)} - 0.36 \cdot \sum_{i=1}^{30} DIV_i^{gr} \\ &= S_t \cdot [1 + r \cdot (T-t)] - 0{,}36 \cdot \sum_{i=1}^{30} DIV_i^{gr} \end{aligned}$$

4. Empirical results

It is assumed that institutional investors incur proportional pre-tax transaction costs of 0.25 %. The total after-tax transaction costs are defined as[12]:

$$TK_t = S_t \cdot \alpha , \quad (17)$$

[12] Since private investors cannot shield transaction costs we calculate arbitrage profits on a pre-tax basis. We ignore additional transaction costs such as the buying or selling stocks caused by dividend payments.

where:

TK_t = total after-tax transaction costs of index arbitrage.

α = transaction costs factor.

Arbitrage is indicated when the absolute difference between the futures price and its fair value minus the total transaction costs exceeds zero, i. e. , when,

$$\left|F_t - F_t^*\right| - TK_t > 0 \tag{18}$$

The empirical tests are based on intraday time-stamped DAX futures contracts transaction prices. The DAX futures contract is traded on the Frankfurt Futures Exchange in Germany. Minute-interval intra-day data are used in computing arbitrage profits.

As the Frankfurt Stock Exchange publishes the opening quotation of the DAX index when the opening prices of at least 15 stocks and 70 % of the index capitalisation are available (also using the previous day's closing prices of the other index constituents), the early index quotations do not necessarily show the actual market value of the index portfolio. Chung (1991) has emphasised the problems inherent in early trades in the stock market. Arbitrage profits based on index data can overestimate the attainable arbitrage gains during early trading in the stock market. In order to prevent stale prices from influencing our results we exclude the first 15 minutes of stock trading.

Since the stocks quoted on the Frankfurt Stock Exchange are traded directly without the use of market makers the implementation of the day's latest trades of the day is not guaranteed. Therefore, we exclude trades within the last five minutes of the trading day.

In this paper we focus on all trading days of the futures market between January 1991 and December 1992 and we use transaction data for the period between 10.45 a.m. and 1.25 p.m. Previous research has shown the impact of early and late transactions on cash and carry arbitrage profits (see Bamberg/Röder 1994b)[13].

The results presented here[14] are based on the "Deutsche Kapitalmarktdaten-bank DFDB Karlsruhe - Mannheim - Aachen". The DAX values were directly

---

[13] Effects on reverse cash and carry arbitrage are negligible.

[14] We would like to thank W. Bühler and H. Göppl and the Deutsche Börse AG for providing us with the requested data.

obtained from the Frankfurt Stock Exchange. The daily listing of the 3 month FIBOR (new) is used as proxy for the risk-free interest rate.

The data are divided into two periods of equal length. The one is the calendar year 1991 and the other is the calendar year 1992. The sample contains 241 trading days in 1991 and 246 trading days in 1992[15]. The Frankfurt Futures Market simultaneously lists three contracts with different maturities. We divided the contracts into three groups. The first group always contains the contract with the nearest to maturity date. The second group consists of all transactions in the contract with a medium term maturity date. Finally, the transactions relating to the contract with the most distant to maturity date form the third group.

Since the DAX futures contract with the nearest maturity date is the most actively traded and has the highest liquidity, we exclusively calculate the ex-ante arbitrage profits attainable from this contract.

4.1 Reverse cash and carry arbitrage

This section focuses on the ex-ante index arbitrage gain of a reverse cash and carry strategy. We assume a one minute time-lag for realising arbitrage transactions after ex-post mispricings have been observed. The futures market is regarded as efficient if the expected value of ex-ante reverse cash and carry arbitrage is not positive, i. e., when,

$$E\left(F^*_{t+\Delta} - F_{t+\Delta} - TK_{t+\Delta} \,\middle|\, F^*_t - F_t - TK_t > 0\right) \leq 0, \tag{19}$$

where:

Δ = reaction time lag after the detection of a mispricing signal (one or two minutes).

Adopting formula (19) we test the following hypotheses[16]:

H_0: $E(\cdot) \leq 0$

versus

H_1: $E(\cdot) > 0$.

We compare empirical tests for the three different pricing models enumerated in Table 1.

---

[15] There were 10 days for which no data were available.

[16] The results of the empirical tests are presented in Bamberg/Röder (1994c). Here we extract the most important empirical results relating to arbitrage profits.

Table 1: Different pricing models

Assumptions about market participants[17]	F_t^{**} according to formula
• institutional investor, $k = 0.5$, ignoring dividends	(15)
• institutional investor, $k = 0.5$, including exact dividends	(10)
• institutional investor, $k = 0.5$, including exact dividends and security lending costs for reverse cash and carry arbitrage	(14)

4.1.1 Ignoring dividends

The figures in this paper illustrate the life cycles of 8 futures contracts. As the maturity day of the DAX futures contract is the third Friday in the maturity month, all contracts considered here span four calendar months[18]. Results relating to the first calendar month include all transactions following the maturity of the previous contract. Results presented for the fourth month include all trades up to the maturity day of the contract under consideration. Therefore, the first and the fourth months include fewer trading days than both second and third.

Figure 1 depicts ex-ante reverse cash and carry results ignoring dividend payments. The arbitrage profits of ‘92 contracts are lower than those for ‘91 contracts. Contracts which include relatively high dividends generate relatively high arbitrage profits. Even when dividends are ignored, the maximum annual arbitrage profits are obtained from the long maturity June contract prices.

4.1.2 Including dividends

Figure 2 shows the impact of dividend payments on arbitrage profits. Dividends reduce the average arbitrage profit in the first month of the June 91 contract from 836 DM to 39 DM per contract and the number of arbitrage possibilities from 3,076 to 99. Figure 2 also illustrates the absence of arbitrage possibilities from March 1992 to June 1992. This is caused by the negative influence of dividend payments on arbitrage profits. Ignoring dividends overestimates the arbitrage profits of the months which include dividend payments.

---

[17] The fair value for institutional investors nearly equals the fair value for tax-exempt investors. Therefore, we only calculate the fair futures value assuming corporate taxes.

[18] E.g. in accordance with the June 92 DAX futures, we analyse the transaction data in March, April, May and June 1992.

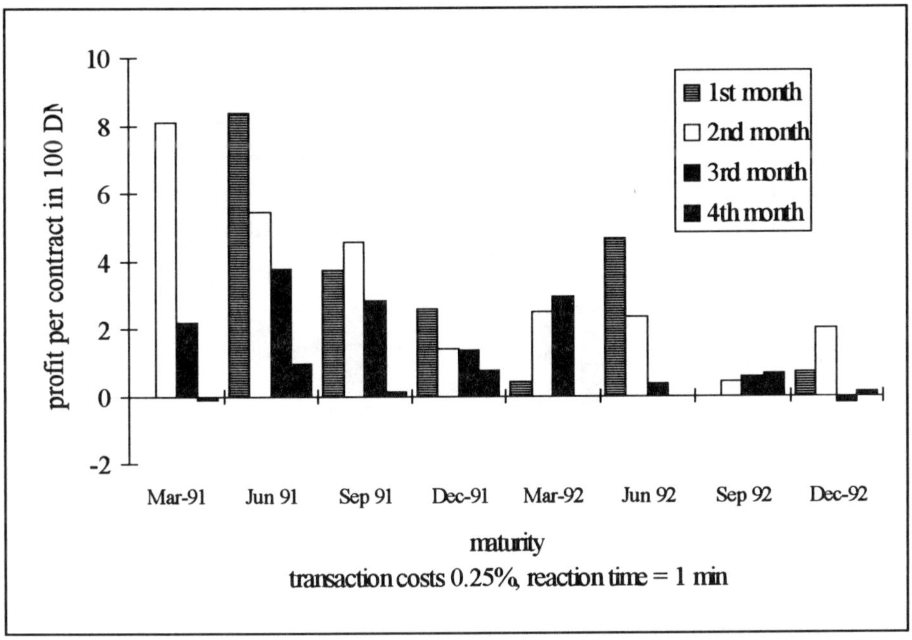

Figure 1: Ex-ante arbitrage profit from reverse CAC arbitrage ignoring dividends and stock lending costs - comparing maturity dates -

Most of the annual reverse cash and carry arbitrage profits in 1991 an 1992 were earned during the lifetime of March contracts. The March 91 contract is the only contract in the sample containing no dividend payments[19]. This might explain the extraordinary arbitrage profits from this contract that are depicted in figure 2.

It should be noted that slightly negative average arbitrage profits during the lifetimes of June 91 and December 92 contracts are based on only 38 and 76 arbitrage possibilities respectively, whereas the relatively high arbitrage profit in January 1991 results from 5,470 arbitrage opportunities.

---

[19] The March 91 contract is the only contract not containing dividend payments during the final months to maturity following the maturity of the previous December 90 contract. The March 92 contract includes dividend payments because of earlier dividend distribution of the Siemens AG.

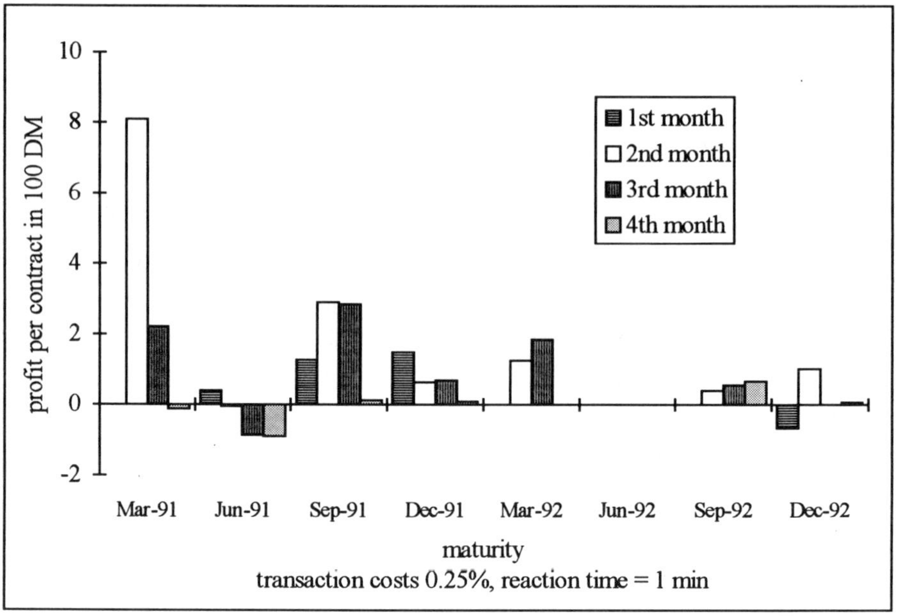

Figure 2: Ex-ante arbitrage profit from reverse CAC arbitrage including dividends and ignoring stock lending costs - comparing maturity dates -

4.1.3 Including dividends and security lending costs

Previous Germany researchers have reported significant ex-ante reverse cash and carry arbitrage profits (see Bühler/Kempf 1993 or Bamberg/Röder 1993, 1994b). Formula (11) implies that dividend payments have a negative effect on arbitrage profits of institutional investors who pay corporate taxes. The seasonality of dividends could therefore be expected to have a negative effect on the ex-ante reverse cash and carry arbitrage profits of institutional investors.

The impact of security lending on arbitrage profits is proportional to the level of stock lending costs[20] and the time to maturity. We can only report that the arbitrage profits earned by the March 91 and September 91/92 contracts are worth mentioning.

Pope/Yadav (1994) analyze the impact of short sales constraints on stock index futures prices in the UK. Their research presents evidence on "short sales constraints and costs being a significant factor leading to underpricing relative to

[20] Like transaction costs the security lending costs vary from person to person. Since the price of security lending dramatically fell from 1991 to 1992 an average security lending price was chosen.

the cash index". We have in fact disregarded the following dividend induced costs.

- Additional transaction costs for selling and buying odd-lot numbers of stocks.
- Additional transaction costs for security lending or risk adjustment caused by the impossibility of additional stock borrowing.
- Security borrowing problems caused by odd-lot orders.
- Additional risk induced by small order prices in the stock market.

Therefore, our reverse cash and carry arbitrage results can overestimate true profits. However, we also believe that traditional models as introduced above, overestimate arbitrage profits when dividend payments are relatively high.

4.2 Cash and carry arbitrage

By analogy with section 4.1, we examine the ex-ante arbitrage profit of the cash and carry index arbitrage. Here it is not necessary we do not have to consider short sales restrictions. In an arbitrage-free economy the expected value of the ex-ante arbitrage profit should not exceed zero.

$$E\left(F_{t+\Delta} - F^{*}_{t+\Delta} - TK_{t+\Delta} \;\middle|\; F_t - F_t^{*} - TK_t > 0\right) \leq 0\,. \tag{20}$$

Previous research indicates that only arbitrageurs with very low transaction costs can profit from cash and carry arbitrage (see Bamberg/Röder 1994b).

4.2.1 Ignoring dividends

Figures 3 and 4 contain results of ex-ante cash and carry arbitrage ignoring and including dividends respectively. Average arbitrage profits and the number of arbitrage possibilities in general are less than the profits and the number of arbitrage signals in the case of reverse cash and carry arbitrage.

Notice that only arbitrageurs with 0.25 % transaction costs can profit from cash and carry arbitrage. Figure 3 illustrates the results of cash and carry arbitrage assuming 0.25 % transaction costs and one minute reaction time. Arbitrage profits appear to be random observations.

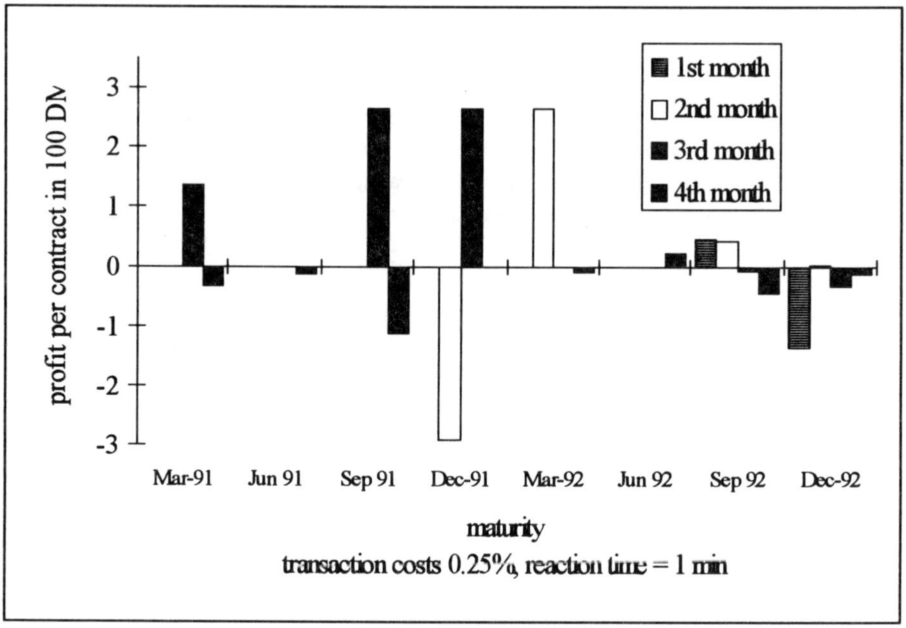

Figure 3: Ex-ante arbitrage profit from CAC arbitrage ignoring dividends
- comparing maturity dates -

4.2.2 Including dividends

According to formulae (10) and (7) dividend payments should have positive effects on arbitrage profits for both institutional investors and tax-exempt arbitrageurs.

Figure 4 illustrates that cash and carry arbitrage becomes more profitable when dividend payments are included. The arbitrage results of June contracts are particularly influenced by dividend payments. Figure 3 underestimates true profits.

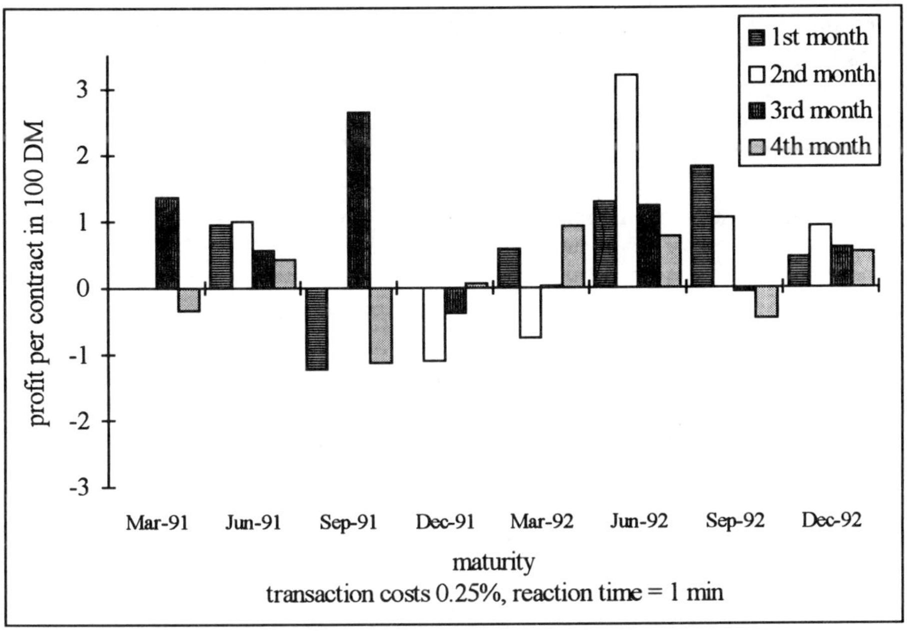

Figure 4: Ex-ante arbitrage profit from CAC arbitrage including dividends
- comparing maturity dates -

5. Summary of results

This paper exploits the seasonality of the dividend payments in Germany to test for their impact on stock index arbitrage profits. The standard cash and carry model for stock index futures contracts was adapted to the specifications of the German market and taxation system. Valuation models were derived for the DAX futures contracts listed on the Frankfurt Options and Futures Exchange taking account of income taxes and corporate taxes in the case of institutional and private investors respectively. The efficiency of the futures market for tax-exempt investors and institutional investors using intraday transaction data was also tested. Ignoring interest payments on the dividend difference account, the fair value of a DAX futures contract for tax-exempt investors equals the fair value for arbitrageurs who pay corporate taxes. The tests presented in this paper allow for German short sales restrictions, transaction costs and market participants' reaction times.

The underlying of the DAX futures contract is a performance index which is corrected for dividends, capital increases etc.. The impact of dividends in

Germany is not negligible the differing tax positions of market participants necessitate different adjustments to the index replicating portfolio. This taxation effect is intensified by the seasonality in the dividend payments on German stocks. Neglecting dividends overestimates arbitrage profits on reverse cash and carry arbitrage in Germany.

The main results of this paper in respect of reverse cash and carry arbitrage are:

- Arbitrage profits and the number of arbitrage possibilities declined in 1992, compared with 1991.
- Independent of variations in transaction costs and reaction time institutional investors can generate significant earnings from index arbitrage.
- Life cycle analysis explains the impact of dividend payments on reverse arbitrage profits. June 91 and June 92 contracts did not earn arbitrage profits. These contracts contain the (relatively) highest part of dividends paid.
- Stock lending costs dramatically reduce reverse cash and carry arbitrage profits.

The main results relating to cash and carry arbitrage are:

- Only arbitrageurs with transaction costs of less than 0.25 % can profit from index arbitrage.
- Arbitrage profits and the number of arbitrage possibilities did not decline in 1992 compared with 1991.
- Dividend payments dramatically increase arbitrage profits and the number of arbitrage possibilities.

The results emphasise the importance of allowing for the seasonality of dividend payments in the German DAX futures market. But the figures presented in this paper may tend to overestimate the true results. Nevertheless, a strategy that takes account of seasonality in German dividends apparently achieves extraordinary arbitrage profits.

References

Bamberg, G. and Röder, K. (1993): Arbitrage am DAX-Futures Markt unter Berücksichtigung von Einkommensteuern, in: Kredit und Kapital 26, 575-607.

Bamberg, G. and Röder, K. (1994a): Arbitrage institutioneller Anleger am DAX-Futures Markt unter Berücksichtigung von Körperschaftsteuern und Dividenden, in: Zeitschrift für Betriebswirtschaft 64, 1533-1566.

Bamberg. G. and Röder, K. (1994b): The Intraday ex ante Profitability of DAX-Futures Arbitrage for institutional Investors in Germany - The Case of Early and Late Transactions, in: Financial Markets and Portfolio Management 8, 50-62.

Bamberg. G. and K. Röder (1994c): Seasonality in Ex Ante German Stock Index Futures Arbitrage - Where Do Arbitrage Profits in Germany Come from?, Arbeitspapiere zur Mathematischen Wirtschaftsforschung, No. 120, University of Augsburg.

Bröker, K. (1991): Neue DTB-Produkte, Anlage Praxis, 20-21.

Bühler, W. and Kempf, A. (1993): Der DAX-Future: Kursverhalten und Arbitragemöglichkeiten, in: Kredit und Kapital 26, 533-574.

Chung, P. (1991): A Transactions Data Test of Stock Index Futures Market Efficiency and Index Arbitrage Profitability, in: Journal of Finance 66, 1791-1809.

Cornell, B. and French, K. (1983a): The Pricing of Stock Index Futures, in: Journal of Futures Markets 3, 1-14.

Cornell, B. and French, K. (1983b): Taxes and the Pricing of Treasury Bill Futures Contracts, in: Journal of Finance 38, 675-694.

Deutscher Kassenverein AG (1992): Technische Richtlinien für Leihgeschäfte - Banken. Frankfurt, 1992.

Grünbichler, A. and T. Callahan (1993): Stock Index Futures Arbitrage in Germany: The Behavior of the DAX Index Futures Prices, Working Paper, University of California, Los Angeles.

Hoffmann, P. and R. Ramke (1990): Finanzinnovationen an der Deutschen Terminbörse (DTB): Chancen und Risiken des Handels mit Optionen und Finanzterminkontrakten, Grundlagen und Praxis des Bank- und Börsenwesens, No. 23. Berlin (Erich Schmidt).

Hohmann, R. (1991): Der Einfluß der Wertpapierleihe auf die Bewertung des DAX-Futures, in: Kapitalanlagen Wirtschaft Recht Steuern 4, 574-582.

Janßen, B. and B. Rudolph (1992): Der Deutsche Aktienindex DAX, Konstruktion und Anwendungsmöglichkeiten. Frankfurt (Frankfurt Stock Exchange).

Jung, J. and Redanz, U. (1993): Zur Besteuerung der DTB-Geschäfte von Privatanlegern im Gewerbebetrieb und in der privaten Vermögensverwaltung, in: Zeitschrift für Bankrecht und Bankwirtschaft, 68-89.

Kawaller, I. (1987): A Note: Debunking the Myth of the Risk-Free Return, in: Journal of Futures Markets 7, 327-331.

Loistl, O. and M. Kobinger (1992): Index-Arbitrage insbesondere mit DAX-Futures, Beiträge zur Wertpapieranalyse (der DVFA), No.28.

Modest, D. and Sundaresan, M. (1983): The Relationship between Spot and Futures Prices in Stock Index Futures Markets: Some Preliminary Evidence, in: Journal of Futures Markets 3, 15-41.

Prigge, J. and Schlag, C. (1992): Die Bewertung des DAX-Future-Kontrakts an der Deutschen Terminbörse, in: Zeitschrift für Bankrecht und Bankwirtschaft, 299-307.

Impact of Stock Price Jumps on Option Values

Siegfried Trautmann and Michaela Beinert
University of Mainz

1. Introduction

Many empirical papers document the fact that the distribution of stock returns exhibits fatter tails than would be expected from a normal distribution. This might explain some of the pricing biases of the Black/Scholes model, which is based on a normal return distribution. Given this result, alternative option pricing models should be based on one of the following three classes of return models: (1) a stationary process, such as a paretian stable or a student's t-distribution, (2) a mixture of stationary distributions, such as two normal distributions with different means or variances, or a mixture of a diffusion and a pure jump process, or (3) a distribution such as a normal distribution with time-varying parameters. Although any of these choices could improve on the fit of the normal distribution, only a few are economically as appealing as the mixed jump diffusion model. According to this model, the total change in the price of a stock is equal to the sum of two components: (1) the normal fluctuations in price due to new information that causes only marginal changes in stock's value (*'diffusion component'*), and (2) the abnormal price changes due to the infrequent arrival of new information that has more than a marginal effect on price (*'jump component'*). This mixed jump diffusion model was first studied by Press (1967) and incorporated into the theory of option valuation by Merton (1976a). Although a considerable number of papers report a statistically significant jump component in stock returns as well as in index returns (Jarrow/Rosenfeld 1984, Ball/Torous 1985, Akgiray/Booth/Loistl 1989, Beinert/Trautmann 1991), few papers have investigated the effect of jumps in the underlying stock price process on option values. In the first published empirical paper on this subject, Ball/Torous (1985) find no operationally significant pricing differences between the Black/Scholes model and Merton's *idiosyncratic* jump risk model when pricing options on NYSE stocks. By contrast, Bates (1991) finds that a *systematic* jump risk model fits the actual data markedly better than the Black/Scholes model in the case of the transaction prices of S&P 500 futures options.

The purpose of this paper is threefold. First, we provide an economic rationale for the differences between Black/Scholes values and jump model values when jump risk is systematic and idiosyncratic, respectively. Second, we use a comprehensive sample of stock options traded at the *Frankfurt Options Market,* between March 1983 and June 1990, and at the *Deutsche Terminbörse* between January 1990 and December 1991, to examine the historical stock price jump impact on option values. Third, we take the systematic jump risk model to infer the stock price distributions implicit in observed option prices before, during, and after crash periods. The paper is organized as follows. Section 2 presents different formulae for valuing stock options when the underlying stock process includes systematic and idiosyncratic jumps, respectively. We also compare the model values for representative parameters. Section 3 examines the impact of stock price jumps on option values when using historical parameter estimates. The stock price distributions implicit in option prices according to the systematic jump risk model of Bates (1991) are presented in section 4. Section 5 concludes the paper.

2. Option valuation when jump risk is present

Options are usually priced as the discounted expected value of their future payoffs where the expectation is taken over the risk-neutral, rather than the true, distribution of the underlying asset. As long as the option's payoff can be replicated by a dynamic trading strategy in the underlying asset and a riskless bond, the equivalent risk-neutral distribution can be derived via no-arbitrage conditions. Unfortunately such a replication is *not* possible if the stock price, S_t, follows a general jump-diffusion process of the form

$$\frac{dS_t}{S_{t-}} = \alpha_D\, dt + \sigma\, dB_t + L\, dN_t , \tag{1}$$

where

α_D drift rate of the diffusion component,

σ volatility of the diffusion component, $\sigma>0$,

B $\{B_t;\ t\geq 0\}$ is a standard Brownian motion,

N $\{N_t;\ t\geq 0\}$ is a Poisson counting process (independent of B) with parameter $\lambda>0$, denoting the expected number of jumps per unit time,

L $(S_t - S_{t-})/S_{t-}$ represents the percentage change in the price of a stock due to a jump at time t, with $\ln(1+L) \sim N(\mu_J, \sigma_J^2)$, and $k \equiv E(L)=e^{\alpha_J}-1$ with $\alpha_J = \mu_J + (1/2)\,\sigma_J^2$.

Deriving the appropriate risk-neutral probability distribution requires additional restrictions on distributions and/or on preferences. Merton's (1976a) idiosyncratic jump risk model (henceforth *IJD-model*) assumes, for instance, that jump risk is *diversifiable*. Under this simplifying assumption Merton derives an option valuation formula that is independent of investors' preferences. Unfortunately, several papers report that Merton's assumption of diversifiable jump risk might not be realistic. For instance, Beinert/Trautmann (1991) report that DAX returns have a statistically significant jump component implying that jump risk must be deemed to be systematic in the German stock market. If jump risk is assumed to be systematic, then all stock prices and the market index jump simultaneously, albeit by possibly different amounts. To price the additional risk when jump risk is *systematic*, Bates (1991) extends the equilibrium-based model of Cox/Ingersoll/Ross (1985), while the alternative model of Amin/Ng (1993) is an extension of the pure exchange model proposed by Rubinstein (1976). Both of the resulting formulae depend on risk preferences. The following analysis is based on Bates' version of the systematic jump risk model (henceforth *SJD-model*). We first present the valuation formulae of Bates and Merton and then compare the two models with the Black/Scholes model (henceforth *BS-model*).

2.1 Systematic jump risk call formulae

Bates (1991) assumes the existence of a representative investor who seeks to maximize his expected utility of lifetime consumption and whose optimal invested wealth, W_t, follows a jump diffusion process

$$\frac{dW_t}{W_{t-}} = \left(\alpha_W - \lambda\, k_W - \frac{Y_t}{W_t} \right) dt + \sigma_W B_t + L_W dN_t , \tag{2}$$

where Y_t represents the optimal consumption at time t. One plus the percentage wealth jump sizes, $(1+L_w)$, is log-normally distributed, $\ln(1+L_w) \sim N(\mu_{J,W}, \sigma^2_{J,W})$. Like in the IJD-model jump sizes are independent and identically distributed. The covariance between the stock returns and the change in the optimal invested wealth, conditional on no jumps, is given by $\sigma_{D,SW}$, while the covariance between jumps is defined as $Cov(\ln(1+L), \ln(1+L_W)) = \sigma_{J,SW}$. Under the assumption that the investor's direct utility function is given by $U(Y_t) = Y_t^{-R}/(1-R)$, with R as coefficient of relative risk aversion[1], Bates derives the following 'risk-neutral' valuation formula for European calls:[2]

---

[1] Risk-neutrality obtains for R=0, and R→1 results in logarithmic preferences.

[2] Although formula (3) is written in a 'risk-neutralized' fashion, the call value depends via $\lambda*$ and $k*$ on the risk aversion parameter R. Like in the pure diffusion environment, there is no known analytic solution for American puts when the underlying stock obeys a jump diffusion process. Bates (1991) generalizes McMillan's (1987) quadratic approximation to

$$C^{SJD} = e^{-rT} \sum_{n=0}^{\infty} \frac{e^{-\lambda^* T}(\lambda^* T)^n}{n!} \quad [\ S\, e^{r_n T}\, \Phi(d_{1,n}) \ -\ K\ \Phi(d_{2,n})\ ] \qquad (3)$$

,

where

$$d_{1,n} \equiv \left[\ln(S/K) + r_n T + \left(\sigma^2 T + n\,\sigma_J^2\right)/2\right] / \left(\sigma^2 T + n\,\sigma_J^2\right)^{1/2},$$

$$d_{2,n} \equiv d_{1,n} - \left(\sigma^2 T + n\,\sigma_J^2\right)^{1/2},$$

$$\lambda^* \equiv \lambda \exp\left(-R\,\alpha_{W,J} + \left(R(1+R)\sigma_{J,W}^2\right)/2\right),$$

$$r_n \equiv r - \lambda^* k^* + \left(n\,\mu_J^*\right)/T,$$

$$k^* \equiv \exp\left(\alpha_J^*\right) - 1,$$

$$\alpha_J^* \equiv \alpha_J - R\,\sigma_{J,SW},$$

$\Phi(.) \equiv$ standard normal cumulative density function.

Within this equilibrium framework the drift of the stock price process, α, and the riskless interest rate, r, are endogenously determined. The terminal stock price, $\widetilde{S}_T$, resulting from the 'risk-neutral' process is given by:

$$\widetilde{S}_T = S_0 \exp\left\{\left(r - \tfrac{1}{2}\sigma^2 - \lambda^* k^*\right)T + \sigma\, B_T + \sum_{i=1}^{N_T} \ln(1 + L^*)\right\}. \qquad (4)$$

Bates' option formula (3) can be specialized to all known option formulae proposed for a jump diffusion framework. Assuming an investor with logarithmic utility (R=1), the above formula collapses to that presented by Ahn (1992). If the call is written on a proxy of the market portfolio, we have $\sigma_{J,SW} = \sigma_{D,SW} = 1$, $\sigma_W = \sigma$, $\mu_W = \mu$, $\sigma_{J,W} = \sigma_J$ and $\mu_{J,W} = \mu_J$, and we obtain the formula proposed by Naik/Lee (1990). Furthermore, if the jump risk is *diversifiable* (idiosyncratic), i. e., $\alpha_{J,W} = \sigma_{J,W} = \sigma_{J,WS} = 0$, *or* the representative investor is risk-neutral, i. e., R=0, the call formula (3) collapses to Merton's idiosyncratic jump risk formula for European Calls:

$$C^{IJD} = \sum_{n=0}^{\infty} \frac{e^{-\lambda(1+k)T}\left(\lambda(1+k)T\right)^n}{n!} \left[S\,\Phi\left(d_{1,n}\right) - K e^{-r_n T}\,\Phi\left(d_{2,n}\right)\right]. \qquad (5)$$

American option values for jump-diffusion process. Amin (1993) approximates the jump-diffusion processes with sufficient accuracy using a Markov chain.

Finally, in the special case of a Geometric Brownian Motion governing the underlying stock price, i.e., for $\lambda = 0$ or $\lambda \to \infty$ (while the jump coefficients tend to zero), we have $d_{1,n} = d_1 \equiv [\ln(S/K) + (r + \sigma^2/2)T]/\sigma\sqrt{T}$, and $d_{2,n} = d_2 \equiv d_1 - \sigma\sqrt{T}$ and the formulae (3) and (5) specialize to the Black/Scholes formula for European calls:

$$C^{BS} = S\,\Phi(d_1) - e^{-rT} K\,\Phi(d_2). \tag{6}$$

2.2 A comparison of Black/Scholes-values and jump-diffusion values

The impact of jumps on option values is illustrated for an investor who erroneously adopts the BS-formula, when either the SJD-formula or the IJD-formula should be used. We also demonstrate the valuation errors which risk averse investors using the IJD-formula take into account when jump risk is systematic and the SJD-formula with $R>0$ should be used.[3] We calculate model values for calls written on a stock index. The annualized volatility estimate of the pure diffusion process, VOLA, corresponds to the total volatility of the jump-diffusion process, VOLA$=\sqrt{\sigma^2 + \lambda(\mu_J^2 + \sigma_J^2)} = 30\%$, the strike price is $K = 100$, the riskless interest rate is $r = 10\%$, and 80% of the total variance is due to the jump component, i. e., $\gamma \equiv \lambda(\mu_J^2 + \sigma_J^2) / (\sigma^2 + \lambda(\mu_J^2 + \sigma_J^2)) = 0.80$. Besides a symmetric distribution of actual stock returns (when $\mu_J = 0$), we allow for negative skewness (when $\mu_J = -0.20$ or $\mu_J = -0.10$) and positive skewness (when $\mu_J = 0.20$ or $\mu_J = 0.10$) in the actual return distribution.[4] Since substantial differences between the BS-value and the SJD-value occur only for a low jump intensity, we choose the rather low jump intensity of $\lambda = 1$, that is, on average one jump per year.[5]

In Table 1 the numbers in *bold face* correspond to a *symmetric* distribution of actual stock returns. The column headed 'BS' gives BS-values for short-term ($\tau = 1/12$, i. e., one month) and long-term ($\tau = 1$, i. e., one year) out-the-money (OTM) calls, at-the-money (ATM) calls, and in-the-money (ITM) calls,

---

[3] The same error occurs if risk averse investors erroneously value options as if they were risk-neutral when recognizing that jump risk is systematic.

[4] Recall that in the BS-model the actual, as well as the risk-neutral, return distribution are symmetric. In the case of the Poisson-jump diffusion model, skewness specializes to [λ μJ (μJ2 + 3 σJ2)] / [(T)1/2 [(σ2 + λ(μJ 2 + σJ2)]3/2]; and, for R > 0 the risk-neutral return distribution will always be skewed.

[5] For a jump intensity of $\lambda = 100$, Trautmann/Beinert (1995) demonstrate that the deviations of the SJD-values from BS-values are negligible, even for short-term ATM options exhibiting the largest absolute differences in value.

respectively. The columns headed 'IJD' and 'SJD' contain the corresponding call values according to the IJD-model and to the SJD-model (for $R = 3$), respectively. While for the BS-model and IJD-model there is no difference between the shapes of the actual and the risk-neutral return distributions, the shape of the risk-neutral return distribution underlying the SJD-model depends on R as depicted in column 1 of Table 2 for options with one year to maturity. Since $\mu_J^* = \mu_J - R\,\sigma_J^2 < 0$ for $\mu_J = 0$ and $R > 0$, the risk-neutral return distribution is skewed to the left. The columns headed 'Diff' contain the difference between the corresponding jump diffusion model value according to the *symmetric actual* return distribution and the model value according to *skewed* distributions. Table 2 depicts the differences between the BS-values and the IJD-values (middle column) as well as the differences between the BS-values and SJD-values for $R = 3$ (right hand column) with respect to different money ratios, for options with one month and one year to maturity, respectively. As distinguished from Table 1, we consider in addition to a symmetric actual return distribution, only one negatively skewed (when $\mu_J = -0.20$) and only one positively skewed (when $\mu_J = 0.20$) actual return distribution.

Turning first to the *symmetric* return distributions; a comparison of BS-values and IJD-values shows that, for options with one month to maturity, the BS-value exceeds the IJD-value for ATM options, while the opposite is true for OTM options and for ITM options. But only in the case of the OTM options can the percentage difference[6] almost amount to 100%. This v-shaped relationship between the IJD-value and the BS-value was first documented by Merton (1976b). For options with one year to maturity, all BS-values exceed the IJD-values. Clearly, these effects are explained by the shape of the underlying risk-neutral return distributions, as depicted in column 1 of Table 2 .

In the case of a symmetric return distribution, the SJD-value exceeds the BS-value, except for short-term OTM options. The interaction between the so-called *volatility effect* and *skewness effect* may explain this. For index options, the risk-neutralized volatility[7], $\text{VOLA}^* \equiv \sqrt{\sigma^2 + \lambda^*\left((\mu_J^*)^2 + \sigma_J^2\right)}$, exceeds the actual volatility for $\mu_J < (1/2)\,R\sigma_J^2$ and $R > 0$. For $\mu_J > (1/2)\,R\,\sigma_J^2$ and $R > 0$ the opposite is true. Since we have $\text{VOLA}^* > \text{VOLA}$ for $\mu_J = 0$, the SJD-value exceeds the BS-value. The skewness effect describes the shift to the left of the risk-neutralized return distribution if $\mu_J < (1/2)\,R\sigma_J^2$, and the shift to the right for $\mu_J > (1/2)\,R\,\sigma_J^2$. Since we have $\mu_J^* < \mu_J = 0$, the negatively skewed risk-neutral return distribution causes the SJD-value of OTM calls to be smaller, while the SJD-value for ATM calls and ITM calls are higher by comparison with a symmetric risk-neutral return distribution. The skewness effect leads to a smaller SJD-

[6] The mean percentage difference is defined as the mean of [(CIJD - CBS) / CIJD] 100.

[7] Recall that λ∗ = λexp(−R μJ +σJ2 R2/2) and μJ∗ = μJ − R σJ2

value, compared to the BS-value for OTM calls with a short time to maturity, because of the smaller risk-neutral probability to end up in-the-money.

Table 1: Calls written on the market index: Influence of the jump component (Fixed parameters:[a] $K=100$, $r=10\%$, $\lambda=1$, $\gamma=0.8$, VOLA=30%)

Parameters of the RN[b] distribution	BS	LJD (equals SJD-value for R = 0)					SJD for R=3 (Strong risk aversion)				
[c] λ^*	**0**	1.00	1.00	**1.00**	1.00	1.00	2.10	1.78	**1.38**	0.98	0.63
[d] μ_J^*	**0**	−0.20	−0.10	**0.00**	0.10	0.20	−0.30	−0.29	**−0.22**	−0.09	0.10
[e] $\lambda^* k^*$	**0**	−0.17	−0.07	**0.03**	0.14	0.24	−0.52	−0.41	**−0.23**	−0.06	0.08
[f] VOLA*	**0.30**	0.30	0.30	**0.30**	0.30	0.30	0.52	0.53	**0.43**	0.29	0.21
Option specification	C^{BS}	Diff[g]	Diff	C^{LJD}	Diff	Diff	Diff[g]	Diff	C^{SJD}	Diff	Diff
OTM $\tau=1/12$	**0.02**	−0.30	−0.18	**0.31**	0.18	0.26	−0.09	−0.05	**0.09**	0.04	0.08
(S=80) $\tau=1$	**5.76**	−1.40	−1.08	**5.52**	1.08	1.50	3.21	2.90	**7.19**	−2.80	−3.52
ATM $\tau=1/12$	**3.87**	0.08	−0.01	**2.74**	0.07	0.19	1.22	0.80	**3.41**	−0.72	−1.05
(S=100) $\tau=1$	**16.73**	0.48	0.15	**15.89**	0.29	0.79	3.12	3.01	**20.10**	−4.29	−6.88
ITM $\tau=1/12$	**20.88**	0.26	0.15	**21.11**	−0.16	−0.27	0.71	0.64	**21.94**	−0.71	−1.08
(S=120) $\tau=1$	**32.41**	0.70	0.50	**32.19**	−0.58	−0.81	2.69	2.70	**36.12**	−3.64	−6.02

[a] The drift parameters α_D and α_{DY} are determined endogenously by the Euler conditions.
[b] RN denotes the *risk-neutral* return distribution.
[c] The 'risk-neutral' jump intensity is defined as $\lambda^*=\lambda\exp(-R\mu_J + R\,\sigma_J^2/2)$.
[d] The 'risk-neutral' mean of $\ln(L+1)$ is: $\mu_J^* = \mu_J - R\,\sigma_J^2$.
[e] The 'risk-neutral' mean jump size per year.
[f] The 'risk-neutral' volatility is given by: $\text{VOLA}^* = [(\sigma^2 + \lambda^*((\mu_J^*)^2+\sigma_J^2))]^{1/2}$.
[g] $\text{Diff} \equiv C^{SJD}(\mu_J \neq 0) - C^{SJD}(\mu_J = 0)$.

Table 2: Calls written on the market index: Deviations from Black/Scholes-values (Fixed parameters[a]: K=100, r=10%, VOLA=30%, λ=1, γ=0.8)

Shapes of the risk-neutralized return distribution (T=1)	Deviations from Black/Scholes-values if jump risk is idiosyncratic[b] (or R=0)	Deviations from Black/Scholes-values if jump risk is systematic[b] and R=3
Panel A: $\mu_J = 0$ (i. e. the *actual* return distribution is symmetric)		
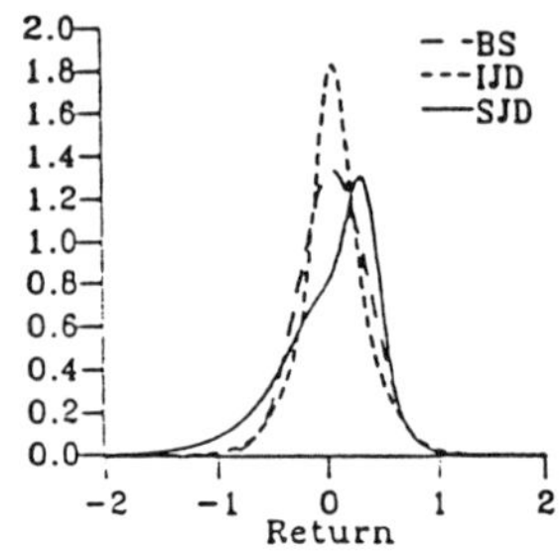	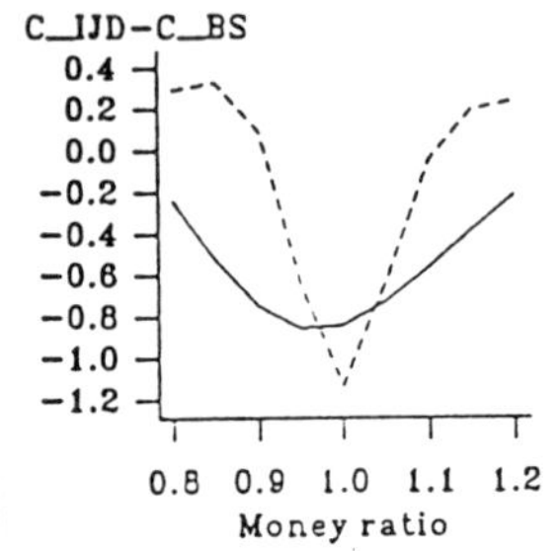	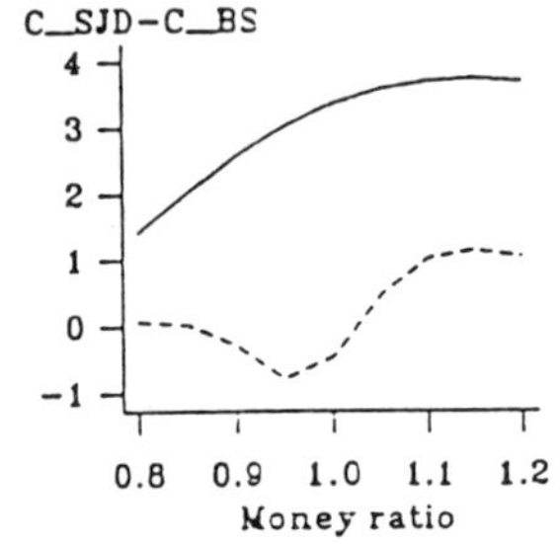
Panel B: $\mu_J = -0.20$ (i. e. the *actual* return distribution is negatively skewed)		
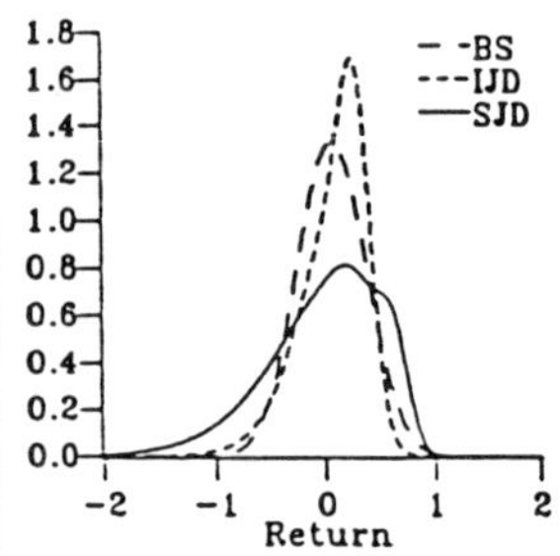	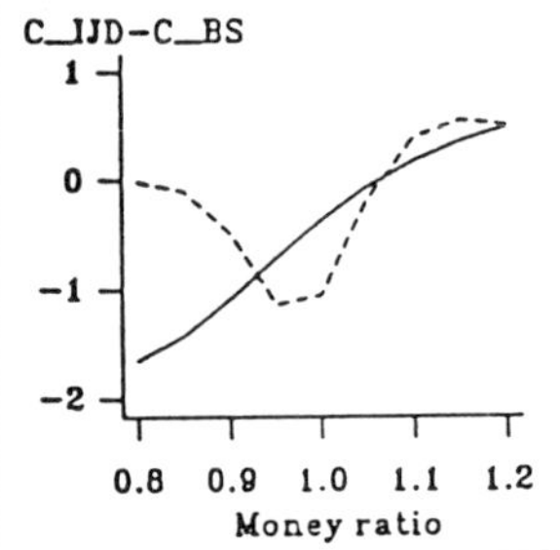	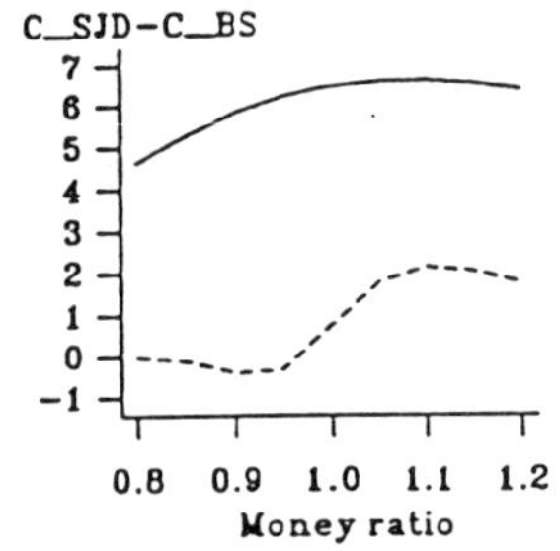
Panel C: $\mu_J = 0.20$ (i. e. the *actual* return distribution is positively skewed)		
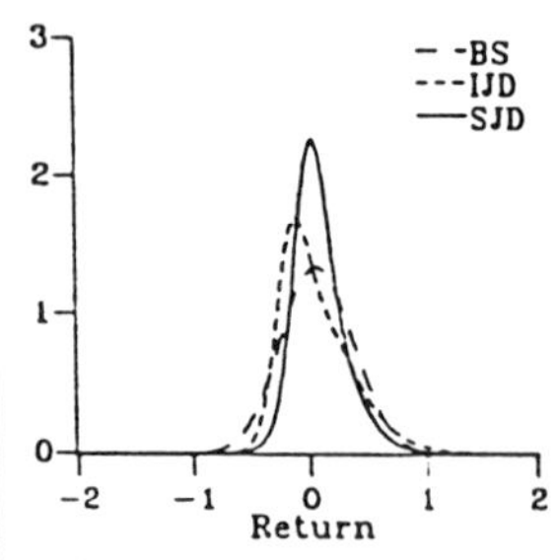	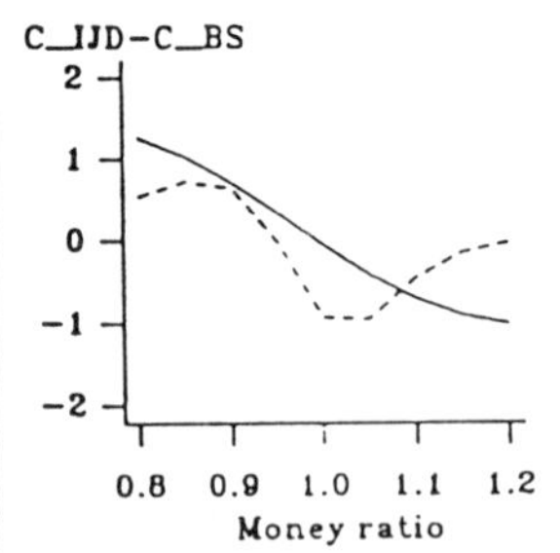	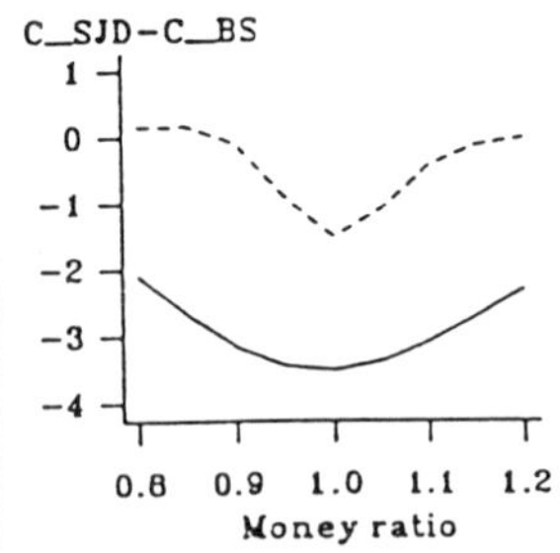

[a] The resulting risk-neutralized parameters of the SJD-model are the same as in table 1.
[b] Deviations are plotted only for options with one month (dashed line) and one year (solid line) time to maturity, respectively.

A comparison between IJD-values and the SJD-values (with $R = 3$) for symmetric return distributions (numbers in bold face in Table 1) shows, that for ITM and ATM options the SJD-value is higher than the IJD-value. The same is true for long-term OTM options, while for short-term OTM calls the IJD-value exceeds the SJD-value. According to Amin/Ng (1993), the interaction between the so called '*drift-effect*' and '*discounting-effect*' explains this difference. As long as the correlation between stock price jumps and wealth jumps is positive, the stock price drifts upwards at a faster rate since the stock return premium is higher under systematic jump risk relative to the diversifiable jump risk case. Therefore, the 'drift-effect' causes the options to be worth more under systematic jump risk than under idiosyncratic jump risk. In contrast, the 'discounting effect' causes the value under systematic jump risk to be smaller than the value under diversifiable jump risk. Wealth tends to jump with the stock return when jump risk is systematic, while jumps in the stock price that increase the value of the call tend to decrease the interest rate.[8] The direction of these effects depends on the assumption about the sign of the correlation between wealth jumps and asset jumps. Therefore, the above effects reverse themselves when a negative correlation is assumed.

Skewness of the actual return distribution changes the sign and magnitude of the differences between the BS-value and the IJD- or SJD-value.[9] According to Tables 1 and 2, the v-shaped relationship between the BS-value and IJD-value still exists for short-term options, but depending upon the sign of the skewness the v-shape is tilt to the right or to the left. For long-term calls the difference in value increases (decreases) with the money ratio if the skewness is negative (positive). In contrast to the IJD-value, the SJD-value increases slightly if the return distribution becomes negatively skewed, except for short-term OTM calls. For positively skewed return distributions the SJD-value is dramatically lower compared to the symmetric case. This is mainly due to the volatility effect; the risk-neutralized volatility is significantly smaller compared to that of the actual return distribution. The shape of the risk-neutral return distribution, as depicted in Table 2 column 1, serves as an explanation.

While the foregoing analysis is restricted to European calls, the same differences in model values also hold for otherwise identical European puts because of the put-call parity.

---

[8] According to Cox/Ingersoll/Ross (1985), the endogenous riskless interest rate is equal the negative of the expected rate of change in the marginal utility of wealth.

[9] This is explained by the shape of skewed return distributions. Return distributions with a negative (positive) skewness exhibit a larger probability for returns far below (above) the mean than for returns far above (below) the mean. This implies that the mean return lies above (below) the median if the return distribution has a negative (positive) skewness.

3. Historical jump risk impact on option values

3.1 Data and estimation

A substantial jump risk impact on option values can only be expected if the estimated model parameters reflect the statistical and economic significance of the jump risk. We therefore pay particular attention to the values of calls whose underlying parameter estimates are based on the extremely volatile stock returns around the crash periods in October 1987 and October 1989.[10] The option price data consist of options written on five actively traded stocks: *Daimler Benz, Deutsche Bank, Siemens, Thyssen and VW.* Henceforth this sample is called BIG5. More precisely, we examine only the subsample BIG5/NODIV since price observations are eliminated if dividends were paid, or stock splits took place, during the lifetime of the option. All option prices, stock prices, dividend and split data, as well as daily stock returns, were taken, or generated, from the *Karlsruher Kapitalmarktdatenbank.* The riskless interest rate appropriate to each option was estimated from the interest rate on three-month inter-bank time deposits.[11]

The time-consuming parameter estimation for the Poisson jump-diffusion process, which was performed only once a month during the sample period, is based on 250 daily returns preceding the estimation date.[12] Figure 1 shows the monthly reestimated parameter values of the skewness and kurtosis according to

---

[10] The total sample covers the period from April 1983 to December 1991. During the post-crash periods, to which particular attention was paid, trading took place on the Frankfurt Options Market (FOM). But, since the opening of the Deutsche Terminbörse (DTB) in January 1990, trading in the most liquid 'blue chips' is no longer possible on the older Frankfurt Options Market (FOM).

[11] Recall that in the SJD-model the riskless interest rate is endogenously determined. In order to be able to compare the SJD-model with models whose r is exogenously given, we endogenize instead the drift rate of wealth: the choice of αW is such that the 'endogenous' r is equal to the observable r.

[12] The parameters of the pure diffusion process were estimated daily, using the 250 preceding daily stock returns and DAX-returns, respectively. Although the SJD-model requires a simultaneous estimation of the jump diffusion parameters of all stocks' returns and the returns on the market proxy, we estimate them independently. The required correlation structure of jumps in the stock price, and in the wealth, is estimated with the following two-step procedure: (1) We identify the return of the DAX or an individual stock as a 'jump return' if at least one of the two returns either exceeds 3% or is lower than –3%, and (2) the correlation between these selected returns serves as proxy for the true correlation between jumps in stock return and aggregate wealth. Typically there is a strong positive correlation between individual stock returns and DAX-returns.

the jump diffusion process for SIEMENS returns. The historical return distributions are negatively skewed during the crash month October 1989 and during the year 1992, thus reflecting the stock price decline in both periods. Beinert/Trautmann (1991) show that the estimated jump component is statistically significant for returns of single stocks as well as for DAX-returns.

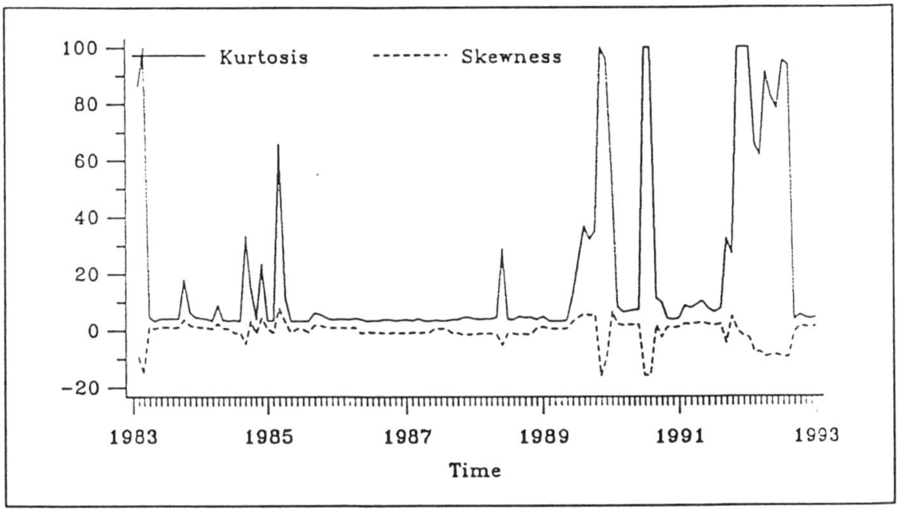

Figure 1: Skewness and kurtosis resulting from the parameter estimates of the Poisson-jump diffusion process of Siemens returns

3.2 Results

Figure 2 depicts the mean differences (in DM) between *BS-values and IJD-values* with respect to different money ratios (left hand scale) for the post-crash period from November 1987 to January 1988 and from November 1989 to January 1990.[13] In these post-crash periods, the pattern resembles that of the *positively* skewed returns which are depicted in Table 2. This *unexpected* result is due to the large positive returns after the October 1989 market crash which obviously cause a positive skewness of the estimated return distributions for some stocks. Figure 1 confirms the positive skewness of the Siemens return distribution after the October 1989 crash. The expected v-shaped relationship obtains for short-term and medium-term options, but the differences are

[13] The right hand scale corresponds to the plotted frequency distribution of observed money ratios.

significant only for OTM options. On an average basis, the differences between BS-values and IJD-values for OTM calls with a short, medium, and long maturity are 0.30 DM (9.5%), 0.61 DM (3.9%), and 0.76 DM (3.3%), respectively. For ATM calls the BS-values are 0.20 DM (0.5%) higher than the IJD-values. For ITM calls with a long maturity the mean IJD-value exceeds the mean BS-value, but the percentage difference is negligible. This deviation pattern contradicts those reported in Tables 1 and 2 when the return distribution is positively skewed. The answer to this puzzle reads as follows: the call values in the period from November 1987 to January 1988 and November 1989 to January 1990 are based on 30 (5x6) different sets of parameter estimates. Unfortunately, some sets of parameter estimates imply a positively skewed return distribution while other sets result in a negatively skewed return distribution.

Figure 3 shows the mean differences (in DM) between *IJD-values and SJD-values* (for R=3) for different money ratios in the post-crash period. The SJD-values substantially exceed the corresponding IJD-values.[14] According to the findings in the foregoing section, the 'drift effect' leads to extremely high SJD-values when the underlying return distributions are symmetric, or negatively skewed, while the opposite is true for return distributions with positive skewness. The observed pattern is therefore consistent with symmetric or negatively skewed return distributions. In contrast to Figure 2, the estimated positive skewness of some of the five underlyings does not influence the expected result. The differences between BS-values and SJD-values are therefore larger than the differences between BS-values and IJD-values, with one exception. Thus, in the case of OTM calls with a short maturity, the IJD-value exceeds the SJD-value and therefore reduces the deviation from the BS-value. This effect is due to the 'discounting effect' as explained in the previous section. On average, the SJD-value is 0.66 DM (5.08%) higher than the BS-value. The percentage difference is 11.39% for OTM calls while for ATM and ITM options the differences are only 1.70% and 0.60%, respectively.

Recall that the put-call parity guarantees that the differences between the BS-value and alternative values for a European call are the same as for an otherwise identical European put. But even if the American puts examined were to be of a European type, we could not expect the same deviation pattern with respect to *S/K* unless for each call there is an otherwise identical put (and conversely) in the sample. Nonetheless, the deviations are very similar and are therefore not presented here.[15]

---

[14] The differences are much smaller for R=1, that is, for a representative investor with logarithmic utility function (figures are not presented here).

[15] More detailed empirical results for calls, as well as for puts, can be found in Trautmann/Beinert (1995).

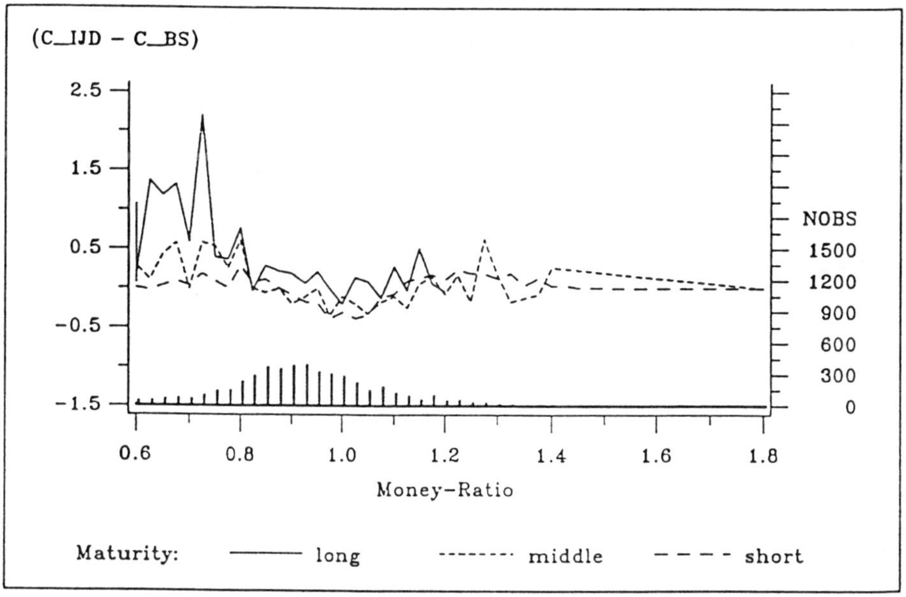

Figure 2: Mean differences (in DM) between B/S-value and IJD-value (BIG5/NODIV Calls, in the post-crash periods 87/11- 88/1 and 89/11 - 90/1)

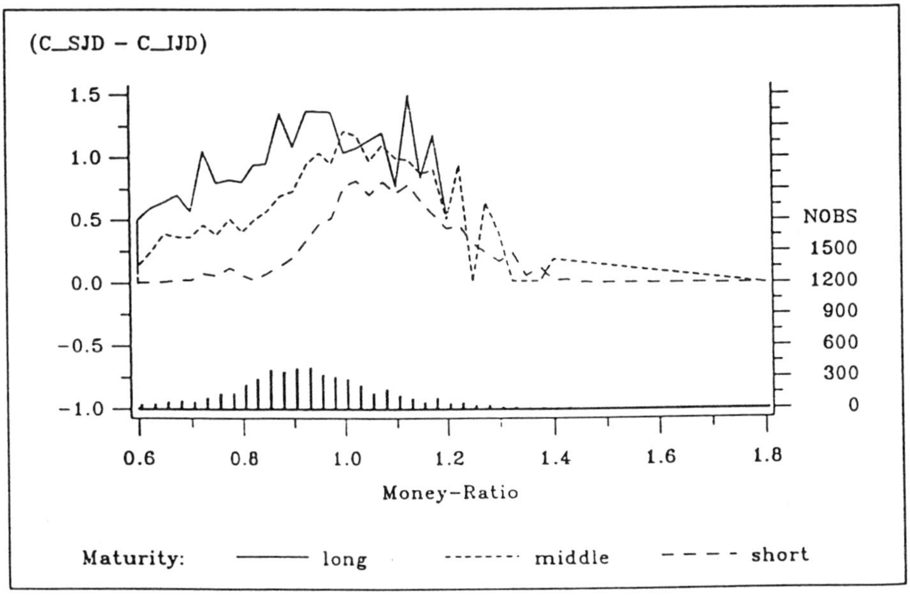

Figure 3: Mean differences (in DM) between the IJD-value and the SJD-value (R=3, BIG5/NODIV Calls, in the post-crash periods 87/11- 88/1 and 89/11 - 90/1)

4. Jump risk implicit in option prices

We now estimate the implicit process parameters by setting observed option prices equal to SJD-values to examine whether stock price jumps were expected by market participants. The subperiods of special interest are therefore the periods before, and after, the market crashes in October 1987 and in October 1989, respectively. Recall that according to the SJD-model a perceived risk of a market crash implies a negatively skewed return distribution which will lead to higher prices for OTM puts and lower prices for OTM calls compared to a symmetric model like the BS-model. Therefore, the parameter estimates, that are implicit in calls and puts according to the SJD-model, give direct effect to market participants' crash fears or hopes of a trend reversion. This is the main advantage of the SJD-model compared to alternative models based on symmetric return distributions, as in the case of the BS-model. Jump intensity, jump size, and risk aversion *implicit* in option prices, determined in accordance with the SJD-model, are reported below.

4.1 Data and estimation

The calculation of SJD-model values reported in the preceding section required either, the seven parameters σ, λ, α_J, σ_J, $\alpha_{J,W}$, $\sigma_{J,W}$, and $\sigma_{J,WS}$ of the *true* stock price distribution and *true* wealth distribution, respectively, as well as the risk aversion parameter R; *or*, the four parameters σ, σ_J, $k^* \equiv \exp\{\alpha_J - R\,\sigma_{J,WS}\}$ and $\lambda^* \equiv \lambda\,\exp\{-R\,\alpha_{J,W} + (1/2)\,R\,(1+R)\,\sigma^2_{J,W}\}$ characterizing the distribution of the *risk-neutral* terminal stock price. To get parameter estimates of the true distribution a two step procedure is used. First, the parameters of the risk-neutral return distribution are inferred from observed option prices. Second, these estimates of the risk-neutral distribution serve as starting points in inferring the parameters of the true distribution.

The parameters corresponding to the true, or risk-neutral, return distribution are estimated via nonlinear least squares[16]. We minimize

$$\sum_{j=1}^{n}\left[C_j - C^{\mathrm{SJD}}\left(S_j, K_j, T_j, R, \sigma, \lambda, \sigma_J, \mu_J, \sigma_{J,W}, \mu_{J,W}\right)\right]^2, \qquad (7)$$

where C_j denotes the market price of call $j=1,\ldots,n$. This minimization is done for every trading day during the observation period.[17] This procedure needs at least four price observations. Since this condition is not always fulfilled for the

---

[16] We used the FORTRAN routine BCLSF available in the IMSL program library.

[17] Since nonlinear least squares do not converge in all cases, we used four different parameter vectors as starting values in order to arrive at the global minimum.

FOM-sample, the corresponding price observations of up to four trading days preceding the trading day under consideration are, if necessary, also used.

4.2 Results

The following figures present the implicit jump frequency per year (IJF), λ, and the implicit jump size per year (IJSY), λk. As long as IJF is small enough, positive and negative values for IJSY imply positive and negative skewness of the implicit return distribution indicating strong crash fears and hopes of a trend reversion, respectively,. Figures 4 and 5 illustrate the parameter estimates implied by the prices of *Deutsche Bank* calls and puts, respectively, for all trading days in the period from July 1987 to December 1987, that is, before and after the market crash on October 19, 1987.

Figure 4 highlights the crash fears in July 1987, confirming the findings of Bates (1991) when examining the implicit distribution of the S&P 500 futures price. The IJSY is quite large while the IJF is relatively small. Therefore the market participants expected a jump with a large negative amplitude (i. e., a market crash). In contrast to the findings of Bates for the US market, German call market participants also expected a crash at the beginning of October 1987. But immediately before the crash on October 1987, crash fears were not strong, since the implicit jump frequency was too high. While the crash fears reflected by the S&P 500 futures option prices returned after the stock market crashed, German option market participants did not expect a further stock price drop. Surprisingly, the IJSY and IJF implicit in call prices indicated an upward stock price correction. The graphs evince this dramatic change in implicit stock price distributions after the crash. The different time series of skewness in return distributions implicit in US and German option prices can be explained by the corresponding historical stock price and index price movement. While the US market peaked in August 1987 after a dramatic upward movement during the preceding twelve months, the German stock market peaked already in December 1985 and declined during the years 1986 and 1987. The October 1987 crash left the US stock market at the end of the year at essentially the same level as in January 1987, while the German market fell back to its January 1985 level. Therefore, while US market participants feared a further drop, the German price level was so low that a further price drop was not expected by the options market participants.

The findings for the implicit parameters of the calls are not identical to those of the puts. Figure 5 shows this difference. First of all, the crash fears in July 1987 are insignificant. Furthermore, since the IJF is low immediately after the crash in October 1987 the parameters implicit in puts mainly reflect rebound hopes. Figure 6 depicts the estimated risk aversion parameter implicit in

Deutsche Bank calls. The average value of the implicit risk aversion parameter R is 9.6, indicating that the risk aversion of the representative investor was relatively high. Evidently, the October 1987 crash did not have a substantial influence on the implicit risk aversion. The same is true for Deutsche Bank puts. With an average value of 10.9, the risk aversion is even higher.

Figure 7 shows the differences in root mean squared errors (RMSE) between the BS-model and SJD-model (upper scale) for the pooled sample of Deutsche Bank calls and puts. The lower scale of Figure 7 shows the difference in RMSE when the parameter estimation is based on the *pooled* sample and when the parameters are *separately* estimated for calls and puts, respectively. The sample period starts in April 1987 and ends in December 1987. The observed root mean squared errors are quite large. This is obviously due to the fact that (1) all transaction prices of one day are used to estimate the implicit parameters, and because (2) price data for this period are not time-stamped. Unfortunately, most of the time the SJD-model does not yield a substantially better fit of the market prices compared to the BS-model. Nonetheless, the SJD-model fits the data much better than does the BS-model *after* the October 1987 crash. The difference between the parameter estimates implicit in Deutsche Bank calls and the parameter estimates implicit in Deutsche Bank puts (compare Figures 4 and 5) is reflected in the increase of the RMSE between late August 1987 and October 1987.

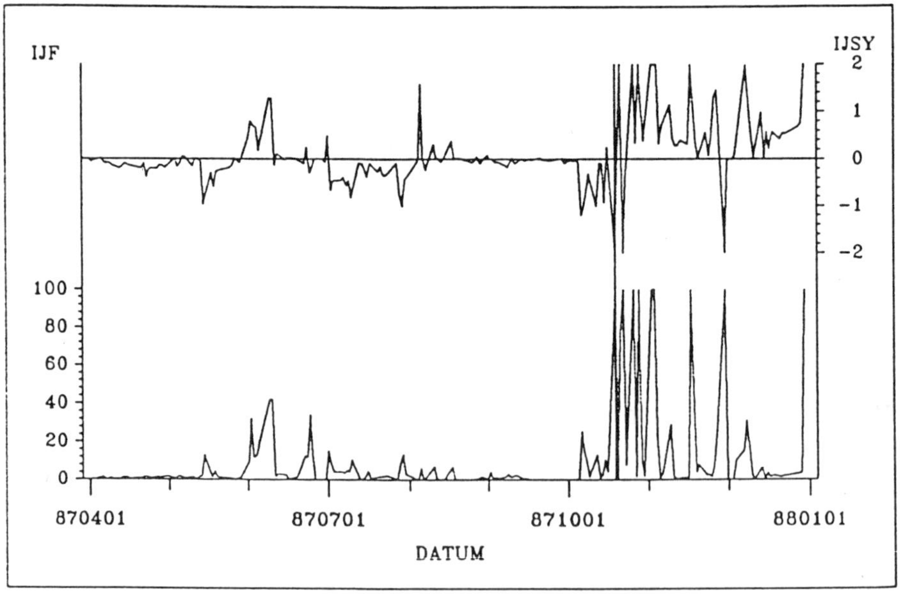

Figure 4: Jump frequency and jump size per year implicit in Deutsche Bank calls observed between April and December in the market crash year 1987

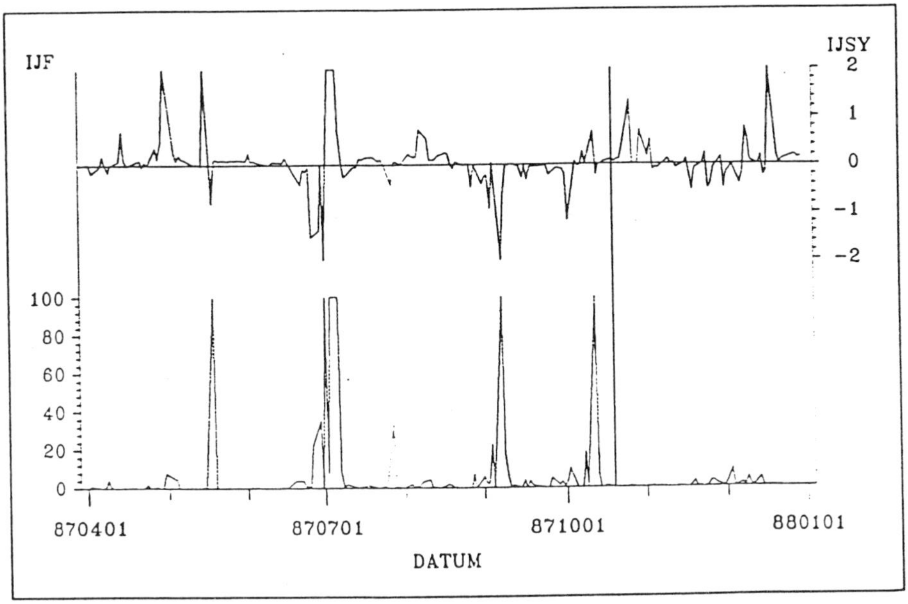

Figure 5: Jump frequency and jump size per year implicit in Deutsche Bank puts observed between April and December in the market crash year 1987

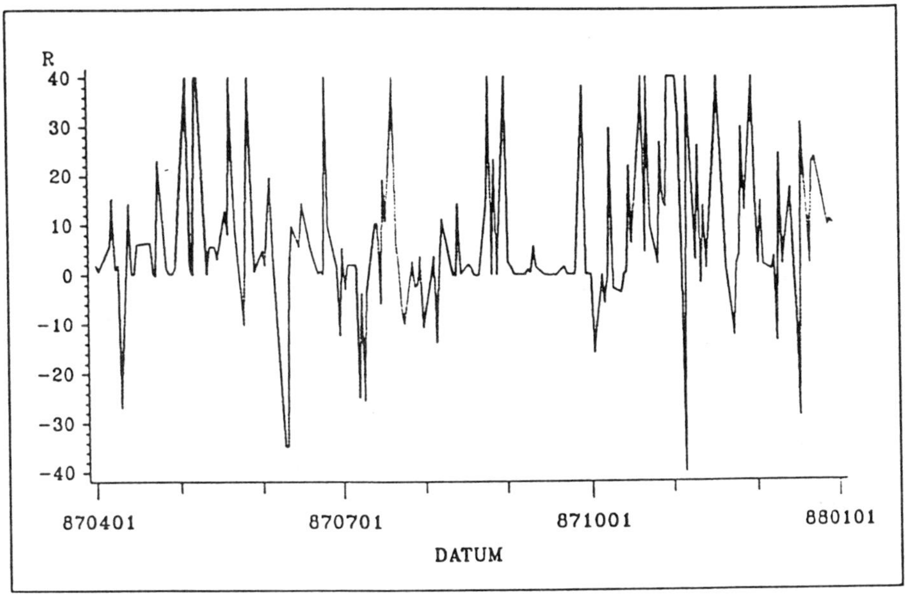

Figure 6: Risk aversion implicit in Deutsche Bank calls observed between April and December in the market crash year 1987

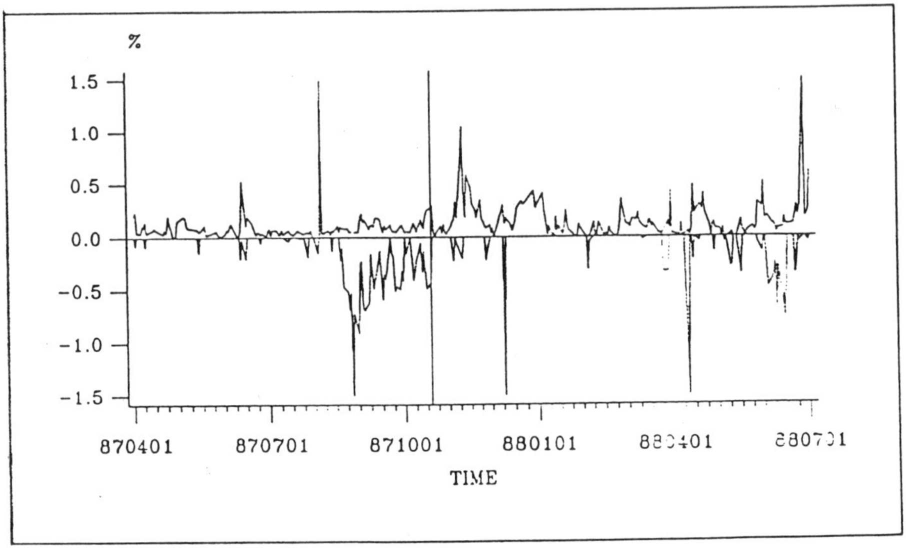

Figure 7: Differences in RMSE as % of the stock price for Deutsche Bank
Upper scale: RMSE (BS-model) minus RMSE (SJD-model) for calls and puts pooled
Lower scale: RMSE (SJD-model calls and puts pooled) minus RMSE(SJD-model unpooled)

5. Conclusions

In conclusion, we list several contributions of this study. In the first place, we have presented a *detailed analysis of the impact of stock price jumps on option values for representative model parameters.* The shapes of the risk-neutral return distributions plotted in Table 2 help to explain the deviation of the jump diffusion values from the BS-values. While the economic rationale behind the difference between SJD-value and IJD-value relies on the interaction between the drift and discounting effect, the interaction between the volatility and skewness effect explains the difference between BS-values and SJD-values.

In the second place, we have examined the *historical impact of jumps on option values*. In the case of options written on 30 NYSE listed common stocks, Ball/Torous (1985) find no operationally significant differences between BS-value and IJD-value, although statistically significant jumps were present in the underlying stock returns. In their sample, the mean percentage deviation for OTM calls is only 2.98%. In contrast to their result, we find a more substantial historical stock price impact. When using the IJD-model in the post-crash period from November 1987 to January 1988, and from November 1989 to January

1990, we find a mean percentage difference between the BS-model and the IJD-model of 6.3% for OTM calls (and –0.81% and 0.19% for ATM calls and ITM calls, respectively). Moreover, the mean percentage difference between the SJD-value (for R=3) and the Black/Scholes value is 7.62% for long-term calls in general and even 11.39% for OTM calls, respectively.

In the third place, we have inferred the *jump intensity, jump size, and risk aversion implicit in option prices* that were quoted before and after market crashes. The time pattern of the implied jump size per year suggests that the market participants feared a stock market crash in July 1987, thus confirming the findings of Bates (1991) for the US market. However, in contrast to Bates, the implicit parameters also suggest crash fears at the beginning of October 1987 and hopes of a stock market rebound after the market crash. Finally, consistent with the findings of Bates (1991), the fit of the SJD-values to the option prices before the October 1987 crash is not significantly better than that of the BS-values (as depicted by the differences in RMSE), while after the October 1987 crash the RMSE for the SJD-model is significantly smaller.

References

Ahn, Ch.M. (1992): Option Pricing when Jump Risk is Systematic, in: Mathematical Finance 2, 299-308.

Akgiray, V. and Booth, G.G. (1986): Stock Price Processes with Discontinuous Time Path, An Empirical Examination, in: The Financial Review 2, 163-168.

Akgiray, V. and Booth, G.G. and Loistl, O. (1989): Statistical Models of German Stock Returns, in: Journal of Economics 50, 17-33.

Amin, K. (1993): Jump Diffusion Option Valuation in Discrete Time, in: Journal of Finance 48, 1833-1863.

Amin, K. and Ng, V. (1993): Option Valuation with Systematic Stochastic Volatility, in: Journal of Finance 48, 881-910.

Ball, C.A. and Torous, W.N. (1985): On Jumps in Common Stock Prices and Their Impact on Call Option Pricing, in: Journal of Finance 40, 155-173.

Bates, D.S. (1991): The Crash of '87, Was It Expected? The Evidence from Options Markets, in: Journal of Finance 46, 1009-1044.

Beckers, S. (1981): A Note on Estimating the Parameters of the Diffusion-Jump Model of Stock Returns, in: Journal of Financial and Quantitative Analysis 16, 127-129.

Beinert, M. and Trautmann, S. (1991): Jump-Diffusion Models of German Stock Returns - A Statistical Investigation, in: Statistical Papers 32, 269-280.

Beinert, M. (1995): Aktienkurssprünge und ihre Auswirkungen auf den Optionswert - eine empirische Überprüfung für den deutschen Aktien- und Optionsmarkt. Mainz (Diss.).

Black, F. and Scholes, M. (1973): The Pricing of Options and Corporate Liabilities, in: Journal of Political Economy 81, 637-654.

Cox, J.C., Ingersoll, J.E. and Ross, S.S. (1985): An Intertemporal General Equilibrium Model of Asset Prices, Econometrica 53, 363-384.

Jarrow, R.A. and Rosenfeld, E. (1984): Jump Risks and the Intertemporal Capital Asset Pricing Model, in: Journal of Business 57, 337-351.

Jones, E.P. (1984): Option Arbitrage and Strategy with Large Price Changes, in: Journal of Financial Economics 13, 91-113.

MacMillan, L.W. (1987): Analytic Approximation for the American Put Option, in: Fabozzi, F.J. (ed.), Advances in Futures and Options Research 1A. Greenwich/Conn. (JAI Press), 119-139.

Merton, R.C. (1976a): Option Pricing when Underlying Stock Returns are Discontinuous, in: Journal of Financial Economics 3, 125-144.

Merton, R.C. (1976b): The Impact on Option Pricing of Specification Error in the Underlying Stock Price Returns, in: Journal of Finance 31, 333-350.

Naik, V. and Lee, M. (1990): General Equilibrium Pricing of Options on the Market Portfolio with Discontinuous Returns, in: Review of Financial Studies 3, 443-521.

Press, J.S. (1967): A Compound Events Model for Security Prices, in: Journal of Business 40, 317-335.

Rubinstein,M. (1976): The Valuation of Uncertain Income Streams and the Pricing of Options, in: Bell Journal of Economics 7, 407-425.

Trautmann, S. (1986): Finanztitelbewertung bei arbitragefreien Finanzmärkten - Theoretische Analyse sowie empirische Überprüfung für den deutschen Markt für Aktienoptionen und Optionsscheine. Karlsruhe (Habil.).

Trautmann, S. (1989): Aktienoptionspreise an der Frankfurter Optionsbörse im Lichte der Optionsbewertungstheorie, Finanzmarkt und Portfoliomanagement 3, 210-225.

Trautmann, S., Beinert M. (1995): Stock Price Jumps and Their Impact on Option Valuation. Working Paper, University of Mainz.

Printing: Weihert-Druck GmbH, Darmstadt
Binding: Buchbinderei Schäffer, Grünstadt